Spring Boot 3 Recipes

A Problem-Solution Approach for Java Microservices and Cloud-Native Applications

Second Edition

Marten Deinum

Apress®

Spring Boot 3 Recipes: A Problem-Solution Approach for Java Microservices and Cloud-Native Applications, Second Edition

Marten Deinum
Meppel, Drenthe, The Netherlands

ISBN-13 (pbk): 979-8-8688-0112-9   ISBN-13 (electronic): 979-8-8688-0113-6
https://doi.org/10.1007/979-8-8688-0113-6

Managing Director, Apress Media LLC: Welmoed Spahr
Acquisitions Editor: Melissa Duffy
Development Editor: Laura Berendson
Editorial Assistant: Jessica Vakili
Copyeditor: Kim Wimpsett

Cover designed by eStudioCalamar

Cover image designed by Freepik.com

Distributed to the book trade worldwide by Springer Science+Business Media New York, 1 New York Plaza, Suite 4600, New York, NY 10004-1562, USA. Phone 1-800-SPRINGER, fax (201) 348-4505, e-mail orders-ny@ springer-sbm.com, or visit www.springeronline.com. Apress Media, LLC is a California LLC and the sole member (owner) is Springer Science + Business Media Finance Inc (SSBM Finance Inc). SSBM Finance Inc is a **Delaware** corporation.

For information on translations, please e-mail booktranslations@springernature.com; for reprint, paperback, or audio rights, please e-mail bookpermissions@springernature.com.

Apress titles may be purchased in bulk for academic, corporate, or promotional use. eBook versions and licenses are also available for most titles. For more information, reference our Print and eBook Bulk Sales web page at http://www.apress.com/bulk-sales.

Any source code or other supplementary material referenced by the author in this book is available to readers on GitHub. For more detailed information, please visit https://www.apress.com/gp/services/source-code.

Paper in this product is recyclable

For my wife and daughters, I love you.

Table of Contents

About the Author

Marten Deinum is a submitter on the open-source Spring Framework project. He is also a Java/software consultant working for Conspect. He has developed and architected software, primarily in Java, for small and large companies. He is an enthusiastic open-source user and longtime fan, user, and advocate of the Spring Framework. He has held a number of positions including software engineer, development lead, coach, and Java and Spring trainer.

Introduction

Welcome to *Spring Boot 3 Recipes*!

Who This Book Is For

This book is for developers who want to make it easier to work with their Spring applications. If your project uses Spring, introducing Spring Boot will simplify your application configuration, deployment, and management.

This book assumes that you are familiar with Java and Spring and that you have an integrated development environment (IDE) of some sort. This book doesn't explain all the internals and in-depth workings of Spring or the related projects; for that you might want to pick up a copy of *Spring 6 Recipes*.

How This Book Is Structured

There are 10 chapters in this book.

Chapter 1, "Introduction to Spring Boot," gives a quick overview of Spring Boot and how to get started.

Chapter 2, "The Basics of Spring Boot," covers the foundations of how to define and configure a bean and do dependency injection with Spring Boot.

Chapter 3, "Spring MVC," covers web-based application development using Spring MVC.

Chapter 4, "Spring Webflux," covers reactive web-based application development using Spring Webflux.

Chapter 5, "Spring Security," provides an overview of how to secure your Spring Boot application using Spring Security.

Chapter 6, "Data Access," explains how to access data storage such as a database or No-SQL store.

Chapter 7, "Java Enterprise Services," introduces how to use enterprise services such as JMX, Mail, and JFR with Spring Boot

Chapter 8, "Messaging," introduces how to do messaging with several different messaging technologies.

Chapter 9, "Spring Boot Actuator," explains how to use the production-ready features such as health and metrics from Spring Boot Actuator.

Chapter 10, "Packaging," shows how to package and deploy your Spring Boot applications by making them executable and how use Docker and GraalVM.

Conventions

We use the following code conventions in this book:

- Sometimes, when we want you to pay particular attention to a certain part of a code example, we will put the code in bold. Please note that the bold doesn't necessarily reflect a code change from the previous version.

- When a code line is too long to fit within the page's width, we will break it with a code continuation character. Please note that when you try to type the code, you have to concatenate the line without any spaces.

Prerequisites

Because the Java programming language is platform independent, you are free to choose any supported operating system. However, some of the examples in this book use platform-specific paths. Translate them as necessary to your operating system's format before typing the examples.

To make the most out of this book, install JDK version 21. You should have a Java IDE installed to make development easier. For this book, most of the sample code is Maven based, and most IDEs have built-in support for Maven to manage the classpath.

The samples sometimes need additional libraries installed such as PostreSQL, ActiveMQ, etc. For this, the book uses Docker. Of course, you can install the libraries on your machine instead of using Docker, but for ease of use (and not polluting your system) using Docker is preferred.

Contacting the Author

We always welcome your questions and feedback regarding the contents of this book. You can contact Marten Deinum by email at marten@deinum.biz or via X at @mdeinum.

CHAPTER 1

Introduction to Spring Boot

In this chapter, you will learn about the fundamentals of Spring Boot. At the heart of Spring Boot lies the Spring Framework, which Spring Boot extends to make auto-configuration, among other features, possible.

> Spring Boot makes it easy to create stand-alone, production-grade Spring-based applications that you can "just run." We take an opinionated view of the Spring platform and third-party libraries so you can get started with minimum fuss. Most Spring Boot applications need very little Spring configuration.
>
> —Spring Boot Reference Guide

Spring Boot has auto-configuration for infrastructure like JMS, JDBC, JPA, RabbitMQ, and more, and it comes with auto-configuration for different frameworks such as Spring Integration, Spring Batch, Spring Security, and many others. When these frameworks or capabilities are detected, Spring Boot will auto-configure them with opiniated but sensible defaults.

The source code uses Maven for its build. Maven will take care of getting the necessary dependencies, compiling the code, and creating the artifact (generally a JAR file). Furthermore, if a recipe illustrates more than one approach, the source code is classified with various examples with roman letters (e.g., `recipe_2_1_i`, `recipe_2_1_ii`, `recipe_2_1_iii`, etc.).

© Marten Deinum 2024
M. Deinum, *Spring Boot 3 Recipes*, https://doi.org/10.1007/979-8-8688-0113-6_1

> 💡 To build each application, go in the recipe directory (e.g., ch2/ recipe_2_1_i/) and execute the mvnw command to compile the source code. Once the source code is compiled, a target subdirectory is created with the application executable. You can then run the application JAR from the command line (e.g., java -jar target/Recipe_2_1_i.jar).

1-1. Create a Spring Boot Application Using Maven

Problem

You want to start developing an application using Spring Boot and Maven.

Solution

Create a Maven build file, pom.xml, and add the needed dependencies. To launch the application, create a Java class containing a main method to bootstrap the application.

How It Works

Suppose you are going to create a simple application that bootstraps SpringApplication, gets all the beans from ApplicationContext, and outputs them to the console.

Create the pom.xml File

Before you can start coding, you need to create the pom.xml file used by Maven to determine what needs to be done. The easiest way to use Spring Boot is to use spring-boot-starter-parent as the parent for your application (see Listing 1-1).

Listing 1-1. Spring Boot Starter Parent

```
<parent>
  <groupId>org.springframework.boot</groupId>
  <artifactId>spring-boot-starter-parent</artifactId>
  <version>3.2.1</version>
</parent>
```

Next, you need to add some Spring dependencies to get started using Spring. For this, add `spring-boot-starter` as a dependency to your `pom.xml` file (see Listing 1-2).

Listing 1-2. Spring Boot Dependency

```
<dependency>
  <groupId>org.springframework.boot</groupId>
  <artifactId>spring-boot-starter</artifactId>
</dependency>
```

Notice that there is no version or other information needed; all this is managed for you because `spring-boot-starter-parent` is used as the parent for the application. This will pull in all the core dependencies needed to start a very basic Spring Boot application; this includes dependencies such as the Spring Framework, Logback for logging, and Spring Boot itself.

Finally, to be able to create a JAR file that is executable, you will need to add the `spring-boot-maven-plugin` (Listing 1-3). This plugin takes care of creating an executable JAR file. If you have ever used the Maven Shade plugin, this should be familiar. It takes the original JAR file and repackages it with all the dependencies inside it (a so-called JAR with dependencies). That way, you can just hand over the JAR file to the operations team, which only needs to use the command `java -jar <your-application>.jar` to launch the application. There's no need to deploy it to a servlet container or JEE container.

Listing 1-3. Spring Boot Maven Plugin

```
<plugin>
  <groupId>org.springframework.boot</groupId>
  <artifactId>spring-boot-maven-plugin</artifactId>
</plugin>
```

The full `pom.xml` should now look like Listing 1-4.

Listing 1-4. Full pom.xml

```xml
<?xml version="1.0" encoding="UTF-8"?>
<project xmlns="http://maven.apache.org/POM/4.0.0"
         xmlns:xsi="http://www.w3.org/2001/XMLSchema-instance"
         xsi:schemaLocation="http://maven.apache.org/POM/4.0.0
         http://maven.apache.org/xsd/maven-4.0.0.xsd">
  <modelVersion>4.0.0</modelVersion>
  <groupId>com.apress.springboot3recipes</groupId>
  <artifactId>recipe_1_1_i</artifactId>
  <version>6.0.0-SNAPSHOT</version>
  <parent>
    <groupId>org.springframework.boot</groupId>
    <artifactId>spring-boot-starter-parent</artifactId>
    <version>3.2.1</version>
  </parent>
  <properties>
    <java.version>21</java.version>
  </properties>
  <dependencies>
    <dependency>
      <groupId>org.springframework.boot</groupId>
      <artifactId>spring-boot-starter</artifactId>
    </dependency>
  </dependencies>
  <build>
    <plugins>
      <plugin>
        <groupId>org.springframework.boot</groupId>
        <artifactId>spring-boot-maven-plugin</artifactId>
      </plugin>
    </plugins>
  </build>
</project>
```

Create the Application Class

Let's create a DemoApplication class with a main method. The main method calls
SpringApplication.run with DemoApplication.class and arguments from the main
method. The run method returns an ApplicationContext, and the bean names can be
retrieved from it. Use the getBeanDefinitionNames method to retrieve the names, iterate
over them and get the actual beans from the ApplicationContext, and print some
information about the bean.

The resulting class will look like Listing 1-5.

Listing 1-5. DemoApplication Class

```java
package com.apress.springboot3recipes.demo;

import java.util.Arrays;

import org.springframework.boot.SpringApplication;
import org.springframework.boot.autoconfigure.SpringBootApplication;

@SpringBootApplication
public class DemoApplication {
  public static void main(String[] args) {
    try (var ctx = SpringApplication.run(DemoApplication.class, args)) {

      System.out.println("# Beans: " + ctx.getBeanDefinitionCount());

      var names = ctx.getBeanDefinitionNames();
      Arrays.sort(names);
      Arrays.asList(names).forEach(System.out::println);
    }
  }
}
```

This class is a regular Java class with a main method, so you can just run this class
from your IDE. When the application runs, it will show output similar to Figure 1-1.

```
    .   ____          _            __ _ _
   /\\ / ___'_ __ _ _(_)_ __  __ _ \ \ \ \
  ( ( )\___ | '_ | '_| | '_ \/ _` | \ \ \ \
   \\/  ___)| |_)| | | | | || (_| |  ) ) ) )
    '  |____| .__|_| |_|_| |_\__, | / / / /
   =========|_|==============|___/=/_/_/_/
   :: Spring Boot ::                (v3.2.1)

2023-12-27T12:01:21.839+01:00  INFO 19202 --- [           main] c.a.s.demo.DemoApplication
2023-12-27T12:01:21.842+01:00  INFO 19202 --- [           main] c.a.s.demo.DemoApplication
2023-12-27T12:01:22.428+01:00  INFO 19202 --- [           main] c.a.s.demo.DemoApplication
# Beans: 59
applicationAvailability
applicationTaskExecutor
demoApplication
```

Figure 1-1. *Output of running the application*

What happened with this code and annotations? The @SpringBootApplication annotation makes this class the entry point for a Spring Boot application. The @SpringBootApplication class is a so-called composed annotation and is annotated with other annotations (see Figure 1-2). Next to some general Java-based annotations, you see the @SpringBootConfiguration, @EnableAutoConfiguration, and @ComponentScan annotations.

```
@Target(ElementType.TYPE)
@Retention(RetentionPolicy.RUNTIME)
@Documented
@Configuration
@Indexed
public @interface SpringBootConfiguration {
```

```
@Target(ElementType.TYPE)
@Retention(RetentionPolicy.RUNTIME)
@Documented
@Inherited
@AutoConfigurationPackage
@Import(AutoConfigurationImportSelector.class)
public @interface EnableAutoConfiguration {
```

```
@Target(ElementType.TYPE)
@Retention(RetentionPolicy.RUNTIME)
@Documented
@Inherited
@SpringBootConfiguration
@EnableAutoConfiguration
@ComponentScan(excludeFilters = { @Filter(type = FilterType.CUSTOM, classes = TypeExcludeFilter.class),
        @Filter(type = FilterType.CUSTOM, classes = AutoConfigurationExcludeFilter.class) })
public @interface SpringBootApplication {
```

Figure 1-2. *@SpringBootApplication definition*

Let's take a quick look at the different annotations and what they achieve:

- @ComponentScan: This annotation instructs Spring to scan everything in this package and all of its subpackages. It will detect all the @Component annotated classes. The defined filters are so that exclusions can be made, either by using the exclude attribute from @EnableAutoConfiguration or by providing a TypeFilter as a bean in the application context.

- @EnableAutoConfiguration: This registers AutoConfigurationImportSelector, which will load the auto-configuration classes from a file in the classpath (/META-INF/spring/ org.springframework.boot.autoconfigure.AutoConfiguration. imports) and check if the config should be included. It also has an additional @AutoConfigurationPackage annotation, which will also register this package for component scanning, so components in this (and subpackages) will also be automatically detected.

- @SpringBootConfiguration: This class is a specialization of the @Configuration for Spring Boot and will be mainly used to detect the main entrypoint for the application. This is especially useful for testing. Your application should have only one class with the @SpringBootConfiguration annotation, and generally that is the @SpringBootApplication annotated class.

1-2. Create a Spring Boot Application Using Gradle

Problem

You want to start developing an application using Spring Boot and Gradle.

Solution

Create a Gradle build file, build.gradle, and add the needed dependencies. To launch the application, create a Java class containing a main method to bootstrap the application.

How It Works

Suppose you are going to create a simple application that bootstraps
SpringApplication, gets all the beans from ApplicationContext, and outputs them to
the console.

Create the build.gradle File

First you need to create a build.gradle file and use the two plugins needed for Gradle
to properly manage the dependencies for Spring Boot. Spring Boot requires a special
Gradle plugin as well as a plugin to extend the default dependency management
capabilities of Gradle. As this is also a Java project, you will also need the java plugin.

Listing 1-6. Spring Boot Gradle Plugins

```
plugins {
    id 'java'
    id 'org.springframework.boot' version '3.2.1'
    id 'io.spring.dependency-management' version '1-1-4'
}
```

Finally, you will need to add the needed dependencies. Just as with Recipe 1-1, add
the spring-boot-starter dependency.

Listing 1-7. Spring Boot Gradle Dependencies

```
dependencies {
    implementation 'org.springframework.boot:spring-boot-starter'
}
```

Notice the absence of the specific version on the dependency. If you are familiar with
Gradle, this might come as a surprise. You do not have to specify the version because it is
automatically managed by the io.spring.dependency-management plugin. Just as with
Maven, this allows for easier dependency management.

The full build.gradle file should now look something like Listing 1-8.

Listing 1-8. Full Gradle Build File

```
plugins {
    id 'java'
    id 'org.springframework.boot' version '3.2.1'
    id 'io.spring.dependency-management' version '1-1-4'
}

sourceCompatibility = 21

repositories {
    mavenCentral()
}

dependencies {
    implementation 'org.springframework.boot:spring-boot-starter'
}

tasks.named('test') {
    useJUnitPlatform()
}
```

Create the Application Class

Let's create a DemoApplication class with a main method. The main method calls SpringApplication.run with DemoApplication.class and arguments from the main method. The run method returns an ApplicationContext, which can be used to retrieve the bean names. Use the getBeanDefinitionNames method to retrieve the names, iterate over them and get the actual beans from ApplicationContext, and print some information about the bean.

The resulting class will look like Listing 1-9.

Listing 1-9. DemoApplication Class

```
package com.apress.springboot3recipes.demo;

import java.util.Arrays;

import org.springframework.boot.SpringApplication;
import org.springframework.boot.autoconfigure.SpringBootApplication;
```

```java
@SpringBootApplication
public class DemoApplication {

  public static void main(String[] args) {
    try (var ctx = SpringApplication.run(DemoApplication.class, args)) {

      System.out.println("# Beans: " + ctx.getBeanDefinitionCount());

      var names = ctx.getBeanDefinitionNames();
      Arrays.sort(names);
      Arrays.asList(names).forEach(System.out::println);
    }
  }
}
```

This class is a regular Java class with a `main` method, so you can just run this class from your IDE. When the application runs, it will show output similar to Figure 1-3.

```
  .   ____          _            __ _ _
 /\\ / ___'_ __ _ _(_)_ __  __ _ \ \ \ \
( ( )\___ | '_ | '_| | '_ \/ _` | \ \ \ \
 \\/  ___)| |_)| | | | | || (_| |  ) ) ) )
  '  |____| .__|_| |_|_| |_\__, | / / / /
 =========|_|==============|___/=/_/_/_/
 :: Spring Boot ::                (v3.2.1)

2023-12-27T12:01:21.839+01:00  INFO 19202 --- [           main] c.a.s.demo.DemoApplication
2023-12-27T12:01:21.842+01:00  INFO 19202 --- [           main] c.a.s.demo.DemoApplication
2023-12-27T12:01:22.428+01:00  INFO 19202 --- [           main] c.a.s.demo.DemoApplication
# Beans: 59
applicationAvailability
applicationTaskExecutor
demoApplication
```

Figure 1-3. *Output of running the application*

What happened with this code and annotations? The `@SpringBootApplication` annotation makes this class the entry point for a Spring Boot application. The `@SpringBootApplication` class is a so-called composed annotation and is annotated with other annotations (see Figure 1-4). Next to some general Java-based annotations, you see the `@SpringBootConfiguration`, `@EnableAutoConfiguration`, and `@ComponentScan` annotations.

```
@Target(ElementType.TYPE)
@Retention(RetentionPolicy.RUNTIME)
@Documented
@Configuration
@Indexed
public @interface SpringBootConfiguration {
```

```
@Target(ElementType.TYPE)
@Retention(RetentionPolicy.RUNTIME)
@Documented
@Inherited
@AutoConfigurationPackage
@Import(AutoConfigurationImportSelector.class)
public @interface EnableAutoConfiguration {
```

```
@Target(ElementType.TYPE)
@Retention(RetentionPolicy.RUNTIME)
@Documented
@Inherited
@SpringBootConfiguration
@EnableAutoConfiguration
@ComponentScan(excludeFilters = { @Filter(type = FilterType.CUSTOM, classes = TypeExcludeFilter.class),
        @Filter(type = FilterType.CUSTOM, classes = AutoConfigurationExcludeFilter.class) })
public @interface SpringBootApplication {
```

Figure 1-4. *@SpringBootApplication definition*

Let's take a quick look at the different annotations and what they achieve:

- @ComponentScan: This annotation instructs Spring to scan everything in this package and all of its subpackages. It will detect all @Component annotated classes. The defined filters are so that exclusions can be made, either by using the exclude attribute from the @EnableAutoConfiguration or by providing a TypeFilter as a bean in the application context.

- @EnableAutoConfiguration: This registers AutoConfigurationImportSelector, which will load the auto-configuration classes from a file in the classpath (/META-INF/spring/ org.springframework.boot.autoconfigure.AutoConfiguration. imports) and check if the config should be included. It also has an additional @AutoConfigurationPackage annotation, which will also register this package for component scanning, so components in this package (and subpackages) will also be automatically detected.

- @SpringBootConfiguration: This class is a specialization of the @Configuration for Spring Boot and will be mainly used to detect the main entry point for the application; this is especially useful for testing. Your application should have only one class with the @SpringBootConfiguration annotation, and generally that is the @SpringBootApplication annotated class.

1-3. Create a Spring Boot Application Using Spring Initializr

Problem

You want to start a Spring Boot application using Spring Initializr

Solution

Go to `https://start.spring.io`, select the Spring Boot version and the different dependencies you think you need, and download the project.

How It Works

First go to `https://start.spring.io`, which will open the Spring Initializr (see Figure 1-5).

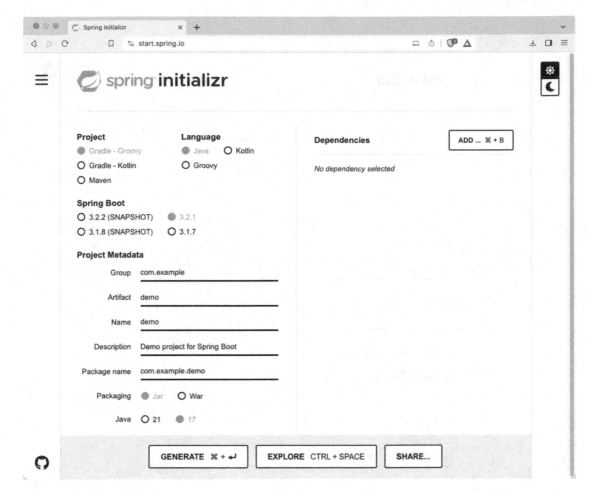

Figure 1-5. *Spring Initializr*

Now select what you want to generate (Maven or Gradle) and select the Spring Boot version you want to use (probably the most recent one). For the group, enter com.apress.springboot3recipes, and as an artifact leave the default demo value (see Figure 1-6).

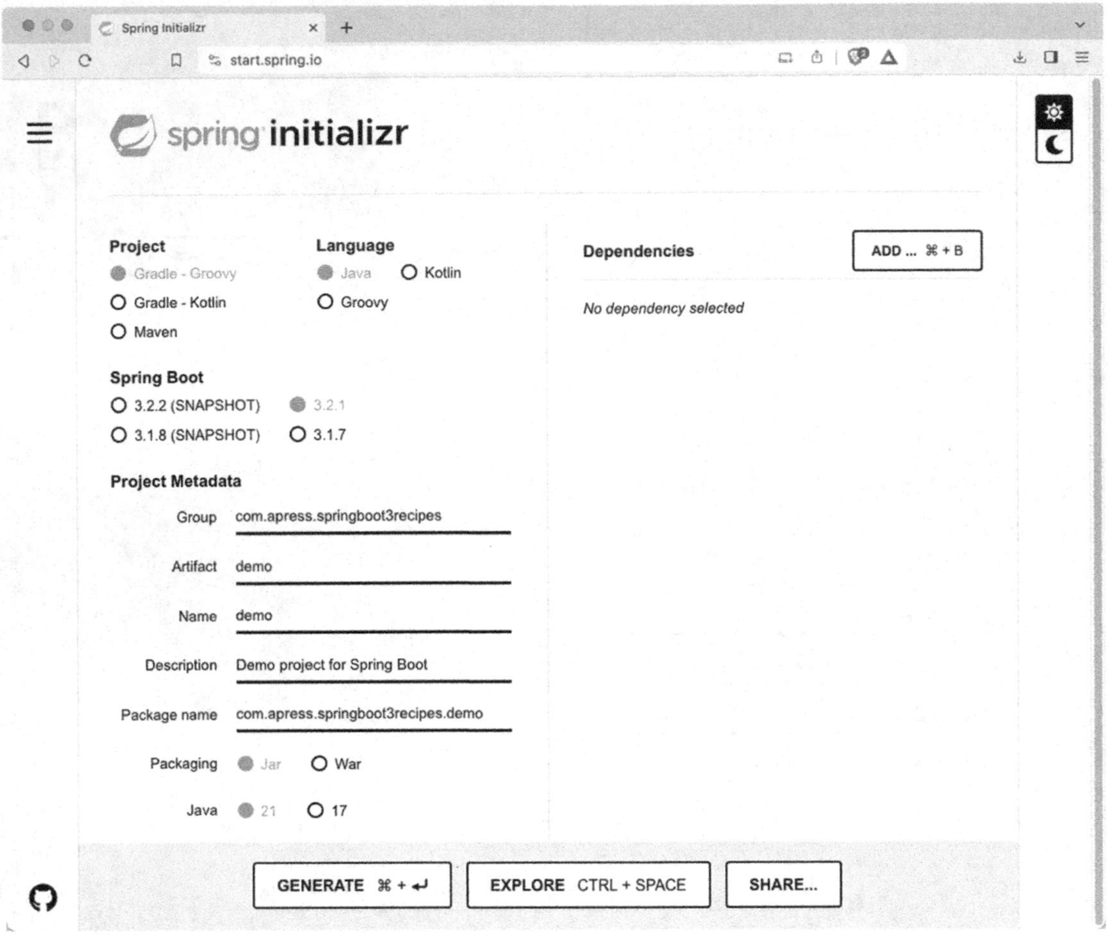

Figure 1-6. *Spring Initializr with values*

Finally, click the Generate button, which will trigger a download of a `demo.zip` file. Extract this zip file and import the project into your IDE. After importing, you should have a structure like what's shown in Figure 1-7.

Figure 1-7. *Imported project*

Open the `pom.xml` file and compare it to the one from Recipe 1-1. It is quite similar; however, there are differences to note. There is an additional dependency, `spring-boot-starter-test`. This pulls in the needed test dependencies like Spring Test, Mockito, JUnit, and AssertJ. With this single dependency, you are ready to start testing.

Building the JAR File

When using the Spring Initializr, all projects come with the Maven Wrapper (or Gradle Wrapper when using Gradle) to make it easier to build the application. You don't need to have Maven pre-installed to build the application. To use these scripts, open a command line, navigate to the directory the project is in, and execute `./mvnw verify` or `./mvnw package`. This should create the executable artifact in the target.

🛈   Running the `verify` goal is recommended for local development by the Maven team; it will run more checks on the results of the tests and other plugins that might run.

Now that the JAR file has been built, let's execute it and see what happens. Type `java -jar target/demo-0.0.1-SNAPSHOT.jar` and watch the application start and shut down, as the application itself doesn't do much, as shown in Figure 1-8. Depending on the dependencies you choose to use, the output might differ (like starting a Tomcat server, initializing an H2 database, etc.).

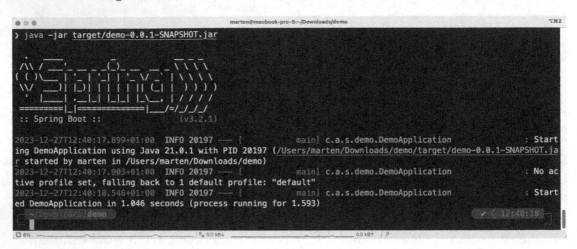

Figure 1-8. *Console output of running the JAR file*

Summary

In this chapter, you looked at how to bootstrap your development using Spring Boot. We looked at how to get started using Maven as well as Gradle, and finally we looked at how to get started using the Spring Initializr.

In the next chapter, we will take a look at the basic configuration of a Spring Boot application, how to define a bean, how to use property files, and how to override properties.

CHAPTER 2

The Basics of Spring Boot

In this chapter, we will take a look at the foundational features of Spring Boot.

ⓘ   Use the Spring Initializr to create a project; no additional dependencies are required.

2-1. Configure a Bean
Problem

You want Spring Boot to use your class as a bean.

Solution

Depending on your needs, either you can leverage `@ComponentScan` to automatically detect your class and create an instance, using it with `@Autowired` and `@Value` to inject dependencies or properties, or you can use a method annotated with `@Bean` in an `@Configuration` class to maintain more control over the bean being created.

How It Works

Recipe 1-1 explained that `@SpringBootApplication` includes both `@ComponentScan` and `@Configuration`. This means that any `@Component` annotated class will be automatically detected and instantiated by Spring Boot; it also allows for `@Bean` methods to be defined to declare beans.

© Marten Deinum 2024
M. Deinum, *Spring Boot 3 Recipes*, https://doi.org/10.1007/979-8-8688-0113-6_2

Configure a Bean Using @Component

First create a class to bootstrap the application. Create a HelloWorldApplication instance that is annotated with @SpringBootApplication. See Listing 2-1.

Listing 2-1. HelloWorldApplication Source

```
package com.apress.springboot3recipes.helloworld;

import org.springframework.boot.SpringApplication;
import org.springframework.boot.autoconfigure.SpringBootApplication;

@SpringBootApplication
public class HelloWorldApplication {

  public static void main(String[] args) {
    SpringApplication.run(HelloWorldApplication.class, args);
  }
}
```

💡 Place the @SpringBootApplication annotated class in a top-level package. This way it will automatically detect all your annotated components, configuration classes, etc.[1]

This will bootstrap the application, detect all @Component annotated classes, and detect which libraries are on the classpath (see also Chapter 1). When running this HelloWorldApplication, you will see that it won't do much, as there is nothing to detect or to run. Let's create a simple class that Spring Boot will automatically detect.

---

[1] https://docs.spring.io/spring-boot/docs/current/reference/htmlsingle/#using-boot-locating-the-main-class

```
package com.apress.springboot3recipes.helloworld;

import jakarta.annotation.PostConstruct;
import org.springframework.stereotype.Component;

@Component
public class HelloWorld {

  @PostConstruct
  public void sayHello() {
    System.out.println("Hello World, from Spring Boot 3!");
  }
}
```

This class will automatically be detected by Spring Boot due to the @Component annotation. The @PostConstruct annotation tells Spring to invoke this method after constructing the bean and injecting all the dependencies. Simply put, at startup the sayHello method will be run, and the console will print the line Hello World, from Spring Boot 3!.

💡   When you need to scan packages not covered by the default component scanning, you can use scanBasePackages or scanBasePackagesClasses on the @SpringBootApplication annotation to define additional packages to scan.

Configure a Bean Using an @Bean Method

Instead of automatically detecting components, you can also use a factory method to create beans. This is useful if you want or need more control over the construction of your bean. A factory method is a method annotated with @Bean,[2] and it will be used to register a bean in the application context. By default, the name of the bean is the same as the name of the method. The method can also have arguments, and they will be automatically resolved to other beans in the application context.

---

[2] https://docs.spring.io/spring/docs/current/spring-framework-reference/core.html#beans-java-bean-annotation

Let's create an application that can do some basic calculations for integers. First let's write the `Calculator`. It will get a collection of `Operation` beans in the constructor. `Operation` is an interface, and the different implementations will do the actual calculation. See Listing 2-2.

Listing 2-2. Calculator Class Source

```
package com.apress.springboot3recipes.calculator;

import org.springframework.stereotype.Component;

import java.util.Collection;

@Component
public class Calculator {

  private final Collection<Operation> operations;

  public Calculator(Collection<Operation> operations) {
    this.operations = operations;
  }

  public void calculate(int lhs, int rhs, char op) {
    operations.stream()
        .filter((operation) -> operation.handles(op))
        .map((operation) -> operation.apply(lhs, rhs))
        .peek( (result) -> System.out.printf("%d %s %d = %s%n", lhs, op,
        rhs, result))
        .findFirst()
        .orElseThrow(() ->
        new IllegalArgumentException("Unknown operation " + op));
  }
}
```

In the `calculate` method, the right `Operation` is detected using the `Operation.handles` method; when the right one is found, the `Operation.apply` method is called to do the actual calculation. If we pass in an operation that the calculator cannot handle, a method is thrown.

The Operation interface is a simple interface with the earlier mentioned two methods. See Listing 2-3.

Listing 2-3. Operation Interface Source

```
package com.apress.springboot3recipes.calculator;

public interface Operation {

  int apply(int lhs, int rhs);
  boolean handles(char op);
}
```

Now let's add two operations: one for adding values and one for multiplying values. See Listing 2-4 and Listing 2-5.

Listing 2-4. Addition Operation Class Source

```
package com.apress.springboot3recipes.calculator.operation;

import com.apress.springboot3recipes.calculator.Operation;
import org.springframework.stereotype.Component;

@Component
class Addition implements Operation {

    @Override
    public int apply(int lhs, int rhs) {
        return lhs + rhs;
    }

    @Override
    public boolean handles(char op) {
        return '+' == op;
    }
}
```

Listing 2-5. Multiplication Operation Class Source

```java
package com.apress.springboot3recipes.calculator.operation;

import com.apress.springboot3recipes.calculator.Operation;
import org.springframework.stereotype.Component;

@Component
class Multiplication implements Operation {

    @Override
    public int apply(int lhs, int rhs) {
        return lhs * rhs;
    }

    @Override
    public boolean handles(char op) {
        return '*' == op;
    }
}
```

These are all the components we need to make a calculator that can do addition and multiplication and still have an extensible mechanism.

Finally, let's make an application that configures and uses the Calculator. To make an instance of the Calculator, an @Bean method is needed; this method can be added to the class annotated with @SpringBootApplication or a regular @Configuration. See Listing 2-6.

Listing 2-6. CalculatorApplication Source

```java
package com.apress.springboot3recipes.calculator;

import org.springframework.boot.SpringApplication;
import org.springframework.boot.autoconfigure.SpringBootApplication;
import org.springframework.context.annotation.Bean;

import java.util.Collection;
```

```
@SpringBootApplication
public class CalculatorApplication {

  public static void main(String[] args) {
    var ctx = SpringApplication.run(CalculatorApplication.class, args);

    var calculator = ctx.getBean(Calculator.class);
    calculator.calculate(137, 21, '+');
    calculator.calculate(137, 21, '*');
    calculator.calculate(137, 21, '-');
  }

  @Bean
  public Calculator calculator(Collection<Operation> operations) {
    return new Calculator(operations);
  }
}
```

The calculator factory method takes a Collection<Operation>, and we use that to construct the Calculator. When using parameters in the @Bean annotated method, those will automatically be resolved. When injecting a generic collection, Spring will automatically detect all instances of the beans required and use that to invoke the calculator factory method.

In the main method, we retrieve the Calculator and call its calculate method with different numbers and operations. The first two will nicely print some output to the console. The last one will throw an exception as there is no suitable operation to do subtractions (Figure 2-1).

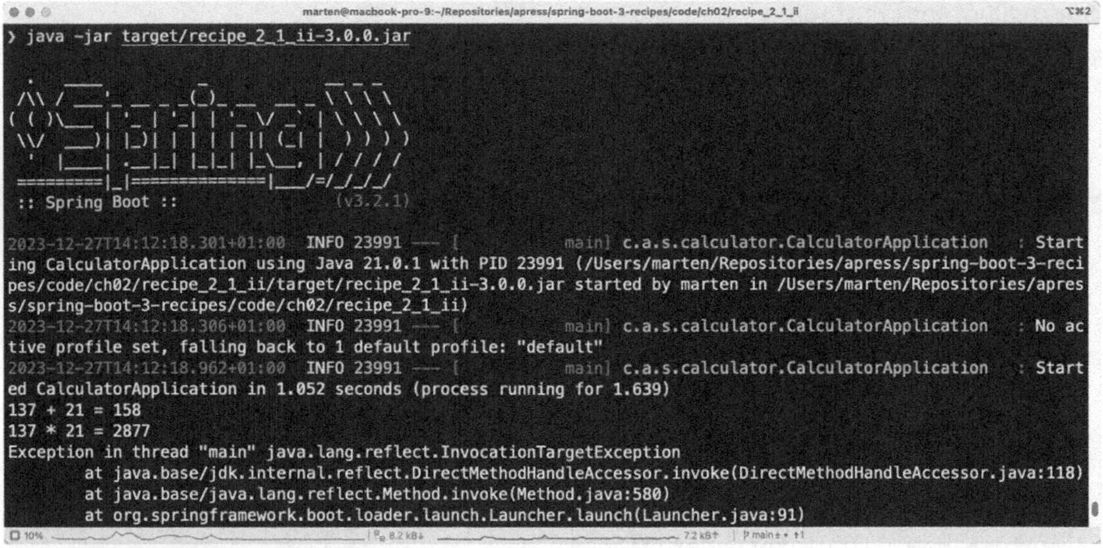

Figure 2-1. *Calculator application output*

Although you created a factory method for the `Calculator`, this isn't actually needed, as it has been annotated with `@Component`, and Spring will automatically use the single constructor in the class and try to detect all dependencies. Another thing that isn't really nice about this code is that beans are retrieved manually, which could be considered a bad practice. Generally, you want to use dependency injection. Spring Boot has an `ApplicationRunner` interface that can be used to run some code after the application starts. When Spring Boot detects a bean of type `ApplicationRunner`, it will invoke its method as soon as the application has fully started. Let's clean up the code by using this interface. See Listing 2-7.

Listing 2-7. CalculatorApplication Source (Updated)

```
package com.apress.springboot3recipes.calculator;

import org.springframework.boot.ApplicationRunner;
import org.springframework.boot.SpringApplication;
import org.springframework.boot.autoconfigure.SpringBootApplication;
import org.springframework.context.annotation.Bean;

@SpringBootApplication
public class CalculatorApplication {
```

```
public static void main(String[] args) {
  SpringApplication.run(CalculatorApplication.class, args);
}

@Bean
public ApplicationRunner calculationRunner(Calculator calculator) {
  return args -> {
    calculator.calculate(137, 21, '+');
    calculator.calculate(137, 21, '*');
    calculator.calculate(137, 21, '-');
  };
}
}
```

The method to create a `Calculator` has been replaced by an `ApplicationRunner`.
This `ApplicationRunner` receives the automatically configured `Calculator` and runs
some operations on it. When running this class, the output should still be the same as
before (Figure 2-1). The major difference and advantage is that it is no longer needed to
manually get beans from the `ApplicationContext` as Spring will take care of getting the
correct beans.

2-2. Externalize Properties

Problem

You want to use properties to configure your application for different environments or
executions.

Solution

Spring Boot supports getting properties from numerous locations. By default it will
load a file named `application.properties` and also use the OS environment variables
as well as Java `System` properties. When running from the command line, it will also
take command-line arguments into consideration. There are more locations that are
taken into account depending on the type of application and availability or capabilities

(like JNDI, for instance).[3] For our application, the following resources are taken into consideration in a given order:

- `application.properties`/`application.yaml` outside of the packaged application

- `application.properties`/`application.yaml` packaged inside the application

- OS environment variables

- Java system properties

- Command-line arguments

💡 Instead of `.properties` files, you could also use a YAML file to express the configuration properties. The same rules as with `.properties` files still apply.

In addition, for the first two options, you can also load a profile-specific one based on the active profiles. The profiles to activate can be passed through the `spring.profiles.active` property. The profile-specific `application-{profile}.properties` profiles take precedence over the non-profile-specific ones. Each will get loaded, and with that you can override properties. Therefore, this list is a bit longer:

- `application-{profile}.properties` outside the packaged application

- `application.properties` outside of the packaged application

- `application-{profile}.properties` packaged inside the application

- `application.properties` packaged inside the application

- OS environment variables

- Java system properties

- Command-line arguments

---

[3] https://docs.spring.io/spring-boot/docs/current/reference/html/boot-features-external-config.html#boot-features-external-config

How It Works

The Calculator created for Recipe 2-1 is pretty flexible; however, the CalculatorApplication has hard-coded values when it comes to the calculations it does. Now when we want to calculate something different, we would need to modify the code, recompile, and run the newly compiled code. We probably want to use properties for this so that we are able to change them when needed.

First modify the application to use the values from properties instead of hard-coded values. For this, change the @Bean method for the ApplicationRunner to accept three additional parameters, which are going to be annotated with @Value. See Listing 2-8.

Listing 2-8. CalculatorApplication Source with Properties

```
package com.apress.springboot3recipes.calculator;

import org.springframework.beans.factory.annotation.Value;
import org.springframework.boot.ApplicationRunner;
import org.springframework.boot.SpringApplication;
import org.springframework.boot.autoconfigure.SpringBootApplication;
import org.springframework.context.annotation.Bean;

@SpringBootApplication
public class CalculatorApplication {

  public static void main(String[] args) {
    SpringApplication.run(CalculatorApplication.class, args);
  }

  @Bean
  public ApplicationRunner calculationRunner(Calculator calculator,
                      @Value("${lhs}") int lhs,
                      @Value("${rhs}") int rhs,
                      @Value("${op}") char op) {
    return args -> calculator.calculate(lhs, rhs, op);
  }
}
```

The @Value will instruct Spring to look up the property and use the value of that property. For instance, if we would use a @Value("${lhs}"), Spring would try to detect a property named lhs and use the value. You could also specify a default value by adding a semicolon with the value @Value("${lhs:12}"). Now, if no value can be found, it will use 12. If there is no default value specified, an exception will be thrown. If we started the application now, an exception would be thrown explaining that no property called lhs can be found.

Add application.properties in src/main/resources and put values in there for lhs, rhs, and op. See Listing 2-9.

Listing 2-9. Default Properties

```
lhs=12
rhs=15
op=*
```

Spring Boot will load the application.properties at startup, and with that the properties are available. Now when running the application, it should again create output honoring the values given in application.properties (Figure 2-2).

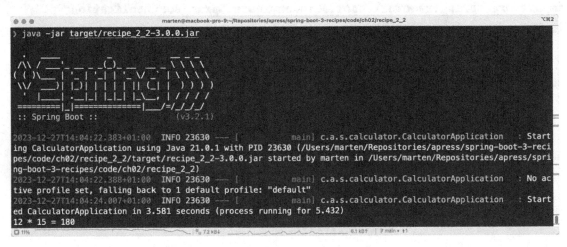

Figure 2-2. Calculator application output

Although you now have externalized the properties into application.properties, those properties are still packaged up inside the application. That would mean you still would need to change them to do a different calculation. Imagine doing this for a real production system and creating new artifacts just because your configuration needs to change. There are different ways in which Spring Boot can help you with that.

Override Properties Using an External application.properties File

First build the artifact and launch the application with `java -jar`
`recipe_2_2-3.0.0.jar`. It will still run and use the supplied and packaged `application.`
`properties`. Now in the same location as the artifact, add `application.properties` and
put values in there for the different properties. See Listing 2-10.

Listing 2-10. Example Overridden Properties

```
lhs=26
rhs=952
op=*
```

When launching the application again, it will now use the values from this
`application.properties`. See Figure 2-3.

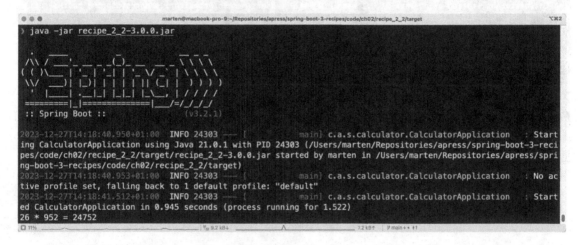

Figure 2-3. *Calculator application output - using overridden properties*

Override Properties Using Profiles

Spring Boot can use the active profiles to load additional configuration files that can
totally replace or override parts of the general configuration. Let's add `application-`
`add.properties` in `src/main/resources`, which contains a different value for `op`. See
Listing 2-11.

Listing 2-11. Profile-Specific Properties

```
op=+
```

Now build the artifact (a JAR file) and launch it from the command line with
`java -jar recipe_2_2-3.0.0.jar --spring.profiles.active=add`, and it will start
and use the properties from both `application.properties` and `application-add.
properties` to configure the application. Notice how an addition operation is done
instead of multiplication (Figure 2-4), which indicates that the `application-add.
properties` properties take precedence over the general `application.properties`
properties.

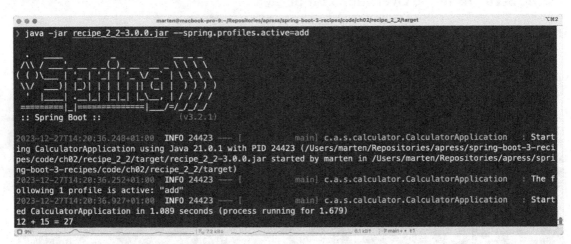

Figure 2-4. *Calculator application output - overridden properties using profiles*

💡 This also works when working with an external `application.properties`
and `application-{profile}.properties` files.

Override Properties Using Command-Line Arguments

The last option is to use command-line arguments to override properties. In the previous
section, you already used the command-line argument `--spring.profile.active=add`
to specify the active profile. You can also specify `lhs` and other arguments that way. Use
`java -jar recipe_2_2-3.0.0.jar --lhs=22 --rhs=25 --op=+` to run the application;
you will see that it does the calculation based on the arguments passed in through the
command line (Figure 2-5). Arguments from the command line always override all other
configurations.

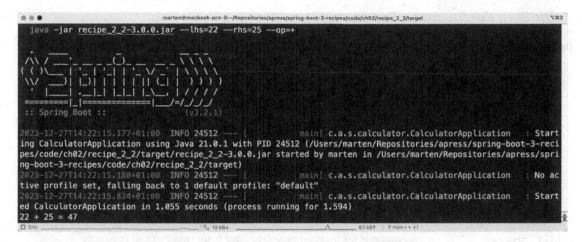

Figure 2-5. *Calculator application output - overridden properties using arguments*

Load Properties from Different Configuration Files

If you are using a different file than `application.properties` or you have some component that comes with an embedded file you want to load, you can always use an additional `@PropertySource` annotation on your `@SpringBootApplication` annotated class to load that additional file. See Listing 2-12.

Listing 2-12. Application Class with @PropertySource

```
@PropertySource("classpath:your-external.properties")
@SpringBootApplication
public class MyApplication { ... }
```

The `@PropertySource` annotation allows you to add additional property files to be loaded during startup. You can also specify the behavior when the file isn't found by specifying the `ignoreResourceNotFound` attribute and setting it to `true` (the default is `false`).

Although adding an additional `@PropertySource` annotation would work, it doesn't rely on Spring Boot to load it and as such wouldn't get the same treatment. You wouldn't be able to load a different configuration for another profile. However, instead of using an `@PropertySource` annotation, you can instruct Spring Boot to load additional property files using command-line parameters (see Table 2-1).

31

Table 2-1. *Configuration Parameters*

Parameter	Description
`spring.config.name`	Comma-separated string of filenames to load; the default is `application`.
`spring.config.location`	Comma-separated string of resource locations (or files) to consider for loading property files from; the default is `classpath:/,classpath:/config/,file:./,file:./config/`.
`spring.config.additional-location`	Comma-separated string of additional resource locations (or files) to consider for loading property files from; the default is empty.

> 🛈   When using `spring.config.location` or `spring.config.additional-location` with a file location, this will be used as is, and a profile-specific one won't be loaded. When using a directory, the profile-specific files will be loaded.

Using `--spring.config.name=your-external` would be sufficient to load the your-external.properties file; however, this will break loading `application.properties`, so it is better to use `--spring.config.name=application,your-external`. Now all the locations will be searched for both `application.properties` and `your-external.properties`, and also the profile-specific versions will be taken into consideration.

2-3. Configure Testing

Problem

You want to write a test for a component or part of your Spring Boot application.

Solution

Spring Boot extends the range of features of the Spring Testing framework. It adds support for mocking and spying (through Mockito) on beans as well as provides autoconfiguration for web tests. It also introduces easy ways of testing slices of your application by bootstrapping only what is needed (through the use of @WebMvCTest or @JdbcTest, for instance) or to write full-blown integration tests with @SpringBootTest.

How It Works

Spring Boot extended the auto-configuration to parts of the test framework as well. It integrates with Mockito for easy mocking (or spying) on beans. It also provides auto-configuration for web-based tests using either the Spring MockMvc testing framework or WebDriver-based testing.

Write a Unit Test

First let's write a simple unit test for one of the components of the calculator, MultiplicationTest, which will test the Multiplication class. See Listing 2-13.

Listing 2-13. Basic Unit Test

```
package com.apress.springboot3recipes.calculator.operation;

import org.junit.jupiter.api.Test;

import static org.junit.jupiter.api.Assertions.assertEquals;
import static org.junit.jupiter.api.Assertions.assertFalse;
import static org.junit.jupiter.api.Assertions.assertTrue;

public class MultiplicationTest {

  private final Multiplication operation = new Multiplication();

  @Test
  public void shouldMatchSign() {
    assertTrue(operation.handles('*'));
    assertFalse(operation.handles('/'));
  }
```

```
@Test
public void shouldCorrectlyApplyFormula() {
    assertEquals(4, operation.apply(2, 2));
    assertEquals(120, operation.apply(12, 10));
  }
}
```

This is a basic unit test. Once `Multiplication` is instantiated, we call methods on it, and finally we validate the outcome. The first test will test if it really reacts to the * operator and not something else. The second test will test the actual multiplication logic. To make a method a test method, you will have to annotate it with `@Test`.

Mock Dependencies in a Unit Test

Sometimes a class needs dependencies; however, you want your test to test only a single component (when writing a unit test). Spring Boot automatically brings in the Mockito framework. Mockito is a nice library to mock classes and record behavior on them. Writing a test for the `Calculator` application requires additional components as it delegates the actual calculation to the available `Operation` classes. To test the correct behavior of the `Calculator`, we would need to create a mock of the `Operation` and inject that into the `Calculator`. See Listing 2-14.

Listing 2-14. Unit Test with Mock

```
package com.apress.springboot3recipes.calculator;

import static org.junit.jupiter.api.Assertions.assertThrows;
import static org.mockito.Mockito.anyChar;
import static org.mockito.Mockito.times;
import static org.mockito.Mockito.verify;
import static org.mockito.Mockito.when;

import java.util.Collections;

import org.junit.jupiter.api.BeforeEach;
import org.junit.jupiter.api.Test;
import org.mockito.Mockito;

public class CalculatorTest {
```

```java
private Calculator calculator;
private Operation mockOperation;

@BeforeEach
public void setup() {
  mockOperation = Mockito.mock(Operation.class);
  calculator = new Calculator(Collections.singletonList(mockOperation));
}

@Test
public void throwExceptionWhenNoSuitableOperationFound() {
  when(mockOperation.handles(anyChar())).thenReturn(false);
  assertThrows(IllegalArgumentException.class,
          () -> calculator.calculate(2, 2, '*'));
}

@Test
public void shouldCallApplyMethodWhenSuitableOperationFound() {
  when(mockOperation.handles(anyChar())).thenReturn(true);
  when(mockOperation.apply(2, 2)).thenReturn(4);

  calculator.calculate(2, 2, '*');

  verify(mockOperation, times(1)).apply(2, 2);
 }
}
```

In the @BeforeEach class, we mock the Operation by calling Mockito.mock, and we construct the Calculator using the mocked operation. The mock is used in the test methods to have a certain behavior. In the first test method, we want to test the situation where no suitable operation can be found, and hence we instruct the mock to return false when the handles method is being called. The test will expect an exception; if the exception occurs, the test will succeed. The second test is to test if the correct flow is followed; we want to test the correct behavior. The mock is instructed to return true for the handles method and a return value for the apply method.

Perform Integration Testing with Spring Boot

Spring Boot provides several annotations to aid in testing. The first is @SpringBootTest, which will make the test a Spring Boot–driven test, which means that the test context framework will be searching for the class annotated with @SpringBootApplication (if no specific configuration is passed) and will use that to actually start the application. See Listing 2-15.

Listing 2-15. Spring Boot Integration Test

```
package com.apress.springboot3recipes.calculator;

import static org.junit.jupiter.api.Assertions.assertThrows;
import static org.junit.jupiter.api.Assertions.assertTrue;

import org.junit.jupiter.api.Test;
import org.junit.jupiter.api.extension.ExtendWith;
import org.springframework.beans.factory.annotation.Autowired;
import org.springframework.boot.test.context.SpringBootTest;

@SpringBootTest(classes = CalculatorApplication.class)
public class CalculatorApplicationTests {

  @Autowired
  private Calculator calculator;

  @Test
  public void doingDivisionShouldFail() {
    assertThrows(IllegalArgumentException.class,
          () -> calculator.calculate(12,13, '/'));
  }
}
```

The previous test will start the CalculatorApplication and inject the fully configured Calculator. We can then write a test, in this case a situation that the calculator cannot handle, and write expectations for it.

When doing a calculation, the output is printed to the console. Using the OutputCaptureExtension JUnit extension, we could also write a success test and test the written output. See Listing 2-16.

Listing 2-16. Spring Boot Integration Test (Extended)

```
package com.apress.springboot3recipes.calculator;

import static org.junit.jupiter.api.Assertions.assertThrows;
import static org.junit.jupiter.api.Assertions.assertTrue;

import org.junit.jupiter.api.Test;
import org.junit.jupiter.api.extension.ExtendWith;
import org.springframework.beans.factory.annotation.Autowired;
import org.springframework.boot.test.context.SpringBootTest;
import org.springframework.boot.test.system.CapturedOutput;
import org.springframework.boot.test.system.OutputCaptureExtension;

@ExtendWith(OutputCaptureExtension.class)
@SpringBootTest(classes = CalculatorApplication.class)
public class CalculatorApplicationTests {

  @Autowired
  private Calculator calculator;

  @Test
  public void doingMultiplicationShouldSucceed(CapturedOutput capture) {
    calculator.calculate(12,13, '*');
    assertTrue(capture.getOut().contains("12 * 13 = 156"));
  }

  @Test
  public void doingDivisionShouldFail() {
    assertThrows(IllegalArgumentException.class,
            () -> calculator.calculate(12,13, '/'));
  }
}
```

The `@ExtendWith` will configure the given JUnit extension, in this case the `OutputCaptureExtension` extension, which comes with Spring Boot and intercepts `System.out` and `System.err` so that assertions can be written on the output generated on those streams. To inspect the output, use the `CapturedOutput` class. This can be injected into the method automatically by the extension. In this case, we do multiplication, and the output should reflect that.

Perform Integration Testing with Spring Boot and Mocks

Spring Boot makes it easy to replace a bean with a mock in the application context. For this, Spring Boot has the @MockBean annotation. See Listing 2-17.

Listing 2-17. MockBean Annotation Sample

```
@MockBean
private Calculator calculator
```

This would replace the whole calculator with a mocked instance. To be able to use it, you would need to define the behavior using the regular Mockito way. When there are multiple beans of a certain type, you need to specify the name attribute of the bean you want to replace. See Listing 2-18.

Listing 2-18. MockBean Annotation with Name Sample

```
@MockBean(name ="addition")
private Operation mockOperation;
```

This would replace the regular Addition bean with a mocked instance, which we can then use to register mock behavior on. When a bean with that name cannot be found, the mocked bean will be registered as a new instance of that bean. See Listing 2-19.

Listing 2-19. MockBean Annotation with Name Sample (Nonexisting Bean)

```
@MockBean(name ="division")
private Operation mockOperation;
```

This will not replace an existing bean but add a bean to the application context, and as a result, the Calculator would have an additional operation added to the operations it can handle. You could test that using the ReflectionTestUtils helper class from the Spring test framework. See Listing 2-20.

Listing 2-20. Validating the Number of Operations

```
@Test
public void calculatorShouldHave3Operations() {
  var operations = ReflectionTestUtils.getField(calculator,
          "operations");
  assertEquals(3, ((Collection<Operation>) operations).size());
}
```

This will obtain the operations field through reflection and assert that the collection size is 3. When the @MockBean annotation is removed (or the name changed to addition), this test will fail as there are now only two operations registered.

Using the mock is straightforward. See Listing 2-21.

Listing 2-21. Using the Mocked Bean

```
@Test
public void mockDivision(CapturedOutput capture) {
  when(mockOperation.handles('/')).thenReturn(true);
  when(mockOperation.apply(14, 7)).thenReturn(2);

  calculator.calculate(14, 7, '/');
  assertTrue(capture.getOut().contains("14 / 7 = 2"));
}
```

Here we instruct Mockito to return true when a division (/) is being tested and return a value when the apply method is called. Next the method is called, and we assert that the output is what is expected from this test.

Perform Integration Testing with Spring Boot Using Slices

Instead of using @SpringBootTest, you can also test part of your application. For this, Spring Boot has so-called slices. With the dedicated @*Test annotation (see Table 2-2), it will load an ApplicationContext with only the parts of the configuration that are needed. For instance, when using @JdbcTest, it will create an ApplicationContext with only the JDBC-related beans like a DataSource, JdbcTemplate, etc. It will not create all non-related beans like your web server or web-related beans.

Table 2-2. *Test Slice Annotations*

Annotation	Description
@JsonTest	Auto-configure the available JSON mappers and apply the found JSON configuration.
@WebMvcTest	Auto-configure the web-related parts of your application (filters, controllers, security, etc.) and set up MockMvc. This is generally used to test a single controller using @MockBean for the dependencies.
@WebfluxTest	Auto-configure the WebFlux-related parts of your application and set up a WebTestClient based on this. This is generally used to test a single controller using @MockBean for the dependencies.
@GraphQlTest	Auto-configure Spring GraphQL.
@DataCassandraTest	Auto-configure Spring Data Cassandra.
@DataCouchbaseTest	Auto-configure Spring Data Couchbase.
@DataElasticsearchTest	Auto-configure Spring Data ElasticSearch.
@DataJdbcTest	Auto-configure Spring Data JDBC and by default will configure an in-memory database if present.
@DataJpaTest	Auto-configure Spring Data JPA and by default will configure an in-memory database if present.
@DataLdapTest	Auto-configure Spring Data LDAP; by default it will set up an in-memory LDAP server for testing.
@DataMongoTest	Auto-configure Spring Data MongoDB.
@DataNeo4jTest	Auto-configure Spring Data Neo4J.
@DataR2dbcTest	Auto-configure Spring Data R2DBC.
@DataRedisTest	Auto-configure Spring Data Redis.
@JdcbTest	Auto-configure JDBC and by default will configure an in-memory database if present.
@JooqTest	Auto-configure JOOQ and by default will configure an in-memory database if present.
@RestClientTest	Auto-configure REST clients and set up MockRestServiceServer.

(*continued*)

Table 2-2. (*continued*)

Annotation	Description
@WebServiceClientTest	Auto-configure WebServiceTemplate and set up MockWebServiceServer.
@WebServiceServerTest	Auto-configure the Spring web service and set up a MockWebServiceClient.

As an example, let's take a look at @WebMvcTest and use that to test a controller, without bootstrapping the whole application. Listing 2-22 contains a sample controller that allows us to execute a calculation through the Web. It will take the parameters and call the calculator. For more information on controllers and web-related recipes, see Chapters 3 and 4. See Listing 2-22.

Listing 2-22. Calculator Controller

```
package com.apress.springboot3recipes.calculator.web;

import com.apress.springboot3recipes.calculator.Calculator;
import org.springframework.web.bind.annotation.GetMapping;
import org.springframework.web.bind.annotation.RestController;

@RestController
public class CalculatorController {

    private final Calculator calculator;

    public CalculatorController(Calculator calculator) {
        this.calculator = calculator;
    }

    @GetMapping("/calculate")
    public int calculate(Calculation calc) {
        return calculator.calculate(calc.lhs(), calc.rhs(), calc.op());
    }
}

record Calculation(int lhs, int rhs, char op) {}
```

41

To test this, we can use the @WebMvcTest annotation on a test and use a mocked instance of the Calculator, as that won't be part of the context. See Listing 2-23.

Listing 2-23. @WebMvcTest for the CalculatorController

```
package com.apress.springboot3recipes.calculator.web;

import com.apress.springboot3recipes.calculator.Calculator;
import org.junit.jupiter.api.Test;
import org.springframework.beans.factory.annotation.Autowired;
import org.springframework.boot.test.autoconfigure.web.servlet.WebMvcTest;
import org.springframework.boot.test.mock.mockito.MockBean;
import org.springframework.test.web.servlet.MockMvc;
import org.springframework.test.web.servlet.request.MockMvcRequestBuilders;
import org.springframework.test.web.servlet.result.MockMvcResultMatchers;

import static org.mockito.Mockito.*;

@WebMvcTest(CalculatorController.class)
class CalculatorControllerTest {

    @Autowired
    private MockMvc mockMvc;

    @MockBean
    private Calculator calculator;

    @Test
    void successfulCalculation() throws Exception {

        when(calculator.calculate(10,5,'*')).thenReturn(50);

        var request = MockMvcRequestBuilders.get("/calculate")
                .param("lhs", "10")
                .param("rhs", "5")
                    .param("op", "*");

        mockMvc.perform(request)
```

```
        .andExpect(MockMvcResultMatchers.status().isOk())
        .andExpect(MockMvcResultMatchers.content().string("50"));

    verify(calculator, times(1)).calculate(10, 5, '*');
    }
}
```

With the `@WebMvcTest(CalculatorController.class)`, we instruct the test framework to create a minimal Spring Boot application with the web-based classes needed for the `CalculatorController`. It will also set up `MockMvc` to make it easier to call the endpoint and validate it. When now running it, it will bootstrap a Spring Boot application with only the web-related parts and the given mocks. Now in this small sample, there isn't a large difference in executing an `@SpringBootTest` or an `@WebMvcTest`, but in a larger application the performance difference will be quite notable. The sample, of course, applies to the other slice-based tests.

Use Testcontainers with Spring Boot Testing

You might have heard of the Testcontainers library, and you might want to use it in your Spring Boot application for testing. With the Testcontainers library, it becomes easy to write your tests and use your actual database, messaging solution, or mail provider (and many more) that you are using in production. So instead of reverting to an in-memory or embedded solution, you get your fully fledge solution as used in production. Testcontainers uses Docker to make this possible, and it, by default, binds the life cycle of the container to your tests.

To be able to use this, you will need to add a dependency, `spring-boot-testcontainers`, to your dependency management (Maven or Gradle), and you need to include the modules from Testcontainers that you want to utilize. The sample we are using will utilize a PostgreSQL container to execute some JDBC queries on it; it will also leverage the aforementioned slice support to set up a JDBC-based test. See Listing 2-24.

Listing 2-24. Maven Dependencies for Testcontainers and PostgreSQL

```
<dependency>
    <groupId>org.springframework.boot</groupId>
    <artifactId>spring-boot-testcontainers</artifactId>
    <scope>test</scope>
</dependency>
```

43

```xml
<dependency>
    <groupId>org.testcontainers</groupId>
    <artifactId>junit-jupiter</artifactId>
    <scope>test</scope>
</dependency>
<dependency>
    <groupId>org.testcontainers</groupId>
    <artifactId>postgresql</artifactId>
    <scope>test</scope>
</dependency>
<dependency>
    <groupId>org.postgresql</groupId>
    <artifactId>postgresql</artifactId>
    <scope>runtime</scope>
</dependency>
```

We add the `spring-boot-testcontainers` dependency as well as the PostgreSQL JDBC driver and the PostgreSQL and JUnit Testcontainers modules. With this we can use the `@TestContainers` annotation to start a PostgreSQL database for our test. See Listing 2-25.

Listing 2-25. @JdbcTest with Regular Testcontainers Usage

```java
package com.apress.springboot3recipes.calculator;

import org.junit.jupiter.api.Test;
import org.springframework.beans.factory.annotation.Autowired;
import
org.springframework.boot.test.autoconfigure.jdbc.AutoConfigureTestDatabase;
import org.springframework.boot.test.autoconfigure.jdbc.JdbcTest;
import org.springframework.jdbc.core.JdbcTemplate;
import org.springframework.test.context.DynamicPropertyRegistry;
import org.springframework.test.context.DynamicPropertySource;
import org.springframework.test.jdbc.JdbcTestUtils;
import org.testcontainers.containers.PostgreSQLContainer;
import org.testcontainers.junit.jupiter.Container;
import org.testcontainers.junit.jupiter.Testcontainers;
```

```java
import static org.junit.jupiter.api.Assertions.assertEquals;

@JdbcTest
@AutoConfigureTestDatabase(replace = AutoConfigureTestDatabase.Replace.NONE)
@Testcontainers
public class JdbcTestWithTestcontainers {

    @Container
    static PostgreSQLContainer<?> postgres = new PostgreSQLContainer<>(
    "postgres:15.2");

    @Autowired
    private JdbcTemplate jdbc;

    @DynamicPropertySource
    public static void properties(DynamicPropertyRegistry props) {
        props.add("spring.datasource.url", postgres::getJdbcUrl);
        props.add("spring.datasource.username", postgres::getUsername);
        props.add("spring.datasource.password", postgres::getPassword);
    }

    @Test
    void retrieveTables() {
        var tables = JdbcTestUtils.countRowsInTable(jdbc, "pg_catalog.
        pg_tables");
        assertEquals(68, tables);
    }
}
```

On the test, we added @Testcontainers, which is a special Junit extension for Testcontainers. It will now detect fields annotated with @Container and automatically start them. As we are using a container, we need to instruct Spring Boot to use it. For JDBC, we need to configure the spring.datasource.url property (and the username and password). To do this, we can utilize the @DynamicPropertySource, which can be placed on a static method in the test, and it can then retrieve the settings from the container and register them as properties.

Finally, notice the @AutoConfigureTestDatabase, which is needed for database-driven tests as by default Spring Boot will try to start an embedded container and use that as a `Datasource`. If we didn't add this, the test case would fail. Now when running the test, Testcontainers will kick in and download the container and start it, and the test will execute. Afterward, the container will be stopped and destroyed.

Although this works and is a valid way to work with Testcontainers, it could be better. Spring Boot introduced a so-called service connection. This is an abstraction over various different services you can connect to, like a database or message broker. To make use of this, there is the `@ServiceConnection` annotation, which can be placed on the container you want to use. When using this, you don't need to add a method to dynamically register the properties for the context. See Listing 2-26.

Listing 2-26. @JdbcTest with Spring Boot @ServiceConnection

```
package com.apress.springboot3recipes.calculator;

import org.junit.jupiter.api.Test;
import org.springframework.beans.factory.annotation.Autowired;
import
org.springframework.boot.test.autoconfigure.jdbc.AutoConfigureTestDatabase;
import org.springframework.boot.test.autoconfigure.jdbc.JdbcTest;
import org.springframework.boot.testcontainers.service.connection.
ServiceConnection;
import org.springframework.jdbc.core.JdbcTemplate;
import org.springframework.test.jdbc.JdbcTestUtils;
import org.testcontainers.containers.PostgreSQLContainer;
import org.testcontainers.junit.jupiter.Container;
import org.testcontainers.junit.jupiter.Testcontainers;

import static org.junit.jupiter.api.Assertions.assertEquals;

@JdbcTest
@AutoConfigureTestDatabase(replace = AutoConfigureTestDatabase.
Replace.NONE)
@Testcontainers
public class JdbcTestWithTestcontainersServiceConnection {

    @Container
    @ServiceConnection
```

```
static PostgreSQLContainer postgres = new PostgreSQLContainer(
"postgres:15.2");

@Autowired
private JdbcTemplate jdbc;

@Test
void retrieveTables() {
    var tables = JdbcTestUtils.countRowsInTable(jdbc, "pg_catalog.
    pg_tables");
    assertEquals(68, tables);
}
}
```

The test will still behave the same: download the container (if needed), start the container, run the test, and stop and destroy the container. However, there is no more need to explicitly configure the properties. This reduces the code we have to write and maintain.

The @ServiceConnection annotation doesn't work for all containers, only for a selection of well-known containers. At the moment of writing, the following containers are supported:

- Containers of type CassandraContainer
- Containers of type CouchbaseContainer
- Containers of type ElasticSearchContainer
- Containers of type JdbcDatabaseContainer
- Containers of type KafkaContainer/RedpandaContainer
- Containers of type MongoDBContainer
- Containers of type Neo4jContainer
- Containers of type RabbitMQContainer
- Containers named redis
- Containers named openzipkin/zipkin

💡   By default the service connection infrastructure will use the `Container.`
`getDockerImageName` to determine which connection details to expose. This can
be problematic in case of custom images (especially for those based on name
instead of type). For these circumstances, you can specify the `name` attribute of the
`@ServiceConnection` to match the proper name.

When there are multiple tests using the same containers, you can also specify the
containers in an interface or abstract base class and let the test classes import/extend
that. This allows for easier reuse of the containers and saves you from defining the
containers in each test that would need them. An additional benefit is that you could
also use these containers when running Spring, and with the reuse you can make sure
your tests as well as your application are using the same containers (see Recipe 2-6). See
Listing 2-27.

Listing 2-27. Inteface with Container Definitions

```
package com.apress.springboot3recipes.calculator;

import org.springframework.boot.testcontainers.service.connection.
ServiceConnection;
import org.testcontainers.containers.PostgreSQLContainer;
import org.testcontainers.junit.jupiter.Container;

public interface TestcontainersConfig {

    @ServiceConnection
    @Container
    PostgreSQLContainer<?> postgres = new PostgreSQLContainer<>(
    "postgres:15.2");
}
```

Next you can just let your test class implement this interface to reuse the container
definitions. See Listing 2-28.

Listing 2-28. Test Class with Reused Definitions

```
package com.apress.springboot3recipes.calculator;

import org.junit.jupiter.api.Test;
import org.springframework.beans.factory.annotation.Autowired;
import
org.springframework.boot.test.autoconfigure.jdbc.AutoConfigureTestDatabase;
import org.springframework.boot.test.autoconfigure.jdbc.JdbcTest;
import org.springframework.jdbc.core.JdbcTemplate;
import org.springframework.test.jdbc.JdbcTestUtils;
import org.testcontainers.junit.jupiter.Testcontainers;

import static org.junit.jupiter.api.Assertions.assertEquals;

@JdbcTest
@AutoConfigureTestDatabase(replace = AutoConfigureTestDatabase.Replace.NONE)
@Testcontainers
public class JdbcTestWithTestcontainersReuse implements TestcontainersConfig {

    @Autowired
    private JdbcTemplate jdbc;

    @Test
    void retrieveTables() {
        var tables = JdbcTestUtils.countRowsInTable(jdbc, "pg_catalog.
        pg_tables");
        assertEquals(66, tables);
    }
}
```

2-4. Configure Logging

Problem

You want to configure log levels for certain loggers.

Solution

With Spring Boot you can configure the logging framework and configuration.

How It Works

Spring Boot ships with a default configuration for the supported log providers (Logback, Log4J2, and Java Util Logging). In addition to the default configuration, it adds support for configuring the logging levels through the regular `application.properties` as well as specifing patterns and where to, optionally, write log files to.

Spring Boot uses SLF4J as the logging API, and when writing components, you should use those interfaces to write your logging. That way, you have a choice in which logging framework to use.

Configure Logging

One of the general things to do with a logging framework is to enable or disable logging for parts of the framework. With Spring Boot, you can do this by adding some lines to your `application.properties` file. The lines need to be prefixed with `logging.level.` followed by the name of the logger and finally the level you want it to be.

```
logging.level.org.springframework.web=DEBUG
```

The previous line will enable DEBUG logging for the `org.springframework.web` logger (generally all classes in that package and subpackages). To set the level of the ROOT logger, use `logging.level.ROOT=<level>`. This will set the default level of logging.

Log to a File

By default Spring Boot will log only to the console. If you want to write to a file as well, you need to specify either `logging.file` or `logging.path`. The first takes the name of the file, and the second takes the path. The default filename used is `spring.log`, and the default directory used is the Java temp dir.

```
logging.file=application.log
logging.path=/var/log
```

With this configuration, a logfile named `application.log` will be written to the /var/log directory.

When writing logs to a file, you might want to prevent the logfiles from flooding your system. You can specify how many files to retain with `logging.file.max-history` (the default is 0, meaning unlimited) and `logging.file.max-size` to specify the file size (the default is 10 MB).

Use Your Preferred Logging Provider

Spring Boot by default uses Logback as the provider for the logging. It also supports Java Util Logging as well as Log4j 2. To use another logging framework, you will have to first exclude the default framework and then include your own. Spring Boot has `spring-boot-starter-log4j2` to include all the necessary dependencies for Log4j 2. To exclude the default Logback logging, you need to add an exclusion rule to the `spring-boot-starter` dependency. This is the main dependency that brings in the logging.

```
<dependency> ①
  <groupId>org.springframework.boot</groupId>
  <artifactId>spring-boot-starter</artifactId>
  <exclusions>
    <exclusion>
      <groupId>org.springframework.boot</groupId>
      <artifactId>spring-boot-starter-logging</artifactId>
    </exclusion>
  </exclusions>
</dependency>
<dependency> ②
  <groupId>org.springframework.boot</groupId>
  <artifactId>spring-boot-starter-log4j2</artifactId>
</dependency>
```

① Include the dependency for `spring-boot-starter` with an exclusion for `spring-boot-starter-logging`.

② Include the `spring-boot-starter-log4j` to bring in the necessary dependencies for Log4j 2.

ⓘ   Spring Boot 3 doesn't support the older Log4j framework. It supports its successor Log4j 2.

2-5. Reuse an Existing Configuration

Problem

You have an existing application or module, and you want to reuse the configuration with Spring Boot.

Solution

To import an existing configuration, add the `@Import` or `@ImportResource` annotation to your `@Configuration` or `@SpringBootApplication` annotated class.

How It Works

On your main application class, the one with `@SpringBootApplication`, place the `@Import` or `@ImportResource` annotation to let Spring load the additional files.

Reuse an Existing XML Configuration

Find the class with the `@SpringBootApplication` annotation and add the `@ImportResource` annotation to it.

```
@SpringBootApplication
@ImportResource("classpath:application-context.xml")
public class Application { ... }
```

This configuration will load the `application-context.xml` file from the classpath because of the `classpath:` prefix. If the file is somewhere on the file system, you can use the `file:` prefix, i.e., `file:/var/conf/application-context.xml`.

When bootstrapping the application, Spring Boot will load the additional configuration from the mentioned XML file.

Reuse an Existing Java Configuration

Find the class with the `@SpringBootApplication` annotation and add the `@Import` annotation to it.

```
@SpringBootApplication
@Import(ExistingConfiguration.class)
public class Application { ... }
```

The `@Import` annotation will take care of adding the mentioned class to the configuration. This can be needed if you want to include things not covered in the component scan or if you have disabled the auto-detection of `@Configuration` classes.

2-6. Use Docker with Spring Boot During Development

Docker has become a popular technology to drive the development using a containerized environment for both development and production.

Problem

You have some containerized infrastructure (such as database, messaging providers, email, etc.) that you want to use during development and local testing as well.

Solution

Spring Boot supports a dockerized environment in two ways. First, it has optional support for Docker Compose, and second, it can utilize Testcontainers to bootstrap containers just as with tests (see Recipe 2-3).

The Docker Compose support can be enabled by including the `spring-boot-docker-componse` dependency. When it detects a `docker-compose.yml` or `compose.yml` in the root of your application folder, it will use that to start the containers before starting the application. It will use the `ConnectionProvider` abstraction and `@ServiceConnection` support (see Recipe 2-3 on Testcontainers and Docker support) to determine which containers are started and will make the metadata (like URL, username, password, etc.) available to Spring Boot automatically.

ℹ️   By default the Docker Compose support is disabled for testing in favor of using Testcontainers.

The other option is to define some containers using Testcontainers and use the `@ImportTestcontainers` annotation to use them to start the dockerized environment. The added benefit of this is that you can reuse the same container definitions as used when writing tests.

How It Works

Spring Boot Docker Compose Support

To start, you would need a `docker-compose.yaml` file to determine which services need to run. Let's create one that bootstraps Postgresql with a database and a given username/password combination (see Listing 2-29).

Listing 2-29. Docker Compose File

```
services:
  postgres:
    image: 'postgres:15.2'
    environment:
      - 'POSTGRES_DB=springboot3recipes'
      - 'POSTGRES_USER=springboot3'
      - 'POSTGRES_PASSWORD=recipes'
    ports:
      - '5432'
```

To enable the support, the `spring-boot-docker-compose` dependency needs to be added as a dependency. See Listing 2-30 and Listing 2-31.

Listing 2-30. Spring Boot Additional Dependency

```
<dependency>
    <groupId>org.springframework.boot</groupId>
    <artifactId>spring-boot-docker-compose</artifactId>
</dependency>
```

Finally, one would need an application that uses the database to do something. Let's write a simple JDBC program that lists the tables available in PostgreSQL.

Listing 2-31. Spring Boot Application Using a Docker Container

```
package com.apress.springboot3recipes.docker;

import org.springframework.boot.ApplicationRunner;
import org.springframework.boot.SpringApplication;
import org.springframework.boot.autoconfigure.SpringBootApplication;
import org.springframework.context.annotation.Bean;
import org.springframework.jdbc.core.JdbcTemplate;

@SpringBootApplication
public class DockerApplication {

    public static void main(String[] args) {
        SpringApplication.run(DockerApplication.class, args);
    }

    @Bean
    public ApplicationRunner lister(JdbcTemplate jdbc) {
        return (args) -> {
            jdbc.query("select * from pg_catalog.pg_tables", rs -> {
                System.out.printf("Table: %s.%s%n", rs.getString(1),
                rs.getString(2));
            });
        };
    }
}
```

The `DockerApplication` class contains a simple `ApplicationRunner` that at startup will query the PostgreSQL `pg_tables` system table to retrieve the names of the available tables and print them to the console. After that, it will stop. Notice how there is nothing Docker specific here nor that we have specified anything for the database as a configuration.

Now when running the application, there will be some output stating that a Docker compose file has been found and that it will start the containers. When the containers have started, the application will continue and list the tables. See Figure 2-6.

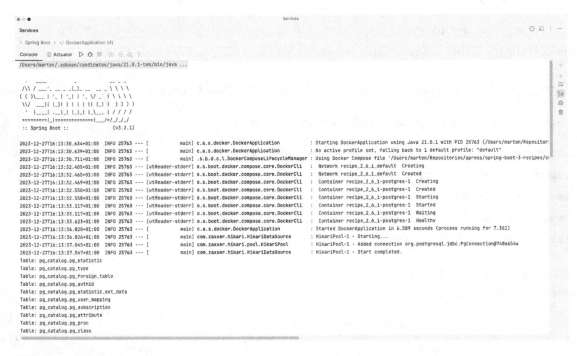

Figure 2-6. *Docker application output*

There was/is no manually starting the containers anymore with `docker compose up` or by modifying your build (or `main` method) to start the containers.

By default the Spring Boot Docker Compose support will look for a `docker-compose.yaml/compose.yml` file. This can be changed using the `spring.docker.compose.file` property. You can point it to a specific file on your file system. There are more properties (see Table 2-3) that you can use to modify the behavior.

Table 2-3. *Docker Compose Configuration Parameters*

Parameter	Description
`spring.docker.compose.enabled`	Sets whether Docker Compose support is enabled; default is `true`.
`spring.docker.compose.file`	Path to a specific Docker Compose file.
`spring.docker.compose.lifecycle-management`	Docker Compose life cycle; default is START_AND_STOP.
`spring.docker.compose.host`	Hostname/IP address of the machine where the Docker containers will start and run.
`spring.docker.compose.start.command`	The Docker Compose command used when starting; the default is UP.
`spring.docker.compose.start.loglevel`	Log level for Docker Compose output.
`spring.docker.compose.stop.command`	The Docker Compose command used when stopping; the default is STOP.
`spring.docker.compose.stop.duration`	Timeout for stopping Docker Compose; the default is 10 seconds. Set it to 0 for forced stop.
`spring.docker.compose.profiles.active`	Docker compose profiles that should be activated.
`spring.docker.compose.skip.in-tests`	Sets whether Docker Compose support is enabled in tests; the default is `false`.
`spring.docker.compose.readiness.wait`	The wait strategy to use; the default is ALWAYS.
`spring.docker.compose.readiness.timeout`	Timeout for the readiness check; the default is 2 minutes.
`spring.docker.compose.readiness.tcp.connect-timeout`	Timeout for connections.
`spring.docker.compose.readiness.tcp.read-timeout`	Timeout for reads.

> ⚠️ `spring.docker.compose.profiles.active` is to set/enable the
> profiles to use with Docker Compose. These profiles aren't related to Spring
> profiles.

The Docker Compose support in Spring Boot uses the names of the Docker images
to determine what to configure. See Table 2-4 for the names and supported technologies.

Table 2-4. *Docker Compose Supported Containers*

Technology	Container Image Name(s) Matched
Cassandra	`cassandra`
ElasticSearch	`elasticsearch`
JDBC and R2DBC	• `gvenzl/oracle-xe` • `mariadb` • `mssql/server` • `mysql` • `postgres`
MongoDB	`mongo`
RabbitMQ	`rabbitmq`
Redis	`redis`
Zipkin	`openzipkin/zipkin`

Spring Boot Docker Compose Support: Custom Container Images

As Table 2-4 shows, the names of the container matter. But what if you want to use a
customized container, for instance with a preconfigured and filled PostgreSQL database
or a preconfigured and secured message broker? With the Spring Docker Compose
Support, this is still possible, with some additional configuration in the Docker Compose
file. With Docker Compose, it is possible to specify labels. The Spring Boot Docker
Compose support will read the `org.springframework.boot.service-connection` label;
the value it has will be used as the name of the container. See Listing 2-32.

Listing 2-32. Docker Compose File with Label

```
services:
  postgres:
    image: 'postgres:15.2'
    environment:
      - 'POSTGRES_DB=springboot3recipes'
      - 'POSTGRES_USER=springboot3'
      - 'POSTGRES_PASSWORD=recipes'
    ports:
      - '5432'
    labels:
      org.springframework.boot.service-connection: redis
```

There are more labels that can be used to configure/influence the Docker Compose support (see Table 2-5).

Table 2-5. *Docker Compose Labels*

Parameter	Description
org.springframework.boot.service-connection	The name of the container image to use (see Table 2-4).
org.springframework.boot.ignore	Ignore this container for the Docker Compose support.
org.springframework.boot.readiness-check.tcp.disable	Disable the TCP readiness check.
org.springframework.boot.readiness-check.tcp.connect-timeout	The connection timeout.
org.springframework.boot.readiness-check.tcp.read-timeout	The read timeout.

Spring Boot Testcontainers Support

To utilize the Testcontainers support during development time, a dependency on the `spring-boot-testcontainers` module is needed as well as the various Testcontainers modules (in this case for PostgreSQL). See also Recipe 2-3 for testing support.

In this sample, we will use the PostgreSQL container and the JUnit Jupiter integration. As we are using PostgreSQL, we will also need the JDBC driver for this. See Listing 2-33.

Listing 2-33. Testcontainers Support Dependencies

```
<dependency>
    <groupId>org.springframework.boot</groupId>
    <artifactId>spring-boot-testcontainers</artifactId>
    <scope>test</scope>
</dependency>
<dependency>
    <groupId>org.testcontainers</groupId>
    <artifactId>junit-jupiter</artifactId>
    <scope>test</scope>
</dependency>
<dependency>
    <groupId>org.testcontainers</groupId>
    <artifactId>postgresql</artifactId>
    <scope>test</scope>
</dependency>
<dependency>
    <groupId>org.postgresql</groupId>
    <artifactId>postgresql</artifactId>
    <scope>runtime</scope>
</dependency>
```

As we want to use Testcontainers, we need to add a Java configuration class containing our container definitions. In this case, it is just one as we need only PostgreSQL, but it can be as many as you need. The containers need to be Spring managed beans, accomplished by adding @Bean to the methods as well as with @ServiceConnection. The latter makes it visible to the Spring Testcontainers support, and it will extract the needed information for the container and make it available to the application. The information that will be extracted depends on the type of container. For our PostgreSQL container, it will be the information needed to configure a JDBC data source, like `spring.datasource.url`, `spring.datasource.username`, and `spring.datasource.password`. See Listing 2-34.

Listing 2-34. Testcontainers Java Configuration

```
package com.apress.springboot3recipes.calculator;

import org.springframework.boot.test.context.TestConfiguration;
import org.springframework.boot.testcontainers.service.connection.
ServiceConnection;
import org.springframework.context.annotation.Bean;
import org.testcontainers.containers.PostgreSQLContainer;

@TestConfiguration(proxyBeanMethods = false)
public class TestContainersConfig {

    @Bean
    @ServiceConnection
    public PostgreSQLContainer<?> postgres() {
        return new PostgreSQLContainer<>("postgres:15.2");
    }
}
```

Next we can reuse the Spring Boot application class from the previous section (see Listing 2-31). To use the Testcontainers support, we will need to add another class with a `main` method in the test directory. See Listing 2-35.

💡 When using this with Spring Boot Devtools (see Recipe 2-7), you might want to add the `@RestartScope` annotation. This will reuse and keep the container instead of stopping it and restart. This will also keep the data that is in the container between updates.

Listing 2-35. Spring Boot Testcontainers Main

```
package com.apress.springboot3recipes.calculator;

import org.springframework.boot.SpringApplication;

public class TestDockerApplication {

    public static void main(String[] args) {
        SpringApplication.from(DockerApplication::main)
                .with(TestContainersConfig.class).run(args);
    }

}
```

Notice that this class bears no annotations and just has a simple main method. In this method, we reference the main method of our actual @SpringBootApplication annotation class with the from. Next, we augment the configuration with our TestContainersConfig. class using the with method. Finally, we call run to start the actual application.

A common way to define Testcontainers is to declare them as static fields in a class or interface. When you use an interface to define the container(s), you can reuse them between your tests and your specialized application runner. To reuse the interface-based definitions, you can use the @ImportTestContainers annotation on your configuration class. See Listing 2-36.

Listing 2-36. Testcontainers Definitions on Interface

```
package com.apress.springboot3recipes.calculator;

import org.springframework.boot.testcontainers.service.connection.
ServiceConnection;
import org.testcontainers.containers.PostgreSQLContainer;
import org.testcontainers.junit.jupiter.Container;

public interface OurContainersConfig {

    @ServiceConnection
    @Container
    PostgreSQLContainer<?> postgres = new PostgreSQLContainer<>(
    "postgres:15.2");
}
```

Now use the @ImportTestContainers annotation to reuse this interface. See Listing 2-37.

Listing 2-37. Testcontainers Definitions on Interface

```
package com.apress.springboot3recipes.calculator;

import org.springframework.boot.test.context.TestConfiguration;
import
org.springframework.boot.testcontainers.context.ImportTestcontainers;

@TestConfiguration(proxyBeanMethods = false)
@ImportTestcontainers(OurContainersConfig.class)
public class TestContainers2Config { }
```

2-7. Use Spring Boot Devtools to Speed Up Development

Problem

You want to have fast feedback during development and not have to rebuild and restart the application.

Solution

You can use Spring Boot Devtools. Devtools allows you to detect classpath changes, and when a change is detected, it will restart the application. This restart will be much faster than a cold start. It will also set certain properties to values that make sense during development (such as disabling caching for Thymeleaf templates, including full error details in error responses). Table 2-6 lists the properties with their default values as set by Spring Boot Devtools. If you want to disable these defaults, add spring.devtools.add-properties with the value of false to your application.properties.

Table 2-6. *Spring Boot Devtools Default Properties*

Property	Value	Description
`server.error.include-binding-errors`	always	Show full info on binding errors.
`server.error.include-message`	always	Include the custom error message in error response.
`server.error.include-stacktrace`	always	Show full stacktrace in error response.
`server.servlet.jsp.init-parameters.development`	true	JSP development parameter, allows reload.
`server.servlet.session.persistent`	true	Persist session information during restarts.
`spring.docker.compose.readiness.wait`	only-if-started	Wait for Docker containers to be ready.
`spring.freemarker.cache`	false	Disable Freemarker template caching.
`spring.graphql.graphiql.enabled`	true	Enable the GraphiQL UI.
`spring.groovy.template.cache`	false	Disable Groovy template caching.
`spring.h2-console.enabled`	true	Enable the H2 console, when available.
`spring.mustache.servlet.cache`	false	Disable Mustache template cache.
`spring.mvc.log-resolved-exception`	true	Log exceptions.
`spring.reactor.netty.shutdown-quiet-period`	0s	Shut down Netty immediately instead of waiting.
`spring.template.provider.cache`	false	Disable template caching.
`spring.thymeleaf.cache`	false	Disable Thymeleaf template caching.
`spring.web.resource.cache.period`	0s	Disable static resource caching.
`spring.web.resource.chain.cache`	0s	Disable static resource caching.

How It Works

To enable and reload Spring Boot Devtools, you would first need a dependency on the `spring-boot-devtools` module. See Listing 2-38.

Listing 2-38. Devtools Dependency

```
<dependency>
    <groupId>org.springframework.boot</groupId>
    <artifactId>spring-boot-devtools</artifactId>
    <optional>true</optional>
</dependency>
```

Notice how the dependency is marked as optional. This means to not include it in the runnable artifact that is created by Spring Boot.

Now let's write a simple controller that lists the tables in a PostgreSQL database. It will directly access the database through a `JdbcTemplate` and fire a query to obtain the `tablename` from the `pg_tables` table in PostgreSQL. Finally, it will turn this into a response.

First we need some dependencies to make this work. In addition to the dependencies for the controller and JDBC classes, we also use the Docker Compose support to bootstrap a PostgreSQL container (see recipe 2-6).

```
<dependency>
    <groupId>org.springframework.boot</groupId>
    <artifactId>spring-boot-starter-web</artifactId>
</dependency>
<dependency>
    <groupId>org.springframework.boot</groupId>
    <artifactId>spring-boot-starter-jdbc</artifactId>
</dependency>
<dependency>
    <groupId>org.springframework.boot</groupId>
    <artifactId>spring-boot-docker-compose</artifactId>
</dependency>
```

Next comes the controller, shown here:

```
package com.apress.springboot3recipes;

import org.springframework.jdbc.core.JdbcTemplate;
import org.springframework.web.bind.annotation.GetMapping;
import org.springframework.web.bind.annotation.RestController;
```

```java
import java.util.List;

@RestController
public class ShowTablesController {

  private final JdbcTemplate jdbc;

  public ShowTablesController(JdbcTemplate jdbc) {
    this.jdbc = jdbc;
  }

  @GetMapping("/show-tables")
  public List<String> showTables() {
    var sql = "select tablename from pg_catalog.pg_tables";
    return jdbc.queryForList(sql, String.class);
  }
}
```

This will use a JdbcTemplate to retrieve the tablename from the PostgreSQL pg_tables table and return it as a response. To launch, we need a basic Spring Boot application.

```java
package com.apress.springboot3recipes;

import org.springframework.boot.SpringApplication;
import org.springframework.boot.autoconfigure.SpringBootApplication;

@SpringBootApplication
public class DevtoolsApplication {

  public static void main(String[] args) {
    SpringApplication.run(DevtoolsApplication.class, args);
  }
}
```

With all of this in place, we can launch the application, either in our IDE or through the command line using Maven or Gradle. Here we will use the IDE. In Figure 2-7, you can see that it took about 4 seconds to start this simple application. This does include some time to start the PostgreSQL container.

```
/\\ / ___'_ __ _ _(_)_ __  __ _ \ \ \ \
( ( )\__ | '_ | '_| | '_ \/ _` | \ \ \ \
 \\/  ___)| |_)| | | | | || (_| |  ) ) ) )
  '  |____| .__|_| |_|_| |_\__, | / / / /
 =========|_|==============|___/=/_/_/_/
 :: Spring Boot ::       (v3.2.0-SNAPSHOT)

2023-07-11T20:06:25.984+02:00  INFO 51778 --- [  restartedMain] c.a.s.DevtoolsApplication                : Starting DevtoolsApplication using Java 21-ea with PID 51778 (/Users/marten
2023-07-11T20:06:25.908+02:00  INFO 51778 --- [  restartedMain] c.a.s.DevtoolsApplication                : No active profile set, falling back to 1 default profile: "default"
2023-07-11T20:06:26.005+02:00  INFO 51778 --- [  restartedMain] .s.b.d.c.l.DockerComposeLifecycleManager : Using Docker Compose file '/Users/marten/Repositories/apress/spring-boot-3-
2023-07-11T20:06:26.880+02:00  INFO 51778 --- [utReader-stderr] o.s.boot.docker.compose.core.DockerCli   :  Container recipe_2_7_1-postgres-1  Created
2023-07-11T20:06:26.885+02:00  INFO 51778 --- [utReader-stderr] o.s.boot.docker.compose.core.DockerCli   :  Container recipe_2_7_1-postgres-1  Starting
2023-07-11T20:06:27.158+02:00  INFO 51778 --- [utReader-stderr] o.s.boot.docker.compose.core.DockerCli   :  Container recipe_2_7_1-postgres-1  Started
2023-07-11T20:06:27.158+02:00  INFO 51778 --- [utReader-stderr] o.s.boot.docker.compose.core.DockerCli   :  Container recipe_2_7_1-postgres-1  Waiting
2023-07-11T20:06:27.666+02:00  INFO 51778 --- [utReader-stderr] o.s.boot.docker.compose.core.DockerCli   :  Container recipe_2_7_1-postgres-1  Healthy
2023-07-11T20:06:28.137+02:00  INFO 51778 --- [  restartedMain] .e.DevToolsPropertyDefaultsPostProcessor : Devtools property defaults active! Set 'spring.devtools.add-properties' to
2023-07-11T20:06:28.138+02:00  INFO 51778 --- [  restartedMain] .e.DevToolsPropertyDefaultsPostProcessor : For additional web related logging consider setting the 'logging.level.web'
2023-07-11T20:06:29.041+02:00  INFO 51778 --- [  restartedMain] o.s.b.w.embedded.tomcat.TomcatWebServer   : Tomcat initialized with port 8080 (http)
2023-07-11T20:06:29.054+02:00  INFO 51778 --- [  restartedMain] o.apache.catalina.core.StandardService   : Starting service [Tomcat]
2023-07-11T20:06:29.054+02:00  INFO 51778 --- [  restartedMain] o.apache.catalina.core.StandardEngine    : Starting Servlet engine: [Apache Tomcat/10.1.10]
2023-07-11T20:06:29.100+02:00  INFO 51778 --- [  restartedMain] o.a.c.c.C.[Tomcat].[localhost].[/]        : Initializing Spring embedded WebApplicationContext
2023-07-11T20:06:29.100+02:00  INFO 51778 --- [  restartedMain] w.s.c.ServletWebServerApplicationContext : Root WebApplicationContext: initialization completed in 962 ms
2023-07-11T20:06:29.453+02:00  INFO 51778 --- [  restartedMain] o.s.b.d.a.OptionalLiveReloadServer       : LiveReload server is running on port 35729
2023-07-11T20:06:29.479+02:00  INFO 51778 --- [  restartedMain] o.s.b.w.embedded.tomcat.TomcatWebServer   : Tomcat started on port 8080 (http) with context path ''
2023-07-11T20:06:29.485+02:00  INFO 51778 --- [  restartedMain] c.a.s.DevtoolsApplication                : Started DevtoolsApplication in 3.993 seconds (process running for 5.418)
```

Figure 2-7. *Output for first launch*

Notice the [restartedMain] in the logging output. Spring Boot Devtools uses a
separate thread and additional classloader to enable the reload of modified classes.
While in general this works well, it can sometimes be problematic in larger multimodule
projects and with other technologies that use classloading as well (like Hibernate for
instance) to modify classes.

Now let's change the controller and instead of returning just the tablename, let's
include the schemaname. For this, we would need to modify the query and the mapping of
the result as we need to concatenate two strings.

```java
package com.apress.springboot3recipes;

import org.springframework.jdbc.core.JdbcTemplate;
import org.springframework.web.bind.annotation.GetMapping;
import org.springframework.web.bind.annotation.RestController;

import java.util.List;

@RestController
public class ShowTablesController {

  private final JdbcTemplate jdbc;

  public ShowTablesController(JdbcTemplate jdbc) {
    this.jdbc = jdbc;
  }
```

```
@GetMapping("/show-tables")
public List<String> showTables() {
    var sql = "select schemaname, tablename from pg_catalog.pg_tables";
    return jdbc.query(sql,
        (rs, row) -> rs.getString("schemaname") + "." +
        rs.getString("tablename"));
}
}
```

Now when the changes are built and propagated to the classpath, this will be detected by Spring Boot Devtools, and it will restart the application. This restart will take a fraction of the time it took to start the whole application (Figure 2-8). In this case, it took now 0.681 seconds, a little less than a second. This is a great boost for writing code and getting direct feedback in your IDE.

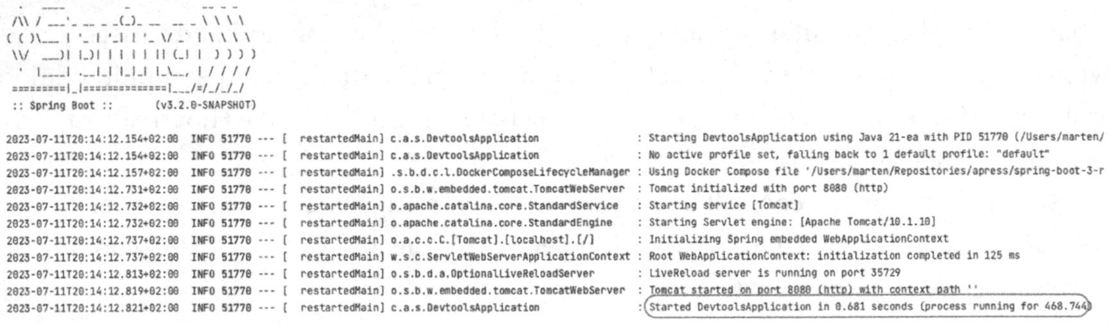

Figure 2-8. *Output after restart*

Summary

In this chapter, we looked at configuring beans in Spring Boot and how to provide Spring Boot with configuration properties through property files and command-line arguments. Next we took a quick look at writing unit tests with and without Spring Boot and using Mockito as a mocking library. Finally, we introduced logging into our application and showed how to configure it through the earlier mentioned properties as well as how to switch to a different log provider (Log4j 2 instead of Logback).

The next chapter will walk you through Spring Boot and Spring MVC.

CHAPTER 3

Spring MVC

Spring Boot will automatically configure a web application when it finds classes on the classpath. It will also start an embedded server (by default it will launch an embedded Tomcat instance).

3-1. Get Started with Spring MVC
Problem

You want to use Spring Boot to power a Spring MVC application.

Solution

Spring Boot will auto-configure the components needed for Spring MVC. Spring Boot needs to detect the Spring MVC classes on its classpath. For this you need to add `spring-boot-starter-web` as a dependency.

How It Works

In your project, add the dependency for `spring-boot-starter-web`. See Listing 3-1.

Listing 3-1. Spring Boot Starter for Spring MVC

```
<dependency>
  <groupId>org.springframework.boot</groupId>
  <artifactId>spring-boot-starter-web</artifactId>
</dependency>
```

69

© Marten Deinum 2024
M. Deinum, *Spring Boot 3 Recipes*, https://doi.org/10.1007/979-8-8688-0113-6_3

This adds the needed dependencies for Spring MVC, `spring-web` and `spring-webmvc`. Now that Spring Boot can detect these classes, it will do additional configuration to set up `DispatcherServlet`. It will also add all the JAR files needed to be able to start an embedded Tomcat server. See Listing 3-2.

Listing 3-2. Spring Boot Application to Launch Spring MVC

```
package com.apress.springboot3recipes.library;

import org.springframework.boot.SpringApplication;
import org.springframework.boot.autoconfigure.SpringBootApplication;

@SpringBootApplication
public class HelloWorldApplication {

        public static void main(String[] args) {
                SpringApplication.run(HelloWorldApplication.class, args);
        }

}
```

These few lines of code are enough to start the embedded Tomcat server and set up a preconfigured Spring MVC. When you start the application, you will see output similar to that in Figure 3-1.

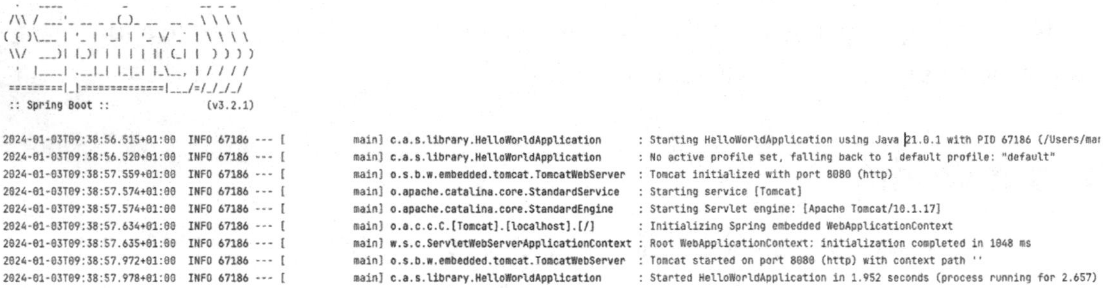

Figure 3-1. *Startup output*

Spring Boot does the following when you start `HelloWorldApplication`:

1. Start an embedded Tomcat server on port 8080 (by default).

2. Register and enable a couple of default servlet filters (see Table 3-1).

3. Set up static resource handling for things like *.css, *.js, and favicon.ico.

4. Enable integration with web JARs.

5. Set up basic error handling features.

6. Configure the DispatcherServlet with the needed components (i.e., ViewResolvers, I18N, etc.).

Table 3-1. *Automatically Registered Servlet Filters*

Filter	Description
DefaultCharacterEncodingFilter	Forces the encoding to be UTF-8 by default. Can be configured by setting the spring.http.encoding. charset property. Can be disabled by setting server. servlet.encoding.enabled to false.
FormContentFilter	Wraps the request with FormContentRequestWrapper for PUT, PATCH, and DELETE requests so there is consistent handling of those requests and to be able to use bindings with them. Can be disabled by setting the spring.mvc. formcontent.enabled property to false.
RequestContextFilter	Exposes the current request to the current thread so that you can use RequestContextHolder and LocaleContextHolder even in a non-Spring MVC application like Jersey.

In the current state, HelloWorldApplication doesn't do anything but start the server. Let's add a controller to return some information. See Listing 3-3.

Listing 3-3. HelloWorld Controller

```
package com.apress.springboot3recipes.library;

import org.springframework.boot.SpringBootVersion;
import org.springframework.web.bind.annotation.GetMapping;
import org.springframework.web.bind.annotation.RestController;
```

```
@RestController
public class HelloWorldController {

        @GetMapping("/")
        public String hello() {
                var version = SpringBootVersion.getVersion();
                return String.format("Hello World, from Spring Boot %s!",
                version);
        }
}
```

This `HelloWorldController` controller will be registered at the / URL and when called will return the phrase `Hello World, from Spring Boot` with the Spring Boot version included. `@RestController` indicates that this is an `@Controller` and as such will be detected by Spring Boot. Additionally, it adds the `@ResponseBody` annotation to all request handling methods. `@GetMapping` maps the `hello` method to every GET request that arrives at /. We could also have written `@RequestMapping(path="/",` `method=RequestMethod.GET)`.

When restarting `HelloWorldApplication`, the `HelloWorldController` controller will be detected and processed. Now when using something like `curl` or `HTTPie` to access `http://localhost:8080/`, the result should look like Figure 3-2.

Figure 3-2. *Output of controller*

Test the Controller

Now that the application is running and returning results, it's time to add a test for the controller. Spring already has some impressive testing features, and Spring Boot adds even more. Testing a controller has become pretty easy with Spring Boot. See Listing 3-4.

Listing 3-4. WebMvcTest Slice Test for HelloWorldController

```
package com.apress.springboot3recipes.library;

import org.hamcrest.Matchers;
import org.junit.jupiter.api.Test;
import org.springframework.beans.factory.annotation.Autowired;
import org.springframework.boot.test.autoconfigure.web.servlet.WebMvcTest;
import org.springframework.http.MediaType;
import org.springframework.test.web.servlet.MockMvc;
import org.springframework.test.web.servlet.request.MockMvcRequestBuilders;

import static org.springframework.test.web.servlet.result.
MockMvcResultMatchers.content;
import static org.springframework.test.web.servlet.result.
MockMvcResultMatchers.status;

@WebMvcTest(HelloWorldController.class)
class HelloWorldControllerTest {

        @Autowired
        private MockMvc mockMvc;

        @Test
        void testHelloWorldController() throws Exception {
                var expected = "Hello World, from Spring Boot ";
                mockMvc.perform(MockMvcRequestBuilders.get("/"))
                        .andExpect(status().isOk())
                        .andExpect(content().string(Matchers.
                        containsString(expected)))
                        .andExpect(content().contentTypeCompatibleWith(
                        MediaType.TEXT_PLAIN));
        }
}
```

The @WebMvcTest annotation instructs the Spring Test framework to set up an application context for testing this specific controller. It will start a minimal Spring Boot application with only the web-related beans like @Controller, @ControllerAdvice, etc. In addition, it will preconfigure the Spring Test Mock MVC support, which can then be autowired.

Spring Test Mock MVC can be used to simulate making an HTTP request to the controller and to do some operations on the result. Here we call / with GET and expect an HTTP 200 (thus OK) response with a text message containing Hello World, from Spring Boot.

3-2. Expose REST Resources with Spring MVC

Problem

You want to use Spring MVC to expose REST-based resources.

Solution

You will need a JSON library to do the JSON marshaling (although you could use XML and other formats as well, as content negotiation is part of REST as originally described). In this recipe, we will use the Jackson library to take care of the JSON conversion.

How It Works

Imagine you are working at a public library and you need to develop a REST API to make it possible to list and search for books.

First you need to add the dependencies of the Jackson library to your build. Spring Boot has spring-boot-starter-json to add all the needed dependencies. See Listing 3-5.

Listing 3-5. Spring Boot JSON Starter Dependency

```
<dependency>
  <groupId>org.springframework.boot</groupId>
  <artifactId>spring-boot-starter-json</artifactId>
</dependency>
```

> ⓘ   The `spring-boot-starter-web` dependency already has a dependency on `spring-boot-starter-json` and will pull it in automatically. But it can be handy to declare it explicitly to state that you are using/enabling JSON.
>
> You can also use the Google GSON library; just use the appropriate GSON dependency instead and exclude `spring-boot-starter-json` from the `spring-boot-starter-web` dependency.

As you are making an application for a library, it will probably include books, so let's create a Book record. See Listing 3-6.

Listing 3-6. Book Record

```java
package com.apress.springboot3recipes.library;

import java.util.List;
import java.util.Objects;

public record Book(

        String isbn,
        String title,
        List<String> authors) {

  @Override
        public boolean equals(Object o) {

                if (this == o) return true;
                if (o == null || getClass() != o.getClass()) return false;
                Book book = (Book) o;
                return Objects.equals(isbn, book.isbn);

        }

        @Override
        public int hashCode() {
                return Objects.hash(isbn);
        }
}
```

A book is defined by its ISBN number; it has a title and one or more authors. Normally a record creates an `equals`, a `hashCode`, and a `toString` method, which will include all the data from the record (as it is immutable). However, here we want to have an `equals` and `hashCode` based only on the `isbn` field, so we provide the implementation ourselves.

You would also need a service to work with the books in the library. Let's define an interface and implementation for the `BookService`. See Listing 3-7.

Listing 3-7. BookService Interface

```
package com.apress.springboot3recipes.library;

import java.util.Optional;

public interface BookService {

        Iterable<Book> findAll();
        Book create(Book book);
        Optional<Book> find(String isbn);
}
```

The implementation, for now, is a simple in-memory implementation. See Listing 3-8.

Listing 3-8. BookService In-Memory Implementation

```
package com.apress.springboot3recipes.library;

import org.springframework.stereotype.Service;

import java.util.Map;
import java.util.Optional;
import java.util.concurrent.ConcurrentHashMap;

@Service
class InMemoryBookService implements BookService {

        private final Map<String, Book> books = new ConcurrentHashMap<>();

        @Override
        public Iterable<Book> findAll() {
                return books.values();
        }
```

```
@Override
public Book create(Book book) {
        books.put(book.isbn(), book);
        return book;
}

@Override
public Optional<Book> find(String isbn) {
        return Optional.ofNullable(books.get(isbn));
}
}
```

The service has been annotated with @Service so that Spring Boot will detect it and create an instance of it. See Listing 3-9.

Listing 3-9. Application Class with Setup Data

```
package com.apress.springboot3recipes.library;

import java.util.List;

import org.springframework.boot.ApplicationRunner;
import org.springframework.boot.SpringApplication;
import org.springframework.boot.autoconfigure.SpringBootApplication;
import org.springframework.context.annotation.Bean;

@SpringBootApplication
public class LibraryApplication {

        public static void main(String[] args) {
                SpringApplication.run(LibraryApplication.class, args);
        }

        @Bean
        public ApplicationRunner booksInitializer(BookService
        bookService) {
                return args -> {
```

```
                        bookService.create(
                                    new Book("9780061120084", "To
                                            Kill a Mockingbird",
                                            List.of("Harper
                                                    Lee")));
                        bookService.create(
                                    new Book("9780451524935",
                                            "1984",
                                            List.of("George
                                                    Orwell")));
                        bookService.create(
                                    new Book("9780618260300",
                                            "The Hobbit",
                                            List.of("J.R.R.
                                                    Tolkien")));
            };
        }
}
```

The LibraryApplication will detect all the classes and start the server. Upon starting, it will preregister three books so that we have something in our library.

To expose the Book as a REST resource, create a class called BookController and annotate it with @RestController. Spring Boot will detect this class and create an instance of it. Using @RequestMapping (and @GetMapping and @PostMapping), you can write methods to handle the incoming requests.

ⓘ   Instead of @RestController, you could use @Controller and put @ResponseBody on each request handling method. Using @RestController will implicitly add @ResponseBody to the request handling methods.

```
package com.apress.springboot3recipes.library.rest;

import com.apress.springboot3recipes.library.Book;
import com.apress.springboot3recipes.library.BookService;
import org.springframework.http.ResponseEntity;
```

```java
import org.springframework.web.bind.annotation.*;
import org.springframework.web.util.UriComponentsBuilder;

@RestController
@RequestMapping("/books")
public class BookController {

        private final BookService bookService;

        public BookController(BookService bookService) {
                this.bookService = bookService;
        }

        @GetMapping
        public Iterable<Book> all() {
                return bookService.findAll();
        }

        @GetMapping("/{isbn}")
        public ResponseEntity<Book> get(@PathVariable("isbn")
        String isbn) {
                return ResponseEntity.of(bookService.find(isbn));
        }

        @PostMapping
        public ResponseEntity<Book> create(@RequestBody Book book,
                                    UriComponentsBuilder uriBuilder) {
    var created = bookService.create(book);
    var newBookUri = uriBuilder.path("/books/{isbn}").build(created.
    isbn());
    return ResponseEntity.created(newBookUri).body(created);
        }
}
```

The controller will be mapped to the /books path due to the @RequestMapping(
"/books") annotation on the class. The list method will be invoked for GET requests
on /books. When /books/979-8-8688-0112-9 is called with a GET request, the get
method will be invoked and return the result for a single book or, when no book can
be found, a 404 response status. Finally, you can add books to the library using a POST
request on /books. Then the create method will be invoked, and the body of the
incoming request will be converted into a book.

Spring Boot can also show you what mappings are available during startup. For
this to happen, you will need to enable TRACE logging for the web group (a placeholder
in Spring Boot to enable logging for a bunch of packages). By adding logging.level.
web=TRACE to application.properties, it will list all the mappings onto the console. It
will also enable a lot of logging on incoming requests and process those requests, so you
probably don't want to keep this on, but it can be a great tool to debug mapping issues.
See Figure 3-3 for sample output.

```
2023-07-28T10:00:27.726+02:00 DEBUG 95667 --- [          main] o.s.b.w.s.ServletContextInitializerBeans : Mapping servlets: dispatcherServlet urls=[/]
2023-07-28T10:00:27.871+02:00 TRACE 95667 --- [          main] s.w.s.m.m.a.RequestMappingHandlerMapping :
    c.a.s.l.r.BookController:
    {GET [/books/{isbn}]}: get(String)
    {POST [/books]}: create(Book,UriComponentsBuilder)
    {GET [/books]}: all()
2023-07-28T10:00:27.876+02:00 TRACE 95667 --- [          main] s.w.s.m.m.a.RequestMappingHandlerMapping :
    o.s.b.a.w.s.e.BasicErrorController:
    { [/error]}: error(HttpServletRequest)
    { [/error], produces [text/html]}: errorHtml(HttpServletRequest,HttpServletResponse)
2023-07-28T10:00:27.880+02:00 DEBUG 95667 --- [          main] s.w.s.m.m.a.RequestMappingHandlerMapping : 5 mappings in 'requestMappingHandlerMapping'
2023-07-28T10:00:27.883+02:00 DEBUG 95667 --- [          main] o.s.w.s.h.BeanNameUrlHandlerMapping      : Detected 0 mappings in 'beanNameHandlerMapping'
2023-07-28T10:00:27.925+02:00 TRACE 95667 --- [          main] o.s.w.s.f.support.RouterFunctionMapping  : 0 RouterFunction(s) in 'routerFunctionMapping'
2023-07-28T10:00:27.936+02:00 TRACE 95667 --- [          main] o.s.w.s.handler.SimpleUrlHandlerMapping  : Mapped [/webjars/**] onto ResourceHttpRequestHandler [classpath [META-INF/resources/webjars/]]
2023-07-28T10:00:27.936+02:00 TRACE 95667 --- [          main] o.s.w.s.handler.SimpleUrlHandlerMapping  : Mapped [/**] onto ResourceHttpRequestHandler [classpath [META-INF/resources/], classpath [resources/],
2023-07-28T10:00:27.936+02:00 DEBUG 95667 --- [          main] o.s.w.s.handler.SimpleUrlHandlerMapping  : Patterns [/webjars/**, /**] in 'resourceHandlerMapping'
2023-07-28T10:00:27.957+02:00 DEBUG 95667 --- [          main] s.w.s.m.m.a.RequestMappingHandlerAdapter : ControllerAdvice beans: 0 @ModelAttribute, 0 @InitBinder, 1 RequestBodyAdvice, 1 ResponseBodyAdvice
2023-07-28T10:00:27.987+02:00 DEBUG 95667 --- [          main] .m.m.a.ExceptionHandlerExceptionResolver : ControllerAdvice beans: 0 @ExceptionHandler, 1 ResponseBodyAdvice
```

Figure 3-3. *Startup logging with request mappings*

Now that the application has started, you can use HTTPie or curl to retrieve the
books. When using http :8080/books, you should see output similar to Figure 3-4.

```
● ● ●      ■ target — marten@iMac-van-Marten — ..pe_3_2/target — -zsh — 88×31
[→ target git:(master) x http :8080/books                                           ]
HTTP/1.1 200
Content-Type: application/json;charset=UTF-8
Date: Wed, 04 Apr 2018 07:50:40 GMT
Transfer-Encoding: chunked

[
    {
        "authors": [
            "J.R.R. Tolkien"
        ],
        "isbn": "9780618260300",
        "title": "The Hobbit"
    },
    {
        "authors": [
            "George Orwell"
        ],
        "isbn": "9780451524935",
        "title": "1984"
    },
    {
        "authors": [
            "Harper Lee"
        ],
        "isbn": "9780061120084",
        "title": "To Kill a Mockingbird"
    }
]

→ target git:(master) x █
```

Figure 3-4. *JSON output for list of books*

A request to `http://localhost:8080/books/9780451524935` will give you the result
of a single book, in this case for *1984* by George Orwell. Using an unknown ISBN will
result in a 404.

When issuing a POST request, we could add a new book to the list. See Listing 3-10.

Listing 3-10. HTTPie Command

```
http POST :8080/books \
  title="The Lord of the Rings" \
  isbn="9780618640157" \
  authors:='["J.R.R. Tolkien"]'
```

The result of this call, when done correctly, is the freshly added book. Now when
you get the list of books, it should contain four books instead of the three books you
started with.

What happens is that HTTPie translates the parameters into a JSON request body, which in turn is read by the Jackson library and turned into a Book. See Listing 3-11.

Listing 3-11. Book JSON Representation

```
{
  "title": "The Lord of the Rings",
  "isbn": "9780618640157",
  "authors": ["J.R.R. Tolkien"]
}
```

Jackson will detect the Book record we created (see Listing 3-6) and map the properties to the correct constructor argument.

Test an @RestController

As you want to make sure that the controller does what it is supposed to do, write a test to verify the correct behavior of the controller. See Listing 3-12.

Listing 3-12. Integration Test for BookController Using WebMvcTest

```
package com.apress.springboot3recipes.library.rest;

import com.apress.springboot3recipes.library.Book;
import com.apress.springboot3recipes.library.BookService;
import org.hamcrest.Matchers;
import org.junit.jupiter.api.Test;
import org.springframework.beans.factory.annotation.Autowired;
import org.springframework.boot.test.autoconfigure.web.servlet.WebMvcTest;
import org.springframework.boot.test.mock.mockito.MockBean;
import org.springframework.http.MediaType;
import org.springframework.test.web.servlet.MockMvc;
import org.springframework.test.web.servlet.result.MockMvcResultMatchers;

import java.util.Arrays;
import java.util.List;
import java.util.Optional;

import static org.mockito.ArgumentMatchers.any;
import static org.mockito.ArgumentMatchers.anyString;
```

```java
import static org.mockito.Mockito.when;
import static org.springframework.test.web.servlet.request.
MockMvcRequestBuilders.get;
import static org.springframework.test.web.servlet.request.
MockMvcRequestBuilders.post;
import static org.springframework.test.web.servlet.result.
MockMvcResultMatchers.header;
import static org.springframework.test.web.servlet.result.
MockMvcResultMatchers.status;

@WebMvcTest(BookController.class)
public class BookControllerTest {

        @Autowired
        private MockMvc mockMvc;

        @MockBean
        private BookService bookService;

        @Test
        public void shouldReturnListOfBooks() throws Exception {
                when(bookService.findAll()).thenReturn(Arrays.asList(
                                new Book("123", "Spring 5 Recipes", List.
                                of("Marten Deinum", "Josh Long")),
                                new Book("321", "Pro Spring MVC", List.
                                of("Marten Deinum", "Colin Yates"))));

                mockMvc.perform(get("/books"))
                        .andExpect(status().isOk())
                        .andExpect(MockMvcResultMatchers.jsonPath("$",
                        Matchers.hasSize(2)))
                        .andExpect(MockMvcResultMatchers.jsonPath("$[*].
                        isbn", Matchers.containsInAnyOrder("123", "321")))
                        .andExpect(MockMvcResultMatchers.jsonPath("$[*].
                        title", Matchers.containsInAnyOrder("Spring 5
                        Recipes", "Pro Spring MVC")));
        }
```

```
    @Test
    public void shouldReturn404WhenBookNotFound() throws Exception {
        when(bookService.find(anyString())).thenReturn(Optional.
        empty());

        mockMvc.perform(get("/books/123"))
                        .andExpect(status().isNotFound());
    }

    @Test
    public void shouldReturnBookWhenFound() throws Exception {

        when(bookService.find(anyString())).thenReturn(
                                        Optional.of(new Book("123",
                                        "Spring 6 Recipes", List.
                                        of("Marten Deinum", "Josh
                                        Long"))));

        mockMvc.perform(get("/books/123"))
                        .andExpect(status().isOk())
                        .andExpect(MockMvcResultMatche
                        rs.jsonPath("$.isbn", Matchers.
                        equalTo("123")))
                        .andExpect(MockMvcResultMatche
                        rs.jsonPath("$.title", Matchers.
                        equalTo("Spring 6 Recipes")));
    }

    @Test
public void shouldAddBook() throws Exception {

    when(bookService.create(any(Book.class))).thenReturn(new
    Book("123456789", "Test Book Stored", List.of("T. Author")));

    mockMvc.perform(post("/books")
      .contentType(MediaType.APPLICATION_JSON)
      .content("{ \"isbn\" : \"123456789\", \"title\" :
      \"Test Book\", \"authors\" : [\"T. Author\"]}"))
      .andExpect(status().isCreated())
```

```
    .andExpect(header().string("Location", "http://localhost/
        books/123456789"));
  }

}
```

The test uses @WebMvcTest to create a MockMvc-based integration test. It will create a minimal Spring Boot application to be able to run the controller. The controller needs an instance of a BookService, so we let the framework create a mock for this using the @MockBean annotation. In the different test methods, we mock the expected behavior (such as returning a list of books, returning an empty Optional, etc.).

 Spring Boot uses Mockito to create mocks using @MockBean.

Furthermore, the test uses the JsonPath library so that you can use expressions to test the JSON result. JsonPath is to JSON as XPath is to XML.

3-3. Use Thymeleaf with Spring Boot
Problem

You want to use Thymeleaf to render the pages of your application.

Solution

Add the dependency for Thymeleaf and create an @Controller to determine the view and fill the model.

How It Works

To get started, you will first need to add spring-boot-starter-thymeleaf as a dependency to your project to get the desired Thymeleaf dependencies.

```
<dependency>
  <groupId>org.springframework.boot</groupId>
  <artifactId>spring-boot-starter-thymeleaf</artifactId>
</dependency>
```

With the addition of this dependency, you will get the Thymeleaf library as well as the Thymeleaf Spring dialect so that the two integrate nicely. Because of the existence of these two libraries, Spring Boot will automatically configure `ThymeleafViewResolver`.

`ThymeleafViewResolver` requires a Thymeleaf `ITemplateEngine` to be able to resolve and render the views. A special `SpringTemplateEngine` will be preconfigured with `SpringDialect` so that you can use SpEL inside Thymeleaf pages.

💡 To add other Thymeleaf dialects, you only need to create an `@Bean` method for it, and Spring Boot will automatically detect and wire them with Thymeleaf. Some of them are even automatically configured like when integrating with Spring Security (see Chapter 5).

To configure Thymeleaf, Spring Boot exposes several properties in the `spring.thymeleaf` namespace (see Table 3-2).

Table 3-2. *Thymeleaf Properties*

Property	Description
`spring.thymeleaf.cache`	Sets whether resolved templates should be cached; the default is `true`.
`spring.thymeleaf.check-template`	Checks if the template exists before rendering; the default is `true`.
`spring.thymeleaf.check-template-location`	Checks if the template location exists; the default is `true`.
`spring.thymeleaf.enabled`	Sets whether Thymeleaf should be enabled; the default is `true`.
`spring.thymeleaf.enable-spring-el-compiler`	Enables the compilation of SpEL expressions; the default is `false`.
`spring.thymeleaf.encoding`	Sets the encoding of the templates; the default is `UTF-8`.
`spring.thymeleaf.exclude-view-names`	Lists the view names (separated with commas) that are excluded from being resolved.

(continued)

Table 3-2. (*continued*)

Property	Description
`spring.thymeleaf.mode`	Sets the Thymeleaf TemplateMode to use; the default is HTML.
`spring.thymeleaf.prefix`	Sets the `prefix` to use for `ViewResolver`; the default is `classpath:/templates/`.
`spring.thymeleaf.suffix`	Sets the `suffix` to use for `ViewResolver`; the default is `.html`.
`spring.thymeleaf.render-hidden-markers-before-checkbox`	Sets whether hidden inputs for checkboxes should be rendered before the checkbox element itself (the default is `false`).
`spring.thymeleaf.template-resolver-order`	Sets the order of `ViewResolver`; the default is 1.
`spring.thymeleaf.view-names`	Sets the view names (separated with commas) that can be resolved with this `ViewResolver`.
`spring.thymeleaf.servlet.content-type`	Sets the Content-Type used to write the HTTP response; the default is `text/html`.
`spring.thymeleaf.servlet.produce-partial-output-while-processing`	Sets whether writing (partial content) should start as soon as possible or buffer until the template processing finished; the default is `true`.
`spring.thymeleaf.reactive.max-chunk-size`	Sets the maximum size of data buffers used for writing to the response. If this is not set, it uses chunked mode by default.
`spring.thymeleaf.reactive.media-types`	Sets the media types supported by this view technology.
`spring.thymeleaf.reactive.full-mode-view-names`	Contains a comma-separated list of view names (patterns are allowed) that should execute in FULL mode.
`spring.thymeleaf.reactive.chunked-mode-view-names`	Contains a comma-separated list of view names (patterns are allowed) that should execute in CHUNKED mode.

Add an Index Page

First add an index page to our application. Create an `index.html` file inside the `src/main/resources/templates` directory (the default location). See Listing 3-13.

Listing 3-13. Index Page

```
<!DOCTYPE html>
<html xmlns:th="http://www.thymeleaf.org">
<head>
    <meta charset="UTF-8">
    <title>Spring Boot Recipes - Library</title>
</head>
<body>

<h1>Library</h1>

<a th:href="@{/books.html}" href="#">List of books</a>

</body>
</html>
```

This is just a basic HTML5 page with some minor additions for Thymeleaf. First there is `xmlns:th="http://www.thymeleaf.org"` to enable the namespace for Thymeleaf. The namespace is used in the link through `th:href`. The `@{/books.html}` part will be expanded, by Thymeleaf, to a proper link and placed in the actual `href` attribute of the link.

Now when running the application, you should be greeted by a page with a link to the book's overview (see Figure 3-5).

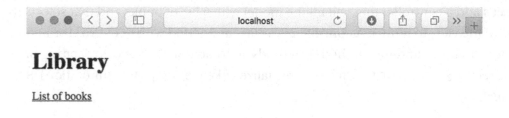

Figure 3-5. *Rendered index page*

Add a Controller and View

When clicking the link provided in the index page, we want to see a page that shows a list of available books in the library (see Figure 3-6). For this, two things need to be added: first a controller that can handle the request and prepare the model and second a view to render the list of books.

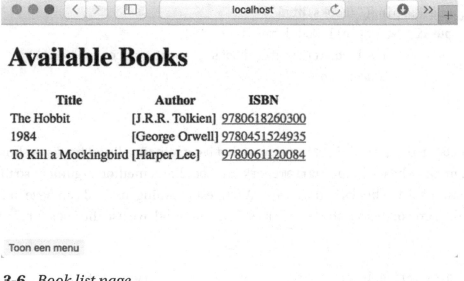

Figure 3-6. *Book list page*

Let's add a controller that will fill the model with a list of books and that selects the name of the view to render. A controller is a class annotated with @Controller and that contains request handling methods (methods annotated with @RequestMapping or as in this recipe @GetMapping, which is a specialized @RequestMapping annotation). See Listing 3-14.

Listing 3-14. BookController

```
package com.apress.springboot3recipes.library.web;

import com.apress.springboot3recipes.library.Book;
import com.apress.springboot3recipes.library.BookService;
import org.springframework.stereotype.Controller;
import org.springframework.ui.Model;
import org.springframework.web.bind.annotation.GetMapping;

@Controller
public class BookController {

        private final BookService bookService;

        public BookController(BookService bookService) {
                this.bookService = bookService;
        }

        @GetMapping("/books.html")
        public String all(Model model) {
                model.addAttribute("books", bookService.findAll());
                return "books/list";
        }
}
```

BookController needs BookService so that it can obtain a list of books to show. The all method has org.springframework.ui.Model as a method argument so that we can put the list of books in the model. A request handling method can have different arguments[1]; one of them is the Model class. In the method, we use the BookService

---

[1]https://docs.spring.io/spring/docs/current/spring-framework-reference/web. html#mvc-ann-arguments

to retrieve all the books from the datastore and add it to the model using model. addAttribute. The list of books is now available in the model under the key books.

Finally, we return the name of the view to render books/list.

Now that the controller together with the request handling method has been added, we need to create the view. Create a list.html file in the src/main/templates/books directory. See Listing 3-15.

Listing 3-15. Book List Page

```html
<!DOCTYPE html>
<html xmlns:th="http://www.thymeleaf.org">
<head lang="en">
    <meta charset="UTF-8">
    <title>Library - Available Books</title>
    <meta http-equiv="Content-Type" content="text/html; charset=UTF-8"/>
</head>
<body>
    <h1>Available Books</h1>
    <table>
        <thead>
            <tr>
                <th>Title</th>
                <th>Author</th>
                <th>ISBN</th>
            </tr>
        </thead>
        <tbody>
            <tr th:each="book : ${books}">
                <td th:text="${book.title}">Title</td>
                <td th:text="${book.authors}">Authors</td>
                <td><a th:href="@{/books.html(isbn=${book.isbn})}"
                th:text="${book.isbn}" href="#">ISBN</a></td>
            </tr>
        </tbody>
    </table>
</body>
</html>
```

This is again an HTML5 page using the Thymeleaf syntax. The page will render a list of books using the th:each expression. It will take all the books from the books property in the model and for each book create a row. Each column in the row will contain some text using the th:text expression; it will print the title, authors, and ISBN of the book. The final column in the table contains a link to the book details. It constructs a URL using the th:href expression. Notice the expression between (); this will add the isbn request parameter.

When launching the application and clicking the link on the index page, you should be greeted with a page showing the contents of the library, as shown earlier in Figure 3-6.

Add a Details Page

Finally, when clicking the ISBN number in the table, you want a page with details to be shown. The link contains a request parameter named isbn, which we can retrieve and use in the controller to find a book. The request parameter can be retrieved through a method argument annotated with @RequestParam.

The following method will handle the GET request, map the request parameter to the method argument, and include the model so that we can add the book to the model.

```
@GetMapping(value = "/books.html", params = "isbn")
public String get(@RequestParam("isbn") String isbn, Model model) {

        bookService.find(isbn)
                            .ifPresent(book -> model.
                            addAttribute("book", book));

        return "books/details";
}
```

The controller will render the books/details page. Add the details.html file to the src/main/resources/templates/books directory. See Listing 3-16.

Listing 3-16. Book Details Page

```
<!DOCTYPE html>
<html xmlns:th="http://www.thymeleaf.org">
<head lang="en">
    <meta charset="UTF-8">
    <title>Library - Available Books</title>
```

```html
    <meta http-equiv="Content-Type" content="text/html; charset=UTF-8"/>
</head>
<body>
    <div th:if="${book != null}">
        <div>
            <div th:text="${book.title}">Title</div>
            <div th:text="${book.authors}">authors</div>
            <div th:text="${book.isbn}">ISBN</div>
        </div>
    </div>

    <div th:if="${book} == null">
        <h1 th:text="'No book found with ISBN: ' + ${param.isbn}">Not
        Found</h1>
    </div>
</body>
</html>
```

This HTML5 Thymeleaf template will render one of the two available blocks on the page. Either the book has been found and then it will display the details or it will show a "not found" message. This is achieved by using the th:if expression. The isbn for the "not found" message is retrieved from the request parameters using the param as a prefix; ${param.isbn} will get the isbn request parameter.

Test an @Controller

As you want to make sure that the controller does what it is supposed to do, write a test to verify the correct behavior of the controller. See Listing 3-17.

Listing 3-17. Integration Test for BookController Using WebMvcTest

```java
package com.apress.springboot3recipes.library.web;

import com.apress.springboot3recipes.library.Book;
import com.apress.springboot3recipes.library.BookService;
import org.hamcrest.Matchers;
import org.junit.jupiter.api.Test;
```

```java
import org.springframework.beans.factory.annotation.Autowired;
import org.springframework.boot.test.autoconfigure.web.servlet.WebMvcTest;
import org.springframework.boot.test.mock.mockito.MockBean;
import org.springframework.test.web.servlet.MockMvc;

import java.util.Arrays;
import java.util.List;
import java.util.Optional;

import static org.mockito.ArgumentMatchers.anyString;
import static org.mockito.Mockito.when;
import static org.springframework.test.web.servlet.request.
MockMvcRequestBuilders.get;
import static org.springframework.test.web.servlet.result.
MockMvcResultMatchers.*;

@WebMvcTest(BookController.class)
public class BookControllerTest {

        @Autowired
        private MockMvc mockMvc;

        @MockBean
        private BookService bookService;

        @Test
        public void shouldReturnListOfBooks() throws Exception {

                when(bookService.findAll()).thenReturn(Arrays.asList(
                        new Book("123", "Spring 6 Recipes", List.
                        of("Marten Deinum", "Josh Long")),
                        new Book("321", "Pro Spring MVC", List.
                        of("Marten Deinum", "Colin Yates"))));

                mockMvc.perform(get("/books.html"))
                                        .andExpect(status().isOk())
                                        .andExpect(view().
                                        name("books/list"))
```

```
                                            .andExpect(model().
                                            attribute("books",
                                            Matchers.hasSize(2)));
    }

    @Test
    public void shouldReturnNoBookWhenNotFound() throws Exception {

            when(bookService.find(anyString())).thenReturn(Optional.
            empty());

            mockMvc.perform(get("/books.html").param("isbn", "123"))
                                            .andExpect(status().isOk())
                                            .andExpect(view().
                                            name("books/details"))
                                            .andExpect(model().attribut
                                            eDoesNotExist("book"));
    }

    @Test
    public void shouldReturnBookWhenFound() throws Exception {

            Book book = new Book("123", "Spring 6 Recipes",
                                            List.of("Marten Deinum", "Josh
                                            Long"));
            when(bookService.find(anyString())).thenReturn(Optional.
            of(book));

            mockMvc.perform(get("/books.html").param("isbn", "123"))
                                            .andExpect(status().isOk())
                                            .andExpect(view().
                                            name("books/details"))
                                            .andExpect(model().
                                            attribute("book", Matchers.
                                            is(book)));
    }
}
```

The test uses @WebMvcTest to create a MockMvc-based integration test. It will create a minimal Spring Boot application to be able to run the controller. The controller needs an instance of a BookService, so we let the framework create a mock for this using the @MockBean annotation. In the different test methods, we mock the expected behavior (like returning a list of books, returning an empty Optional, etc.).

   Spring Boot uses Mockito to create mocks using @MockBean.

With the MockMvc support from the Spring Test framework, we can check if the controller returns what we expect. We can check the HTTP status, the name of the view, and if the Model has the correct entries.

3-4. Handle Exceptions with Spring MVC

Problem

You want to configure the exception handling for Spring MVC and configure it according to your needs.

Solution

Spring MVC provides several ways of handling exceptions, and with Spring Boot it has become pretty easy to modify the default behavior.

For view-related implementations, it is easy to add pages that will be automatically picked up. Add an error.html file as a customized error page, or add specific error pages for specific HTTP error codes, i.e., 404.html and 500.html.

Spring Boot also has exception handling support for REST-based controllers. It will return a response containing the error information, much like the error information that is available with the regular MVC exception handling. Another option is to enable the Problem Detail support (RFC-7807), which is a small standard for defining error responses. To enable it, set the spring.mvc.problemdetails.enabled property to true.

How It Works

Spring Boot by default comes with the error handling enabled and will show a default error page. This can be disabled in full by setting the `server.error.whitelabel.enabled` property to `false`. When disabled, the exception handling will be handled by the servlet container instead of the general exception handling mechanism provided by Spring and Spring Boot.

Handle Exceptions for View Technologies

There are also some other properties that can be used to configure the whitelabel error page, mainly for what is going to be included in the model so that it, optionally, could be used to display additional information. See Table 3-3 for the properties.

Table 3-3. *Error Handling Properties*

Property	Description
server.error. whitelabel.enabled	Sets whether the whitelabel error page is enabled; the default is true.
server.error.path	Sets the path of the error page; the default is /error.
Server.error.include-exception	Sets whether the name of the exception should be included in the model; the default is false.
server.error.include-stacktrace	Sets whether the stack trace should be included in the model; the default is NEVER.
server.error.include-message	Sets whether the message should be included in the model; the default is NEVER.
server.error.include-binding-errors	Sets whether the message should be included in the model; the default is NEVER.

First let's add a method to `BookController` that forces an exception.

```
@GetMapping("/books/500")
public void error() {
        var cause = new NullPointerException("Dummy Exception");
        throw new ServerErrorException(cause.getMessage(), cause);
}
```

This will throw an exception, and as a result the `whitelabel` error page will be shown (see Figure 3-7).

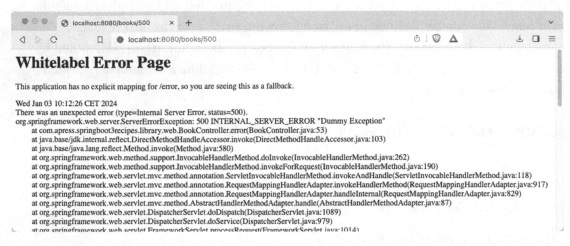

Figure 3-7. *Default whitelabel error page*

This is shown if no error page can be found. To override this, add an `error.html` file to the `src/main/resources/templates` directory. See Listing 3-18.

Listing 3-18. Customized Error Page

```
<!DOCTYPE html>
<html xmlns:th="http://www.thymeleaf.org">
<head>
        <meta charset="UTF-8">
        <title>Spring Boot Recipes - Library</title>
</head>
<body>
<h1>Oops something went wrong, we don't know what but we are going to work
on it!</h1>

<div>
        <div>
                <span><strong>Status</strong></span>
                <span th:text="${status}"></span>
        </div>
        <div>
```

```
            <span><strong>Error</strong></span>
            <span th:text="${error}"></span>
        </div>
        <div th:if="${message != null}">
            <span><strong>Message</strong></span>
            <span th:text="${message}"></span>
        </div>
        <div th:if="${exception != null}">
            <span><strong>Exception</strong></span>
            <span th:text="${exception}"></span>
        </div>
        <div th:if="${trace != null}">
            <h3>Stacktrace</h3>
            <span th:text="${trace}"></span>
        </div>
</div>
</body>
</html>
```

Now when the application starts and an exception occurs, this custom error page will be shown (see Figure 3-8). The page will be rendered by the view technology of your choice (in this case, it uses Thymeleaf).

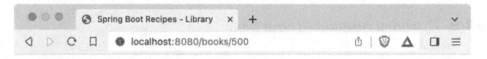

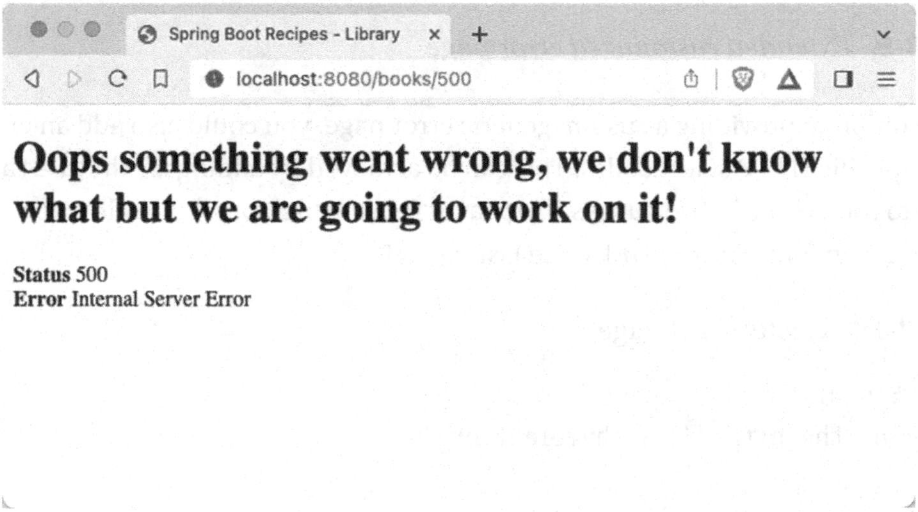

Spring Boot Recipes - Library
localhost:8080/books/500
Oops something went wrong, we don't know what but we are going to work on it!
Status 500
Error Internal Server Error

Figure 3-8. *Customized error page*

If you now set `server.error.include-exception` to `true` and `server.error.include-stacktrace` and `server.error.include-message` to `always`, the customized error page will show the classname of the exception, the message, and the stacktrace (see Figure 3-9).

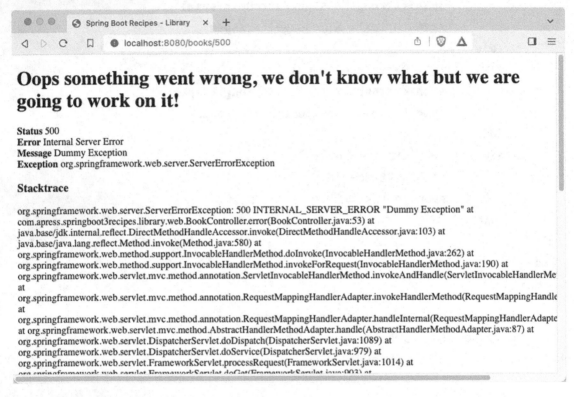

Figure 3-9. *Extended customized error page*

In addition to providing a custom generic error page, you could also add an error page for specific HTTP status codes. This can be achieved by adding an `<http-status>.html` file to the `src/main/resources/templates/error` directory. Let's add a `404.html` file to be shown for unknown URLs. See Listing 3-19.

Listing 3-19. Custom 404 Page

```
<!DOCTYPE html>
<html xmlns:th="http://www.thymeleaf.org">
<head>
    <meta charset="UTF-8">
    <title>Spring Boot Recipes - Library - Resource Not Found</title>
```

```
</head>
<body>
<h1>Oops the page couldn't be located.</h1>
</body>
</html>
```

When navigating to a URL that is unknown, it will render this page, and when triggering the exception, it will still show the customized error page, as shown in Figure 3-8.

💡   You can also add a `4xx.html` or `5xx.html` file for a custom error page for all HTTP status codes in the 400 or 500 range.

Add Attributes to the Model

By default Spring Boot will include the attributes listed in Table 3-4 in the model for the error page.

Table 3-4. *Default Error Model Attributes*

Attribute	Description
timestamp	The time that the errors were extracted
status	The status code
error	The error reason
exception	The class name of the root exception (if configured)
message	The exception message
errors	Any errors from a `BindingResult` (when using binding and/or validation)
trace	The exception stack trace (if configured)
path	The URL path when the exception was raised

This is all done through the use of an `ErrorAttributes` component. The default used and configured is the `DefaultErrorAttributes` component. You can create your own `ErrorAttributes` handler to create a custom model or extend `DefaultErrorAttributes` to add additional attributes. See Listing 3-20.

101

Listing 3-20. Custom ErrorAttributes Implementation

```
package com.apress.springboot3recipes.library;

import org.springframework.boot.web.error.ErrorAttributeOptions;
import org.springframework.boot.web.servlet.error.DefaultErrorAttributes;
import org.springframework.web.context.request.WebRequest;

import java.util.Map;

public class CustomizedErrorAttributes extends DefaultErrorAttributes {

    @Override
    public Map<String, Object> getErrorAttributes(WebRequest
    webRequest,
                                  ErrorAttributeOptions options) {
        var errorAttributes = super.getErrorAttributes(webRequest,
        options);
        errorAttributes.put("parameters", webRequest.
        getParameterMap());
        return errorAttributes;
    }
}
```

CustomizedErrorAttributes will add the original request parameters to the model in addition to the default attributes. The next step is to configure this as a bean so that Spring Boot can detect it and use it instead of configuring the default. Adding the bean definition shown in Listing 3-21 to LibraryApplication will make that possible.

Listing 3-21. Custom ErrorAttributes Bean Definition

```
@Bean
public CustomizedErrorAttributes errorAttributes() {
    return new CustomizedErrorAttributes();
}
```

Finally, you want to use the additional properties in your error.html file. See Listing 3-22.

Listing 3-22. Modification to the Errors Page

```
<div th:unless="${parameters.empty}">
        <h3>Parameters</h3>
        <span th:each="param :${parameters}">
                <div th:text="${param.key} + ' : ' + ${#strings.
                arrayJoin(param.value, ',')}"/>
        </span>
</div>
```

When Listing 3-22 is included in your error.html file, it will print the content of the map of parameters available in the model.

Handle Exceptions for REST Controllers

Write a custom ErrorAttributes to replace the default one (Figure 3-10) and to fill the model that is being written as a response.

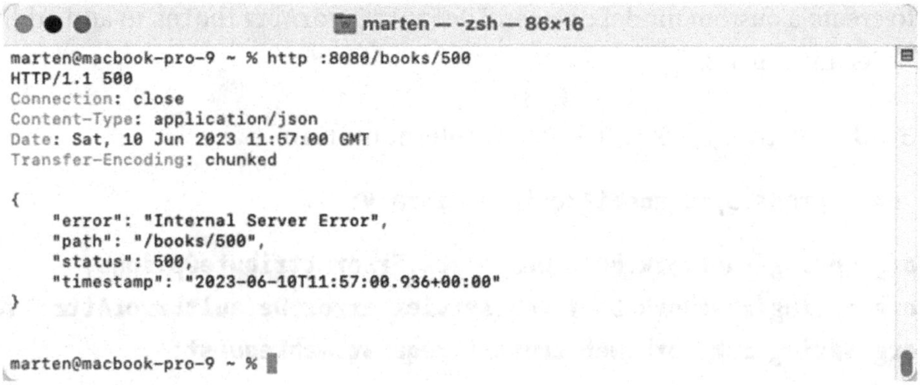

```
marten@macbook-pro-9 ~ % http :8080/books/500
HTTP/1.1 500
Connection: close
Content-Type: application/json
Date: Sat, 10 Jun 2023 11:57:00 GMT
Transfer-Encoding: chunked

{
    "error": "Internal Server Error",
    "path": "/books/500",
    "status": 500,
    "timestamp": "2023-06-10T11:57:00.936+00:00"
}

marten@macbook-pro-9 ~ %
```

Figure 3-10. *Default error response*

By default Spring Boot will include the attributes listed in Table 3-5 in the model for the error response.

Table 3-5. *Default Error Model Attributes*

Attribute	Description
timestamp	The time that the errors were extracted
status	The status code
error	The error reason
exception	The class name of the root exception (if configured)
message	The exception message
errors	Any errors from a BindingResult (when using binding and/or validation)
trace	The exception stack trace (if configured)
path	The URL path when the exception was raised

This is all done through the use of an ErrorAttributes component. The default used and configured is DefaultErrorAttributes. You can create your own ErrorAttributes handler to create a custom model or extend DefaultErrorAttributes to add additional attributes. See Listing 3-23.

Listing 3-23. Custom ErrorAttributes Implementation

```
package com.apress.springboot3recipes.library;

import org.springframework.boot.web.error.ErrorAttributeOptions;
import org.springframework.boot.web.servlet.error.DefaultErrorAttributes;
import org.springframework.web.context.request.WebRequest;

import java.util.Map;

public class CustomizedErrorAttributes extends DefaultErrorAttributes {

        @Override
        public Map<String, Object> getErrorAttributes(WebRequest
        webRequest,
                                        ErrorAttributeOptions options) {
                var errorAttributes = super.getErrorAttributes(webRequest,
                options);
                errorAttributes.put("parameters", webRequest.
                getParameterMap());
```

```
        return errorAttributes;
    }
}
```

The `CustomizedErrorAttributes` bean will add the original request parameters to the model next to the default attributes. The next step is to configure this as a bean so that Spring Boot can detect it and use it instead of configuring the default. Adding the bean definition from Listing 3-24 to `LibraryApplication` will make that possible.

Listing 3-24. Custom ErrorAttributes Bean Defnition

```
@Bean
public CustomizedErrorAttributes errorAttributes() {
        return new CustomizedErrorAttributes();
}
```

This will generate the error shown in Figure 3-11; notice the additional `parameters` attribute.

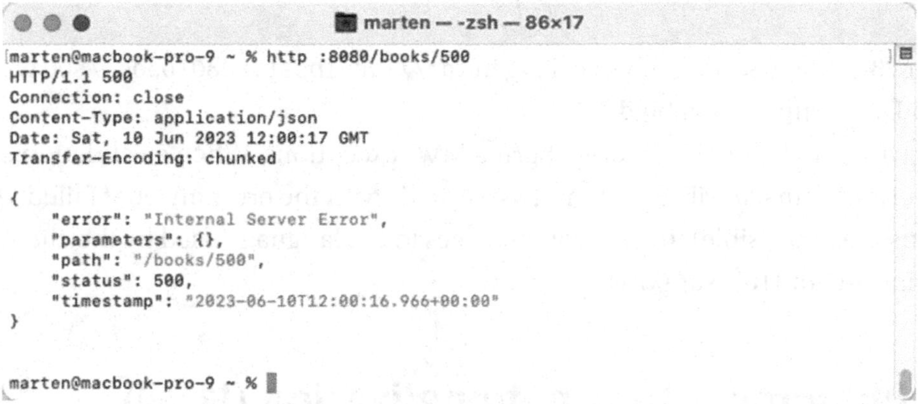

Figure 3-11. *Customized error response*

Enable and Use Problem Details

Spring 6 added support for the Problem Details for HTTP API (RFC-7807), and with Spring Boot it is quite easy to enable it. By adding `spring.mvc.problemdetails.enabled=true` (or `spring.webflux.problemdetails.enabled=true` for WebFlux-based applications), this support will be enabled.

When this is enabled, Spring Boot will register `ProblemDetailsExceptionHandler` as an additional `ExceptionHandler` with a higher order. `ProblemDetailsExceptionHandler` will handle some well-known exception (all the Spring-related web exceptions) and return a result containing more information including the type `application/problem+json` (see Figure 3-12).

```
marten@macbook-pro-9 ~ % http :8080/books/500
HTTP/1.1 500
Connection: close
Content-Type: application/problem+json
Date: Fri, 28 Jul 2023 09:35:46 GMT
Transfer-Encoding: chunked

{
    "detail": "Dummy Exception",
    "instance": "/books/500",
    "status": 500,
    "title": "Internal Server Error",
    "type": "about:blank"
}

marten@macbook-pro-9 ~ %
```

Figure 3-12. *Problem detail error response*

Figure 3-12 shows the result of calling `http://localhost:8080/books/500` with Problem Detail support enabled.

This will work for all the different Spring MVC exceptions. When a validation or binding error occurs, it will also show a list of fields with the error on what failed. It will even translate (if possible) those error messages to the language used by the client (see also Recipe 3-6 for I18N support).

3-5. Implement Internationalization (I18N)

Problem

When developing an internationalized web application, you have to display your web pages in a user's preferred locale. You don't want to create different versions of the same page for different locales.

Solution

To avoid creating different versions of a page for different locales, you should make your web page independent of the locale by externalizing locale-sensitive text messages. Spring is able to resolve text messages for you by using a message source, which has to implement the `MessageSource` interface. In your page templates, you can then either use special tags or do lookups for the messages.

How It Works

Spring Boot automatically configures a `MessageSource` when it finds a `messages.properties` file in `src/main/resources` (the default location). This `messages.properties` file contains the default messages to be used in your application. Spring Boot will use the `Accept-Language` header from the request to determine which locale to use for the current request (see Recipe 3-6 on how to change that).

There are some properties that change the way the `MessageSource` reacts to missing translations, caching, etc. See Table 3-6 for an overview of the properties.

Table 3-6. *I18N Properties*

Property	Description
spring.messages.basename	Comma-separated list of base names; the default is `messages`.
spring.messages.encoding	Message bundle encoding; the default is `UTF-8`.
spring.messages.always-use-message-format	Sets whether `MessageFormat` should be applied to all messages; the default is `false`.
spring.messages.fallback-to-system-locale	Fallback to the system's locale when no resource bundle for the detected locale can be found. When disabled, this will load the defaults from the default file. The default is `true`.
spring.messages.use-code-as-default-message	Use the message code as a default message when no message can be found instead of throwing a `NoSuchMessageException`. The default is `false`.
spring.messages.cache-duration	Cache duration; the default is `forever`.

💡 It can be useful to set `spring.messages.fallback-to-system-locale` to `false` when deploying your application to the cloud or other external hosting parties. That way you control what the default language of your application is, instead of the (out of your control) environment you are deploying on.

Add a `messages.properties` file to the `src/main/resources` directory. See Listing 3-25.

Listing 3-25. Default Messages

```
main.title=Spring Boot Recipes - Library

index.title=Library
index.books.link=List of books

books.list.title=Available Books
books.list.table.title=Title
books.list.table.author=Author
books.list.table.isbn=ISBN
```

Now change the templates to use the translations. See Listing 3-26.

Listing 3-26. Index Page with I18N Support

```html
<!DOCTYPE html>
<html xmlns:th="http://www.thymeleaf.org">
<head>
    <meta charset="UTF-8">
    <title th:text="#{main.title}">Spring Boot Recipes - Library</title>
</head>
<body>

<h1 th:text="#{index.title}">Library</h1>

<a th:href="@{/books.html}" href="#" th:text="#{index.books.link}">List of
books</a>

</body>
</html>
```

For Thymeleaf, you can use an #{...} expression in the th:text attribute; this will (due to the automatic Spring integration) resolve the messages from the MessageSource. When restarting the application, it appears as if nothing has changed in the output. However, all the texts now come from the messages.properties.

Now let's add a messages_nl.properties for the Dutch translation of the website. See Listing 3-27.

Listing 3-27. Dutch Messages

```
main.title=Spring Boot Recipes - Bibliotheek

index.title=Bibliotheek
index.books.link=Lijst van boeken

books.list.title=Beschikbare Boeken
books.list.table.title=Titel
books.list.table.author=Auteur
books.list.table.isbn=ISBN
```

Now when changing the accept header to Dutch, the website will magically translate to Dutch (see Figure 3-13).

Changing the language for your browser might not be that easy; for Chrome and Firefox there are plugins that allow you to switch the Accept-Language header easily.

Figure 3-13. *Dutch translated index page*

3-6. Change User Locales

Problem

For your web application to support internationalization, you have to identify each user's preferred locale and display contents according to this locale.

Solution

In a Spring MVC application, a user's locale is identified by component, which has to implement the `LocaleResolver` interface. Spring MVC comes with several `LocaleResolver` implementations for you to resolve locales by different criteria. Alternatively, you may create your own custom locale resolver by implementing this interface.

You can define a locale resolver by registering a bean of type `LocaleResolver` in the web application context. You must set the bean name of the locale resolver to `localeResolver` so it can be autodetected.

How It Works

Spring MVC ships with several default implementations of the LocaleResolver interface, some of which allow the Locale to be changed. To change the Locale, one can use a specific HandlerInterceptor to allow users to override the locale they want to use, the LocaleChangeInterceptor.

Resolve Locales with an HTTP Request Header

The default locale resolver registered by Spring Boot is the AcceptHeaderLocaleResolver. It resolves locales by inspecting the Accept-Language header of an HTTP request. This header is set by a user's web browser according to the locale setting of the underlying operating system. See Listing 3-28.

ℹ   The AcceptHeaderLocaleResolver cannot change a user's locale because it is unable to modify the locale setting of the user's operating system.

Listing 3-28. AcceptHeaderLocaleResolver Bean Definition

```
@Bean
public LocaleResolver localeResolver () {
  return new AcceptHeaderLocaleResolver();
}
```

Resolve Locales with a Session Attribute

Another option of resolving locales is by SessionLocaleResolver. It resolves locales by inspecting a predefined attribute in a user's session. If the session attribute doesn't exist, this locale resolver determines the default locale from the Accept-Language HTTP header. See Listing 3-29.

Listing 3-29. SessionLocaleResolver Bean Definition

```
@Bean
public LocaleResolver localeResolver () {
    var localeResolver = new SessionLocaleResolver();
    localeResolver.setDefaultLocale(Locale.forLanguageTag("en"));
    return localeResolver;
}
```

You can set the `defaultLocale` property for this resolver in case the session attribute doesn't exist. Note that this locale resolver is able to change a user's locale by altering the session attribute that stores the locale.

Resolve Locales with a Cookie

You can also use `CookieLocaleResolver` to resolve locales by inspecting a cookie in a user's browser. If the cookie doesn't exist, this locale resolver determines the default locale from the `Accept-Language` HTTP header. See Listing 3-30.

Listing 3-30. CookieLocaleResolver Bean Definition

```
@Bean
public LocaleResolver localeResolver() {
    return new CookieLocaleResolver();
}
```

The cookie used by this locale resolver can be customized by configuring the properties in Table 3-7 on `CookieLocaleResolver`. See Listing 3-31.

Table 3-7. *CookieLocaleResolver Properties*

Property	Description
cookieDomain	Sets the value for the Domain attribute of a cookie.
cookieHttpOnly	Adds the HttpOnly attribute to the cookie.
cookieMaxAge	Sets the Max-Age attribute of the cookie, -1 will persist until browser shutdown (the default).
cookieName	Sets the name of the cookie (deprecated; uses the constructor instead).
cookiePath	Sets the Path attribute of the cookie; the default is /.
cookieSameSite	Sets the Same-Site attribute of the cookie; the default is Lax.
cookieSecure	Sets the Secure attribute of the cookie; the default is false.
langagueTagCompliant	Sets whether the resolver should be BCP47 language tag compliant versus the Java Legacy locals; the default is true.
rejectInvalidCookies	Sets whether we reject invalid/corrupt cookies; the default is true.

Listing 3-31. Example with Properties Set

```
@Bean
public LocaleResolver localeResolver() {
    var cookieLocaleResolver = new CookieLocaleResolver("language");
    cookieLocaleResolver.setCookieMaxAge(Duration.ofMinutes(30));
    cookieLocaleResolver.setDefaultLocale(Locale.forLanguageTag("en"));
    return cookieLocaleResolver;
}
```

You can also set the defaultLocale property for this resolver in case the cookie doesn't exist in a user's browser. This locale resolver is able to change a user's locale by altering the cookie that stores the locale.

Change a User's Locale

In addition to changing a user's locale by calling `LocaleResolver.setLocale()` explicitly, you can also apply `LocaleChangeInterceptor` to your handler mappings. This interceptor detects if a special parameter is present in the current HTTP request. The parameter name can be customized with the `paramName` property of this interceptor (the default is `locale`). If such a parameter is present in the current request, this interceptor changes the user's locale according to the parameter value.

To be able to change the locale, a `LocaleResolver` that allows change has to be used.

```
@Bean
public LocaleResolver localeResolver() {
  return new CookieLocaleResolver();
}
```

To change the locale, add the `LocaleChangeInterceptor` as a bean and register it as an interceptor; for the latter, use the `addInterceptors` method from the `WebMvcConfigurer`. See Listing 3-32.

ℹ   Instead of adding it to the `@SpringBootApplication`, you could also create a specialized `@Configuration` annotated class to register the interceptors. Be aware of *not* adding `@EnableWebMvc` to that class as that will disable the auto-configuration from Spring Boot!

Listing 3-32. LocaleChangeInterceptor Beans and Configuration

```
@SpringBootApplication
public class LibraryApplication implements WebMvcConfigurer {

    public static void main(String[] args) {
        SpringApplication.run(LibraryApplication.class, args);
    }

    @Override
    public void addInterceptors(InterceptorRegistry registry) {
        registry.addInterceptor(new LocaleChangeInterceptor());
    }
```

```
    @Bean
    public LocaleResolver localeResolver() {
            return new CookieLocaleResolver();
    }
}
```

Now add the snippet to the `index.html` file, as shown in Listing 3-33.

Listing 3-33. Language Change Modifications for Index Page

```
<h3>Language</h3>
<div>
    <a href="?locale=nl" th:text="#{main.language.nl}">NL</a> |
    <a href="?locale=en" th:text="#{main.language.en}">EN</a>
</div>
```

Now when selecting one of the languages, the page will rerender and display in the selected language. When you continue browsing, the remainder of the pages will also be shown in the selected language (as in Figure 3-13).

3-7. Select and Configure the Embedded Server
Problem

You want to use Jetty as an embedded container instead of the default Tomcat container.

Solution

Exclude the Tomcat runtime and include the Jetty runtime. Spring Boot will automatically detect whether Tomcat, Jetty, or Undertow is on the classpath and configure the container accordingly.

How It Works

Spring Boot has out-of-the-box support for Tomcat, Jetty, and Undertow as embedded servlet containers. By default Spring Boot uses Tomcat as the container (expressed through the `spring-boot-starter-tomcat` dependency in the `spring-boot-starter-`

115

web artifact). The container can be configured using properties for which some apply to all containers and others to a specific container. The global properties are prefixed with `server.` or `server.servlet`, whereas the container ones start with `server.<container>` (where `container` is either `tomcat`, `jetty`, or `undertow`).

Set General Configuration Properties

Several general server properties are available, as shown in Table 3-8.

Table 3-8. *General Server Properties*

Property	Description
`server.port`	Specifies the HTTP server port; the default is 8080.
`server.address`	Specifies the IP address to bind to; the default is 0.0.0.0, i.e., all adapters.
`server.server-header`	Specifies the name of the header to send the server name; the default is empty.
`server.max-http-header-size`	Specifies the maximum size of a HTTP header; the default is 0 (unlimited).
`server.connection-timeout`	Specifies the timeout for HTTP connectors to wait for the next request before closing. The default is empty leaving it to the container; a value of -1 means infinite and never time out.
`server.http2.enabled`	Enables Http2 support if the current container supports it. The default is false.
`server.forward-headers-strategy`	Strategy for the X-Forward-* headers support; one of native, framework, none.
`server.compression.enabled`	Specifies whether the HTTP compression should be enabled; the default is false.
`server.compression.mime-types`	Contains a comma-separated list of MIME types that compression applies to.
`server.compression.excluded-user-agents`	Contains a comma-separated of user agents for which compression should be disabled.

(continued)

Table 3-8. (*continued*)

Property	Description
`server.compression.min-response-size`	Sets the minimum size of the request for compression to be applied; the default is 2048.
`server.servlet.context-path`	Sets the main context path of the application; the default is launched as the root application.
`server.servlet.application-display-name`	Sets the name used as the display name in the container; the default is `application`.
`server.servlet.context-parameters`	Sets the servlet container context/init parameters.
`server.shutdown`	Server shutdown mode; one of `immediate` or `graceful`. The default is `immediate`.

As the embedded containers all adhere to the Servlet specification, there is also support for JSP pages, and that support is enabled by default. Spring Boot makes it easy to change the JSP provider or even disable the support in full. See Table 3-9 for the exposed properties.

Table 3-9. *JSP-Related Server Properties*

Property	Description
`server.servlet.jsp.registered`	Specifies whether the JSP servlet should be registered; the default is `true`.
`server.servlet.jsp.class-name`	Sets the JSP servlet classname; the default is `org.apache.jasper.servlet.JspServlet` as both Tomcat and Jetty use Jasper as the JSP implementation.
`server.servlet.jsp.init-parameters`	Sets the context parameters for the JSP servlet.

The use of JSP with a Spring Boot application is discouraged and limited.[2]

When using Spring MVC, you might want to use the HTTP session to store attributes (generally with Spring Security to store CSFR tokens, etc.). The general servlet configuration also allows you to configure the HTTP session and the way it will be stored (cookie, URL, etc.). See Table 3-10 for the properties.

Table 3-10. *Servlet Container HTTP Session Properties*

`server.servlet.session.timeout`	Sets a session timeout; the default is 30 minutes.
`server.servlet.session.tracking-modes`	Session tracking modes; one or more of `cookie`, `url`, and `ssl`. The default is empty, leaving it to the container.
`server.servlet.session.persistent`	Sets whether session data should be persisted between restarts; the default is `false`.
`server.reactive.session.cookie.name`	Specifies the name of the cookie to store the session identifier. The default is empty, leaving it to the container default.
`server.reactive.session.cookie.domain`	Specifies the domain value to use for the session cookie. The default is empty, leaving it to the container default.
`server.reactive.session.cookie.path`	Specifies the path value to use for the session cookie. The default is empty, leaving it to the container default.
`server.reactive.session.cookie.http-only`	Specifies whether the session cookie should be HTTP-only accesible. The default is empty, leaving it to the container default.
`server.reactive.session.cookie.secure`	Specifies whether the cookie should be sent through SSL only. The default is empty, leaving it to the container default.
`server.reactive.session.cookie.max-age`	Sets the lifetime of the session cookie. The default is empty, leaving it to the container default.

(continued)

---

[2]https://docs.spring.io/spring-boot/docs/current/reference/html/web.html#web.
 servlet.embedded-container.jsp-limitations

Table 3-10. (*continued*)

`server.reactive.session.cookie.same-site`	Sets the Same-Site policy to use (NONE/LAX/STRICT); the default is NONE.
`server.servlet.session.session-store-directory.directory`	Sets the name of the directory to use for persistent cookies. This has to be an existing directory.

> ℹ When using a Spring session, only the `server.servlet.session.timeout` property applies!

Finally, Spring Boot makes it easy to configure SSL by exposing a few properties. See Table 3-11 and Recipe 3-8 for how to configure SSL.

Table 3-11. *Servlet Container SSL Properties*

Property	Description
`server.ssl.enabled`	Specifies whether SSL should be enabled; the default is `true`.
`server.ssl.bundle`	Sets the name of the SSL bundle to use.
`server.ssl.ciphers`	Specifies the supported SSL ciphers; the default is empty.
`server.ssl.client-auth`	Sets the SSL client authentication, one of none, want, or need. The default is empty.
`server.ssl.protocol`	Sets the SSL protocol to use; the default is TLS.
`server.ssl.enabled-protocols`	Sets which SSL protocols are enabled; the default is empty.
`server.ssl.key-alias`	Sets the alias to identify the key in the keystore; the default is empty.
`server.ssl.key-password`	Sets the password to access the key in the keystore; the default is empty.
`server.ssl.key-store`	Sets the location of the keystore, typically a JKS file; the default is empty.

(*continued*)

Table 3-11. (*continued*)

Property	Description
`server.ssl.key-store-password`	Sets the password to access the keystore; the default is empty.
`server.ssl.key-store-type`	Sets the type of the keystore; the default is empty.
`server.ssl.key-store-provider`	Sets the provider of the keystore; the default is empty.
`server.ssl.trust-store`	Sets the location of the trust store.
`server.ssl.trust-store-password`	Sets the password to access the trust store; the default is empty.
`server.ssl.trust-store-type`	Sets the type of the trust store; the default is empty.
`server.ssl.trust-store-provider`	Sets the provider of the trust store; the default is empty.

ℹ️   All the properties mentioned in the previous tables apply *only* when using an embedded container to run your application. When deploying to an external container (i.e., deploying a WAR file), the settings do not apply!

Change the Runtime Container

When including the `spring-boot-starter-web` dependency, it will automatically include a dependency to the Tomcat container as it has a dependency on the `spring-boot-starter-tomcat` artifact. To enable a different servlet container, `spring-boot-starter-tomcat` needs to be excluded, and one of `spring-boot-starter-jetty` or `spring-boot-starter-undertow` needs to be included. See Listing 3-34.

Listing 3-34. Exclusion of Tomcat and Use of Jetty

```
<dependency>
    <groupId>org.springframework.boot</groupId>
    <artifactId>spring-boot-starter-web</artifactId>
    <exclusions>
        <exclusion>
```

```xml
            <groupId>org.springframework.boot</groupId>
            <artifactId>spring-boot-starter-tomcat</artifactId>
         </exclusion>
      </exclusions>
   </dependency>
   <dependency>
      <groupId>org.springframework.boot</groupId>
      <artifactId>spring-boot-starter-jetty</artifactId>
   </dependency>
```

In Maven, you can use an <exclusion> element inside your <dependency> to exclude a dependency.

Now when the application is started, it will start with Jetty instead of using Tomcat (see Figure 3-14).

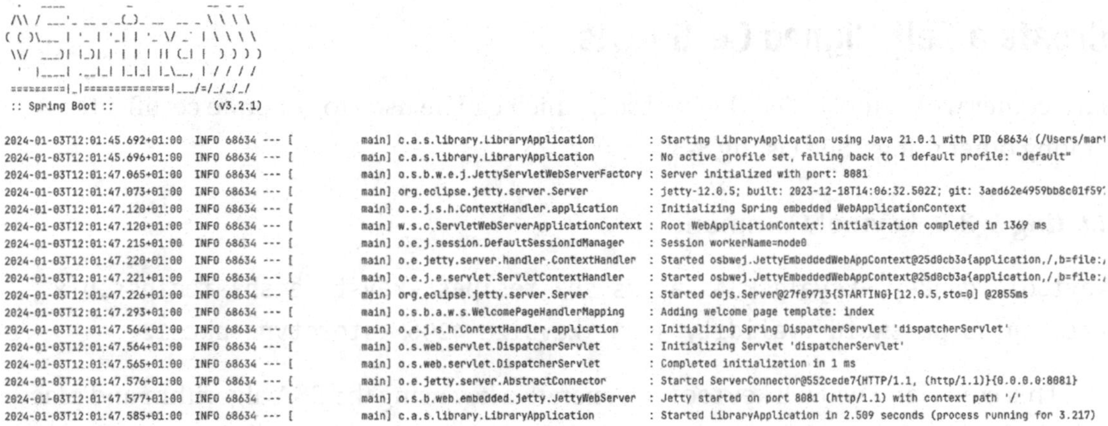

Figure 3-14. *Bootstrap logging with the Jetty container*

3-8. Configure SSL for the Servlet Container
Problem

You want your application to be accessible through HTTPS next (or instead of) HTTP.

Solution

Get a certificate, place it in a keystore, and use the `server.ssl` properties to configure the keystore. Spring Boot will then automatically configure the server to be accesible through HTTPS only.

How It Works

Using the `server.ssl.keystore` (and related properties), you can configure the embedded container to accept only an HTTPS connection. Before you can configure SSL, you will need to have a certificate to secure your application with. Generally, you will want to get a certificate from a certificate authority like Verisign or Let's Encrypt. However, for development purposes, you can use a self-signed certificate (see the section "Create a Self-Signed Certificate").

Create a Self-Signed Certificate

Java comes with a tool called the `keytool`, which can be used to generate certificates, among other things. See Listing 3-35.

Listing 3-35. keytool Command

```
keytool -genkey -keyalg RSA -alias sb3-recipes -keystore sb3-recipes.pfx
-storepass password -validity 3600 -keysize 4096 -storetype pkcs12
```

This command will tell `keytool` to generate a key using the RSA algorithm and place it in the keystore named `sb3-recipes.pfx` with the alias `sb3-recipes`, and it will be valid for 3,600 days. When running the command, it will ask a few questions. Answer them accordingly (or leave them empty). After that, there will be a file called `sb3-recipes.pfx` containing the certificate and protected with a password.

Place this file in the `src/main/resources` folder so that it is packaged as part of your application and Spring Boot can easily access it.

⚠️   Using a self-signed certificate will produce a warning in the browser that the website isn't safe and protected.

Configure Spring Boot to Use the Keystore

Spring Boot will need to know about the keystore to be able to configure the embedded container. For this use the `server.ssl.keystore` property. You will also need to specify the type of keystore (`pkcs12`) and the password. See Listing 3-36 and Figure 3-15.

Listing 3-36. SSL Properties

```
server.ssl.key-store=classpath:sb3-recipes.pfx
server.ssl.key-store-type=pkcs12
server.ssl.key-store-password=password
server.ssl.key-password=password
server.ssl.key-alias=sb2-recipes
```

Available Books

Title	Author	ISBN
The Hobbit	[J.R.R. Tolkien]	9780618260300
1984	[George Orwell]	9780451524935
To Kill a Mockingbird	[Harper Lee]	9780061120084

Figure 3-15. *Library accessed through HTTPS*

Support Both HTTP and HTTPS

Spring Boot by default starts only one connector, either HTTP or HTTPS, but not both. If you want to support both HTTP and HTTPS, you will manually have to add an additional connector. It is easiest to create the HTTP connector yourself and let Spring Boot set up the SSL part.

First let's configure Spring Boot to start the server on port 8443. See Listing 3-37.

Listing 3-37. Server Property for the Port

```
server.port=8443
```

To add an additional connector to the embedded Tomcat, you will need to add TomcatServletWebServerFactory as a bean to our context. Normally Spring Boot would detect the container and select the WebServerFactory to use; however, as a customization needs to be done, we need to add it manually. See Listing 3-38.

Listing 3-38. Additional Tomcat Connector

```
@Bean
public TomcatServletWebServerFactory tomcatServletWebServerFactory() {
  var factory = new TomcatServletWebServerFactory();
  factory.addAdditionalTomcatConnectors(httpConnector());
  return factory;
}

private Connector httpConnector() {
  var connector = new Connector(TomcatServletWebServerFactory.DEFAULT_
  PROTOCOL);
  connector.setScheme("http");
  connector.setPort(8080);
  connector.setSecure(false);
  return connector;
}
```

This will add an additional connector on port 8080, and the application will now be usable from ports 8080 and 8443. Using Spring Security, you could now force access to parts of your application over HTTPS instead of HTTP. See Listing 3-39.

 If you don't want to explicitly configure the TomcatServletWebServerFactory, you could use a BeanPostProcessor to register the additional Connector with the TomcatServletWebServerFactory. That way, you could implement this for different embedded containers instead of being tied to a single container.

Listing 3-39. Additional Tomcat Connector: Using BeanPostProcessor

```
@Bean
public BeanPostProcessor addHttpConnectorProcessor() {
  return new BeanPostProcessor() {
    @Override
    public Object postProcessBeforeInitialization(Object bean, String
    beanName)
    throws BeansException {
      if (bean instanceof TomcatServletWebServerFactory factory) {
        factory.addAdditionalTomcatConnectors(httpConnector());
      }
      return bean;
    }
  };
}
```

Redirect HTTP to HTTPS

Instead of supporting both HTTP and HTTPS, another option is to support only HTTPS and redirect the traffic from HTTP to HTTPS. The configuration is similar to that when supporting both HTTP and HTTPS. However, you now configure the connector to redirect all traffic from 8080 to 8443. See Listing 3-40.

Listing 3-40. Additional Tomcat Connector: With Redirect

```
@Bean
public TomcatServletWebServerFactory tomcatServletWebServerFactory() {
  var factory = new TomcatServletWebServerFactory();
  factory.addAdditionalTomcatConnectors(httpConnector());
  factory.addContextCustomizers(securityCustomizer());
  return factory;
}

private Connector httpConnector() {
  var connector = new Connector(TomcatServletWebServerFactory.DEFAULT_
  PROTOCOL);
  connector.setScheme("http");
```

```
  connector.setPort(8080);
  connector.setSecure(false);
  connector.setRedirectPort(8443);
  return connector;
}

private TomcatContextCustomizer securityCustomizer() {
  return context -> {
    var collection = new SecurityCollection();
    collection.addPattern("/*");
    var securityConstraint = new SecurityConstraint();
    securityConstraint.setUserConstraint("CONFIDENTIAL");
    securityConstraint.addCollection(collection);
    context.addConstraint(securityConstraint);
  };
}
```

The httpConnector now has a redirectPort set so that it knows which port to use. Finally, you need to secure all URLs with a SecurityConstraint. With Spring Boot, you can use a specialized TomcatContextCustomizer to post process the Context from Tomcat before it is started. The constraint makes everything (due to the use of /* as pattern) confidential (one of NONE, INTEGRAL, or CONFIDENTIAL is allowed), and the result is that everything will be redirected.

3-9. Implement Asynchronous Request Handling with Controllers and TaskExecutor

Problem

To increase the throughput on the servlet container, you want to asynchronously handle the request so resources can be assigned more efficiently.

Solution

When a request comes in, it is handled synchronously, which blocks the HTTP request handling thread. The response stays open and is available to be written to. This is useful when a call, for instance, takes some time to finish, and instead of blocking threads, you can have this processed in the background and return a value to the user when finished.

How It Works

Spring MVC supports a number of return types from methods; the return types in Table 3-12 are processed in an asynchronous way.

Table 3-12. *Asynchronously Return Types*

Type	Description
DeferredResult<?>	Async result produced later from another thread.
ListenableFuture<?>	Async result produced later from another thread, an equivalent alternative for DeferredResult. As of Spring 6.0, this is deprecated in favor of a CompletableFuture<?>.
CompletionStage<?>/Comp letableFuture<?>	Async result produced later from another thread, an equivalent alternative for DeferredResult.
Callable<?>	An async computation with the result produced after the computation finishes.
ResponseBodyEmitter	Can be used to write multiple objects to the response asynchronously.
SseEmitter	Can be used to write Server-Sent event asynchronously.
StreamingResponseBody	Can be used to write to the OutputStream asynchronously.

The generic return types in turn can return any of the return types for the controller, so either an object to be added to the model, a name of the view, or even a ModelAndView.

Configure Async Processing

Async request handling support has been added to the servlet specification in version 3. To enable it, you have to tell all your filters and servlets to behave asynchronously. In a Spring Boot application, this is done by default for the `DispatcherServlet` and detected `Filter` beans.

Spring Boot by default configures an `AsyncTaskExecutor` for use with Spring MVC. You can, however, depending on your needs, configure an `AsyncTaskExecutor`, and wire that in the MVC configuration. See Listing 3-41.

Listing 3-41. Explicit TaskExecutor Configuration

```
@SpringBootApplication
public class HelloWorldApplication implements WebMvcConfigurer {

  public static void main(String[] args) {
    SpringApplication.run(HelloWorldApplication.class, args);
  }

  @Override
  public void configureAsyncSupport(AsyncSupportConfigurer configurer) {
    configurer.setDefaultTimeout(5000);
    configurer.setTaskExecutor(mvcTaskExecutor());
  }

  @Bean
  public ThreadPoolTaskExecutor mvcTaskExecutor() {
    ThreadPoolTaskExecutor taskExecutor = new ThreadPoolTaskExecutor();
    taskExecutor.setThreadNamePrefix("mvc-executor-");
    return taskExecutor;
  }
}
```

> 💡 When Spring Boot detects that you have access to virtual threads (Java 21) and the property `spring.threads.virtual.enabled` is set to `true`, it will automatically set this up for Virtual Thread usage.

To configure async processing, you override the `configureAsyncSupport` method of `WebMvcConfigurer`. Overriding this method gives you access to the `AsyncSupportConfigurer`. This allows you to set `defaultTimeout` and the `AsyncTaskExecutor` to use. The timeout is set to 5 seconds, and as an executor you will use a `ThreadPoolTaskExecutor`.

💡 The `defaultTimeout` can also be set by setting `spring.mvc.async.request-timeout` in the `application.properties`. Adding `spring.mvc.async.request-timeout=5s` is the same as in the `@Bean` method.

Write an Asynchronous Controller

Writing a controller and having it handle the request asynchronously is as simple as changing the return type of the controller's handler method (see Table 3-12). Let's imagine that the call to `HelloWorldController.hello` takes some time, but we don't want to block the server for that.

Use a Callable

Listing 3-42 shows how to use a callable.

Listing 3-42. Async Controller Using a Callable

```
package com.apress.springboot3recipes;

import org.springframework.boot.SpringBootVersion;
import org.springframework.web.bind.annotation.GetMapping;
import org.springframework.web.bind.annotation.RestController;

import java.util.concurrent.Callable;
import java.util.concurrent.ThreadLocalRandom;

@RestController
public class HelloWorldController {

        @GetMapping
        public Callable<String> hello() {
```

```
return () -> {
    Thread.sleep(ThreadLocalRandom.current().
    nextInt(5000));
    var version = SpringBootVersion.getVersion();
    return String.format("Hello World, from Spring Boot
    %s!", version);
};
}
}
```

The hello method now returns a `Callable<String>` instead of returning a `String` directly. Inside the newly constructed `Callable<String>` there is a random wait to simulate a delay before the message is returned to the client.

Now when making a reservation, you will see something similair in the logs (see Figure 3-16).

ℹ   To enable this logging, you need to enable DEBUG level logging for the web-related groups. You can do this by adding `logging.level.web=DEBUG` to your `application.properties`.

```
2018-09-09 10:06:14.957 DEBUG 82160 ---- [nio-8080-exec-1] o.s.web.servlet.DispatcherServlet          : GET "/hello", parameters={}
2018-09-09 10:06:14.972 DEBUG 82160 ---- [nio-8080-exec-1] s.w.s.m.m.a.RequestMappingHandlerMapping : Mapped to public java.util.concurrent.Callable<java.lar
2018-09-09 10:06:14.996 DEBUG 82160 ---- [nio-8080-exec-1] o.s.w.c.request.async.WebAsyncManager     : Started async request
2018-09-09 10:06:14.998 DEBUG 82160 ---- [nio-8080-exec-1] o.s.web.servlet.DispatcherServlet          : Exiting but response remains open for further handling
2018-09-09 10:06:15.708 DEBUG 82160 ---- [      task-1] o.s.w.c.request.async.WebAsyncManager     : Async result set, dispatch to /hello
2018-09-09 10:06:15.716 DEBUG 82160 ---- [nio-8080-exec-2] o.s.web.servlet.DispatcherServlet          : "ASYNC" dispatch for GET "/hello", parameters={}
2018-09-09 10:06:15.716 DEBUG 82160 ---- [nio-8080-exec-2] s.w.s.m.m.a.RequestMappingHandlerAdapter : Resume with async result ["Hello World, from Spring Boo
2018-09-09 10:06:15.730 DEBUG 82160 ---- [nio-8080-exec-2] m.m.a.RequestResponseBodyMethodProcessor : Using 'text/plain', given [*/*] and supported [text/pla
n]
2018-09-09 10:06:15.731 DEBUG 82160 ---- [nio-8080-exec-2] m.m.a.RequestResponseBodyMethodProcessor : Writing ["Hello World, from Spring Boot 2!"]
2018-09-09 10:06:15.740 DEBUG 82160 ---- [nio-8080-exec-2] o.s.web.servlet.DispatcherServlet          : Exiting from "ASYNC" dispatch, status 200
```

Figure 3-16.   *Logging output with async enabled*

You notice that request handling is started on a certain thread (here `nio-8080-exec-2`). Another thread is doing the processing and returning the result (here `task-1`). Finally, the request is dispatched to `DispatcherServlet` again to handle the result on yet another thread.

Use a CompletableFuture

Change the signature of the method to return `CompletableFuture<String>` and use the `AsyncTaskExecutor` to async execute the code. See Listing 3-43.

Listing 3-43. Async Controller Using a CompletableFuture

```java
package com.apress.springboot3recipes;

import org.springframework.boot.SpringBootVersion;
import org.springframework.core.task.AsyncTaskExecutor;
import org.springframework.web.bind.annotation.GetMapping;
import org.springframework.web.bind.annotation.RestController;

import java.util.concurrent.CompletableFuture;
import java.util.concurrent.ThreadLocalRandom;

@RestController
public class HelloWorldController {

    private final AsyncTaskExecutor taskExecutor;

    public HelloWorldController(AsyncTaskExecutor taskExecutor) {
        this.taskExecutor = taskExecutor;
    }

    @GetMapping
    public CompletableFuture<String> hello() {
        return taskExecutor.submitCompletable(() -> {
            randomDelay();
            var version = SpringBootVersion.getVersion();
            return String.format("Hello World, from Spring Boot
            %s!", version);
        });
    }

    private void randomDelay() {
        try {
            Thread.sleep(ThreadLocalRandom.current().
            nextInt(5000));
        } catch (InterruptedException e) {
            Thread.currentThread().interrupt();
        }
    }
}
```

The task is executed on a thread from the `AsyncTaskExecutor`. We pass the task using the `submitCompletable`, which returns a `CompletableFuture`. When returning a `CompletableFuture`, you can take advantage of all the features of it, like composing and chaining multiple `CompletableFuture` instances.

Test Async Controllers

Just like regular controllers, the Spring MVC Test framework can be used to test async controllers.

Create a test class and annotate it with `@WebMvcTest(HelloWorldController.class)`. The `@WebMvcTest` will bootstrap a minimal Spring Boot application containing the things needed to test the controller. It automatically configures Spring `MockMvc`, which is autowired into the test. See Listing 3-44.

Listing 3-44. Test for the HelloWorldController

```
package com.apress.springboot3recipes;

import org.junit.jupiter.api.Test;
import org.springframework.beans.factory.annotation.Autowired;
import org.springframework.boot.test.autoconfigure.web.servlet.WebMvcTest;
import org.springframework.http.MediaType;
import org.springframework.test.web.servlet.MockMvc;
import org.springframework.test.web.servlet.MvcResult;
import org.springframework.test.web.servlet.request.MockMvcRequestBuilders;
import org.springframework.test.web.servlet.result.MockMvcResultHandlers;

import static org.hamcrest.Matchers.startsWith;
import static org.springframework.test.web.servlet.request.
MockMvcRequestBuilders.asyncDispatch;
import static org.springframework.test.web.servlet.result.
MockMvcResultMatchers.content;
import static org.springframework.test.web.servlet.result.
MockMvcResultMatchers.request;
import static org.springframework.test.web.servlet.result.
MockMvcResultMatchers.status;
```

```
@WebMvcTest(HelloWorldController.class)
public class HelloWorldControllerTest {

    @Autowired
    private MockMvc mockMvc;

    @Test
    public void testHelloWorldController() throws Exception {
MvcResult mvcResult = mockMvc.perform(MockMvcRequestBuilders.get("/"))
        .andExpect(request().asyncStarted())
        .andDo(MockMvcResultHandlers.print())
        .andReturn();

mockMvc.perform(asyncDispatch(mvcResult))
  .andExpect(status().isOk())
  .andExpect(content().contentTypeCompatibleWith(MediaType.TEXT_PLAIN))
  .andExpect(content().string(startsWith("Hello World, from Spring
  Boot ")));
    }
}
```

The main difference between an async web test and a regular web test is the fact that the async dispatching needs to be initiated. First the initial request is performed and validated for the async to start. For debugging purposes, you could log the result. Next the asyncDispatch is applied. Finally, we can assert the expected response.

ℹ️   Instead of using asyncDispatch, you could also use mvcResult. getAsyncResult (with or without a timeout) to directly get the result. However, generally you want to write additional assertions on the response.

3-10. Create Response Writers

Problem

You have a service, or multiple calls, and want to send the response in chunks to the client.

Solution

Use a `ResponseBodyEmitter` (or its sibling `SseEmitter`) to send the response in chunks.

How It Works

Here's how it works.

Send Multiple Results in a Response

Spring MVC has a class named `ResponseBodyEmitter` that is particularly useful if instead of a single result you want to return multiple objects to the client. When sending an object, it is converted to a result using an `HttpMessageConverter`. To use the `ResponseBodyEmitter`, you have construct it and return it from the request handling method.

Create an `OrderController` with an `orders` method that returns a `ResponseBodyEmitter` and send the results one by one to the client. See Listing 3-45.

Listing 3-45. OrderController Using ResponseBodyEmitter

```
package com.apress.springboot3recipes.order.rest;

import com.apress.springboot3recipes.order.Order;
import com.apress.springboot3recipes.order.OrderService;
import org.springframework.core.task.TaskExecutor;
import org.springframework.http.MediaType;
import org.springframework.web.bind.annotation.GetMapping;
import org.springframework.web.bind.annotation.RestController;
import org.springframework.web.servlet.mvc.method.annotation.
ResponseBodyEmitter;
```

```java
import java.io.IOException;
import java.util.concurrent.ThreadLocalRandom;

@RestController
public class OrderController {

    private final OrderService orderService;
    private final TaskExecutor executor;

    public OrderController(OrderService orderService, TaskExecutor
    executor) {
        this.orderService = orderService;
        this.executor = executor;
    }

    @GetMapping("/orders")
    public ResponseBodyEmitter orders() {
        var emitter = new ResponseBodyEmitter();
        executor.execute(() -> {
            var orders = orderService.findAll();
    try {
      for (var order : orders) {
        sendAndDelay(emitter, order);
      }
      emitter.complete();
    } catch (IOException ex) {
      emitter.completeWithError(ex);
    }
        });
        return emitter;
    }

    private void sendAndDelay(ResponseBodyEmitter emitter, Order order)
    throws IOException{
    emitter.send(order, MediaType.APPLICATION_JSON);
    randomDelay();
    }
```

```java
    private void randomDelay() {
        try {
            Thread.sleep(ThreadLocalRandom.current().
            nextInt(150));
        } catch (InterruptedException e) {
            Thread.currentThread().interrupt();
        }
    }
}
```

First a `ResponseBodyEmitter` is created and in the end returned from this method. Next a task is executed, which will query the reservations using the `OrderService.findAll` method. All the results from that call are returned one by one using the `send` method of the `ResponseBodyEmitter`. When all the objects have been sent, the `complete()` method needs to be called so that the thread responsible for sending the response can complete the request and be freed up for the next response to handle. When an exception occurs and you want to inform the user of this, you call the `completeWithError`. The exception will pass through the normal exception handling of Spring MVC, and after that the response is completed.

When using a tool like `HTTPie` or `curl`, calling the URL `http://localhost:8080/orders` will yield the results shown in Figure 3-17. The result will be chunked and has a status of 200 (OK).

```
● ● ●                              ▣ marten — marten@imac-van-marten — ~ — -zsh — 122×32
▷ http :8080/orders -v
GET /orders HTTP/1.1
Accept: */*
Accept-Encoding: gzip, deflate
Connection: keep-alive
Host: localhost:8080
User-Agent: HTTPie/0.9.9


HTTP/1.1 200
Date: Sun, 09 Sep 2018 08:34:38 GMT
Transfer-Encoding: chunked
```

{"id":"a3e2c659-6d61-4f72-81a2-9386767901c7","amount":964.3303264760648}{"id":"68e353b9-69b0-44cc-a0a5-c9d811a61f5e","amou
nt":630.5819945932226}{"id":"7cd568aa-4168-40cb-996c-051e5fa82457","amount":247.3223213836674}{"id":"964a6124-f993-43eb-ba
17-908bfc5097aa","amount":808.549237068922}{"id":"5ecc62bc-9f3c-473b-9966-d5c9f37555fd","amount":661.3744699952401}{"id":"
f676d1bc-dde0-4f8c-83b5-e3101642c123","amount":857.9818651414307}{"id":"2c4f7232-83f5-41b3-9633-4f71a48e3364","amount":891
.7136746089751}{"id":"d20b0c31-8dcd-46d1-aea3-9d0fac9f14c0","amount":332.49993916867015}{"id":"b683f8ee-011b-4390-8973-80a
a17509d7a","amount":800.6509712001965}{"id":"3cd778f0-9e25-4d2a-b29e-92d239a9189d","amount":801.3667308438916}{"id":"abd8e
7da-9d76-42d9-a0f0-0455e0518fb1","amount":554.321571430265}{"id":"7769e9a4-f951-447c-961c-d715c8a18ab8","amount":115.50183
059747442}{"id":"5b1fc94f-853b-4f32-b01c-1f4af7ce41dd","amount":686.6941002940033}{"id":"05d36d52-786a-4a5e-b02a-915958b89
37e","amount":748.0382636058531}{"id":"6564f567-d9ad-4486-b5dd-b77ce1e1b06c","amount":879.4838692645402}{"id":"be6c103d-f0
9a-4afe-9f5f-992d522b42ba","amount":447.45108559657245}{"id":"46a39e54-bb29-43dc-9417-c17fc7462574","amount":419.547649244
9695}{"id":"51a7c85c-b35a-4269-9b52-e2dd7ef2d08c","amount":421.8349910257171}{"id":"35564e73-b7ee-46ca-9438-fdc9637d63d4",
"amount":975.0530454514776}{"id":"6f0eb0fa-1c60-4a9c-8299-1d592204dd30","amount":338.355915281261}{"id":"5542e1a6-d500-44
4d-b889-ad0cd98d17a7","amount":402.66337491090167}{"id":"47087519-3e98-4f10-8719-61aa581f06a6","amount":702.9394273793404}
{"id":"11b96b15-d4eb-4f56-b14b-1b3f9ff77d61","amount":176.0339216118647}{"id":"697b74c3-8e35-4514-beb9-3e35d4a7b935","amou
nt":297.7516547391046}{"id":"c058b00d-b09f-442f-8f7b-3c8469f49720","amount":588.2887029367946}

~

Figure 3-17. *Chunked result*

Finally, let's write a test for this controller. Annotate a class with `@WebMvcTest(OrderController.class)` to get a web slice test. `OrderController` needs an `OrderService` that is mocked by using `@MockBean` on the `OrderService` field. See Listing 3-46.

Listing 3-46. Test for OrderController

```java
package com.apress.springboot3recipes.order.rest;

import com.apress.springboot3recipes.order.Order;
import com.apress.springboot3recipes.order.OrderService;
import org.junit.jupiter.api.Test;
import org.springframework.beans.factory.annotation.Autowired;
import org.springframework.boot.test.autoconfigure.web.servlet.WebMvcTest;
import org.springframework.boot.test.mock.mockito.MockBean;
import org.springframework.test.web.servlet.MockMvc;
import org.springframework.test.web.servlet.MvcResult;
import org.springframework.test.web.servlet.result.MockMvcResultHandlers;

import java.math.BigDecimal;
import java.util.List;
```

```
import static org.mockito.Mockito.when;
import static org.springframework.test.web.servlet.request.
MockMvcRequestBuilders.asyncDispatch;
import static org.springframework.test.web.servlet.request.
MockMvcRequestBuilders.get;
import static org.springframework.test.web.servlet.result.
MockMvcResultMatchers.content;
import static org.springframework.test.web.servlet.result.
MockMvcResultMatchers.request;
import static org.springframework.test.web.servlet.result.
MockMvcResultMatchers.status;

@WebMvcTest(OrderController.class)
public class OrderControllerTest {

        @Autowired
        private MockMvc mockMvc;

        @MockBean
        private OrderService orderService;

        @Test
        public void shouldReturnOrdres() throws Exception {

                when(orderService.findAll())
                        .thenReturn(List.of(new Order("1234",
                        BigDecimal.TEN)));

                MvcResult mvcResult = mockMvc.perform(get("/orders"))
                        .andExpect(request().asyncStarted())
                        .andDo(MockMvcResultHandlers.log())
                        .andReturn();

                mockMvc.perform(asyncDispatch(mvcResult))
                        .andDo(MockMvcResultHandlers.log())
                        .andExpect(status().isOk())
                        .andExpect(content().json("{\"id\":\"1234\",
                        \"amount\":10}"));
        }
}
```

The test method first registers the behavior on the mocked `OrderService` to return a single instance of an `Order`. Next, we use `MockMvc` to perform a get on the `/orders` endpoint. As this is an async controller, the request should start async processing, which is asserted here. Next, we mimic the async dispatching and write assertions for the actual response. The result should be a single JSON element containing the `id` and `amount`.

Send Multiple Results as Events

`ResponseBodyEmitter` is a sibling of the `SseEmitter` that can deliver events from the server to the client. For this Server-Sent-Events are used. Server-Sent-Events are messages from the server to the client. They have a `Content-Type` header of `text/event-stream`. They are quite lightweight with only four fields (see Table 3-13).

Table 3-13. *Allowed Fields for Server-Sent-Events*

Field	Description
Id	The ID of the event
Event	The type of event
Data	The event data
Retry	Reconnection time for the event stream

To send events from a request handling method, you need to create an instance of `SseEmitter` and return it from the request handling method. Then use the `send` method to send individual elements to the client. See Listing 3-47.

Listing 3-47. OrderController with SseEmitter

```
@GetMapping("/orders")
public SseEmitter orders() {
        var emitter = new SseEmitter();
        executor.execute(() -> {
                var orders = orderService.findAll();
                try {
                        for (var order : orders) {
                                sendAndDelay(emitter, order);
                        }
```

```
                        emitter.complete();
                } catch (IOException ex) {
                        emitter.completeWithError(ex);
                }
        });
        return emitter;
    }

    private void sendAndDelay(ResponseBodyEmitter emitter, Order order)
        throws IOException{
        emitter.send(order, MediaType.APPLICATION_JSON);
        randomDelay();
    }
}
```

ℹ️   There is a delay in sending each item to the client, just so you can see the different events coming in. You wouldn't do this in real code.

Now when the URL http://localhost:8080/orders is called, you see events coming in one by one (Figure 3-18).

Figure 3-18. *Server-Sent-Events result*

Note the Content-Type header. It has a value of text/event-stream to indicate that we get a stream of events. The stream can be kept open and to receive event notifications. Each object written is converted to JSON. This is done with an HttpMessageConverter just as with a plain ResponseBodyEmitter. Each object is written in the data tag as the event data.

If you want to add more info to the event (fill one of the other fields as mentioned in Table 3-13), use the SseEventBuilder. The event() factory method of the SseEmitter creates an instance. Use it to fill in the id and event fields. See Listing 3-48.

Listing 3-48. OrderController with SseEmitter: Extended Events

```
private void sendAndDelay(ResponseBodyEmitter emitter, Order order)
throws IOException{
  var eventBuilder = SseEmitter.event();
  emitter.send(
      eventBuilder
```

```
            .data(order, MediaType.APPLICATION_JSON)
            .name("order-created")
            .id(String.valueOf(order.hashCode())).build());
    randomDelay();
  }
}
```

Now when calling the URL http://localhost:8080/orders, events contain id, event, and data fields. See Figure 3-19.

```
● ● ●                ▇ marten — marten@imac-van-marten — ~ — -zsh — 92×29
[▷ http :8080/orders                                                                    ]
HTTP/1.1 200
Content-Type: text/event-stream;charset=UTF-8
Date: Wed, 11 Jul 2018 10:07:49 GMT
Transfer-Encoding: chunked

data:{"id":"8b32ffa1-9108-4135-a1f1-b576ffab9cbc","amount":571.7930067888439}
event:order-created
id:1253900499

data:{"id":"2be2f24d-fd82-4f56-994b-c7c0f65de1ed","amount":337.4862782201099}
event:order-created
id:1820233767

data:{"id":"17153887-5304-43ff-9088-62b1a4cb63db","amount":489.9123343382062}
event:order-created
id:2096994301

data:{"id":"e515b3b8-a5bc-4f8d-aa3f-2c6576e77913","amount":234.7290986199768}
event:order-created
id:1747749104

data:{"id":"93b87a4a-b145-4306-a589-c0eae8458757","amount":167.13027374188226}
event:order-created
id:616835188

data:{"id":"d48b5a1f-d5b7-41da-8374-00a3d9f56c1f","amount":467.42611999725835}
event:order-created
id:1239837839
```

Figure 3-19. *Server-Sent-Events extended results*

Test Server-Sent Events

Testing the output for Server-Sent Events is much like a regular async test. The main difference is the content type that is being returned (text/event-stream) and the assertions that are being done (on the id, event, and data fields). See Listing 3-49.

Listing 3-49. OrderControllerTest for Server-Sent Events Test

```
package com.apress.springboot3recipes.order.rest;

import com.apress.springboot3recipes.order.Order;
import com.apress.springboot3recipes.order.OrderService;
import org.junit.jupiter.api.Test;
import org.springframework.beans.factory.annotation.Autowired;
import org.springframework.boot.test.autoconfigure.web.servlet.WebMvcTest;
import org.springframework.boot.test.mock.mockito.MockBean;
import org.springframework.test.web.servlet.MockMvc;
import org.springframework.test.web.servlet.result.MockMvcResultHandlers;

import java.util.List;

import static java.math.BigDecimal.TEN;
import static org.hamcrest.Matchers.allOf;
import static org.hamcrest.Matchers.containsString;
import static org.mockito.Mockito.when;
import static org.springframework.http.MediaType.TEXT_EVENT_STREAM_VALUE;
import static org.springframework.test.web.servlet.request.
MockMvcRequestBuilders.asyncDispatch;
import static org.springframework.test.web.servlet.request.
MockMvcRequestBuilders.get;
import static org.springframework.test.web.servlet.result.
MockMvcResultMatchers.content;
import static org.springframework.test.web.servlet.result.
MockMvcResultMatchers.request;
import static org.springframework.test.web.servlet.result.
MockMvcResultMatchers.status;

@WebMvcTest(OrderController.class)
public class OrderControllerTest {

  @Autowired
  private MockMvc mockMvc;

  @MockBean
  private OrderService orderService;
```

```java
@Test
public void ordersEventStream() throws Exception {
  var orders = List.of(new Order("1234", TEN));
  when(orderService.findAll()).thenReturn(orders);

  var mvcResult = mockMvc.perform(get("/orders"))
    .andExpect(request().asyncStarted())
    .andDo(MockMvcResultHandlers.log())
    .andReturn();

  mockMvc.perform(asyncDispatch(mvcResult))
    .andDo(MockMvcResultHandlers.log())
    .andExpect(status().isOk())
    .andExpect(content().contentTypeCompatibleWith(TEXT_EVENT_
    STREAM_VALUE))
    .andExpect(content().string(
      allOf(
        containsString("data:{\"id\":\"1234\",\"amount\":10}"),
        containsString("event:order-created"),
        containsString("id:"))));
  }
}
```

3-11. Consume REST Resources with Spring MVC

Problem

You need to connect to a REST resource for your application and want to use a
RestTemplate or RestClient for this.

Solution

Spring Boot provides the configuration and builders to help construct the needed
classes. This recipe is going to build an application that can be used to consume the API,
as shown in Recipe 3-2.

You can use either the `RestTemplateBuilder` to create a `RestTemplate` and use that in your application or the exposed `RestClient.Builder` to create a `RestClient`. A final option is to use a declarative client using an `@HttpExchange`.

ℹ️   The `RestClient` is a more fluent approach to building, executing, and processing REST calls than the `RestTemplate` is. It is built as a blocking variant of the `WebClient` for Webflux (see Chapter 4).

How It Works

Although each approach differs in the classes in use, we are still going to need a dependency on the web classes for Spring MVC. For this, we can add the `spring-boot-starter-web` dependency. See Listing 3-50.

Listing 3-50. Spring Boot Starter Web Dependency

```
<dependency>
        <groupId>org.springframework.boot</groupId>
        <artifactId>spring-boot-starter-web</artifactId>
</dependency>
```

ℹ️   If you are writing a stand-alone client not in need of a servlet container, you might want to add an exclusion for `spring-boot-starter-tomcat`.

We are going to use Recipe 3-2 as our server API, and we will write an application that looks up a book on that API, calls another API (on `https://openlibrary.org`) to retrieve additional information for the book, and returns an enriched response.

`EnrichedBook` looks like Listing 3-51.

Listing 3-51. EnrichedBook Record

```
package com.apress.springboot3recipes.library;

import java.util.List;
import java.util.Objects;
```

```java
public record EnrichedBook(
        String isbn,
        String title,
        String published,
        List<String> authors) {

    @Override
        public boolean equals(Object o) {
                if (o instanceof EnrichedBook book) {
                        return Objects.equals(isbn, book.isbn);
                }
                return false;
        }

    @Override
    public int hashCode() {
                return Objects.hash(isbn);
        }
}
```

It is a slightly extended version of the Book class created in Recipe 3-2 (see Listing 3-6). For the Open Library API we will use a HashMap to put the response in and retrieve the elements we needed.

Use a RestTemplate

To create a RestTemplate, we can use the RestTemplateBuilder, ideally as an argument in an @Bean method. With this we can create a new RestTemplate as a bean. The RestTemplateBuilder takes care of configuring the RestTemplate we need. See Listing 3-52.

Listing 3-52. RestTemplate Configuration

```java
@Bean
public RestTemplate restTemplate(RestTemplateBuilder builder) {
        return builder.build();
}
```

This will construct a new `RestTemplate` for use in our application.

It is also possible to specify additional configuration for the `RestTemplateBuilder` through the helper methods. Each method will construct a new `RestTemplateBuilder` as the `RestTemplateBuilder` itself is immutable. So, changes set will not be reflected in other places that use a `RestTemplateBuilder`. See Table 3-14.

Table 3-14. *RestTemplateBuilder Configuration Methods*

Method	Description
additionalCustomizers	Adds additional `RestTemplateCustomizer` that should be applied to the created `RestTemplate`. Applied in the order as added on the configuration.
additionalInterceptors	Adds additional `ClientHttpRequestInterceptors` that should be added/configured on the created `RestTemplate`.
additionalMessageConverters	Adds additional `HttpMessageConverter` that should be used with the created `RestTemplate`.
additionalRequestCustomizers	Adds additional `RestTemplateRequestCustomizer` instances to be used to modify the `ClientHttpRequest` for the created `RestTemplate`.
basicAuthentication	Sets a basic authentication header with `username` and `password`.
customizers	Replaces the `RestTemplateCustomizers` that are used by the created `RestTemplate`.
defaultHeader	Adds a header with a default value.
detectRequestFactory	Sets whether the request factory should be detected; the default is `true`. Set to `false` when explicitly configuring the `requestFactory`.
errorHandler	Sets the `ResponseErrorHandler` that should be used with the created `RestTemplate`.
interceptors	Replaces the interceptors that are used by the created `RestTemplate`.

(*continued*)

Table 3-14. (*continued*)

Method	Description
messageConverters	Replaces the HttpMessageConverter that should be used with the created RestTemplate.
requestCustomizers	Replaces the RestTemplateRequestCustomizer instances to be used to modify the ClientHttpRequest for the created RestTemplate.
requestFactory	Sets the ClientHttpRequestFactory to be used with the created RestTemplate, by default auto-detected.
rootUri	Sets the root URL to be used with requests; the default is null.
setConnectTimeout	Sets the connection timeout to use on the RestTemplate.
setReadTimeout	Sets the read timeout to use on the RestTemplate.
setSslBundle	If SSL in use, use this to set the SSL configuration.
uriTemplateHandler	Sets the UriTemplateHandler to use.

Let's write a controller that will fetch a Book from our own server (see Recipe 3-2) and will also call the Open Library API to fetch the date the book was published. See Listing 3-53.

Listing 3-53. Controller Using a RestTemplate

```
package com.apress.springboot3recipes.library.rest;

import com.apress.springboot3recipes.library.Book;
import com.apress.springboot3recipes.library.EnrichedBook;
import org.springframework.http.ResponseEntity;
import org.springframework.web.bind.annotation.GetMapping;
import org.springframework.web.bind.annotation.PathVariable;
import org.springframework.web.bind.annotation.RequestMapping;
import org.springframework.web.bind.annotation.RestController;
import org.springframework.web.client.RestClientException;
import org.springframework.web.client.RestClientResponseException;
import org.springframework.web.client.RestTemplate;
```

```java
import java.util.Map;

@RestController
@RequestMapping("/books")
public class EnrichedBookController {

    private static final String BOOKS_URL = "http://localhost:8080/
    books/{isbn}";
    private static final String OL_API = "https://openlibrary.org/isbn/
    {isbn}.json";

    private final RestTemplate rest;

    public EnrichedBookController(RestTemplate rest) {
        this.rest = rest;
    }

    @GetMapping("/{isbn}")
    public ResponseEntity<EnrichedBook> get(@PathVariable("isbn")
    String isbn) {

        try {
            var book = rest.getForObject(BOOKS_URL, Book.
            class, isbn);
            var library = rest.getForObject(OL_API, Map.
            class, isbn);
            var published = extractPublishData(library);
            var enriched = enrich(book, published);
            return ResponseEntity.ok(enriched);
        } catch (RestClientException ex) {
            if (ex instanceof
            RestClientResponseException rex) {
                return ResponseEntity.status(rex.
                getStatusCode()).build();
            }
            return ResponseEntity.internalServerError().
            build();
        }
    }
```

```
    private EnrichedBook enrich(Book book, String publishDate) {
        return new EnrichedBook(book.isbn(), book.title(),
        publishDate, book.authors());
    }
    private String extractPublishData(Map json) {
        return (String) json.getOrDefault("publish_date", "");
    }
}
```

The controller first retrieves a Book using the getForObject method on the RestTemplate (there are various other ones as well). Next we use the same method to retrieve additional information from the Open Library API, and with both responses we write a result.

When you call http://localhost:8090/books/9780618260300 from the command line using curl or HTTPie, you will get output similar to that of Figure 3-20.

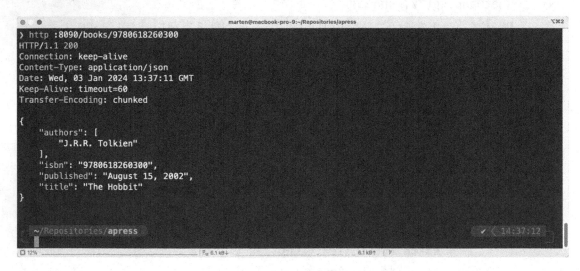

Figure 3-20. *Enriched book result*

Use a RestClient

Instead of using a RestTemplate, it is also possible to use a more fluent RestClient. Spring Boot exposes the RestClient.Builder automatically. See Listing 3-54.

Listing 3-54. RestClient Bean Definition with Builder

```
@Bean
public RestClient restClient(RestClient.Builder builder) {
        return builder.build();
}
```

RestClient.Builder provides some methods to enhance the configuration. Each method will result in a new RestClient.Builder instance. See Table 3-15 and Listing 3-55.

Table 3-15. *RestTemplateBuilder Configuration Methods*

Method	Description
baseUrl	The root URL to be used with requests; the default is null.
defaultHeader / defaultHeaders	Adds a header with a default value.
defaultRequest	Consumer to customize every request that is being built.
defaultStatusHandler	Registers a default status handler to be applied to each response.
defaultUriVariables	Default values for URI variables.
messageConverters	Replaces the HttpMessageConverter that should be used with the created RestTemplate.
observationConvention	Configures the ObservationConvention used to collect metadata for the request observation/metrics. The default will be set to DefaultClientRequestObservationConvention.
observationRegistry	Configures the ObservationRegistry to use for recording HTTP client observations. Generally, this is automatically set by Spring Boot.
requestFactory	Sets the ClientHttpRequestFactory to be used with the created RestClient, by default auto-detected.
requestInitializer / requestInitializers	Adds the given ClientHttpRequestInitializer instances to the end of the initializer chain.
requestInterceptor / requestInterceptors	Adds the given ClientHttpRequestInterceptor instances to the end of the interceptor chain.
uriBuilderFactory	Sets the UriBuilderFactory to use.

Listing 3-55. Controller Using a RestClient

```
package com.apress.springboot3recipes.library.rest;

import com.apress.springboot3recipes.library.Book;
import com.apress.springboot3recipes.library.EnrichedBook;
import org.springframework.http.ResponseEntity;
import org.springframework.web.bind.annotation.GetMapping;
import org.springframework.web.bind.annotation.PathVariable;
import org.springframework.web.bind.annotation.RequestMapping;
import org.springframework.web.bind.annotation.RestController;
import org.springframework.web.client.RestClient;
import org.springframework.web.client.RestClientException;
import org.springframework.web.client.RestClientResponseException;

import java.util.Map;

@RestController
@RequestMapping("/books")
public class EnrichedBookController {

        private static final String BOOKS_URL = "http://localhost:8080/
        books/{isbn}";
        private static final String OL_API = "https://openlibrary.org/isbn/
        {isbn}.json";

        private final RestClient rest;

        public EnrichedBookController(RestClient rest) {
                this.rest = rest;
        }

        @GetMapping("/{isbn}")
        public ResponseEntity<EnrichedBook> get(@PathVariable("isbn")
        String isbn) {

                try {
                        var book = rest.get().uri(BOOKS_URL, isbn).
                        retrieve().body(Book.class);
```

```
                var library = rest.get().uri(OL_API, isbn).
                retrieve().body(Map.class);
                var published = extractPublishData(library);
                var enriched = enrich(book, published);
                return ResponseEntity.ok(enriched);
        } catch (RestClientException ex) {
                if (ex instanceof
                RestClientResponseException rex) {
                        return ResponseEntity.status(rex.
                        getStatusCode()).build();
                }
                return ResponseEntity.internalServerError().
                build();
        }
    }

    private EnrichedBook enrich(Book book, String publishDate) {
            return new EnrichedBook(book.isbn(), book.title(),
            publishDate, book.authors());
    }

    private String extractPublishData(Map json) {
            return (String) json.getOrDefault("publish_date", "");
    }
}
```

The controller uses RestClient to call the URL. First, we determine what type of request we want in order to make a get() in our case. Next, we specify the URL with the parameters we want to call using the uri() method. That finishes our request that we can now execute through the receive() method. Finally, we map the response body using the body() method.

As the RestClient reuses parts of the same infrastructure that the RestTemplate uses, we can reuse the same exception handling we had. When you call the http://localhost:8090/books/9780618260300 from the command line using curl or HTTPie, you will get output similiar to that of Figure 3-20.

Use a Declarative Client

Spring Framework 6 introduced the declarative HTTP client. With this it is possible to write an interface with some annotations. At runtime a proxy would be created that would handle the request/response including the mapping and exception handling.

The starting point is an interface with an @HttpExchange annotation (or one of the derived annotations like @GetExchange or @PostExchange) on either the class or methods. It functions much in the same way as @RequestMapping from the server API.

Using @HttpExchange, it is possible to set some properties (see Table 3-16).

Table 3-16. *HttpExchange Properties*

Attribute	Description
value or url	Sets the URL for the request; can be a full URL, a path relative to the type-level @HttpExchange; or the preset base URI.
method	The HTTP method to use; DELETE, GET, PATCH, POST, PUT. The default is empty.
contentType	The media type to send for the Content-Type header; the default is empty.
accept	The media type for the Accept header.

In addition to the @HttpExchange annotation, there are also @DeleteExchange, @GetExchange, @PatchExchange, @PostExchange, and @PutExchange. These can be used instead of @HttpExchange with a specific method value. Using those annotations makes it more explicit.

Just like request handling methods with @RequestMapping, the declarative client supports multiple arguments, annotations, and return types. It reuses common parts of the web infrastructure for this. See Table 3-17.

Table 3-17. *HttpExchange Supported Method Arguments*

Type	Description
java.net.URI	Dynamically sets the URL for the request; overrides the url attribute from the @HttpExchange.
UriBuilder Factory	Provides a UriBuilderFactory to expand the URI template and URI variables. Used instead of the UriBuilderFactory of the underlying client.
HttpMethod	Dynamically sets the HTTP method to use for the request; overrides the method attribute from the @HttpExchange.
MultipartFile	Adds a request part from a MultipartFile; typically used with Spring MVC to indicate an uploaded file.
@CookieValue	Adds cookie(s) to the outgoing request. The argument can be a Map<String, ?> or a MultiValueMap<String, ?> with multiple cookies or individual values. Uses the type conversion for non-String values.
@RequestHeader	Adds request headers to the outgoing request. The argument can be a Map<String, ?> or a MultiValueMap<String, ?> with multiple headers or individual values. Uses the type conversion for non-String values.
@PathVariable	Adds a variable to expand a placeholder in the request URL. The argument may be a Map<String, ?> for multiple values or an individual value. Uses the type conversion for non-String values.
@RequestBody	Provides the body of the request either as an Object to be serialized or as a Reactive Streams Publisher such as Mono, Flux, or any other async type supported through the configured ReactiveAdapterRegistry.
@RequestParam	Adds request parameters. Can be a Map<String, ?> / MultiValueMap<String, ?> for multiple values. Or can be an individual type. Uses the type conversion for non-String values. When contentType is application/x-www-form-urlencoded, the parameters are added to the request body.
@RequestPart	Adds a request part that can be a String (becomes a form field), a Resource, an Object to be encoded as JSON (or whatever is configured), an HttpEntity including headers , a Spring Part, or a supported Reactive Streams Publisher.

In addition to the method arguments, there is also support for several method return types. See Table 3-18.

Table 3-18. *HttpExchange Supported Method Return Types*

Type	Description
void	Perform the request; no response.
HttpHeaders	Perform the request and return only the headers.
<T>	Perform the request and return the decoded body as type T.
ResponseEntity<Void>	Perform the request and return a ResponseEntity with the status and headers.
ResponseEntity<T>	Perform the request and return a ResponseEntity with the status and headers and the body decoded as type T.

Given this information, we could provide two interfaces to provide access to the APIs that we need to call. Let's start with the API for the books. See Listing 3-56.

Listing 3-56. BookServiceClient Sources

```
package com.apress.springboot3recipes.library.rest;

import com.apress.springboot3recipes.library.Book;
import org.springframework.web.bind.annotation.PathVariable;
import org.springframework.web.service.annotation.GetExchange;

public interface BookServiceClient {

        @GetExchange("http://localhost:8080/books/{isbn}")
        Book getBook(@PathVariable String isbn);
}
```

The BookServiceClient has one method, which is annotated with @GetExchange. There is a provided value of http://localhost:8080/books/{isbn}, which is a URI template. The method takes a single argument isbn, which has been annotated with @PathVariable. When calling this method, the value we pass in will be placed in the {isbn} part of the URI before executing the request. When the request has been sent, a response comes in that is converted to a Book, just as we did with the RestTemplate or RestClient.

Next we need an interface for the Open Library API as well. See Listing 3-57.

Listing 3-57. OpenLibraryClient Sources

```
package com.apress.springboot3recipes.library.rest;

import org.springframework.web.bind.annotation.PathVariable;
import org.springframework.web.service.annotation.GetExchange;
import org.springframework.web.service.annotation.HttpExchange;

import java.util.Map;

@HttpExchange(url = "https://openlibrary.org/isbn")
public interface OpenLibraryClient {

        @GetExchange("/{isbn}.json")
        Map getInformation(@PathVariable String isbn);
}
```

OpenLibraryClient has an @HttpExchange method with the url attribute set. This will set a base URI for use for all other methods in this interface. This allows us to specify only relative URLs for all other methods. Now there is only a single method with an @GetExchange. This method also takes a single argument, isbn, which is placed in the URI template as well before executing. The response is turned into a Map again just as before.

Now that the interfaces are ready, we need to expose them in our configuration, but we cannot create an instance from an interface. This is where HttpServiceProxyFactory comes into play; it creates a proxy at runtime for these interfaces. To do this, we need to add some configuration to our application. See Listing 3-58.

Listing 3-58. HttpServiceProxyFactory Configuration

```
@Bean
public HttpServiceProxyFactory httpServiceProxyFactory(RestClient.
Builder builder) {
        var adapter = RestClientAdapter.create(builder.build());
        return HttpServiceProxyFactory.builderFor(adapter).build();
}
```

```
@Bean
public BookServiceClient bookServiceClient(HttpServiceProxyFactory
factory) {
        return factory.createClient(BookServiceClient.class);
}

@Bean
public OpenLibraryClient openLibraryClient(HttpServiceProxyFactory
factory) {
        return factory.createClient(OpenLibraryClient.class);
}
```

RestClient.Builder is used to construct a RestClient for use with the HttpServiceProxyFactory. As the RestClient cannot be used directly, we need to wrap it in a RestClientAdapter, which adapts RestClient to the HttpExchangeAdapter interface.

HttpExchangeAdapter has three implementations: RestClientAdapter, RestTemplateAdapter, and WebClientAdapter. The latter is used in Chapter 4 and is nonblocking. However, it is thus also possible to use a RestTemplate to execute the requests instead of a RestClient.

HttpServiceProxyFactory in turn is used to create proxies for BookServiceClient and OpenLibraryClient. This is simply done by calling createClient with the given interface on HttpServiceProxyFactory. See Listing 3-59.

Listing 3-59. EnrichedBookController with Declarative Clients

```
package com.apress.springboot3recipes.library.rest;

import com.apress.springboot3recipes.library.Book;
import com.apress.springboot3recipes.library.EnrichedBook;
import org.springframework.http.ResponseEntity;
import org.springframework.web.bind.annotation.GetMapping;
import org.springframework.web.bind.annotation.PathVariable;
import org.springframework.web.bind.annotation.RequestMapping;
import org.springframework.web.bind.annotation.RestController;
import org.springframework.web.client.RestClientException;
import org.springframework.web.client.RestClientResponseException;
```

```java
import java.util.Map;

@RestController
@RequestMapping("/books")
public class EnrichedBookController {

    private final BookServiceClient bookServiceClient;
    private final OpenLibraryClient openLibraryClient;

    public EnrichedBookController(BookServiceClient bookServiceClient,
                                  OpenLibraryClient
                                  openLibraryClient) {
        this.bookServiceClient = bookServiceClient;
        this.openLibraryClient = openLibraryClient;
    }

    @GetMapping("/{isbn}")
    public ResponseEntity<EnrichedBook> get(@PathVariable("isbn")
    String isbn) {

        try {
            var book = bookServiceClient.getBook(isbn);
            var library = openLibraryClient.
            getInformation(isbn);
            var published = extractPublishData(library);
            var enriched = enrich(book, published);
            return ResponseEntity.ok(enriched);
        } catch (RestClientException ex) {
            if (ex instanceof
            RestClientResponseException rex) {
                return ResponseEntity.status(rex.
                getStatusCode()).build();
            }
            return ResponseEntity.internalServerError().
            build();
        }
    }
```

```
    private EnrichedBook enrich(Book book, String publishDate) {
            return new EnrichedBook(book.isbn(), book.title(),
            publishDate, book.authors());
    }

    private String extractPublishData(Map json) {
            return (String) json.getOrDefault("publish_date", "");
    }
}
```

Notice that we now can call methods on the interface instead of worrying about constructing a proper request. That is all hidden behind the interface facade and inside the proxy. This makes it easier to write reusable API clients for use in your applications.

Finally, notice that the exception handling didn't change, as the declarative clients still use the same infrastructure, as the RestClient exception handling doesn't need to change.

When rerunning the application and requesting the information for the books, the output should still be the same as shown in Figure 3-20.

Test RestTemplate or RestClient-Based Code

To test the client-side code with a RestTemplate or RestClient, the Spring Test framework provides the MockRestServiceServer. The MockRestServiceServer can be used to return a response for a specific request (based on URL, header, content, etc.).

Spring Boot in turn makes it easier to work with this by providing the @RestClientTest annotation. This will set up the MockRestServiceServer so it can be autowired and will configure the class under test as well. See Listing 3-60.

Listing 3-60. Test for Rest Client Setup

```
package com.apress.springboot3recipes.library.rest;

import org.junit.jupiter.api.Assertions;
import org.junit.jupiter.api.Test;
import org.springframework.beans.factory.annotation.Autowired;
import org.springframework.boot.test.autoconfigure.web.client.
RestClientTest;
import org.springframework.http.HttpStatusCode;
```

```java
import org.springframework.http.MediaType;
import org.springframework.test.web.client.MockRestServiceServer;

import static org.springframework.test.web.client.match.
MockRestRequestMatchers.requestTo;
import static org.springframework.test.web.client.response.
MockRestResponseCreators.withSuccess;

@RestClientTest(EnrichedBookController.class)
class EnrichedBookControllerTest {

    private static final String BOOK_JSON = """
                {
                "authors": [
                    "T. Author"
                ],
                "isbn": "123456789",
                "title": "The Client Test"
            }
            """;

    private static final String OL_JSON = """
            "{ "publish_date": "2024"}"
            """;

    @Autowired
    private MockRestServiceServer mockServer;

    @Autowired
    private EnrichedBookController controller;

    @Test
    void enrichBook() {

        mockServer
                .expect(requestTo("http://localhost:8080/
                books/123456789"))
                .andRespond(withSuccess(BOOK_JSON, MediaType.
                APPLICATION_JSON));
```

```
mockServer
        .expect(requestTo("https://openlibrary.org/
        isbn/123456789.json"))
        .andRespond(withSuccess(OL_JSON, MediaType.
        APPLICATION_JSON));

var response = controller.get("123456789");
var enrichedBook = response.getBody();
Assertions.assertNotNull(enrichedBook);
Assertions.assertEquals(HttpStatusCode.valueOf(200),
response.getStatusCode());
Assertions.assertEquals(enrichedBook.published(), "2024");

mockServer.verify();
    }
}
```

The test uses the @RestClientTest to set up the server and prepare
EnrichedBookController for testing. Both the MockRestServiceServer and the
EnrichedBookController are injected so that they are available for the test.

In the actual test method, we start by setting up the MockRestServiceServer with the
behavior we want. Here we only match the URL and set them up to return a certain JSON
response with the HTTP 200 OK (see Table 3-19 for more possibilities). After the test has
run, we call verify() on the MockRestServiceServer to validate if the requests as we
recorded them are also being issued, indicating that our client is working as expected.

Table 3-19. *MockRestRequestMatchers Setup Methods*

anything()	Matches any request.
content()	Setup matches for the content, like Content-Type or the actual body of the request.
header()	Matches request with given header, with either a value or Hamcrest Matcher.
headerDoesNotExist	Matches request where the given header doesn't exist.
headerList()	Matches request with given header, with values or Hamcrest Matcher.
jsonPath	Setup matches for the request body with JsonPath.
method	Matches the HttpMethod of the request.
queryParam	Match the request parameter with either a value or Hamcrest Matcher.
queryParamList	Match the request parameter with given values or Hamcrest Matcher.
requestTo	Match the request using the expected URI (can be a String or URI).
requestToUriTemplate	Match the request using a URI template.
xpath	Setup matches for the request body with XPath.

The response is created through the use of MockRestResponseCreators, and currently we only use withSuccess, but it is also possible to set up error scenarios (Table 3-20).

Table 3-20. *MockRestResponseCreators Setup Methods*

withAccepted()	Response with a 202 (ACCEPTED) HTTP status code.
withBadGateway()	Response with a 502 (BAD_GATEWAY) HTTP status code.
withBadRequest()	Response with a 400 (BAD_REQUEST) HTTP status code.
withCreatedEntity(URI)	Response with a 201 (CREATED) HTTP status code and Location header.
withException(IOException)	Response with an internal application IOException. It is useful to simulate read or connection timeouts.

(continued)

Table 3-20. (*continued*)

withForbiddenRequest()	Response with a 403 (FORBIDDEN) HTTP status code.
withGatewayTimeout()	Response with a 504 (GATEWAY_TIMEOUT) HTTP status code.
withNoContent	Response with a 204 (NO_CONTENT) HTTP status code.
withRawStatus(int)	Response with the given status.
withRequestConflict()	Response with a 409 (CONFLICT) HTTP status code.
withResourceNotFound()	Response with a 404 (NOT_FOUND) HTTP status code.
withServerError()	Response with a 500 (SERVER_ERROR) HTTP status code.
withServiceUnavailable()	Response with a 503 (SERVICE_UNAVAILABLE) HTTP status code.
withSuccess() withSuccess(byte[], MediaType) withSuccess(Resource, MediaType) withSuccess(String, MediaType)	Response with a 200 (OK) HTTP status code and (optionally) body and Content-Type header.
withTooManyRequests() withTooManyRequests(int)	Response with a 429 (TOO_MANY_REQUESTS) HTTP status code., optionally with a Retry-After header.
withUnauthorizedRequest()	Response with a 401 (UNAUTHORIZED) HTTP status code..

After the setup method is called, a DefaultResponseCreator is being returned that can be used to further define the response, by adding headers, cookies, or even a body.

ℹ️   Instead of using @RestClientTest, we could have also used an @WebMvcTest as the EnrichedBookController is a controller. Automatically setting up the MockRestServiceServer would require an additional annotation, @AutoConfigureMockRestServiceServer; otherwise, it won't be configured.

CHAPTER 4

WebFlux

Spring WebFlux is a reactive web framework included with Spring. It supports fully nonblocking and support Reactive Streams backpressure. It runs on servers like Netty, Undertow or Servlet Containers. When such a server is detected Spring Boot will automatically configure the server for you.

4-1. Develop a Reactive Application with Spring WebFlux

Problem

You want to develop a simple reactive web application with Spring WebFlux to learn the basic concepts and configurations of this framework.

Solution

The lowest component of Spring WebFlux is `org.springframework.http.server.reactive.HttpHandler`. The `HttpHandler` interface has a single `handle` method. See Listing 4-1.

Listing 4-1. HttpHandler Interface

```
public interface HttpHandler {

  Mono<Void> handle(ServerHttpRequest request, ServerHttpResponse response);

}
```

© Marten Deinum 2024
M. Deinum, *Spring Boot 3 Recipes*, https://doi.org/10.1007/979-8-8688-0113-6_4

The `handle` method returns `Mono<Void>`, which is the reactive way of saying it returns `void`. It takes a `ServerHttpRequest` interface and a `ServerHttpResonse` interface, both from the `org.springframework.http.server.reactive` package. Depending on the container used, the proper implementation is created. For this several adapters or bridges for containers exist. When running on a Servlet 5.0 container (supporting nonblocking I/O), `ServletHttpHandlerAdapter` (or one of its subclasses) is used to adapt from the plain Servlet world to the Reactive world. When running on a native Reactive engine like Netty, the `ReactorHttpHandlerAdapter` is used.

When a web request is sent to a Spring WebFlux application, `HandlerAdapter` first receives the request. Then it organizes the different components configured in Spring's application context that are needed to handle the request.

To define a controller class in Spring WebFlux, a class has to be marked with the `@Controller` or `@RestController` annotation (just as with Spring MVC; see Chapter 3).

When an `@Controller` annotated class (i.e., a controller class) receives a request, it looks for an appropriate handler method to handle the request. This requires that a controller class map each request to a handler method by one or more handler mappings. To do this, a controller class's methods are decorated with the `@RequestMapping` annotation, making them handler methods.

The signature for these handler methods—as you can expect from any standard class—is open-ended. You can specify an arbitrary name for a handler method and define a variety of method arguments. Equally, a handler method can return any of a series of values (e.g., `String` or `void`), depending on the application logic it fulfills. The following is only a partial list of valid argument types, just to give you an idea:

- `ServerHttpRequest` or `ServerHttpResponse`

- Request parameters from the URL of arbitrary type, annotated with `@RequestParam`

- Model attributes of arbitrary type, annotated with `@ModelAttribute`

- Cookie values included in an incoming request, annotated with `@CookieValue`

- Request header values of any arbitrary type, annotated with `@RequestHeader`

- Request attribute of arbitrary type, annotated with `@RequestAttribute`

- `Map` or `ModelMap`, for the handler method to add attributes to the model

- `Errors` or `BindingResult`, for the handler method to access the binding and validation result for the command object

- `WebSession`, for the session

Once the controller class has picked an appropriate handler method, it invokes the handler method's logic with the request. Usually, a controller's logic invokes back-end services to handle the request. In addition, a handler method's logic is likely to add or remove information from the numerous input arguments (e.g., `ServerHttpRequest`, `Map`, or `Errors`) that will form part of the ongoing flow.

After a handler method has finished processing the request, it delegates control to a view, which is represented as the handler method's return value. To provide a flexible approach, a handler method's return value doesn't represent a view's implementation (e.g., `user.html` or `report.pdf`) but rather a logical view (e.g., `user` or `report`)—note the lack of file extension.

A handler method's return value can be either a `String`—representing a logical view name—or void, in which case a default logical view name is determined on the basis of a handler method's or controller's name.

To pass information from a controller to a view, it's irrelevant that a handler's method returns a logical view name—`String` or a `void`—since the handler method input arguments will be available to a view.

For example, if a handler method takes `Map` and `Model` objects as input parameters—modifying their contents inside the handler method's logic—these same objects will be accessible to the view returned by the handler method.

When the controller class receives a view, it resolves the logical view name into a specific view implementation (e.g., `user.html` or `report.fmt`) by means of a view resolver. A view resolver is a bean configured in the web application context that implements the `ViewResolver` interface. Its responsibility is to return a specific view implementation for a logical view name.

Once the controller class has resolved a view name into a view implementation, per the view implementation's design, it renders the objects (e.g., `ServerHttpRequest`, `Map`, `Errors`, or `WebSession`) passed by the controller's handler method. The view's responsibility is to display the objects added in the handler method's logic to the user.

How It Works

Let's write a reactive version of `HelloWorldApplication` from Recipe 3-1. See Listing 4-2.

Listing 4-2. Reactive HelloWorldController

```
package com.apress.springboot3recipes.helloworld;

import org.springframework.boot.SpringBootVersion;
import org.springframework.web.bind.annotation.GetMapping;
import org.springframework.web.bind.annotation.RestController;
import reactor.core.publisher.Mono;

@RestController
public class HelloWorldController {

  @GetMapping
  public Mono<String> hello() {
    var version= SpringBootVersion.getVersion();
    var msg = String.format("Hello World, from Reactive Spring Boot %s!",
    version);
    return Mono.just(msg);
  }
}
```

Notice the Mono<String> is a return type for the hello method, instead of a plain String. Mono is what makes it reactive.

Set Up a Spring WebFlux Application

To be able to handle requests in a reactive way, you need to enable WebFlux. This is done by adding a dependency on spring-boot-starter-webflux.

```
<dependency>
    <groupId>org.springframework.boot</groupId>
    <artifactId>spring-boot-starter-webflux</artifactId>
</dependency>
```

This brings in the needed dependencies such as spring-webflux and the Project Reactor dependencies. It also includes a reactive runtime, which by default is Netty.

Now that everything is configured, the final thing to do is create an application class. See Listing 4-3.

Listing 4-3. HelloWorldApplication

```
package com.apress.springboot3recipes.helloworld;

import org.springframework.boot.SpringApplication;
import org.springframework.boot.autoconfigure.SpringBootApplication;

@SpringBootApplication
public class HelloWorldApplication {

    public static void main(String[] args) {
        SpringApplication.run(HelloWorldApplication.class, args);
    }
}
```

Spring Boot will detect the reactive runtime and configure it using the `server.*` properties (see Recipe 3-1).

Create Spring WebFlux Controllers

An annotation-based controller class can be an arbitrary class that doesn't implement a particular interface or extend a particular base class. You can annotate it with the `@Controller` or `@RestController` annotation. There can be one or more handler methods defined in a controller to handle single or multiple actions. The signature of the handler methods is flexible enough to accept a range of arguments. (See also Recipe 4-2 for more information on request mapping.)

```
package com.apress.springboot3recipes.helloworld;

import org.springframework.boot.SpringBootVersion;
import org.springframework.web.bind.annotation.GetMapping;
import org.springframework.web.bind.annotation.RestController;
import reactor.core.publisher.Mono;

@RestController
public class HelloWorldController {

    @GetMapping
    public Mono<String> hello() {
        var version= SpringBootVersion.getVersion();
```

```
    var msg = String.format("Hello World, from Reactive Spring Boot %s!",
    version);
    return Mono.just(msg);
  }
}
```

The annotation @GetMapping is used to decorate the hello method as the controller's HTTP GET handler method. It's worth mentioning that if no default HTTP GET handler method is declared, a ServletException is thrown. Hence, it's important for a controller to have at a minimum a URL route and at least one handler method. The method is bound to /hello because of the expression in @GetMapping.

When a request is made to http://localhost:8080/hello, it will reactively return Hello World, from Reactive Spring Boot 3!. However, the client won't notice this. For the client, it still is a regular HTTP request.

Do Unit Testing for Reactive Controllers

You have two ways of doing an integration test for a controller. The first approach is to simply write a test that creates an instance of HelloWorldController, calls the method, and does expectations on the result. The second is to use the @WebFluxTest annotation to create the test. The latter will start a minimal application context containing the web infrastructure, and you can use MockMvc to test the controller. This last approach sits between a plain unit test and a full-blown integration test. See Listing 4-4.

Listing 4-4. HelloWorldController Unit Test

```
package com.apress.springboot3recipes.helloworld;

import org.junit.jupiter.api.Test;
import reactor.test.StepVerifier;

class HelloWorldControllerUnitTest {

  private final HelloWorldController controller = new
  HelloWorldController();

  @Test
  void shouldSayHello() {
    var result = controller.hello();
```

```
StepVerifier.create(result)
        .expectNext("Hello World, from Reactive Spring Boot 3.2.1!")
        .verifyComplete();
  }
}
```

This is a basic unit test. It instantiates the controller and simply calls the method to be tested. It uses `StepVerifier` from the `reactive-test` module to make it easier to test. The `hello` method is called, and the result is then verified using `StepVerifier`.

Adding the `reactive-test` dependency is done by adding the following dependency:

```
<dependency>
    <groupId>io.projectreactor</groupId>
    <artifactId>reactor-test</artifactId>
    <scope>test</scope>
</dependency>
```

The second option is to use @WebFluxTest for a specific controller.

```
package com.apress.springboot3recipes.helloworld;

import org.hamcrest.Matchers;
import org.junit.jupiter.api.Test;
import org.springframework.beans.factory.annotation.Autowired;
import org.springframework.boot.test.autoconfigure.web.reactive.We
bFluxTest;
import org.springframework.http.MediaType;
import org.springframework.test.web.reactive.server.WebTestClient;

@WebFluxTest(HelloWorldController.class)
class HelloWorldControllerSliceTest {

  @Autowired
  private WebTestClient webClient;

  @Test
  void shouldSayHello() {
```

```
    webClient
        .get().uri("/").accept(MediaType.TEXT_PLAIN).exchange()
        .expectStatus().isOk()
        .expectBody(String.class)
        .value(Matchers.startsWith("Hello World, from Reactive Spring Boot"));
    }
}
```

This test will start a minimal Spring Boot context and auto-detect all WebFlux-related beans in your project, like @ControllerAdvice. Instead of now directly calling the HelloWorldController, you can use the special WebTestClient to declare a request .get().uri("/") and send that nonblocking using exchange(). Finally, the assertions/expectations are verified. The request is expected to have an OK status and to contain the specified body.

Do Integration Testing for Reactive Controllers

The integration test looks very much like @WebFluxTest in the previous section. The main difference is the use of @SpringBootTest instead of @WebFluxText. Using @SpringBootTest, this will bootstrap the full application including all other beans (services, repositories, etc.). With the webEnvironment, you can specify which environment to use. The values are RANDOM_PORT, MOCK (default), DEFINED_PORT, and NONE. Here we use a random port and again use the WebTestClient to fire off a request:

```
package com.apress.springboot3recipes.helloworld;

import org.hamcrest.Matchers;
import org.junit.jupiter.api.Test;
import org.springframework.beans.factory.annotation.Autowired;
import org.springframework.boot.test.autoconfigure.web.reactive.
AutoConfigureWebTestClient;
import org.springframework.boot.test.context.SpringBootTest;
import org.springframework.http.MediaType;
import org.springframework.test.web.reactive.server.WebTestClient;

@SpringBootTest
@AutoConfigureWebTestClient
class HelloWorldControllerIntegrationTest {
```

```
@Autowired
private WebTestClient webClient;

@Test
void shouldSayHello() {
  webClient
    .get().uri("/").accept(MediaType.TEXT_PLAIN).exchange()
    .expectStatus().isOk()
    .expectBody(String.class)
      .value(Matchers.containsString("Hello World, from Reactive Spring
      Boot"));
  }
}
```

The request is sent to the embedded server after which the result is verified to have the correct status and body content.

ⓘ   When using MOCK (also the default) as the webEnvironment, you must add the @AutoConfigureWebTestClient annotation to get the WebTestClient for testing.

4-2. Publish and Consume with Reactive REST Services

Problem

You want to write a reactive REST endpoint that will produce JSON.

Solution

Just as with a regular @RestController, you can return a regular object or a list of objects, and they will be sent to the client. To make them reactive, you will have to wrap those return values in their reactive counterparts, a Mono or a Flux.

How It Works

Let's start by writing a Reactive BookService. Each method will return either a Mono<Book> or a Flux<Book>. See Listing 4-5.

Listing 4-5. Reactive BookService Interface

```
package com.apress.springboot3recipes.library;

import reactor.core.publisher.Flux;
import reactor.core.publisher.Mono;

public interface BookService {

  Flux<Book> findAll();
  Mono<Book> create(Book book);
  Mono<Book> find(String isbn);
}
```

For the BookService interface, we can write an in-memory implementation. See Listing 4-6.

Listing 4-6. Reactive BookService Implementation (In-Memory)

```
package com.apress.springboot3recipes.library;

import org.springframework.stereotype.Service;
import reactor.core.publisher.Flux;
import reactor.core.publisher.Mono;

import java.util.Map;
import java.util.concurrent.ConcurrentHashMap;

@Service
class InMemoryBookService implements BookService {

  private final Map<String, Book> books = new ConcurrentHashMap<>();

  @Override
  public Flux<Book> findAll() {
    return Flux.fromIterable(books.values());
  }
```

```
@Override
public Mono<Book> create(Book book) {
  books.put(book.isbn(), book);
  return Mono.just(book);
}

@Override
public Mono<Book> find(String isbn) {
  return Mono.justOrEmpty(books.get(isbn));
}
}
```

InMemoryBookService has some simple methods to obtain or save a book. When retrieving all books, it will delay them by 128 milliseconds. The Book class is the same as used in Chapter 3. See Listing 4-7.

Listing 4-7. Book Record

```
package com.apress.springboot3recipes.library;

import java.util.List;
import java.util.Objects;

public record Book(String isbn, String title, List<String> authors) {

  @Override
  public boolean equals(Object o) {
    if (o instanceof Book other) {
      return this.isbn != null && Objects.equals(this.isbn, other.isbn);
    }
    return false;
  }

  @Override
  public int hashCode() {
    return Objects.hash(this.isbn);
  }
}
```

A BookController controller is needed to expose Book as a REST resource.

```
package com.apress.springboot3recipes.library.rest;

import com.apress.springboot3recipes.library.Book;
import com.apress.springboot3recipes.library.BookService;
import org.springframework.http.ResponseEntity;
import org.springframework.web.bind.annotation.GetMapping;
import org.springframework.web.bind.annotation.PathVariable;
import org.springframework.web.bind.annotation.PostMapping;
import org.springframework.web.bind.annotation.RequestBody;
import org.springframework.web.bind.annotation.RequestMapping;
import org.springframework.web.bind.annotation.RestController;
import org.springframework.web.util.UriComponentsBuilder;
import reactor.core.publisher.Flux;
import reactor.core.publisher.Mono;

import java.time.Duration;

@RestController
@RequestMapping("/books")
public class BookController {

  private final BookService bookService;

  public BookController(BookService bookService) {
    this.bookService = bookService;
  }

  @GetMapping
  public Flux<Book> all() {
    return bookService.findAll().delayElements(Duration.ofMillis(64));
  }

  @GetMapping("/{isbn}")
  public Mono<Book> get(@PathVariable("isbn") String isbn) {
    return bookService.find(isbn);
  }
```

```
@PostMapping
public Mono<ResponseEntity<Book>> create(@RequestBody Mono<Book> book,
                                    UriComponentsBuilder
                                    uriBuilder) {
  var created = book.flatMap(bookService::create);
  return created.map((it) -> createResponse(it, uriBuilder));
}

private ResponseEntity<Book> createResponse(Book book,
                                    UriComponentsBuilder ucb) {
  var newBookUri = ucb.path("/books/{isbn}").build(book.isbn());
  return ResponseEntity.created(newBookUri).body(book);
}
}
```

To bootstrap everything, a simple LibraryApplication is needed.

```
package com.apress.springboot3recipes.library;

import org.springframework.boot.ApplicationRunner;
import org.springframework.boot.SpringApplication;
import org.springframework.boot.autoconfigure.SpringBootApplication;
import org.springframework.context.annotation.Bean;
import reactor.core.publisher.Flux;

@SpringBootApplication
public class LibraryApplication {

  public static void main(String[] args) {
    SpringApplication.run(LibraryApplication.class, args);
  }

  @Bean
  public ApplicationRunner initData(BookService books) {
    return (args) -> Flux.fromIterable(BookGenerator.all())
      .map(books::create).subscribe();
  }
}
```

BookController is mapped to /books and supports listing all books or a single one and adding and modifying a book. Using something like HTTPie or curl you can query the endpoint.

The command http http://localhost:8080/books should list all the orders in the system (see Figure 4-1), and http http://localhost:8080/books/{isbn} should list a single one.

```
> http http://localhost:8080/books
HTTP/1.1 200 OK
Content-Type: application/json
transfer-encoding: chunked

[
    {
        "authors": [
            "Gregor Hohp",
            "Bobby Woolf"
        ],
        "isbn": "9780321200686",
        "title": "Enterprise Integration Patterns"
    },
    {
        "authors": [
            "Peter Royal"
        ],
        "isbn": "9781484289921",
        "title": "Building Modern Business Applications"
    },
    {
        "authors": [
            "J.R.R. Tolkien"
        ],
        "isbn": "9780008471293",
        "title": "The Lord of the Rings"
    },
```

Figure 4-1. *Result of getting all books*

Stream JSON

The result of the call to /books isn't streaming, but rather it is blocking. It first collects all the results before sending them out. See also the content-type header in Figure 4-1, which is set to application/json. To stream the result, it should be application/x-ndjson (or another content type that supports streaming). This is something to take into consideration when writing a client to consume this endpoint. For HTTPie we can specify the Accept header to make it streaming. Add 'Accept:application/x-ndjson' to the HTTPie command from earlier, and the result will now be streaming. The result will now gently stream in until there is nothing more to consume (see Figure 4-2).

```
marten@macbook-pro-9:~                                          ⌥⌘2

> http http://localhost:8080/books 'Accept:application/x-ndjson' --stream
HTTP/1.1 200 OK
Content-Type: application/x-ndjson
transfer-encoding: chunked

{
    "authors": [
        "Gregor Hohp",
        "Bobby Woolf"
    ],
    "isbn": "9780321200686",
    "title": "Enterprise Integration Patterns"
}

{
    "authors": [
        "Peter Royal"
    ],
    "isbn": "9781484289921",
    "title": "Building Modern Business Applications"
}

{
    "authors": [
        "J.R.R. Tolkien"
    ],
    "isbn": "9780008471293",
    "title": "The Lord of the Rings"
```

Figure 4-2. *Result of streaming all books*

The result also slightly changes. Instead of returning an array or orders (see Figure 4-1), it now returns single orders (see Figure 4-2).

Write an Integration Test

An integration test for the BookController can be written quite easily using WebTestClient and a MOCK web environment (you could also use RANDOM_PORT instead of MOCK).

```
package com.apress.springboot3recipes.library.rest;

import com.apress.springboot3recipes.library.Book;
import org.junit.jupiter.api.Test;
import org.springframework.beans.factory.annotation.Autowired;
import org.springframework.boot.test.autoconfigure.web.reactive.
AutoConfigureWebTestClient;
import org.springframework.boot.test.context.SpringBootTest;
import org.springframework.test.annotation.DirtiesContext;
import org.springframework.test.web.reactive.server.WebTestClient;
```

```java
import java.util.List;

@SpringBootTest(webEnvironment = SpringBootTest.WebEnvironment.MOCK)
@AutoConfigureWebTestClient
@DirtiesContext(methodMode = DirtiesContext.MethodMode.AFTER_METHOD)
class BookControllerIntegrationTest {

  @Autowired
  private WebTestClient webTestClient;

  @Test
  void listBooks() {

    webTestClient.get().uri("/books")
            .exchange()
              .expectStatus().isOk()
              .expectBodyList(Book.class).hasSize(24);
  }

  @Test
  void addAndGetBook() {

    var book = new Book("BOCBC71PHR", "Testing Spring Boot Applications
    Demystified", List.of("Philip Riecks"));
    webTestClient.post().uri("/books").bodyValue(book)
            .exchange()
              .expectStatus().isCreated()
              .expectBody(Book.class).isEqualTo(book);

    webTestClient.get().uri("/books/{isbn}", book.isbn())
            .exchange()
            .expectStatus().isOk()
            .expectBody(Book.class).isEqualTo(book);
  }
}
```

The @DirtiesContext annotation is needed here because BookService is a stateful
bean. So after adding a Book to the library, it needs to be reset for the next test. The test
will start the full application because of the @SpringBootTest annotation with a mocked
environment. The @AutoConfigureWebTestClient annotation is needed for a mocked

environment to get a `WebTestClient`. The `WebTestClient` makes it easy to build a request and send that to the server. After sending the response, it can do expectations on the result.

ℹ️ `webEnvironment = SpringBootTest.WebEnvironment.MOCK` is also the default, so adding it explicitly isn't strictly needed.

4-3. Use Thymeleaf as a Template Engine
Problem

You want to render a view using Thymeleaf in a WebFlux-based application.

Solution

Add the dependency for Thymeleaf and create a handler to determine the view and fill the model.

How It Works

Add a dependency on `spring-boot-starter-webflux` and `spring-boot-starter-thymeleaf`. This is enough for Spring Boot to automatically configure Thymeleaf for use in a WebFlux application. See Listing 4-8.

Listing 4-8. WebFlux and Thymeleaf Dependencies

```xml
<dependency>
    <groupId>org.springframework.boot</groupId>
    <artifactId>spring-boot-starter-webflux</artifactId>
</dependency>
<dependency>
    <groupId>org.springframework.boot</groupId>
    <artifactId>spring-boot-starter-thymeleaf</artifactId>
</dependency>
```

With the addition of this dependency you will get the Thymeleaf library as well as the Thymeleaf Spring Dialect so that they integrate nicely. Because of the existence of these two libraries, Spring Boot will automatically configure the `ThymeleafReactiveViewResolver`. The `ThymeleafReactiveViewResolver` requires a Thymeleaf `ISpringWebFluxTemplateEngine` to be able to resolve and render the views. A special `SpringWebFluxTemplateEngine` will be preconfigured with `SpringDialect` so that you can use SpEL inside Thymeleaf pages.

Configuring Thymeleaf Spring Boot exposes several properties in the `spring.thymeleaf` and `spring.thymeleaf.reactive` namespaces (see Table 4-1).

Table 4-1. *Thymeleaf Properties*

Property	Description
spring.thymeleaf. prefix	Sets the prefix to use for the ViewResolver; the default is classpath:/templates.
spring.thymeleaf. suffix	Sets the suffix to use for the ViewResolver; the default is .html.
spring.thymeleaf. encoding	Sets the encoding of the templates; the default is UTF-8.
spring.thymeleaf. check-template	Checks if the template exists before rendering; the default is true.
spring.thymeleaf. check-template- location	Checks if the template location exists.
spring.thymeleaf.mode	Sets the Thymeleaf TemplateMode to use; the default is HTML.
spring.thymeleaf.cache	Sets whether resolved templates should be cached; the default is true.
spring.thymeleaf. template-resolver- order	Sets the order of the ViewResolver; the default is 1.
spring.thymeleaf.view- names	Sets the view names (separated by commas) that can be resolved with this ViewResolver.

(continued)

Table 4-1. (*continued*)

Property	Description
`spring.thymeleaf.exclude-view-names`	Sets the view names (separated by commas) that are excluded from being resolved.
`spring.thymeleaf.enabled`	Sets whether Thymeleaf should be enabled; the default is `true`.
`spring.thymeleaf.enable-spring-el-compiler`	Enables the compilation of SpEL expressions; the default is `false`.
`spring.thymeleaf.reactive.max-chunk-size`	Sets the maximum size of the data buffer used to write the response in bytes.
`spring.thymeleaf.reactive.media-types`	Sets the media types supported by this view technology.
`spring.thymeleaf.reactive.full-mode-view-names`	Comma-separated list of view names that should operate in FULL mode. The default is none. FULL mode means basically blocking mode.
`spring.thymeleaf.reactive.chunked-mode-view-names`	Comma-separated list of view names that should operate in chunked mode.

Use Thymeleaf Views

First create an `index.html` file in the `src/main/resources/templates` directory. See Listing 4-9.

Listing 4-9. Index Template

```
<!DOCTYPE html>
<html xmlns:th="http://www.thymeleaf.org">
<head>
    <meta charset="UTF-8">
```

```
    <title>Spring Boot Recipes - Library</title>
</head>
<body>

<h1>Library</h1>

<a th:href="@{/books.html}" href="#">List of books</a>

</body>
</html>
```

This page will render a simple page with a single link, pointing to /books. This URL is rendered using the th:href tag, which will expand /books to a proper URL. Next write a controller that will select the page to render. See Listing 4-10.

Listing 4-10. IndexController

```
package com.apress.springboot3recipes.library.web;

import org.springframework.stereotype.Controller;
import org.springframework.web.bind.annotation.GetMapping;

@Controller
public class IndexController {

  @GetMapping
  public String index() {
    return "index";
  }
}
```

Write a BookController that will return orders/list as the name of the view and add Flux<Book> to the model. See Listing 4-11.

Listing 4-11. BookController to List Books

```
package com.apress.springboot3recipes.library.web;

import com.apress.springboot3recipes.library.Book;
import com.apress.springboot3recipes.library.BookService;
import org.springframework.stereotype.Controller;
```

```
import org.springframework.ui.Model;
import org.springframework.web.bind.annotation.GetMapping;
import org.springframework.web.bind.annotation.ModelAttribute;
import org.springframework.web.bind.annotation.PostMapping;
import org.springframework.web.bind.annotation.RequestParam;
import reactor.core.publisher.Mono;

@Controller
public class BookController {

  private final BookService bookService;

  public BookController(BookService bookService) {
    this.bookService = bookService;
  }

  @GetMapping("/books.html")
  public String all(Model model) {
    model.addAttribute("books", bookService.findAll());
    return "books/list";
  }
}
```

Now that the controller and the other needed components are ready, a view is required. Create a list.html file in the src/main/resources/templates/books directory. This page will render a table with the books showing the ISBN, title, and authors. See Listing 4-12.

Listing 4-12. HTML Page for Book List

```
<!DOCTYPE html>
<html xmlns:th="http://www.thymeleaf.org">
<head lang="en">
  <meta charset="UTF-8">
  <title>Library - Available Books</title>
  <meta http-equiv="Content-Type" content="text/html; charset=UTF-8"/>
</head>
<body>
<h1>Available Books</h1>
```

185

```
<table>
  <thead>
  <tr>
    <th>Title</th>
    <th>Author</th>
    <th>ISBN</th>
  </tr>
  </thead>
  <tbody>
  <tr th:each="book : ${books}">
    <td th:text="${book.title}">Title</td>
    <td th:text="${book.authors}">Authors</td>
    <td><a th:href="@{/books.html(isbn=${book.isbn})}"
           th:text="${book.isbn}" href="#">ISBN</a></td>
  </tr>
  </tbody>
</table>
</body>
</html>
```

Finally, Listing 4-13 shows the `LibraryApplication` to start the application.

Listing 4-13. Library Spring Boot Application

```
package com.apress.springboot3recipes.library;

import org.springframework.boot.ApplicationRunner;
import org.springframework.boot.SpringApplication;
import org.springframework.boot.autoconfigure.SpringBootApplication;
import org.springframework.context.annotation.Bean;
import reactor.core.publisher.Flux;

@SpringBootApplication
public class LibraryApplication {
```

```
public static void main(String[] args) {
  SpringApplication.run(LibraryApplication.class, args);
}

@Bean
public ApplicationRunner initData(BookService books) {
  return (args) -> Flux.fromIterable(BookGenerator.all())
    .map(books::create).subscribe();
}
}
```

Now when launching the application and clicking the link, you will end up with a page showing the books (Figure 4-3).

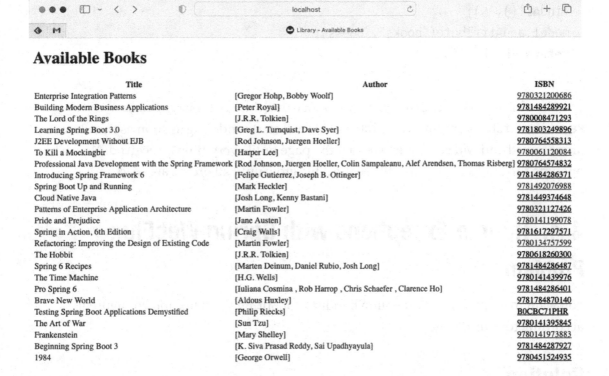

Figure 4-3. *Books list*

Make It More Reactive

When running the application and opening the page, you have to wait some time before the page starts to render. When rendering a page and the model contains `Flux`, it will by default wait until the whole `Flux` is consumed. After that, it will start rendering the page. It basically behaves like you would retrieve a `Collection` instead of a `Flux`. To start rendering the page quicker and get the page streaming, wrap the `Flux` in a `ReactiveDataDriverContextVariable`. See Listing 4-14.

Listing 4-14. Method Using ReactiveDataDriverContextVariable

```
@GetMapping("/books.html")
public String all(Model model) {
  var books = new ReactiveDataDriverContextVariable(bookService.
  findAll(), 5);
  model.addAttribute("books", books);
  return "books/list";
}
```

The `all` method looks the same, but notice that the `Flux` is wrapped in `ReactiveDataDriverContextVariable`. This will start rendering as soon as five elements are received and will continue to render the page until everything is received. Now when opening the books page, you will see the table grow until all orders are read.

4-4. Handle Exceptions with Spring WebFlux

Problem

You want to configure the exception handling for Spring WebFlux and configure it according to your needs.

Solution

Spring WebFlux provides several ways of handling exceptions, and with Spring Boot it has become pretty easy to modify the default behavior.

For view-related implementations, it is easy to add pages that will be automatically picked up. Add `error.html` as a customized error page, or add specific error pages for specific HTTP error codes, i.e., `404.html` and `500.html`.

Spring Boot also has exception handling support for REST-based controllers. It will return a response containing the error information, much like the error information that is available with regular WebFlux exception handling. Another option is to enable Problem Detail support (RFC-7807), which is a small standard for defining error responses. To enable it, set the `spring.webflux.problemdetails.enabled` property to `true`.

How It Works

We'll now explain how it works.

Handle Exceptions Handle Exceptions for REST Controllers

Write a custom `ErrorAttributes` property to replace the default one (Figure 4-4) and to fill the model that is being written as a response.

```
> http :8080/books/500
HTTP/1.1 500 Internal Server Error
Content-Length: 135
Content-Type: application/json

{
    "error": "Internal Server Error",
    "path": "/books/500",
    "requestId": "05e389c9-2",
    "status": 500,
    "timestamp": "2024-01-04T10:31:27.791+00:00"
}
```

Figure 4-4. *Default error response*

By default Spring Boot will include the attributes shown in Table 4-2 in the model for the error response.

Table 4-2. *Default Error Model Attributes*

Attribute	Description
timestamp	The time that the errors were extracted
status	The status code
error	The error reason
exception	The class name of the root exception (if configured)
message	The exception message
errors	Any errors from a `BindingResult` (when using binding and/or validation)
trace	The exception stack trace (if configured)
path	The URL path when the exception was raised

This is all done through the use of an `ErrorAttributes` component. The default is `DefaultErrorAttributes`. You can create your own `ErrorAttributes` handler to create a custom model or extend `DefaultErrorAttributes` to add additional attributes. See Listing 4-20.

Listing 4-20. Custom ErrorAttributes Implementation

```
package com.apress.springboot3recipes.library;

import org.springframework.boot.web.error.ErrorAttributeOptions;
import org.springframework.boot.web.reactive.error.DefaultErrorAttributes;
import org.springframework.web.reactive.function.server.ServerRequest;

import java.util.Map;

public class CustomizedErrorAttributes extends DefaultErrorAttributes {

  @Override
  public Map<String, Object> getErrorAttributes(ServerRequest req,
                                     ErrorAttributeOptions
                                     options) {
    var errorAttributes = super.getErrorAttributes(req, options);
```

```
errorAttributes.put("parameters", req.exchange().getRequest().
getQueryParams());
    return errorAttributes;
  }
}
```

CustomizedErrorAttributes will add the original request parameters to the model next to the default attributes. The next step is to configure this as a bean so that Spring Boot can detect it and use it instead of configuring the default. Adding the bean definition in Listing 4-21 to the LibraryApplication will make that possible.

Listing 4-21. Custom ErrorAttributes Bean Defnition

```
@Bean
public CustomizedErrorAttributes errorAttributes() {
    return new CustomizedErrorAttributes();
}
```

This will generate the error in Figure 4-5; notice the additional parameters attribute.

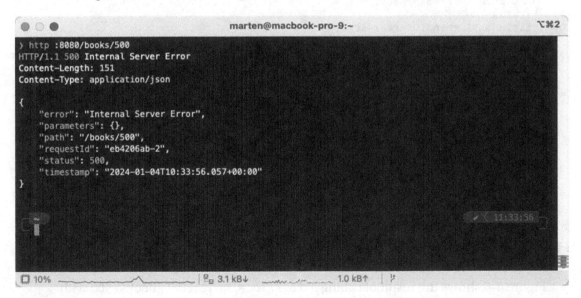

Figure 4-5. *Customized error response*

Enable and Use Problem Details

Spring 6 added support for the Problem Details for HTTP API (RFC-7807), and with Spring Boot it is quite easy to enable it. By adding `spring.webflux.problemdetails.enabled=true` (or `spring.mvc.problemdetails.enabled=true` for MVC-based applications), this support will be enabled.

When this is enabled, Spring Boot will register `ProblemDetailsExceptionHandler` as an additional `ExceptionHandler` with a higher order. The `ProblemDetailsExceptionHandler` will handle some well-known exception (all the Spring-related web exceptions) and return a result containing more information and of the type `application/problem+json`. See Figure 4-6.

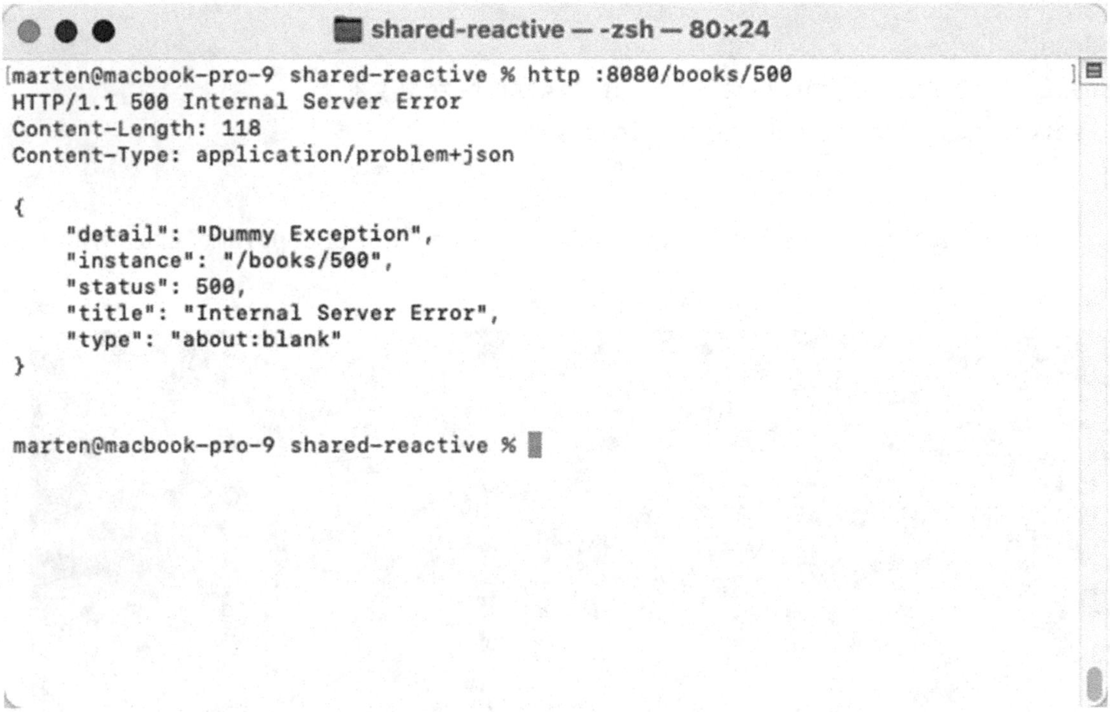

```
● ● ●                      📁 shared-reactive — -zsh — 80×24
[marten@macbook-pro-9 shared-reactive % http :8080/books/500              ]
HTTP/1.1 500 Internal Server Error
Content-Length: 118
Content-Type: application/problem+json

{
    "detail": "Dummy Exception",
    "instance": "/books/500",
    "status": 500,
    "title": "Internal Server Error",
    "type": "about:blank"
}


marten@macbook-pro-9 shared-reactive % █
```

Figure 4-6. *Problem detail error response*

Figure 4-6 shows the result of calling `http://localhost:8080/books/500` with Problem Detail support enabled.

This will work for all the different Spring MVC exceptions. When a validation or binding error occurs, it will also show a list of fields with the error on what failed. It will even translate (if possible) those error messages to the language used by the client (see also Recipes 4-5 and 4-6 for I18N support).

4-5. Implement Internationalization (I18N)

Problem

When developing an internationalized web application, you have to display your web pages in a user's preferred locale. You don't want to create different versions of the same page for different locales.

Solution

To avoid creating different versions of a page for different locales, you should make your web page independent of the locale by externalizing locale-sensitive text messages. Spring is able to resolve text messages for you by using a message source, which has to implement the `MessageSource` interface. In your page templates, you can then either use special tags or do lookups for the messages.

How It Works

Spring Boot automatically configures a `MessageSource` when it finds a `messages.properties` in `src/main/resources` (the default location). This `messages.properties` contains the default messages to be used in your application. Spring Boot will use the `Accept-Language` header from the request to determine which locale to use for the current request (see Recipe 4-6 for how to change that).

Some properties change the way `MessageSource` reacts to missing translations, caching, etc. See Table 4-3 for an overview of the properties.

Table 4-3. I18N Properties

Property	Description
spring.messages. basename	Comma-separated list of base names; the default is messages.
spring.messages. encoding	Message bundle encoding; the default is UTF-8.
spring.messages. always-use- message-format	Sets whether MessageFormat should be applied to all messages; the default is false.
spring.messages. fallback-to- system-locale	Fallback to the system's locale when no resource bundle for the detected locale can be found. When disabled, this will load the defaults from the default file. The default is true.
spring.messages. use-code-as- default-message	Use the message code as a default message when no message can be found instead of throwing a NoSuchMessageException. The default is false.
spring.messages. cache-duration	Cache duration; the default is forever.

💡 It can be useful to set spring.messages.fallback-to-system-locale to false when deploying your application to the cloud or other external hosting parties. That way, you control what the default language of your application is, instead of the (out of your control) environment you are deploying on.

Add a messages.properties file to the src/main/resources directory. See Listing 4-22.

Listing 4-22. Default Messages

```
main.title=Spring Boot Recipes - Library

index.title=Library
index.books.link=List of books
```

```
books.list.title=Available Books
books.list.table.title=Title
books.list.table.author=Author
books.list.table.isbn=ISBN
```

Now change the templates to use message interpolation (the lookup of the text using the `MessageSource`). See Listing 4-23.

Listing 4-23. Index Page with I18N Support

```
<!DOCTYPE html>
<html xmlns:th="http://www.thymeleaf.org">
<head>
    <meta charset="UTF-8">
    <title th:text="#{main.title}">Spring Boot Recipes - Library</title>
</head>
<body>

<h1 th:text="#{index.title}">Library</h1>

<a th:href="@{/books.html}" href="#" th:text="#{index.books.link}">List of
books</a>

</body>
</html>
```

For Thymeleaf you can use an `#{…}` expression in the `th:text` attribute; this will (due to the automatic Spring integration) resolve the messages from the `MessageSource`. When restarting the application, it appears as if nothing has changed in the output. However, all the text now comes from `messages.properties`.

Now let's add a `messages_nl.properties` for the Dutch translation of the website. See Listing 4-24.

Listing 4-24. Dutch Messages

```
main.title=Spring Boot Recipes - Bibliotheek

index.title=Bibliotheek
index.books.link=Lijst van boeken
```

```
books.list.title=Beschikbare Boeken
books.list.table.title=Titel
books.list.table.author=Auteur
books.list.table.isbn=ISBN
```

Now when changing the accept header to Dutch, the website will magically translate to Dutch (see Figure 4-7).

💡   Changing the language for your browser might not be that easy. For Chrome and Firefox there are plugins that allow you to switch the Accept-Language header easily.

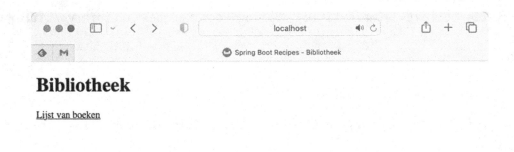

Figure 4-7. *Translated index page*

4-6. Change User Locales

Problem

For your web application to support internationalization, you have to identify each user's preferred locale and display the contents according to this locale.

Solution

In a Spring WebFlux application, a user's locale is identified by a component that has to implement the LocaleContextResolver interface. Spring WebFlux comes with two LocaleContextResolver implementations for you to resolve locales with different criteria. Alternatively, you can create your own custom locale resolver by implementing this interface.

You can define a locale resolver by registering a bean of type LocaleContextResolver in the web application context. You must set the bean name of the locale resolver to localeContextResolver so it can be autodetected.

How It Works

Spring WebFlux ships with several default implementations of the LocaleContextResolver interface, some of which allow the Locale to be changed. To change the Locale, one can use a WebFilter to allow users to override the locale they want to use. None of these is provided by Spring WebFlux (at least not at the moment of writing); hence, you will need to implement them yourself.

Resolve Locales with an HTTP Request Header

The default locale resolver registered by Spring Boot is AcceptHeaderLocaleContextResolver. It resolves locales by inspecting the accept-language header of an HTTP request. This header is set by a user's web browser according to the locale setting of the underlying operating system. See Listing 4-25.

ℹ️   AcceptHeaderLocaleContextResolver cannot change a user's locale because it is unable to modify the locale setting of the user's operating system.

Listing 4-25. AcceptHeaderLocaleContextResolver Bean Definition

```
@Bean
public AcceptHeaderLocaleContextResolver localeContextResolver () {
  return new AcceptHeaderLocaleContextResolver();
}
```

Use a Fixed Locale for Your Application

The other provided LocaleContextResolver is FixedLocaleContextResolver. It doesn't actually resolve a Locale but rather returns a preconfigured one, which is why this resolvers is fixed. It doesn't allow for the Locale to be changed as it is fixed to a single one. See Listing 4-26.

Listing 4-26. FixedLocaleContextResolver Bean Definition

```
@Bean
public FixedLocaleContextResolver localeContextResolver () {
  return new FixedLocaleContextResolver(Locale.GERMANY);
}
```

Change a User's Locale

To change a user's locale, we need to implement a LocaleContextResolver that is allowed to change; however, we want to retain the values between requests from the client. One place to store the value is an HTTP cookie. Another option is to utilize the WebSession. For this code sample, we are going to store the value into a cookie, as this allows our server to remain stateless. See Listing 4-27.

Listing 4-27. Cookie-Based LocaleContextResolver Implementation

```
package com.apress.springboot3recipes.library.i18n;

import org.springframework.context.i18n.LocaleContext;
import org.springframework.context.i18n.SimpleLocaleContext;
import org.springframework.http.ResponseCookie;
import org.springframework.web.server.ServerWebExchange;
import
org.springframework.web.server.i18n.AcceptHeaderLocaleContextResolver;

import java.util.Locale;

public class CookieLocaleContextResolver extends
AcceptHeaderLocaleContextResolver {

  public static final String DEFAULT_NAME =
    CookieLocaleContextResolver.class.getName() + ".LOCALE";
```

```java
@Override
public LocaleContext resolveLocaleContext(ServerWebExchange exchange) {
  parseCookieIfNecessary(exchange);
  return exchange.getAttribute(DEFAULT_NAME);
}

private void parseCookieIfNecessary(ServerWebExchange exchange) {
  if (exchange.getAttribute(DEFAULT_NAME) == null) {
    var cookies = exchange.getRequest().getCookies();
    var cookie = cookies.getFirst(DEFAULT_NAME);
    var attributes = exchange.getAttributes();
    if (cookie != null) {
      var locale = Locale.forLanguageTag(cookie.getValue());
      var context = new SimpleLocaleContext(locale);
      attributes.put(DEFAULT_NAME, context);
    } else
      attributes.put(DEFAULT_NAME, super.resolveLocaleContext(exchange));
  }
}

@Override
public void setLocaleContext(ServerWebExchange exchange,
LocaleContext lc) {
  var cookies = exchange.getResponse().getCookies();
  if (lc != null && lc.getLocale() != null) {
    exchange.getAttributes().put(DEFAULT_NAME, lc);
    var langTag = lc.getLocale().toLanguageTag();
    var cookie = ResponseCookie.from(DEFAULT_NAME, langTag).build();
    cookies.set(DEFAULT_NAME, cookie);
  } else {
    exchange.getAttributes().remove(DEFAULT_NAME, lc);
    cookies.remove(DEFAULT_NAME);
  }
}
}
```

CookieLocaleContextResolver will store, if needed, the user-selected Locale into an HTTP cookie (see the setLocaleContext) method. How this method is called will be shown later. To resolve the Locale, we, if needed, parse the cookie from the request and store the resulting LocaleContext in the attributes for the exchange. This is done to prevent parsing the cookie over and over. The value is also set upon explicitly by setting the LocaleContext in the response to directly activate the selected Locale. Finally, if nothing has been set, a fallback is done to use the accept-header of the browser, which is why it has an extension of AcceptHeaderLocaleContextResolver.

CookieLocaleContextResolver needs to be registered as a bean with the name localeContextResolver so that Spring will pick it up for resolving the Locale. See Listing 4-28.

Listing 4-28. CookieLocaleContextResolver Bean Definition

```
@Bean
public CookieLocaleContextResolver localeContextResolver() {
    return new CookieLocaleContextResolver();
}
```

To change the locale, we need to intercept the incoming request and call the setLocaleContext method of the LocaleContextResolver interface. For this we can use a WebFilter in which we check if a query parameter is present and if so determine the LocaleContext. See Listing 4-29.

Listing 4-29. WebFilter Implementation to Change the Locale

```
package com.apress.springboot3recipes.library.i18n;

import org.springframework.context.i18n.SimpleLocaleContext;
import org.springframework.util.StringUtils;
import org.springframework.web.server.ServerWebExchange;
import org.springframework.web.server.WebFilter;
import org.springframework.web.server.WebFilterChain;
import org.springframework.web.server.i18n.LocaleContextResolver;
import reactor.core.publisher.Mono;

import java.util.Locale;

public class LocaleChangeWebFilter implements WebFilter {
```

```java
public static final String DEFAULT_PARAM_NAME = "locale";

private final LocaleContextResolver resolver;

public LocaleChangeWebFilter(LocaleContextResolver resolver) {
  this.resolver = resolver;
}

@Override
public Mono<Void> filter(ServerWebExchange exchange, WebFilterChain
chain) {
  var params = exchange.getRequest().getQueryParams();
  if (params.containsKey(DEFAULT_PARAM_NAME)) {
    var locale = params.getFirst(DEFAULT_PARAM_NAME);
    var context = StringUtils.hasText(locale) ?
      new SimpleLocaleContext(Locale.forLanguageTag(locale)) : null;
    resolver.setLocaleContext(exchange, context);
  }
  return chain.filter(exchange);
}
}
```

LocaleChangeWebFilter will check if a locale named request parameter (or rather query parameter) is present and if so use that to set the user-selected Locale.

Next, this LocaleChangeWebFilter needs to be registered with Spring WebFlux. Spring WebFlux will automatically detect beans of the type WebFilter and register them with the request processing chain. It is necessary only to make this a bean. See Listing 4-30.

Listing 4-30. LocaleChangeWebFilter Bean Definition

```java
@Bean
public LocaleChangeWebFilter localeChangeWebFilter(LocaleContextResol
ver lcr) {
  return new LocaleChangeWebFilter(lcr);
}
```

To change the locale, add LocaleChangeInterceptor as a bean and register it as an interceptor; for the latter, use the addInterceptors method from WebMvcConfigurer.

ℹ️   Instead of adding it to @SpringBootApplication, you could also create a specialized @Configuration annotated class to register the filters and resolver. Be aware to *not* add @EnableWebFlux to that class as that will disable the auto-configuration from Spring Boot!

Now add the following snippet to the index.html file:

```
<h3>Language</h3>
<div>
    <a href="?locale=nl" th:text="#{main.language.nl}">NL</a> |
    <a href="?locale=en" th:text="#{main.language.en}">EN</a>
</div>
```

Now when selecting one of the languages, the page will rerender and be shown in the selected language. When you continue browsing, the remainder of the pages will also be shown in the selected language.

4-7. Select and Configure the Embedded Server

Problem

You want to use Undertow as an embedded container instead of the default Reactor Netty container.

Solution

Exclude the Reactor Netty runtime and include the Undertow runtime. Spring Boot will automatically detect if Tomcat, Jetty, Reactor Netty, or Undertow is on the classpath and configure the container accordingly.

How It Works

Spring Boot has out-of-the-box support for Tomcat, Jetty, Reactor Netty, and Undertow as embedded reactive containers. By default Spring Boot uses Reactor Netty as the container (expressed through the spring-boot-starter-reactor-netty dependency in the spring-boot-starter-webflux artifact). The container can be configured using properties, some of which apply to all containers and others to a specific container. The global properties are prefixed with server or server.reactive, whereas the containers start with server.<container> (where container is either tomcat, jetty, netty, or undertow).

Set General Configuration Properties

Several general server properties are available, as shown in Table 4-4 and Table 4-5.

Table 4-4. *General Server Properties*

Property	Description
server.port	The HTTP server port; the default is 8080.
server.address	The IP address to bind to; the default is 0.0.0.0, i.e., all adapters.
server.server-header	Name of the header to send the server name; the default is empty.
server.max-http-header-size	Maximum size of an HTTP header; the default is 0 (unlimited).
server.connection-timout	Timeout for HTTP connectors to wait for the next request before closing. The default is empty leaving it to the container; a value of -1 means infinite and to never time out.
server.http2.enabled	Enable Http2 support if the current container supports it. The default is false.
server.forward-headers-strategy	Strategy for the X-Forward-* headers support; one of native, framework, none.
server.compression.enabled	Sets whether HTTP compression should be enabled; the default is false.
server.compression.mime-types	Comma-separated list of MIME types that compression applies to.
server.compression.excluded-user-agents	Comma-separated list of user agents for which compression should be disabled.
server.compression.min-response-size	Minimum size of the request for compression to be applied; the default is 2048.
server.shutdown	Server shutdown mode; one of immediate or graceful. The default is immediate.

Table 4-5. *Reactive Container HTTP Session Properties*

`server.reactive.` `session.timeout`	Session timeout; the default is 30 minutes.
`server.reactive.` `session.cookie.name`	Name of the cookie to store the session identifier. The default is empty leaving it to the container default.

`server.reactive.`
`session.cookie.`
`domain`
	Domain value to use for the session cookie. The default is empty leaving it to the container default.

`server.reactive.` `session.cookie.path`	Path value to use for the session cookie. The default is empty leaving it to the container default.

`server.reactive.`
`session.cookie.`
`http-only`
	Sets whether the session cookie should be http-only accessible. The default is empty leaving it to the container default.

`server.reactive.`
`session.cookie.`
`secure`
	Sets whether the cookie should be sent through SSL only. The default is empty leaving it to the container default.

`server.reactive.`
`session.cookie.`
`max-age`
	Sets the lifetime of the session cookie. The default is empty leaving it to the container default.

`server.reactive.`
`session.cookie.`
`same-site`
	Sets the Same-Site policy to use (NONE/LAX/STRICT); the default is NONE.

ℹ️   When using Spring Session, only the `server.servlet.session.`
`timeout` property applies!

Finally, Spring Boot makes it easy to configure SSL by exposing a few properties; see Table 4-6 and Recipe 4-8 for how to configure SSL.

Table 4-6. *Servlet Container SSL Properties*

Property	Description
server.ssl.enabled	Enables SSL; the default is true.
server.ssl.bundle	Sets the name of the SSL bundle to use.
server.ssl.ciphers	Sets the supported SSL ciphers; the default is empty.
server.ssl.client-auth	Enables SSL client authentication; one of none, want or need. The default is empty.
server.ssl.protocol	Sets the SSL protocol to use; the default is TLS.
server.ssl.enabled-protocols	Sets which SSL protocols are enabled; the default is empty.
server.ssl.key-alias	Sets the alias to identify the key in the keystore; the default is empty.
server.ssl.key-password	Sets the password to access the key in the keystore; the default is empty.
server.ssl.key-store	Sets the location of the keystore, typically a JKS file; the default is empty.
server.ssl.key-store-password	Sets the password to access the keystore; the default is empty.
server.ssl.key-store-type	Sets the type of the keystore; the default is empty.
server.ssl.key-store-provider	Sets the provider of the keystore; the default is empty.
server.ssl.trust-store	Sets the location of the trust store.
server.ssl.trust-store-password	Sets the password to access the trust store; the default is empty.
server.ssl.trust-store-type	Sets the type of the trust store; the default is empty.
server.ssl.trust-store-provider	Sets the provider of the trust store; the default is empty.

> ℹ️   All the properties mentioned in the previous tables apply *only* when using an embedded container to run your application. When deploying to an external container (i.e., deploying a WAR file), the settings do not apply!

Change the Runtime Container

When including the `spring-boot-starter-webflux` dependency, it will automatically include a dependency to the Reactor Netty container as it has a dependency on the `spring-boot-starter-reactor-netty` artifact. To enable a different servlet container, `spring-boot-starter-reactor-netty` needs to be excluded, and one of `spring-boot-starter-jetty` or `spring-boot-starter-undertow` needs to be included. See Listing 4-31.

Listing 4-31. Exclusion of Reactor Netty and Use of Undertow

```xml
<dependency>
    <groupId>org.springframework.boot</groupId>
    <artifactId>spring-boot-starter-webflux</artifactId>
    <exclusions>
        <exclusion>
            <groupId>org.springframework.boot</groupId>
            <artifactId>spring-boot-starter-reactor-netty</artifactId>
        </exclusion>
    </exclusions>
</dependency>
<dependency>
    <groupId>org.springframework.boot</groupId>
    <artifactId>spring-boot-starter-undertow</artifactId>
</dependency>
```

In Maven you can use an `<exclusion>` element inside your `<dependency>` to exclude a dependency.

Now when the application is started, it will start with Undertow instead of using Reactor Netty (see Figure 4-8).

```
/\\/ ___'_ __ _ _(_)_ __ __ _ \ \ \ \
( ( )\___ | '_ | '_| | '_ \/ _` | \ \ \ \
 \\/  ___)| |_)| | | | | || (_| |  ) ) ) )
  '  |____| .__|_| |_|_| |_\__, | / / / /
 =========|_|==============|___/=/_/_/_/
 :: Spring Boot ::             (v3.2.1)

2024-01-04T11:59:01.850+01:00  INFO 79274 --- [    main] c.a.s.library.LibraryApplication       : Starting LibraryApplication using Java 21.0.1 with PID 79274 (/Users/ma
2024-01-04T11:59:01.856+01:00  INFO 79274 --- [    main] c.a.s.library.LibraryApplication       : No active profile set, falling back to 1 default profile: "default"
2024-01-04T11:59:03.370+01:00  INFO 79274 --- [    main] io.undertow                            : starting server: Undertow - 2.3.10.Final
2024-01-04T11:59:03.387+01:00  INFO 79274 --- [    main] org.xnio                               : XNIO version 3.8.8.Final
2024-01-04T11:59:03.402+01:00  INFO 79274 --- [    main] org.xnio.nio                           : XNIO NIO Implementation Version 3.8.8.Final
2024-01-04T11:59:03.448+01:00  INFO 79274 --- [    main] org.jboss.threads                      : JBoss Threads version 3.5.0.Final
2024-01-04T11:59:03.532+01:00  INFO 79274 --- [    main] o.s.b.w.e.undertow.UndertowWebServer   : Undertow started on port 8080 (http)
2024-01-04T11:59:03.538+01:00  INFO 79274 --- [    main] c.a.s.library.LibraryApplication       : Started LibraryApplication in 2.233 seconds (process running for 2.9)
```

Figure 4-8. *Bootstrap logging with Undertow container*

4-8. Configure SSL for the Reactive Container

Problem

You want your application to be accessible through HTTPS next (or instead of) HTTP.

Solution

Get a certificate, place it in a keystore, and use the `server.ssl` properties to configure the keystore. Spring Boot will then automatically configure the server to be accessible through HTTPS only.

How It Works

Using `server.ssl.keystore` (and related properties), you can configure the embedded container to accept only HTTPS connections. Before you can configure SSL, you will need to have a certificate to secure your application. Generally, you will want to get a certificate from a certificate authority such as Verisign or Let's Encrypt. However, for development purposes, you can use a self-signed certificate (see the section "Create a Self-Signed Certificate").

Create a Self-Signed Certificate

Java comes with a tool called `keytool` that can be used to generate certificates among other things. See Listing 4-32.

Listing 4-32. keytool Command

```
keytool -genkey -keyalg RSA -alias sb3-recipes -keystore sb3-recipes.pfx
-storepass password -validity 3600 -keysize 4096 -storetype pkcs12
```

This command will tell `keytool` to generate a key using the RSA algorithm and place it in the keystore named `sb3-recipes.pfx` with the alias `sb3-recipes`, and it will be valid for 3,600 days. When running the command, it will ask a few questions and answer them accordingly (or leave them empty). After that, there will be a file called `sb3-recipes.pfx` containing the certificate protected with a password.

Place this file in the `src/main/resources` folder so that it is packaged as part of your application and Spring Boot can easily access it.

⚠   Using a self-signed certificate will produce a warning in the browser that the website isn't safe or protected.

Configure Spring Boot to Use the Keystore

Spring Boot will need to know about the keystore to be able to configure the embedded container. For this you first create a so-called SSL bundle and use the `server.ssl.bundle` property to link it to the server.

For this use the `server.ssl.keystore` property. You will also need to specify the type of keystore (`pkcs12`) and the password. See Listing 4-33.

Listing 4-33. SSL Properties

```
server.ssl.bundle=server

# SSL Bundle
spring.ssl.bundle.jks.server.key.alias=sb3-recipes
spring.ssl.bundle.jks.server.key.password=password

spring.ssl.bundle.jks.server.keystore.location=classpath:sb3-recipes.pfx
spring.ssl.bundle.jks.server.keystore.password=password
spring.ssl.bundle.jks.server.keystore.type=pkcs12
```

These SSL properties will create an SSL bundle named `server`. It is a JKS type. To pass the alias (as used to create the certificate), use the `key.alias` and for the password the `key.password` property. In addition, we need to link to the actual certificate, which is in the `sb3-recipes.pfx` file. For this use the `keystore.location` as this file is password protected. We need to specify the `keystore.password` property, and finally the type of certificate is needed as well.

Now when accessing the server through HTTPS, you will receive a warning due to the self-signed certificate. When using an official certificate, you obviously wouldn't get this warning. See Figure 4-9.

Figure 4-9. *Library accessed through HTTPS*

4-9. Perform Synchronous Request Handling with Controllers and TaskExecutor

Problem

You have a piece of blocking code that you want to execute in an otherwise totally reactive stack and you don't want to block all the processing.

Solution

When a request comes in, it is handled reactively with an event loop. When calling code that blocks, it will block the event loop and prevent further processing. Spring WebFlux can use a dedicated `TaskExecutor` for processes that would otherwise block the event loop.

How It Works

To configure parts of Spring WebFlux, you can use the `WebFluxConfigurer` interface.
To configure the dedicated `AsyncTaskExecutor` (which generally is a Spring-managed
`AsyncTaskExecutor`), override and implement the `configureBlockingExecution`
method. See Listing 4-34.

Listing 4-34. Spring Boot Application with WebFluxConfigurer

```
package com.apress.springboot3recipes;

import org.springframework.boot.SpringApplication;
import org.springframework.boot.autoconfigure.SpringBootApplication;
import org.springframework.boot.task.SimpleAsyncTaskExecutorBuilder;
import org.springframework.context.annotation.Configuration;
import org.springframework.web.reactive.config.BlockingExecutionConfigurer;
import org.springframework.web.reactive.config.WebFluxConfigurer;

@SpringBootApplication
public class HelloWorldApplication {

  public static void main(String[] args) {
    SpringApplication.run(HelloWorldApplication.class, args);
  }

  @Configuration
  public static class WebFluxConfiguration implements WebFluxConfigurer {

    private final SimpleAsyncTaskExecutorBuilder builder;

    public WebFluxConfiguration(SimpleAsyncTaskExecutorBuilder builder) {
      this.builder = builder;
    }

    @Override
    public void configureBlockingExecution(BlockingExecutionConfigurer
    configurer) {
```

```
      configurer.setExecutor(builder.threadNamePrefix("blocking-").build());
    }
  }

}
```

The inner class `WebFluxConfiguration` implements the `WebFluxConfigurer` interface, and here we override `configureBlockingExecution`. We are using `SimpleAsyncTaskExecutorBuilder` to create an `AsyncTaskExecutor` instance. Using `SimpleAsyncTaskExecutorBuilder`, we can use properties to do some default configuration through application properties (see Recipe 7-1 for more information). We could have created a new `AsyncTaskExecutor`, like `SimpleAsyncTaskExecutor` or `VirtualThreadTaskExecutor` as well.

Using `SimpleAsyncTaskExecutorBuilder`, we set the thread prefix, build the executor, and pass it to `BlockingExecutionConfigurer`. This way, it is automatically detected by Spring WebFlux. Now any nonreactive return type (anything other than the types from Project Reactor, RxJava, Java Flow, or SmallRye Mutiny) will be executed using this executor. See Listing 4-35.

Listing 4-35. HelloWorldController with Blocking and Reactive Handling

```
package com.apress.springboot3recipes;

import org.springframework.boot.SpringBootVersion;
import org.springframework.web.bind.annotation.GetMapping;
import org.springframework.web.bind.annotation.RestController;
import reactor.core.publisher.Mono;

@RestController
public class HelloWorldController {

  @GetMapping("/blocking")
  public String hello() {
    return sayHello();
  }

  @GetMapping("/reactive")
  public Mono<String> helloReactive() {
    return Mono.just(sayHello());
  }
```

```
private static String sayHello() {
  var version = SpringBootVersion.getVersion();
  var thread = Thread.currentThread().getName();
  return String.format("Hello World, from Spring Boot %s on Thread '%s'!"
                       , version, thread);
  }
}
```

HelloWorldController has two methods. The one bound to /blocking returns a regular String, whereas the one bound to /reactive returns a Mono<String>, which is a reactive type.

Now when launching the application and calling the endpoints using HTTPie, curl, or a browser, you should be able to see what is happening as it will return the name of the thread it executed on (see Figure 4-10).

```
marten@macbook-pro-9 ~ % http :8080/blocking
HTTP/1.1 200 OK
Content-Length: 68
Content-Type: text/plain;charset=UTF-8

Hello World, from Spring Boot 3.2.0-SNAPSHOT on Thread 'blocking-1'!


marten@macbook-pro-9 ~ % http :8080/reactive
HTTP/1.1 200 OK
Content-Length: 76
Content-Type: text/plain;charset=UTF-8

Hello World, from Spring Boot 3.2.0-SNAPSHOT on Thread 'reactor-http-nio-3'!


marten@macbook-pro-9 ~ %
```

Figure 4-10. *Blocking and reactive output*

Calling /blocking will be executed on a thread prefixed with blocking, indicating it is indeed executed by the configured AsyncTaskExecutor. The /reactive one is executed on one of the threads of the reactive framework in use (here Project Reactor).

As we are using Spring Boot, it will automatically configure the blocking WebFlux execution for you. By default Spring Boot creates an AsyncTaskExecutor for use in various places in the application including the WebFlux blocking execution. This executor is configurable to various properties (see Recipe 7-1) and could even be switched to virtual threads by setting spring.threads.virtual.enabled to true. See Listing 4-36.

Listing 4-36. Spring Boot Application Without Explicit WebFluxConfigurer

```
package com.apress.springboot3recipes;

import org.springframework.boot.SpringApplication;
import org.springframework.boot.autoconfigure.SpringBootApplication;

@SpringBootApplication
public class HelloWorldApplication {

  public static void main(String[] args) {
    SpringApplication.run(HelloWorldApplication.class, args);
  }
}
```

Without any further configuration, the blocking execution will still happen.

4-10. Create Response Writers

Problem

You have a service, or multiple calls, and want to send the response in chunks to the client.

Solution

Spring WebFlux, like Spring MVC, does content negotiation. When it receives a content type that can be streamed, like application/x-ndjson and text/event-stream, it will switch to a codec that streams the result. For text/event-stream, we could use the SseEventBuilder to add additional information.

How It Works

Let's talk about how it works.

Send Multiple Results in a Response

Spring WebFlux will automatically stream the results when a content type that requires it is detected. Create an `OrderController` with an `orders` method that returns a `Flux<Order>` and send the results one by one to the client.

```java
package com.apress.springboot3recipes.order.rest;
import com.apress.springboot3recipes.order.Order;
import com.apress.springboot3recipes.order.OrderService;
import org.springframework.web.bind.annotation.GetMapping;
import org.springframework.web.bind.annotation.RestController;
import reactor.core.publisher.Flux;

import java.time.Duration;

@RestController
public class OrderController {

  private final OrderService orderService;

  public OrderController(OrderService orderService) {
    this.orderService = orderService;
  }

  @GetMapping("/orders")
  public Flux<Order> orders() {
    return orderService.findAll().delayElements(Duration.ofMillis(32));
  }
}
```

The controller is very simple, because all complexities for returning the correct response are handled by the framework.

ℹ️   There is a delay in sending each item to the client, just so you can see the different events coming in. You wouldn't do this in real code.

When using a tool like HTTPie or curl, calling the URL http://localhost:8080/ orders without specifying a streaming Content-Type will return an array of orders (see Figure 4-11).

```
● ● ●                          marten — -zsh — 108×31
[marten@macbook-pro-9 ~ % http :8080/orders
HTTP/1.1 200 OK
Content-Type: application/json
transfer-encoding: chunked

[
    {
        "amount": 561.89,
        "id": "de27d194-483c-4c84-95a5-3372b2646200"
    },
    {
        "amount": 415.39,
        "id": "b4383150-153a-48d9-8f7b-e191e3c194ca"
    },
    {
        "amount": 445.67,
        "id": "b906a6cd-3be7-45d0-8725-0d747184a552"
    },
    {
        "amount": 425.17,
        "id": "2e8f1fda-4ed5-48e3-beda-f81931c03ed7"
    },
    {
        "amount": 426.32,
        "id": "72380b9c-3386-4e8b-931f-25d0ed23e7ec"
    }
]

marten@macbook-pro-9 ~ % █
```

Figure 4-11. *Response without streaming Content-Type*

When specifying an accept header of application/x-ndjson, the results will be streamed individually instead of collected and sent as an array. Using http :8080/ orders 'Accept:application/x-ndjson' --stream will result in Figure 4-12.

```
● ● ●                        marten — -zsh — 108×33
[marten@macbook-pro-9 ~ % http :8080/orders 'Accept:application/x-ndjson' --stream
HTTP/1.1 200 OK
Content-Type: application/x-ndjson
transfer-encoding: chunked

{
    "amount": 561.89,
    "id": "de27d194-483c-4c84-95a5-3372b2646200"
}

{
    "amount": 415.39,
    "id": "b4383150-153a-48d9-8f7b-e191e3c194ca"
}

{
    "amount": 445.67,
    "id": "b906a6cd-3be7-45d0-8725-0d747184a552"
}

{
    "amount": 425.17,
    "id": "2e8f1fda-4ed5-48e3-beda-f81931c03ed7"
}

{
    "amount": 426.32,
    "id": "72380b9c-3386-4e8b-931f-25d0ed23e7ec"
}


marten@macbook-pro-9 ~ %
```

Figure 4-12. *Response with streaming JSON*

Finally, we could use event streaming by specifying the text/event-stream content
type. Using http :8080/orders 'Accept:text/event-stream' --stream will result in
Figure 4-13.

```
[marten@macbook-pro-9 ~ % http :8080/orders 'Accept:text/event-stream' --stream
HTTP/1.1 200 OK
Content-Type: text/event-stream;charset=UTF-8
transfer-encoding: chunked

data:{
    "amount": 561.89,
    "id": "de27d194-483c-4c84-95a5-3372b2646200"
}

data:{
    "amount": 415.39,
    "id": "b4383150-153a-48d9-8f7b-e191e3c194ca"
}

data:{
    "amount": 445.67,
    "id": "b906a6cd-3be7-45d0-8725-0d747184a552"
}

data:{
    "amount": 425.17,
    "id": "2e8f1fda-4ed5-48e3-beda-f81931c03ed7"
}

data:{
    "amount": 426.32,
    "id": "72380b9c-3386-4e8b-931f-25d0ed23e7ec"
}

marten@macbook-pro-9 ~ %
```

Figure 4-13. *Response with event stream*

Finally let's write a test for this controller. Annotate a class with
@WebFluxTest(OrderController.class) to get a WebFlux slice test. OrderController
needs an OrderService that is mocked by using @MockBean on the OrderService field.
See Listing 4-37.

Listing 4-37. WebFluxTest for the OrderController

```
package com.apress.springboot3recipes.order.rest;

import com.apress.springboot3recipes.order.Order;
import com.apress.springboot3recipes.order.OrderService;
import org.junit.jupiter.api.Test;
import org.springframework.beans.factory.annotation.Autowired;
import org.springframework.boot.test.autoconfigure.web.reactive.WebFluxTest;
import org.springframework.boot.test.mock.mockito.MockBean;
import org.springframework.http.MediaType;
import org.springframework.test.web.reactive.server.WebTestClient;
import reactor.core.publisher.Flux;
```

217

```
import java.math.BigDecimal;

import static org.mockito.Mockito.when;

@WebFluxTest(OrderController.class)
public class OrderControllerTest {

  @Autowired
  private WebTestClient webTestClient;

  @MockBean
  private OrderService orderService;

  @Test
  public void shouldReturnOrdres() throws Exception {

    when(orderService.findAll()).thenReturn(Flux.just((new Order("1234",
    BigDecimal.TEN))));

    webTestClient.get()
        .uri("/orders")
        .accept(MediaType.APPLICATION_NDJSON)
        .exchange()
            .expectStatus().isOk()
        .expectBody().json("{\"id\":\"1234\",\"amount\":10}");
  }
}
```

The test method first registers the behavior on the mocked OrderService to return a single instance of an Order. Next we use a WebTestClient to perform a get on the /orders endpoint with a streaming response type. The result should be a single JSON element containing the id and amount as the OrderService returns just a single element.

Specify What to Send with Server Send Events

Server-Sent-Events are messages from the server to the client. They have a Content-Type header of text/event-stream. They are quite lightweight with only four fields (see Table 4-7).

Table 4-7. *Allowed Fields for Server-Sent-Events*

Field	Description
id	The ID of the event
event	The type of event
data	The event data
retry	Reconnection time for the event stream

By default only the data element is included in the response.

To send events from a request handling method, you use the ServerSentEvent that provided a builder method to actually create the ServerSentEvent instance. To send the ServerSentEvent to the client, you need to convert your object to this. We can extend the OrderController, which was created initially, with a dedicated method for ServerSentEvent instances (see Listing 4-38).

Listing 4-38. OrderController with Special ServerSentEvent Request Handling Method

```
package com.apress.springboot3recipes.order.rest;

import com.apress.springboot3recipes.order.Order;
import com.apress.springboot3recipes.order.OrderService;
import org.springframework.http.MediaType;
import org.springframework.http.codec.ServerSentEvent;
import org.springframework.web.bind.annotation.GetMapping;
import org.springframework.web.bind.annotation.RestController;
import reactor.core.publisher.Flux;

import java.time.Duration;

@RestController
public class OrderController {

  private final OrderService orderService;

  public OrderController(OrderService orderService) {
    this.orderService = orderService;
  }
```

```java
@GetMapping("/orders")
public Flux<Order> orders() {
  return orderService.findAll().delayElements(Duration.ofMillis(32));
}

@GetMapping(value = "/orders", produces = MediaType.TEXT_EVENT_
STREAM_VALUE)
public Flux<ServerSentEvent<Order>> orderEvents() {
  return orderService.findAll()
      .map(this::toEvent)
      .delayElements(Duration.ofMillis(32));
}

private ServerSentEvent<Order> toEvent(Order order) {
  return ServerSentEvent.builder(order)
      .event("order-event")
      .id(order.id()).build();
}
}
```

We create a dedicated ServerSentEvent for each Order we receive. We specify the id
and event. The order is used as the body (the data field). Finally, after calling the build
method, we can use the created ServerSentEvent.

Now when the URL http://localhost:8080/orders with a Content-Type of text/
event-stream is called, you see events coming in one by one (Figure 4-14).

```
●  ●  ●                          marten — -zsh — 108×43

[marten@macbook-pro-9 ~ % http :8080/orders 'Accept:text/event-stream' --stream
HTTP/1.1 200 OK
Content-Type: text/event-stream;charset=UTF-8
transfer-encoding: chunked

id:ef3085bf-27a4-4bc3-aac5-0e013667e678
event:order-event
data:{
    "amount": 756.72,
    "id": "ef3085bf-27a4-4bc3-aac5-0e013667e678"
}

id:0d6950f8-8532-4d14-b904-5d2a28cde3c3
event:order-event
data:{
    "amount": 748.5,
    "id": "0d6950f8-8532-4d14-b904-5d2a28cde3c3"
}

id:06a15c38-d80f-4968-a06a-ea8ff0d0ef0f
event:order-event
data:{
    "amount": 33.58,
    "id": "06a15c38-d80f-4968-a06a-ea8ff0d0ef0f"
}

id:84bf3f98-5688-4eb9-8412-a5e3a06dc9d9
event:order-event
data:{
    "amount": 456.06,
    "id": "84bf3f98-5688-4eb9-8412-a5e3a06dc9d9"
}

id:50246c73-3da5-4909-8587-467a28683d74
event:order-event
data:{
    "amount": 287.36,
    "id": "50246c73-3da5-4909-8587-467a28683d74"
}


marten@macbook-pro-9 ~ % █
```

Figure 4-14. *Server-Sent-Events result*

Note the Content-Type header; it has a value of text/event-stream to indicate that we get a stream of events. The stream can be kept open and receive event notifications. Each object written is converted to JSON; this is done with an Encoder. The object is written in the data tag as the event data.

4-11. Consume REST Resources with Spring WebFlux

Problem

You need to connect to a REST resource for your application and want to use a WebClient for this.

Solution

Spring Boot provides the configuration and builders to help construct the needed classes. This recipe will show how to build an application that can be used to consume the API built in Recipe 4-2.

You can use `WebClient.Builder` to create a `WebClient`. Another option is to use a declarative client using an `@HttpExchange`.

How It Works

Although each approach differs in the classes in use, we are still going to need a dependency on the web classes for Spring MVC. For this we can add the `spring-boot-starter-webflux` dependency. See Listing 4-39.

Listing 4-39. Spring Boot Starter WebFlux Dependency

```
<dependency>
  <groupId>org.springframework.boot</groupId>
  <artifactId>spring-boot-starter-webflux</artifactId>
</dependency>
```

> ℹ️ If you are writing a stand-alone client not in need of a servlet container, you might want to add an exclusion for `spring-boot-starter-netty`.

We are going to use Recipe 4-2 as our server API, and we will write an application that looks up a book on that API, calls another API (on `https://openlibrary.org`) to retrieve additional information for the book, and returns an enriched response.

The `EnrichedBook` looks like Listing 4-40.

Listing 4-40. EnrichedBook Record

```
package com.apress.springboot3recipes.library;

import java.util.List;
import java.util.Objects;
```

```java
public record EnrichedBook(
  String isbn,
  String title,
  String published,
  List<String> authors) {

  @Override
  public boolean equals(Object o) {
    if (o instanceof EnrichedBook book) {
      return Objects.equals(isbn, book.isbn);
    }
    return false;
  }

  @Override
  public int hashCode() {
    return Objects.hash(isbn);
  }
}
```

This is a slightly extended version of the Book class created in Recipe 3-2 (see Listing 3-6). We can reuse the Book class to bind the result from our own server. For the Open Library API, we will use a HashMap to put the response in and retrieve the elements we needed.

Use a WebClient

A WebClient is constructed through a WebClient.Builder, which is exposed by Spring Boot automatically. See Listing 4-41.

Listing 4-41. WebClient Bean Definition with Builder

```java
@Bean
public WebClient restClient(WebClient.Builder builder) {
  var httpClient = HttpClient.create().followRedirect(true);
  var connector = new ReactorClientHttpConnector(httpClient);
  return builder.clientConnector(connector).build();
}
```

RestClient.Builder provides some methods to enhance the configuration. Each method will result in a new RestClient.Builder instance. Here we configure the Project Reactor HttpClient to automatically follow redirects (HTTP status 301/302) as this is disabled by default. The API we are using (from Open Library) uses a redirect to point to the right results. See Table 4-8 and Listing 4-42.

Table 4-8. *WebClient.Builder Configuration Methods*

Method	Description
baseUrl	Sets the root URL to be used with requests; the default is null.
clientConnector	Configures the ClientHttpConnector to be used. Useful for using a preconfigured one in case of (for instance) SSL.
defaultCookie defaultCookies	Adds a cookie(s) with a default value.
defaultHeader defaultHeaders	Adds a header(s) with a default value.
defaultRequest	Consumer to customize every request that is being built.
defaultStatusHandler	Registers a default status handler to be applied to each response.
defaultUriVariables	Default values for URI variables.
messageConverters	Replaces the HttpMessageConverter that should be used with the created RestTemplate.
exchangeFunction	Registers a default ExchangeFunction with a preconfigured Client HttpConnector and ExchangeStrategies.
exchangeStrategies	Configures the ExchangeStrategies to use.
filter	Adds the given filter to the end of the filter chain.
observationConvention	Configures the ObservationConvention used to collect metadata for the request observation/metrics. The default will be set to DefaultClientRequestObservationConvention.
observationRegistry	Configures the ObservationRegistry to use for recording HTTP Client observations. Generally automatically set by Spring Boot.
uriBuilderFactory	Sets the UriBuilderFactory to use.

Listing 4-42. Controller Using a WebClient

```java
package com.apress.springboot3recipes.library.rest;

import com.apress.springboot3recipes.library.Book;
import com.apress.springboot3recipes.library.EnrichedBook;
import org.springframework.http.ResponseEntity;
import org.springframework.web.bind.annotation.GetMapping;
import org.springframework.web.bind.annotation.PathVariable;
import org.springframework.web.bind.annotation.RequestMapping;
import org.springframework.web.bind.annotation.RestController;
import org.springframework.web.client.RestClientResponseException;
import org.springframework.web.reactive.function.client.WebClient;
import reactor.core.publisher.Mono;

import java.util.Map;

@RestController
@RequestMapping("/books")
public class EnrichedBookController {

  private static final String BOOKS_URL = "http://localhost:8080/books/
  {isbn}";
  private static final String OL_API = "https://openlibrary.org/isbn/
  {isbn}.json";

  private final WebClient rest;

  public EnrichedBookController(WebClient rest) {
    this.rest = rest;
  }

  @GetMapping("/{isbn}")
  public Mono<ResponseEntity<EnrichedBook>> get(@PathVariable("isbn")
  String isbn) {
    var book = rest.get().uri(BOOKS_URL, isbn).retrieve().
    bodyToMono(Book.class);
    var library = rest.get().uri(OL_API, isbn).retrieve().
    bodyToMono(Map.class);
```

```java
    var enriched = enrich(book, library);
    return enriched.map(ResponseEntity::ok).onErrorResume(this::han
    dleError);
}

private Mono<ResponseEntity<EnrichedBook>> handleError(Throwable ex) {
    if (ex instanceof RestClientResponseException rex) {
        return Mono.just(ResponseEntity.status(rex.getStatusCode()).build());
    }
    return Mono.just(ResponseEntity.internalServerError().build());
}

private Mono<EnrichedBook> enrich(Mono<Book> book, Mono<Map> ol) {
    return Mono.zip(book, ol)
        .map((res) -> enrich(res.getT1(), res.getT2()));
}

private EnrichedBook enrich(Book book, Map ol) {
    var publishDate = extractPublishData(ol);
    return new EnrichedBook(book.isbn(), book.title(), publishDate, book.
    authors());
}

private String extractPublishData(Map json) {
    return (String) json.getOrDefault("publish_date", "");
}
}
```

The controller uses the WebClient to call the URL. First we determine what type of request we want to make; this is a get() in our case. Next we specify the URL using the uri() method with the parameters we want. That finishes our request, which we can now execute through the receive() method. Finally, we map the response body using the bodyToMono() method.

As this is a reactive implementation, this code doesn't do anything yet. We need to combine the Mono results into a new result. For this we can use zip, extract both results (which will then execute them in parallel), and produce EnrichedBook.

As the `WebClient` reuses parts of the same infrastructure as the rest of WebFlux, we can reuse the same exception handling we used earlier. When calling `http://localhost:8090/books/9780618260300` from the command line using `curl` or `HTTPie`, you will get output similar to Figure 4-15.

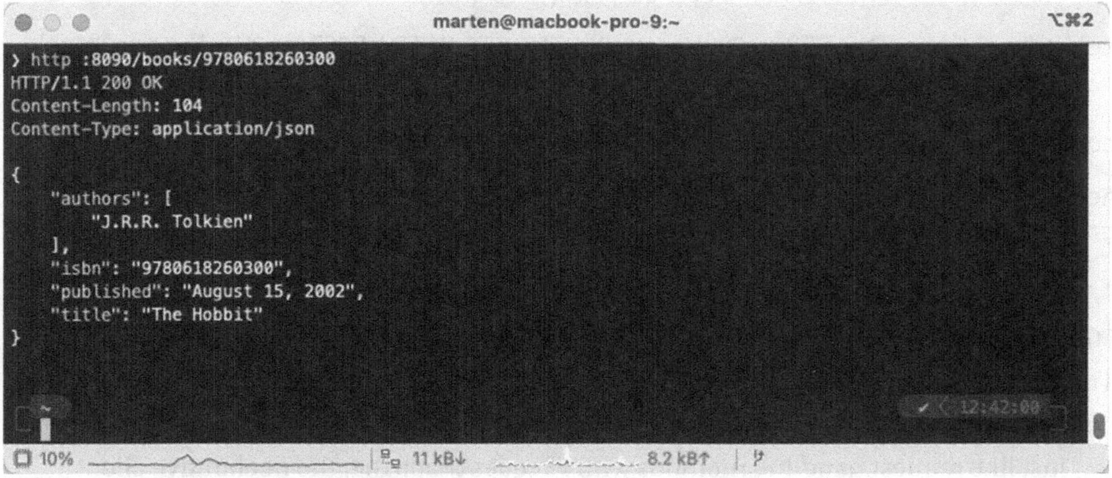
marten@macbook-pro-9:~
⌥⌘2
› http :8090/books/9780618260300
HTTP/1.1 200 OK
Content-Length: 104
Content-Type: application/json
{
"authors": [
"J.R.R. Tolkien"
],
"isbn": "9780618260300",
"published": "August 15, 2002",
"title": "The Hobbit"
}
12:42:00
10%
11 kB↓
8.2 kB↑

Figure 4-15. *Enriched book result*

Use a Declarative Client

Spring Framework 6 introduced the declarative HTTP client. With this it is possible to write an interface with some annotations. At runtime a proxy will be created that will handle the request/response including the mapping and exception handling.

The starting point is an interface with an `@HttpExchange` annotation (or one of the derived annotations like `@GetExchange` and `@PostExchange`) on either the class or the method(s). It functions much in the same way as the `@RequestMapping` annotation from the server API.

Using the `@HttpExchange` annotation, it is possible to set some properties (see Table 4-9).

Table 4-9. *HttpExchange Properties*

Attribute	Description
value or url	The URL for the request; can be a full URL, a path relative to the type level @HttpExchange, or the preset base URI.
Method	The HTTP method to use; DELETE, GET, PATCH, POST, or PUT. The default is empty.
contentType	The media type to send for the Content-Type header; the default is empty.
Accept	The media type for the Accept header.

In addition to the @HttpExchange annotation, there are @DeleteExchange, @GetExchange, @PatchExchange, @PostExchange, and @PutExchange annotations. These can be used instead of @HttpExchange with a specific method value. Using these annotations makes it more explicit.

Just like request handling methods with @RequestMapping, the declarative client supports multiple arguments, annotations, and return types. It reuses common parts of the web infrastructure for this. See Table 4-10.

Table 4-10. *HttpExchange-Supported Method Arguments*

Type	Description
`java.net.URI`	Dynamically sets the URL for the request; overrides the `url` attribute from the `@HttpExchange`.
`UriBuilderFactory`	Provides a `UriBuilderFactory` to expand the URI template and URI variables. Used instead of the `UriBuilderFactory` of the underlying client.
`HttpMethod`	Dynamically sets the HTTP method to use for the request; overrides the `method` attribute from the `@HttpExchange`.
`MultipartFile`	Adds a request part from a `MultipartFile`, typically used with Spring MVC to indicate an uploaded file.
`@CookieValue`	Adds cookies to the outgoing request. The argument can be a `Map<String, ?>` or a `MultiValueMap<String, ?>` with multiple cookies or individual values. Uses the type conversion for non-`String` values.
`@RequestHeader`	Adds request headers to the outgoing request. The argument can be a `Map<String, ?>` or a `MultiValueMap<String, ?>` with multiple headers or individual values. Uses the type conversion for non-`String` values.
`@PathVariable`	Adds a variable to expand a placeholder in the request URL. The argument can be a `Map<String, ?>` for multiple values or an individual value. Uses the type conversion for non-`String` values.
`@RequestBody`	Provides the body of the request either as an `Object` to be serialized or as a Reactive Streams Publisher such as `Mono`, `Flux`, or any other async type supported through the configured `ReactiveAdapterRegistry`.
`@RequestParam`	Adds request parameters. Can be a `Map<String, ?>` / `MultiValueMap<String, ?>` for multiple values. Or can be an individual type. Uses the type conversion for non-`String` values. When `contentType` is `application/x-www-form-urlencoded`, the parameters are added to the request body.
`@RequestPart`	Adds a request part that can be a `String` (becomes a form field), a `Resource`, an `Object` to be encoded as JSON (or whatever is configured), `HttpEntity` including headers, a Spring `Part`, or a supported Reactive Streams Publisher.

In addition to the method arguments, there is support for several method return types. See Table 4-11.

Table 4-11. *HttpExchange Supported Method Return-Types*

Type	Description
void	Performs the request; no response.
HttpHeaders	Performs the request and returns only the headers.
<T>	Performs the request and returns the decoded body as type T.
ResponseEntity<Void>	Performs the request and returns a ResponseEntity with the status and headers.
ResponseEntity<T>	Performs the request and returns a ResponseEntity with the status and headers and the body decoded as type T.
Mono<Void>	Performs the request and drops the body if any.
Mono<HttpHeaders>	Performs the request, drops the body, and returns the headers.
Mono<T>	Performs the request and decodes the body to type T.
Flux<T>	Performs the request and decodes the body to a stream of type T.
Mono<ResponseEntity<Void>>	Performs the request, drops the body, and returns the ResponseEntity with headers and status.
Mono<ResponseEntity<T>>	Performs the request, decodes the body to type T, and returns a ResponseEntity with the body, headers, and status.
Mono<ResponseEntity<FluxT>>>	Performs the request, decodes the body to a stream of type T, and returns a ResponseEntity with a stream of T, headers, and status.

Given this information, we could provide two interfaces to provide access to the APIs that we need to call. Let's start with the API for the books. See Listing 4-43.

Listing 4-43. BookServiceClient Sources

```
package com.apress.springboot3recipes.library.rest;

import com.apress.springboot3recipes.library.Book;
import org.springframework.web.bind.annotation.PathVariable;
import org.springframework.web.service.annotation.GetExchange;
import reactor.core.publisher.Mono;

public interface BookServiceClient {

  @GetExchange("http://localhost:8080/books/{isbn}")
  Mono<Book> getBook(@PathVariable String isbn);
}
```

BookServiceClient has one method, which is annotated with @GetExchange. There is a provided value of http://localhost:8080/books/{isbn}, which is a URI template. The method takes a single argument isbn that has been annotated with @PathVariable. When calling this method, the value we pass in will be placed in the {isbn} part of the URI before executing the request. When the request has been sent, a response comes in that is converted to a Mono<Book>, just as we did with the WebClient.

Next we need an interface for the Open Library API as well. See Listing 4-44.

Listing 4-44. OpenLibraryClient Sources

```
package com.apress.springboot3recipes.library.rest;

import org.springframework.web.bind.annotation.PathVariable;
import org.springframework.web.service.annotation.GetExchange;
import org.springframework.web.service.annotation.HttpExchange;
import reactor.core.publisher.Mono;

import java.util.Map;

@HttpExchange(url = "https://openlibrary.org/isbn")
public interface OpenLibraryClient {

  @GetExchange("/{isbn}.json")
  Mono<Map> getInformation(@PathVariable String isbn);
}
```

OpenLibraryClient has an @HttpExchange method with the url attribute set. This will set a base URI for use for all other methods in this interface. This allows us to specify only relative URLs for all other methods. Now there is only a single method with an @GetExchange. This method also takes a single argument, isbn, which is placed in the URI template before executing. The response is turned into a Mono<Map> again just as before.

Now that the interfaces are ready, we need to expose them in our configuration, but we cannot create an instance from an interface. This is where HttpServiceProxyFactory comes into play; it creates a proxy at runtime for these interfaces. To do this, we need to add some configuration to our application. See Listing 4-45.

Listing 4-45. HttpServiceProxyFactory Configuration

```
@Bean
public WebClient webClient(WebClient.Builder builder) {
  var httpClient = HttpClient.create().followRedirect(true);
  var connector = new ReactorClientHttpConnector(httpClient);
  return builder.clientConnector(connector).build();
}

@Bean
public HttpServiceProxyFactory httpServiceProxyFactory(WebClient client) {
  var adapter = WebClientAdapter.create(client);
  return HttpServiceProxyFactory.builderFor(adapter).build();
}

@Bean
public BookServiceClient bookServiceClient(HttpServiceProxyFactory
factory) {
  return factory.createClient(BookServiceClient.class);
}

@Bean
public OpenLibraryClient openLibraryClient(HttpServiceProxyFactory
factory) {
  return factory.createClient(OpenLibraryClient.class);
}
```

As the WebClient cannot be used directly, we need to wrap it in a WebClientAdapter, which adapts the WebClient to the HttpExchangeAdapter interface.

HttpExchangeAdapter has three implementations: RestClientAdapter, RestTemplateAdapter, and WebClientAdapter. The first two are used in Chapter 3 and are blocking.

HttpServiceProxyFactory in turn is used to create proxies for BookServiceClient and OpenLibraryClient. This is simply done by calling createClient with the given interface on HttpServiceProxyFactory. See Listing 4-46.

Listing 4-46. EnrichedBookController with Declarative Clients

```java
package com.apress.springboot3recipes.library.rest;

import com.apress.springboot3recipes.library.Book;
import com.apress.springboot3recipes.library.EnrichedBook;
import org.springframework.http.ResponseEntity;
import org.springframework.web.bind.annotation.GetMapping;
import org.springframework.web.bind.annotation.PathVariable;
import org.springframework.web.bind.annotation.RequestMapping;
import org.springframework.web.bind.annotation.RestController;
import org.springframework.web.client.RestClientResponseException;
import reactor.core.publisher.Mono;

import java.util.Map;

@RestController
@RequestMapping("/books")
public class EnrichedBookController {

  private final BookServiceClient bookServiceClient;
  private final OpenLibraryClient openLibraryClient;

  public EnrichedBookController(BookServiceClient bookServiceClient,
                                OpenLibraryClient openLibraryClient) {
    this.bookServiceClient = bookServiceClient;
    this.openLibraryClient = openLibraryClient;
  }

  @GetMapping("/{isbn}")
  public Mono<ResponseEntity<EnrichedBook>> get(@PathVariable("isbn")
  String isbn) {
```

```java
    var book = bookServiceClient.getBook(isbn);
    var library = openLibraryClient.getInformation(isbn);
    var enriched = enrich(book, library);
    return enriched.map(ResponseEntity::ok).onErrorResume(this::han
    dleError);
}

private Mono<ResponseEntity<EnrichedBook>> handleError(Throwable ex) {
  if (ex instanceof RestClientResponseException rex) {
    return Mono.just(ResponseEntity.status(rex.getStatusCode()).build());
  }
  return Mono.just(ResponseEntity.internalServerError().build());
}

private Mono<EnrichedBook> enrich(Mono<Book> book, Mono<Map> ol) {
  return Mono.zip(book, ol)
    .map( (res) -> enrich(res.getT1(), res.getT2()));
}

private EnrichedBook enrich(Book book, Map json) {
  var publishDate = extractPublishData(json);
  return new EnrichedBook(book.isbn(), book.title(), publishDate, book.
  authors());
}

private String extractPublishData(Map json) {
  return (String) json.getOrDefault("publish_date", "");
}
}
```

Notice that we now can call methods on the interface instead of worrying about constructing a proper request. That is all hidden behind the interface facade and inside the proxy. This makes it easier to write reusable API clients for use in your applications.

Finally, notice that the exception handling didn't change. As the declarative clients still use the same infrastructure as the WebClient, the exception handling doesn't need to change.

When rerunning the application and requesting the information for the books, the output should still be the same as in Figure 4-15.

CHAPTER 5

Spring Security

In this chapter, we will take a look at the Spring Security integration for Spring Boot. Spring Security can be used for both authenticating and authorizing users for your application. Spring Security has a pluggable mechanism for both the authentication and authorization process and by default supports different mechanisms. For authentication, Spring Security has out-of-the-box support for JDBC, LDAP, and property files.

5-1. Enable Security in Your Spring Boot Application
Problem

You have a Spring Boot–based application and you want to enable security in it.

Solution

Add `spring-boot-starter-security` as a dependency to set up and configure security automatically for your application.

How It Works

To get started, you will need to import the libraries for Spring Security into your application. To do this, you can add `spring-boot-starter-security` to your list of dependencies. See Listing 5-1.

Listing 5-1. Spring Security Starter Dependency

```
<dependency>
  <groupId>org.springframework.boot</groupId>
  <artifactId>spring-boot-starter-security</artifactId>
</dependency>
```

© Marten Deinum 2024
M. Deinum, *Spring Boot 3 Recipes*, https://doi.org/10.1007/979-8-8688-0113-6_5

This will add the `spring-security-core`, `spring-security-config`, and `spring-security-web` dependencies to your project. Spring Boot detects the availability of Spring Security and automatically enables security.

Spring Boot will configure Spring Security with the following:

- Authentication with basic authentication and form login

- HTTP headers for security

- Servlet API integration

- Anonymous login

- Caching of resources disabled

⚠️   Spring Boot will add a default user, named `user` and with a generated password, that is visible in the startup logs. This is intended only to be used for testing, prototyping, or demos. Do not use the generated user in a live system.

When adding the dependency `spring-boot-starter-security` to Recipe 3-2, it will automatically secure all exposed endpoints. At startup, the generated password will be logged (see Figure 5-1).

```
  .   ____          _            __ _ _
 /\\ / ___'_ __ _ _(_)_ __  __ _ \ \ \ \
( ( )\___ | '_ | '_| | '_ \/ _` | \ \ \ \
 \\/  ___)| |_)| | | | | || (_| |  ) ) ) )
  '  |____| .__|_| |_|_| |_\__, | / / / /
 =========|_|==============|___/=/_/_/_/
 :: Spring Boot ::                (v3.2.0)

2023-11-24T11:15:41.242+01:00  INFO 13102 --- [           main] c.a.s.library.LibraryApplication         : Starting LibraryApplication using Java 21.0.1 with PID 131
2023-11-24T11:15:41.247+01:00  INFO 13102 --- [           main] c.a.s.library.LibraryApplication         : No active profile set, falling back to 1 default profile:
2023-11-24T11:15:42.308+01:00  INFO 13102 --- [           main] o.s.b.w.embedded.tomcat.TomcatWebServer  : Tomcat initialized with port 8080 (http)
2023-11-24T11:15:42.324+01:00  INFO 13102 --- [           main] o.apache.catalina.core.StandardService   : Starting service [Tomcat]
2023-11-24T11:15:42.324+01:00  INFO 13102 --- [           main] o.apache.catalina.core.StandardEngine    : Starting Servlet engine: [Apache Tomcat/10.1.16]
2023-11-24T11:15:42.375+01:00  INFO 13102 --- [           main] o.a.c.c.C.[Tomcat].[localhost].[/]        : Initializing Spring embedded WebApplicationContext
2023-11-24T11:15:42.375+01:00  INFO 13102 --- [           main] w.s.c.ServletWebServerApplicationContext : Root WebApplicationContext: initialization completed in 18
2023-11-24T11:15:42.714+01:00  WARN 13102 --- [           main] .s.s.UserDetailsServiceAutoConfiguration :

Using generated security password: 80518386-47d4-40de-be1c-76a59bd54fee

This generated password is for development use only. Your security configuration must be updated before running your application in production.

2023-11-24T11:15:42.834+01:00  INFO 13102 --- [           main] o.s.s.web.DefaultSecurityFilterChain      : Will secure any request with [org.springframework.security
```

Figure 5-1. *Generated password output*

Spring Boot exposes some properties to configure the default user. You can find them in the `spring.security` namespace (see Table 5-1).

Table 5-1. *Properties for Default User*

Property	Description
`spring.security.user.name`	The default username; the default is `user`.
`spring.security.user.password`	Password for the default user; the default is UUID.
`spring.security.user.roles`	Roles for the default user. The default is none.

After adding the dependency and starting `LibraryApplication`, the endpoints are secured. When trying to obtain a list of books from `http://localhost:8080/books`, the result will be an HTTP result with status 401: Unauthorized (see Figure 5-2).

```
●●●                          marten — -zsh — 80×20
HTTP/1.1 401
Cache-Control: no-cache, no-store, max-age=0, must-revalidate
Connection: keep-alive
Content-Length: 0
Date: Fri, 24 Nov 2023 10:20:48 GMT
Expires: 0
Keep-Alive: timeout=60
Pragma: no-cache
Set-Cookie: JSESSIONID=C76410C659E5F950D5C8A17807D7F9D9; Path=/; HttpOnly
Vary: Origin
Vary: Access-Control-Request-Method
Vary: Access-Control-Request-Headers
WWW-Authenticate: Basic realm="Realm"
X-Content-Type-Options: nosniff
X-Frame-Options: DENY
X-XSS-Protection: 0


marten@macbook-pro-9 ~ %
```

Figure 5-2. *Unauthenticated access result*

When adding the correct authentication headers (username `user` with the password from the logging or as specified in the `spring.security.user.password` property), the result will be the regular list of books (see Figure 5-3).

```
● ● ●                    marten — -zsh — 80×30
marten@macbook-pro-9 ~ % http -a user:80518386-47d4-40de-be1c-76a59bd54fee :8080
/books
HTTP/1.1 200
Cache-Control: no-cache, no-store, max-age=0, must-revalidate
Connection: keep-alive
Content-Type: application/json
Date: Fri, 24 Nov 2023 10:21:54 GMT
Expires: 0
Keep-Alive: timeout=60
Pragma: no-cache
Transfer-Encoding: chunked
Vary: Origin
Vary: Access-Control-Request-Method
Vary: Access-Control-Request-Headers
X-Content-Type-Options: nosniff
X-Frame-Options: DENY
X-XSS-Protection: 0

[
    {
        "authors": [
            "J.R.R. Tolkien"
        ],
        "isbn": "9780618260300",
        "title": "The Hobbit"
    },
    {
        "authors": [
            "George Orwell"
        ],
```

Figure 5-3. *Authenticated access result*

Test the Security

When using Spring Security to secure your endpoints with an @WebMvcTest annotation, the security infrastructure will be automatically applied. Spring Security provides some nice annotations to help in writing tests (see Table 5-2).

Table 5-2. *Spring Security Annotations for Testing*

Annotation	Description
@WithMockUser	Run as the user with the given username, password, and roles/authorities
@WithAnonymousUser	Run as an anonymous user
@WithUserDetails	Run as the user with the configured name; does a lookup in the UserDetailsService

> ℹ️ If you want to test your controllers without security, you can disable them by excluding SecurityAutoConfiguration from being run. To do this, specify excludeAutoConfiguration on the @WebMvcTest annotation.

To use these annotations, add a dependency to spring-security-test.

```
<dependency>
    <groupId>org.springframework.security</groupId>
    <artifactId>spring-security-test</artifactId>
    <scope>test</scope>
</dependency>
```

With this dependency, BookControllerTest from Recipe 3-2 can be extended and fixed again. If you don't mind disabling security for your test, you could add @WebMvcTest(value = BookController.class, excludeAutoConfiguration = SecurityAutoConfiguration.class) to the test class. With it, the security filter won't be added, and thus security will be disabled. The tests will run and succeed. See Listing 5-2.

Listing 5-2. Test with Security Disabled

```
@WebMvcTest(value = BookController.class, excludeAutoConfiguration =
SecurityAutoConfiguration.class)
class BookControllerUnsecuredTest {
}
```

If, however, you want to test with security enabled, you will need to make some minor modifications to the test class. First, add @WithMockUser to run with an authenticated user. Second, because Spring Security by default enables CSRF protection, a header or parameter needs to be added to the request. When using Mock MVC, Spring Security provides a RequestPostProcessor for that, the CsrfRequestPostProcessor. SecurityMockMvcRequestPostProcessors contains factory methods to easily use them. See Listing 5-3.

Listing 5-3. Test with Security Enabled

```
package com.apress.springboot3recipes.library.rest;

import org.junit.jupiter.api.Test;
import org.springframework.beans.factory.annotation.Autowired;
import org.springframework.boot.test.autoconfigure.web.servlet.WebMvcTest;
import org.springframework.boot.test.mock.mockito.MockBean;
import org.springframework.security.test.context.support.WithMockUser;

import static org.mockito.ArgumentMatchers.any;
import static org.mockito.Mockito.when;
import static org.springframework.security.test.web.servlet.request.
SecurityMockMvcRequestPostProcessors.csrf;
import static org.springframework.test.web.servlet.request.MockMvcRequest
Builders.post;
import static org.springframework.test.web.servlet.result.MockMvcResult
Matchers.header;
import static org.springframework.test.web.servlet.result.MockMvcResult
Matchers.status;

@WebMvcTest(BookController.class)
@WithMockUser
public class BookControllerSecuredTest {

  @Autowired
  private MockMvc mockMvc;

  @MockBean
  private BookService bookService;

  @Test
```

```
void shouldAddBook() throws Exception {

  when(bookService.create(any(Book.class)))
    .thenReturn(new Book("123456789", "Test Book Stored", List.
    of("T. Author")));

  mockMvc.perform(post("/books")
    .with(csrf())
    .contentType(MediaType.APPLICATION_JSON)
    .content("{ \"isbn\" : \"123456789\"}, \"title\" : \"Test Book\",
    \"authors\" : [\"T. Author\"]"))
    .andExpect(status().isCreated())
    .andExpect(header().string("Location", "http://localhost/
    books/123456789"));
  }
}
```

The test now uses the user as specified in @WithMockUser; here it uses the default user with user as the username and password as the password. The line with(csrf()) takes care of adding the CSRF token to the request.

Which option to use depends on the needs you have. If for instance in your controller you need the current user, then security should probably be enabled, and an @WithMockUser or @WithUserDetails annotation should be used. If that isn't the case and you can test your controller without the security (and you don't have additional security rules, as in Recipe 5-2), you can run with disabled security.

Perform Integration Testing for Security

When using @SpringBootTest to write an integration test it depends on the used webEnvironment if you can use the @With* annotations. With the default mocked environment, it still will work. See Listing 5-4.

Listing 5-4. Integration Test Using Mocks with Security Enabled

```
@SpringBootTest
@WithMockUser
@AutoConfigureMockMvc
class BookControllerIntegrationMockTest {
}
```

This test will create an almost full-blown application but still uses Mock MVC to access the endpoints. It still runs in the same process as the tests, which is why the @WithMockUser annotation and with(csrf()) still work. When running the test on an external port, it won't work anymore.

To test the application on a port, you would need to run the tests through the test client TestRestTemplate and/or WebTestClient and pass the authentication headers or implement the flow by first doing a form-based login in your integration test. To write a successful integration test, inject TestRestTemplate, and before doing the actual request, use the withBasicAuth helper method to set the basic authentication header. See Listing 5-5.

💡 When writing this test and using the default user, you might want to set a default password using spring.security.user.password. This recipe uses @TestPropertySource to do so, but you could add it to the application.properties file as well.

Listing 5-5. Integration Test Using TestRestTemplate with Security Enabled

```
@SpringBootTest(webEnvironment = SpringBootTest.WebEnvironment.RANDOM_PORT)
@TestPropertySource(properties = "spring.security.user.password=s3cr3t")
class BookControllerIntegrationTest {

    @Autowired
    private TestRestTemplate testRestTemplate;

    @MockBean
    private BookService bookService;

    @Test
    void shouldReturnListOfBooks() {

        when(bookService.findAll()).thenReturn(Arrays.asList(
            new Book("123", "Spring 5 Recipes", List.of("Marten Deinum", "Josh
            Long")),
            new Book("321", "Pro Spring MVC", List.of("Marten Deinum", "Colin
            Yates"))));
```

```
ResponseEntity<Book[]> books = testRestTemplate
        .withBasicAuth("user", "s3cr3t")
        .getForEntity("/books", Book[].class);

    assertThat(books.getStatusCode()).isEqualTo(HttpStatus.OK);
    assertThat(books.getBody()).hasSize(2);
  }
}
```

The test uses the default configured TestRestTemplate to issue a request. withBasicAuth uses the default user and presets s3cr3t as the username and password to send to the server. getForEntity can be used to get the result including some additional information about the response. Using ResponseEntity, it is also possible to validate the status code, etc.

When testing a WebFlux-based application instead of TestRestTemplate, you would need WebTestClient (see also Chapter 4 for more information on Spring WebFlux). You can use the headers() function to add additional headers to the request. It exposes the HttpHeaders instance, which in turn has the convenient setBasicAuth method to apply the basic authentication. See Listing 5-6.

Listing 5-6. Integration Test Using WebTestClient with Security Enabled

```
@SpringBootTest(webEnvironment = SpringBootTest.WebEnvironment.RANDOM_PORT)
@TestPropertySource(properties = "spring.security.user.password=s3cr3t")
@AutoConfigureWebTestClient
class BookControllerIntegrationWebClientTest {

  @Autowired
  private WebTestClient webTestClient;

  @MockBean
  private BookService bookService;

  @Test
  void shouldReturnListOfBooks() {

    when(bookService.findAll()).thenReturn(Arrays.asList(
        new Book("123", "Spring 5 Recipes", List.of("Marten Deinum", "Josh
        Long")),
```

```
        new Book("321", "Pro Spring MVC", List.of("Marten Deinum", "Colin
        Yates"))));

    webTestClient
            .get()
              .uri("/books")
              .headers( httpHeaders -> httpHeaders.setBasicAuth("user",
              "s3cr3t"))
            .exchange()
              .expectStatus().isOk()
              .expectBodyList(Book.class).hasSize(2);
    }
```

The request is built and "fired" using exchange(). Then the result is expected to be an HTTP 200 (OK), and the result contains two books.

5-2. Log In to Web Applications
Problem

A secure application requires its users to log in before they can access certain secure functions. This is especially important for applications running on the open Internet, because hackers can easily reach them. Most applications have to provide a way for users to input their credentials to log in.

Solution

Spring Security supports multiple ways for users to log into a web application. It supports form-based login by providing a default web page that contains a login form. You can also provide a custom web page as the login page. In addition, Spring Security supports HTTP Basic authentication by processing the Basic authentication credentials presented in HTTP request headers. HTTP Basic authentication can also be used for authenticating requests made with remoting protocols and web services.

Some parts of your application may allow for anonymous access (e.g., access to the welcome page). Spring Security provides an anonymous login service that can assign a principal and grant authorities to an anonymous user so that you can handle an anonymous user like a normal user when defining security policies.

Spring Security also supports remember-me login, which is able to remember a user's identity across multiple browser sessions so that a user doesn't need to log in again after logging in for the first time.

How It Works

Spring Boot enables the default security settings when no explicit security configuration can be found. When one or more are found, it will use them to configure the security. Security configurations are those with an @EnableWebSecurity and/or @EnableMethodSecurity. Including the @EnableWebSecurity annotation will automatically pull in the HttpSecurityConfiguration class, which contains the default security settings and possibility to customize them.

To help you better understand the various login mechanisms in isolation, let's first discuss the default security configuration. Note that the login services introduced are registered automatically if you include @EnableWebSecurity.

Before enabling the authentication features, you will have to enable the basic Spring Security requirements. You need at least to configure exception handling and security context integration. See Listing 5-7.

Listing 5-7. Security Context Integration and Exception Handling

```
@Configuration
@EnableWebSecurity
public class LibrarySecurityConfig {

  @Bean
  public SecurityFilterChain security(HttpSecurity http) throws Exception {
    http.securityContext(Customizer.withDefaults());
    http.exceptionHandling(Customizer.withDefaults());
    return http.build();
  }
}
```

Without these basics, Spring Security wouldn't store the user after doing a login, and it wouldn't do proper exception translation for security-related exceptions (they would simply bubble up, which might expose some of your internals to the outside world). You also might want to enable the Servlet API integration so that you can use the methods on HttpServletRequest to do checks in your view. See Listing 5-8.

Listing 5-8. Servlet API Defaults

```
@Configuration
@EnableWebSecurity
public class LibrarySecurityConfig {

  @Bean
  public SecurityFilterChain security(HttpSecurity http) throws Exception {
    http.servletApi(Customizer.withDefaults());
    return http.build();
  }
}
```

HTTP Basic Authentication

The HTTP Basic authentication support can be configured via the httpBasic() method. When HTTP Basic authentication is required, a browser will typically display a login dialog box or a browser-specific login page for users to log in. See Listing 5-9.

Listing 5-9. Enabling Basic Authentication with the Defaults

```
@Configuration
@EnableWebSecurity
public class LibrarySecurityConfig {

  @Bean
  public SecurityFilterChain security(HttpSecurity http) throws Exception {
    http.httpBasic(Customizer.withDefaults());
    return http.build();
  }
}
```

Form-Based Login

The form-based login service will render a web page that contains a login form for users to input their login details and process the login form submission. It's configured via the formLogin method. See Listing 5-10.

Listing 5-10. Enable Form-Based Login

```
@Configuration
@EnableWebSecurity
public class LibrarySecurityConfig {

  @Bean
  public SecurityFilterChain security(HttpSecurity http) throws Exception {
    http.formLogin(Customizer.withDefaults());
    return http.build();
  }
}
```

By default, Spring Security automatically creates a login page and maps it to the URL /login. So, you can add a link to your application (e.g., in index.html of Recipe 3-3), referring to this URL for login:

```
<a th:href="/login" href="#">Login</a>
```

If you don't prefer the default login page, you can provide a custom login page of your own. For example, you can create the login.html file in src/main/resources/templates (when using Thymeleaf). See Listing 5-11.

Listing 5-11. Custom Login Page

```
<!DOCTYPE html>
<html xmlns:th="http://www.thymeleaf.org">
<head>
    <title>Login</title>
    <link type="text/css" rel="stylesheet"
          href="https://cdnjs.cloudflare.com/ajax/libs/semantic-ui/2.2.10/
          semantic.min.css">
    <style type="text/css">
```

```
        body {
            background-color: #DADADA;
        }
        body > .grid {
            height: 100%;
        }
        .column {
            max-width: 450px;
        }
    </style>
</head>

<body>
<div class="ui middle aligned center aligned grid">
  <div class="column">
    <h2 class="ui header">Log-in to your account</h2>
    <form method="POST" th:action="@{/login.html}" class="ui large form">
      <input type="hidden"  th:name="${_csrf.parameterName}" th:value="${_
      csrf.token}"/>
      <div class="ui stacked segment">
        <div class="field">
          <div class="ui left icon input">
            <i class="user icon"></i>
            <input type="text" name="username" placeholder="E-mail
            address">
          </div>
        </div>
        <div class="field">
          <div class="ui left icon input">
            <i class="lock icon"></i>
            <input type="password" name="password" placeholder="Password">
          </div>
        </div>
        <button class="ui fluid large submit green button">Login</button>
      </div>
    </form>
```

```
  </div>
</div>
</body>
</html>
```

For Spring Security to display your custom login page when a login is requested, you have to specify its URL in the `loginPage` configuration method (see Listing 5-12).

Listing 5-12. Custom Login Page Configuration

```
@Configuration
@EnableWebSecurity
public class LibrarySecurityConfig {

  @Bean
  public SecurityFilterChain security(HttpSecurity http) throws Exception {
    http.formLogin( (login) ->
            login.loginPage("/login.html")
    return http.build();
  }
}
```

Finally, add a view resolver to map /login to the login.html page. For this you can have the `LibrarySecurityConfig` implement `WebMvcConfigurer` and implement the `addViewControllers` methods.

```
@Configuration
public class LibrarySecurityConfig extends WebSecurityConfigurerAdapter
                                   implements WebMvcConfigurer {

  ...

  public void addViewControllers(ViewControllerRegistry registry) {
    registry.addViewController("/login").setViewName("login");
  }
}
```

If the login page is displayed by Spring Security when a user requests a secure URL, the user will be redirected to the target URL once the login succeeds. However, if the user requests the login page directly via its URL, by default the user will be redirected to the context path's root (i.e., http://localhost:8080/) after a successful login. If you have not defined a welcome page in your web deployment descriptor, you may want to redirect the user to a default target URL when the login succeeds. See Listing 5-13.

Listing 5-13. Custom Login Page Configuration with Success URL

```
@Configuration
@EnableWebSecurity
public class LibrarySecurityConfig {

  @Bean
  public SecurityFilterChain security(HttpSecurity http) throws Exception {
    http.formLogin( (login) ->
            login.loginPage("/login.html")
              .defaultSuccessUrl("/books")
    return http.build();
  }
}
```

If you use the default login page created by Spring Security, then when a login fails, Spring Security will render the login page again with the error message. However, if you specify a custom login page, you will have to configure authentication-failure-url to specify which URL to redirect to when there is a login error. For example, you can redirect to the custom login page again with the error request parameter. See Listing 5-14.

Listing 5-14. Custom Login Page Configuration with Failure Configuration

```
@Configuration
@EnableWebSecurity
public class LibrarySecurityConfig {

  @Bean
  public SecurityFilterChain security(HttpSecurity http) throws Exception {
    http.formLogin( (login) ->
            login.loginPage("/login.html")
              .defaultSuccessUrl("/books")
```

```
        .failureUrl("/login.html?error=true").permitAll());
    return http.build();
  }
}
```

Then your login page should test whether the error request parameter is present. If an error has occurred, you will have to display the error message by accessing the session scope attribute SPRING_SECURITY_LAST_EXCEPTION, which stores the last exception for the current user. See Listing 5-15.

Listing 5-15. Login Page Display Error

```
<div th:if="${param.error}">
  <div class="ui error message" style="display: block;">
    Authentication Failed<br/>
    Reason : <span th:text="${session.SPRING_SECURITY_LAST_EXCEPTION.
    message}">Exception Here</span>
  </div>
</div>
```

The Logout Service

The logout service provides a handler to handle logout requests. It can be configured via the logout() configuration method. See Listing 5-16.

Listing 5-16. Default Logout Configuration

```
@Configuration
@EnableWebSecurity
public class LibrarySecurityConfig {

  @Bean
  public SecurityFilterChain security(HttpSecurity http) throws Exception {
    http.logout(Customizer.withDefaults());
    return http.build();
  }
}
```

By default, it's mapped to the URL /logout and will react to POST requests only. You can add a small HTML form to your page to log out.

```
<form th:action="/logout" method="post"><button>Logout</button><form>
```

ⓘ   When using CSRF protection, don't forget to add the CSRF token to the form; otherwise, logout will fail.

By default, a user will be redirected to the context path's root when the logout succeeds, but sometimes, you may want to direct the user to another URL, which you can do by using the logoutSuccessUrl configuration method. See Listing 5-17.

Listing 5-17. Logout Configuration with Success URL

```
@Configuration
@EnableWebSecurity
public class LibrarySecurityConfig implements WebMvcConfigurer {

  @Bean
  public SecurityFilterChain security(HttpSecurity http) throws Exception {
    http.logout( (logout) -> logout.logoutSuccessUrl("/"));
    return http.build();
  }
}
```

After logout, you might notice that when using the browser back button, you will still be able to see the previous pages, even if your logout was successful. This has to do with the fact that the browser caches the pages. By enabling the security headers, with the headers() configuration method, the browser will be instructed to not cache the page. See Listing 5-18.

Listing 5-18. Security Headers Configuration

```
@Configuration
@EnableWebSecurity
public class LibrarySecurityConfig {

  @Bean
  public SecurityFilterChain security(HttpSecurity http) throws Exception {
    http.headers(Customizer.withDefaults());
    return http.build();
  }
}
```

In addition to the no-cache headers, this will also disable content-sniffing and enable x-frame protection. With this enabled and using the browser back button, you will be redirected to the login page again.

Anonymous Login

The anonymous login service can be configured via the anonymous() method in Java config, where you can customize the username and authorities of an anonymous user, whose default values are anonymousUser and ROLE_ANONYMOUS. See Listing 5-19.

Listing 5-19. Anonymous Login Configuration

```
@Configuration
@EnableWebSecurity
public class LibrarySecurityConfig {

  @Bean
  public SecurityFilterChain security(HttpSecurity http) throws Exception {
    http.anonymous( (anon) ->
        anon.principal("guest").authorities("ROLE_GUEST"));
    return http.build();
  }
}
```

Remember-Me Support

Remember-me support can be configured via the `rememberMe()` method in Java config. By default, it encodes the username, the password, the remember-me expiration time, and a private key as a token, and stores it as a cookie in the user's browser. The next time the user accesses the same web application, this token will be detected so that the user can log in automatically. See Listing 5-20.

Listing 5-20. Remember-Me Configuration

```
@Configuration
@EnableWebSecurity
public class LibrarySecurityConfig {

  @Bean
  public SecurityFilterChain security(HttpSecurity http) throws Exception {
    http.rememberMe(Customizer.withDefaults());
    return http.build();
  }
}
```

However, static remember-me tokens can cause security issues, because they may be captured by hackers. Spring Security supports rolling tokens for more advanced security needs, but this requires a database to persist the tokens. For details about rolling remember-me token deployment, please refer to the Spring Security reference documentation.

5-3. Authenticate Users

Problem

When a user attempts to log into your application to access its secure resources, you have to authenticate the user's principal and grant authorities to this user.

Solution

In Spring Security, authentication is performed by one or more
AuthenticationProviders, connected as a chain. If any of these providers authenticates
a user successfully, that user will be able to log into the application. If any provider
reports that the user is disabled or locked or that the credential is incorrect, or if
no provider can authenticate the user, then the user will be unable to log into this
application.

Spring Security supports multiple ways of authenticating users and includes built-
in provider implementations for them. You can easily configure these providers with
the built-in XML elements. Most common authentication providers authenticate
users against a user repository storing user details (e.g., in an application's memory, a
relational database, or an LDAP repository).

When storing user details in a repository, you should avoid storing user passwords
in clear text, because that makes them vulnerable to hackers. Instead, you should always
store encrypted passwords in your repository. A typical way to encrypt passwords is to
use a one-way hash function to encode the passwords. When a user enters a password
to log in, you apply the same hash function to this password and compare the result
with the one stored in the repository. Spring Security supports several algorithms for
encoding passwords (including BCrypt and SCrypt) and provides built-in password
encoders for these algorithms.

How It Works

Let's talk about how it works.

Authenticate Users with In-Memory Definitions

If you have only a few users in your application and you seldom modify their details, you
can consider defining the user details in Spring Security's configuration file so that they
will be loaded into your application's memory. See Listing 5-21.

Listing 5-21. In-Memory UserDetailsService Configuration

```
@Bean
public UserDetailsService userDetailsService() {
  var adminUser = User.withDefaultPasswordEncoder()
```

```
        .username("admin@books.io").password("secret")
        .authorities("ADMIN","USER").build();

var normalUser = User.withDefaultPasswordEncoder()
        .username("marten@books.io").password("user")
        .authorities("USER").build();

var disabledUser = User.withDefaultPasswordEncoder()
        .username("jdoe@books.io").password("unknown")
        .disabled(true)
        .authorities("USER").build();

return new InMemoryUserDetailsManager(adminUser, normalUser,
disabledUser);
    }
}
```

Using `UserBuild`, obtained through `User.withDefaultPasswordEncoder()`, you can construct users with an encrypted password. It will use the Spring Security default password encoding (which is by default encoded with BCrypt). For each user, you can specify a username, a password, a disabled status, and a set of granted authorities. A disabled user cannot log into an application. When you create the users, you can use them to create an `InMemoryUserDetailsManager`.

Authenticate Users Against a Database

More typically, user details should be stored in a database for easy maintenance. Spring Security has built-in support for querying user details from a database. By default, it queries user details, including authorities, with the SQL statements in Listing 5-22.

Listing 5-22. Default Spring Security SQL Queries

```sql
SELECT username, password, enabled
FROM   users
WHERE  username = ?

SELECT username, authority
FROM   authorities
WHERE  username = ?
```

For Spring Security to query user details with these SQL statements, you have to create the corresponding tables in your database. For example, you can create them in the database with the SQL statements in Listing 5-23.

Listing 5-23. DDL for Default Spring Security Table Structure

```
CREATE TABLE USERS
(
    USERNAME VARCHAR(50) NOT NULL,
    PASSWORD VARCHAR(50) NOT NULL,
    ENABLED  SMALLINT    NOT NULL,
    PRIMARY KEY (USERNAME)
);

CREATE TABLE AUTHORITIES
(
    USERNAME  VARCHAR(50) NOT NULL,
    AUTHORITY VARCHAR(50) NOT NULL,
    FOREIGN KEY (USERNAME) REFERENCES USERS
);
```

> ℹ️   Spring Security provides a `users.ddl` file in the `spring-security-core` JAR, under the `org.springframework.security.userdetails.jdbc` package. You could use this; however, this provided some limitations in the names (max length 50) and relations. So, you might be better off using your own script.

Next, you can input some user details into these tables for testing purposes. The data for these two tables is shown in Tables 5-3 and 5-4.

Table 5-3. *Testing User Data for the USERS Table*

USERNAME	PASSWORD	ENABLED
admin@books.io	{noop}secret	1
marten@books.io	{noop}user	1
jdoe@books.net	{noop}unknown	0

Table 5-4. *Testing User Data for the AUTHORITIES Table*

USERNAME	AUTHORITY
admin@books.io	ADMIN
admin@books.io	USER
marten@books.io	USER
jdoe@books.net	USER

ℹ️   The {noop} in the password field indicates that no encryption has been applied to the stored password. Spring Security uses, by default, delegation to determine which encoding method to use; the values can be {bcrypt}, {scrypt}, {pbkdf2}, and {sha256}. The {sha256} is mainly there for compatibility reasons and should be considered unsecure.

For Spring Security to access these tables, you have to declare a data source to be able to create connections to this database. Spring Security provides an out-of-the-box implementation of a UserDetailsService that can be used (the JdbcDaoImpl). When a UserDetailsService is detected as a bean, this is automatically picked up and used by Spring Security. See Listing 5-24.

Listing 5-24. JDBC Based UserDetailsService Configuration

```
@Bean
public UserDetailsService jdbcUserDetailsService(DataSource datasource) {
  var usd = new JdbcDaoImpl();
  usd.setDataSource(datasource);
  return usd;
}
```

However, in some cases, you may already have your own user repository defined in a legacy database. For example, suppose that the tables are created with the SQL statements in Listing 5-25 and that all users in the MEMBER table have the enabled status.

Listing 5-25. DDL for Custom Spring Security Table Structure (Sample)

```
CREATE TABLE MEMBER
(
    ID       BIGINT      NOT NULL,
    USERNAME VARCHAR(50) NOT NULL,
    PASSWORD VARCHAR(32) NOT NULL,
    PRIMARY KEY (ID)
);

CREATE TABLE MEMBER_ROLE
(
    MEMBER_ID BIGINT      NOT NULL,
    ROLE      VARCHAR(10) NOT NULL,
    FOREIGN KEY (MEMBER_ID) REFERENCES MEMBER
);
```

Suppose you have the legacy user data stored in these tables, as shown in Tables 5-5 and 5-6.

Table 5-5. *Legacy User Data in the MEMBER Table*

ID	USERNAME	PASSWORD
1	admin@ya2do.io	{noop}secret
2	marten@ya2do.io	{noop}user

Table 5-6. *Legacy User Data in the MEMBER_ROLE Table*

MEMBER_ID	ROLE
1	ROLE_ADMIN
1	ROLE_USER
2	ROLE_USER

Fortunately, Spring Security also supports using custom SQL statements to query a legacy database for user details. You can specify the statements for querying a user's information and authorities by setting the usersByUsernameQuery and authoritiesByUsernameQuery properties on the configured JdbcDaoImpl. See Listing 5-26.

Listing 5-26. Configuration for Custom Queries

```
@Configuration
public class LibrarySecurityConfig implements WebMvcConfigurer {

  private static final String USERS_BY_USERNAME_QUERY =
    """
      SELECT username, password, 'true' as enabled
      FROM member WHERE username = ?
      """;

  private static final String AUTHORITIES_BY_USERNAME_QUERY =
    """
      SELECT member.username, member_role.role as authorities
      FROM member, member_role
      WHERE   member.username = ? AND member.id = member_role.member_id
      """;

  @Bean
  public UserDetailsService jdbcUserDetailsService(DataSource datasource) {
    var usd = new JdbcDaoImpl();
    usd.setDataSource(datasource);
    usd.setUsersByUsernameQuery(USERS_BY_USERNAME_QUERY);
    usd.setAuthoritiesByUsernameQuery(AUTHORITIES_BY_USERNAME_QUERY);
    return usd;
  }
}
```

Authenticate Using OAuth2

Instead of manually storing passwords and users, often an external resource is being used, mostly by utilizing OAuth2 or OpenID Connect. This is supported by a large number of providers such as Google, Microsoft, and GitHub but also by companies that specialize in security like Keycloak and Okta. For this part we are going to use GitHub.

To start, register a new OAuth application with GitHub (see Figure 5-4). Make sure the Homepage URL and Authorization Callback URL are as in this image.

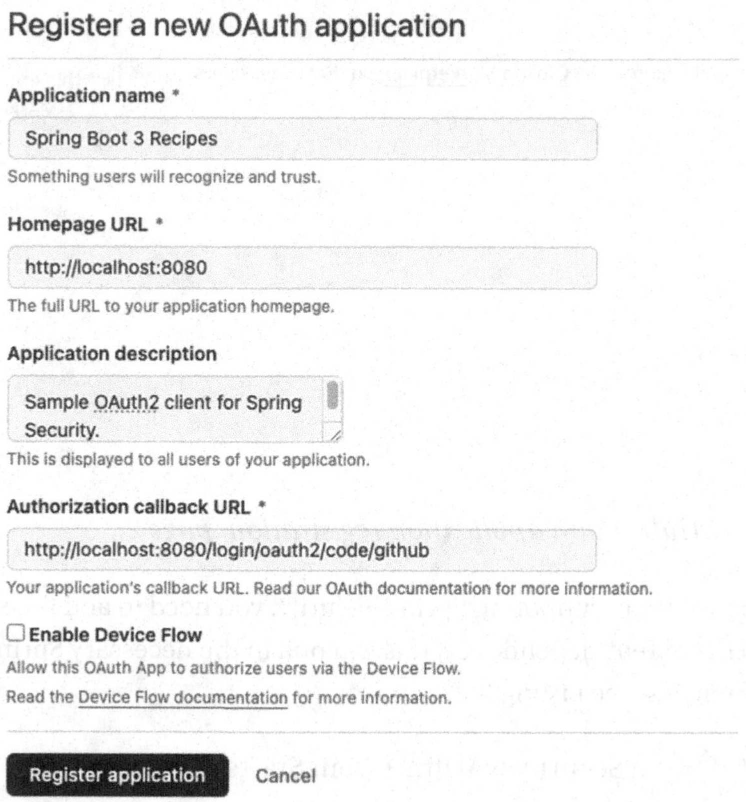

Register a new OAuth application

Application name *

Spring Boot 3 Recipes

Something users will recognize and trust.

Homepage URL *

http://localhost:8080

The full URL to your application homepage.

Application description

Sample OAuth2 client for Spring Security.

This is displayed to all users of your application.

Authorization callback URL *

http://localhost:8080/login/oauth2/code/github

Your application's callback URL. Read our OAuth documentation for more information.

☐ Enable Device Flow

Allow this OAuth App to authorize users via the Device Flow.

Read the Device Flow documentation for more information.

Register application   Cancel

Figure 5-4. *GitHub OAuth application registration*

After the registration on the next page, copy the `clientId` and generate a *secret* and copy that as well, as those are needed in the configuration. See Figure 5-5.

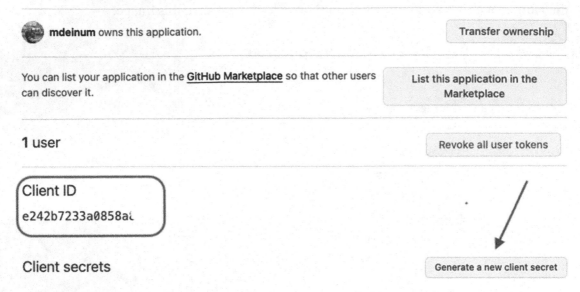

Figure 5-5. GitHub OAuth application registration, page 2

To enable the OAuth support in Spring Security, you need to add the `spring-boot-starter-oauth2-client` dependency; this will pull in the necessary Spring Security and OAuth dependencies. See Listing 5-27.

Listing 5-27. Spring Security OAUth2 Client Starter Dependency

```
<dependency>
  <groupId>org.springframework.boot</groupId>
  <artifactId>spring-boot-starter-oauth2-client</artifactId>
</dependency>
```

Now that this dependency in Spring Boot will automatically detect the classes and, when the proper configuration is given, will set up OAuth2 authentication. To configure it, we need to provide Spring Security with the `clientId` and `secret` from our GitHub OAuth application. See Listing 5-28.

Listing 5-28. Spring Security OAuth2 Client Configuration

```
spring:
  security:
    oauth2:
      client:
        registration:
          github:
            client-id: <clientId-from-Github>
            client-secret:  <secret-from-Github>
```

An important part here is the `github` name in this configuration. Spring Security will automatically configure the proper authentication URLs for certain providers, and GitHub is one of them. The out-of-the-box supported providers are GitHub, Google, Facebook, and Okta. For these providers, automatically `authorizationUri` is being set. This is the URL that you will be redirected to for authentication.

It is of course possible to fully customize the URL or the information retrieved from the OAuth provider if needed. For this, the defaults will suffice.

Now when launching the application and trying to access `http://localhost:8080/books`, you will be redirected to GitHub and will be asked to log in (if you aren't already) and to approve the access for the previously registered application. If you approve, you will be redirected to the application and will see the list of books.

Encrypt Passwords

Until now, you have been storing user details with clear-text passwords. But this approach is vulnerable to hacker attacks, so you should encrypt the passwords before storing them. Spring Security supports several algorithms for encrypting passwords. For example, you can choose BCrypt, a one-way hash algorithm, to encrypt your passwords.

ℹ️   You may need a helper to calculate BCrypt hashes for your passwords. You can do this online through, for example, `https://www.dailycred.com/article/bcrypt-calculator`, or you can simply create a class with a `main` method that uses Spring Security's `BCryptPasswordEncoder`. Another option, not commonly used, is to install the Spring Boot CLI and use that to generate the hashes.

Of course, you have to store the encrypted passwords in the database tables, instead of the clear-text passwords, as shown in Table 5-7. To store BCrypt hashes in the password field, the length of the field has to be at least 68 characters long (that is the length of the BCrypt hash plus the encryption type {bcrypt}).

Table 5-7. *User Data with Encrypted Passwords for the USERS Table*

USERNAME	PASSWORD	ENABLED
admin@ya2do.io	{bcrypt}$2a$10$E3mPTZb50e7sSW15fDx8Ne7hDZpfDjrmM PTTUp8wVjLTu.G5oPYCO	1
marten@ya2do.io	{bcrypt}$2a$10$5VWqjwoMYnFRTTmbWCRZT. iY3WW8ny27kQuUL9yPK1/WJcPcBLFWO	1
jdoe@does.net	{bcrypt}$2a$10$cFKhO.XCUOA9L. in5smIiO2QIOT8.6ufQSwIIC.AVz26WctxhSWC6	0

5-4. Make Access Control Decisions

Problem

In the authentication process, an application will grant a successfully authenticated user a set of authorities. When this user attempts to access a resource in the application, the application has to decide whether the resource is accessible with the granted authorities or other characteristics.

Solution

The decision about whether a user is allowed to access a resource in an application is called an *access control decision*. It is based on the user's authentication status and the resource's nature and access attributes.

How It Works

With Spring Security, it is possible to use Springs Expression Language (SpEL) to create powerful access control rules. Spring Security supports a couple of expressions out of the box (see Table 5-8 for a list). Using constructs such as and, or, and not, you can create very powerful and flexible expressions.

Table 5-8. *Spring Security Built-in Expressions*

Expression	Description
hasRole('role') or hasAuthority('authority')	Returns true if the current user has the given role
hasAnyRole('role1','role2')orhasAnyAuthority('auth1','auth2')	Returns true if the current user has at least one of the given roles
hasIpAddress('ip-address')	Returns true if the current user has the given IP address.
principal	The current user
authentication	Access to the Spring Security authentication object
permitAll()	Always evaluates to true
denyAll()	Always evaluates to false
isAnonymous()	Returns true if the current user is anonymous
isRememberMe()	Returns true if the current user logged in by the means of remember-me functionality
isAuthenticated()	Returns true if this is not an anonymous user
isFullyAuthenticated()	Returns true if the user is not an anonymous or a remember-me user
access()	Use a function to determine whether access is granted

🔥 Although role and authority are almost the same, there is a slight, but important, difference in how they are processed. When using hasRole, the passed-in value for the role will be checked if it starts with ROLE_ (the default role prefix). If not, this will be added before checking the authority. So, hasRole('ADMIN') will actually check if the current user has the authority ROLE_ADMIN. When using hasAuthority, it will check the value as is.

The previous expression would give access to deletion of a book if someone had the ADMIN role or was logged in on the local machine. Writing such an expression can be done through the access method instead of one of the has* methods when defining a matcher. See Listing 5-29.

Listing 5-29. Spring Security with Access Rules

```
public class LibrarySecurityConfig implements WebMvcConfigurer {

  @Override
  public SecurityFilterChain securityFilterChain(HttpSecurity http) throws
  Exception {
    http
      .authorizeRequests()
        .requestMatchers(HttpMethod.GET, "/books*")
          .hasAnyRole("USER", "GUEST")
        .requestMatchers(HttpMethod.POST, "/books*")
          .hasRole("USER")
        .requestMatchers(HttpMethod.DELETE, "/books*")
          .access("hasRole('ADMIN') or hasIpAddress('127.0.0.1') " +
                  "or hasIpAddress('0:0:0:0:0:0:0:1')");
    return http.build();
  }
```

Use an Expression to Make Access Control Decisions Using Spring Beans

Using the @ syntax in the expression, you can call any bean in the application context. So, you could write an expression like @accessChecker.hasLocalAccess(authentication) and provide a bean named accessChecker, which has a hasLocalAccess method that takes an Authentication object. See Listing 5-30.

Listing 5-30. AccessChecker Source

```
package com.apress.springboot3recipes.library.security;

import org.springframework.security.core.Authentication;
import
org.springframework.security.web.authentication.WebAuthenticationDetails;
import org.springframework.stereotype.Component;
```

```
@Component
public final class AccessChecker {

  public boolean hasLocalAccess(Authentication auth) {
    boolean access = false;
    if (auth.getDetails() instanceof WebAuthenticationDetails details) {
      String address = details.getRemoteAddress();
      access = address.equals("127.0.0.1") || address.
      equals("0:0:0:0:0:0:0:1");
    }
    return access;
  }
}
```

Next you can use this AccessChecker in an access method using SpEL. See Listing 5-31.

Listing 5-31. Spring Security with Access Rules Using AccessChecker

```
@Bean
public SecurityFilterChain securityFilterChain(HttpSecurity http) throws
Exception {
  http
    .authorizeRequests()
      .requestMatchers(HttpMethod.GET, "/books*").hasAnyRole("USER", "GUEST")
      .requestMatchers(HttpMethod.POST, "/books*").hasRole("USER")
      .requestMatchers(HttpMethod.DELETE, "/books*")
        .access("hasRole('ADMIN') or @accessChecker.hasLocalAccess(
        authentication)");
  return http.build();
}
```

Secure Methods with Annotations and Expressions

You can use the @PreAuthorize and @PostAuthorize annotations to secure method invocations instead of only securing URLs. With these annotations you can write security-based expressions just as with the URL-based security. To enable the annotation processing, add the @EnableMethodSecurity annotation to the security configuration. See Listing 5-32.

Listing 5-32. Security Configuration with Method Security

```
@Configuration
@EnableMethodSecurity
public class LibrarySecurityConfig implements WebMvcConfigurer {
}
```

Now you can use the @PreAuthorize annotation to secure your application. See Listing 5-33.

Listing 5-33. InMemoryBookService with Authorization Rules

```
package com.apress.springboot3recipes.library;

import org.springframework.security.access.prepost.PreAuthorize;
import org.springframework.stereotype.Service;

import java.util.Map;
import java.util.Optional;
import java.util.concurrent.ConcurrentHashMap;

@Service
class InMemoryBookService implements BookService {

  private final Map<String, Book> books = new ConcurrentHashMap<>();

  @PreAuthorize("isAuthenticated()")
  public Iterable<Book> findAll() {
    return books.values();
  }

  @PreAuthorize("hasAuthority('USER')")
  public Book create(Book book) {
    books.put(book.isbn(), book);
    return book;
  }
```

```
@PreAuthorize("hasAuthority('ADMIN') " +
              "or @accessChecker.hasLocalAccess(authentication)")
public void remove(Book book) {
  books.remove(book.isbn());
}

public Optional<Book> find(String isbn) {
  return Optional.ofNullable(books.get(isbn));
}
}
```

The @PreAuthorize annotation will trigger Spring Security to validate the expression. If it is successful, then access is granted; otherwise, an exception will be thrown that tells the user that access is not granted.

5-5. Add Security to a WebFlux Application

Problem

You have an application built with Spring WebFlux (see Chapter 4) and you want to secure it using Spring Security.

Solution

When adding Spring Security as a dependency to a WebFlux-based application, Spring Boot will automatically enable security. It will add an @EnableWebFluxSecurity configuration class to the application. The @EnableWebFluxSecurity annotation then imports the default Spring Security configuration called WebFluxSecurityConfiguration.

How It Works

A Spring WebFlux application is very different in nature than a regular Spring MVC application. Nonetheless, Spring Boot and Spring Security strive to make it easier to build secure WebFlux-based applications.

To enable security, add spring-boot-starter-security to your WebFlux application (from Recipe 4-3). See Listing 5-34.

Listing 5-34. Spring Security Starter Dependency

```
<dependency>
  <groupId>org.springframework.boot</groupId>
  <artifactId>spring-boot-starter-security</artifactId>
</dependency>
```

This will add the `spring-security-core`, `spring-security-config`, and `spring-security-web` dependencies to your project. Spring Boot detects the availability of some of the classes inside these JAR files and with that will automatically enable security.

Spring Boot will configure Spring Security with the following:

- Authentication with Basic authentication and form login

- HTTP headers for security

- Login requirements to access any resource

⚠️ Spring Boot will add a default user, named `user` and with a generated password, that is visible in the startup logs. This is intended to be used only for testing. Prototyping and demos do not use the generated user in a live system.

When adding the dependency `spring-boot-starter-security` to Recipe 3-3, it will automatically secure all exposed endpoints. At startup, the generated password will be logged (see Figure 5-6).

```
  .   ____          _            __ _ _
 /\\ / ___'_ __ _ _(_)_ __  __ _ \ \ \ \
( ( )\___ | '_ | '_| | '_ \/ _` | \ \ \ \
 \\/  ___)| |_)| | | | | || (_| |  ) ) ) )
  '  |____| .__|_| |_|_| |_\__, | / / / /
 =========|_|==============|___/=/_/_/_/
 :: Spring Boot ::                (v3.2.1)

2024-01-02T13:01:42.133+01:00  INFO 57549 --- [ restartedMain] c.a.s.order.OrderApplication                 : Starting OrderApplication using Java 21.0.1 with PID 57549 (
2024-01-02T13:01:42.139+01:00  INFO 57549 --- [ restartedMain] c.a.s.order.OrderApplication                 : No active profile set, falling back to 1 default profile: "d
2024-01-02T13:01:42.206+01:00  INFO 57549 --- [ restartedMain] .e.DevToolsPropertyDefaultsPostProcessor     : Devtools property defaults active! Set 'spring.devtools.add-
2024-01-02T13:01:42.206+01:00  INFO 57549 --- [ restartedMain] .e.DevToolsPropertyDefaultsPostProcessor     : For additional web related logging consider setting the 'log
2024-01-02T13:01:43.657+01:00  WARN 57549 --- [ restartedMain] o.s.security.core.userdetails.User           : User.withDefaultPasswordEncoder() is considered unsafe for p
2024-01-02T13:01:43.785+01:00  WARN 57549 --- [ restartedMain] o.s.security.core.userdetails.User           : User.withDefaultPasswordEncoder() is considered unsafe for p
2024-01-02T13:01:44.321+01:00  INFO 57549 --- [ restartedMain] o.s.b.d.a.OptionalLiveReloadServer           : LiveReload server is running on port 35729
2024-01-02T13:01:44.445+01:00  INFO 57549 --- [ restartedMain] o.s.b.web.embedded.netty.NettyWebServer      : Netty started on port 8080
2024-01-02T13:01:44.452+01:00  INFO 57549 --- [ restartedMain] c.a.s.order.OrderApplication                 : Started OrderApplication in 2.824 seconds (process running f
```

Figure 5-6. *Secure WebFlux output*

Now when trying to access `http://localhost:8080/`, a login page will be shown (see Figure 5-7).

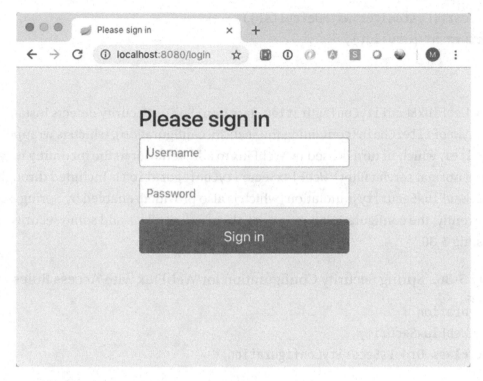

Figure 5-7. *Default login page*

Secure URL Access

Access rules can be configured by adding a custom `SecurityWebFilterChain`. First let's create an `OrdersSecurityConfiguration`. See Listing 5-35.

Listing 5-35. Spring Security Configuration for WebFlux

```
@Configuration
@EnableWebFluxSecurity
public class OrdersSecurityConfiguration {

  @Bean
  public SecurityWebFilterChain springWebFilterChain(ServerHttp
  Security http) {
    http
      .formLogin(Customizer.withDefaults())
      .headers(Customizer.withDefaults())
      .logout(Customizer.withDefaults())
```

```
    .csrf(Customizer.withDefaults());
  return http.build();
  }
}
```

The WebFluxSecurityConfiguration class from Spring Security detects instances of SecurityWebFilterChain (containing the security configuration), which is wrapped as a WebFilter, which in turn is used by WebFlux to add behavior to the incoming request (just as a normal servlet filter). WebFluxSecurityConfiguration is included through the @EnableWebFluxSecurity annotation (which is also provided/enabled by Spring Boot).

Currently, the configuration now only enables security; let's add some security rules. See Listing 5-36.

Listing 5-36. Spring Security Configuration for WebFlux with Access Rules

```
@Configuration
@EnableWebFluxSecurity
public class OrdersSecurityConfiguration {

  @Bean
  public SecurityWebFilterChain springWebFilterChain(ServerHttp
  Security http) {
    http
      .formLogin(Customizer.withDefaults())
      .headers(Customizer.withDefaults())
      .logout(Customizer.withDefaults())
      .csrf(Customizer.withDefaults());

    http
      .authorizeExchange((auth) -> auth
        .pathMatchers("/").permitAll()
        .pathMatchers("/orders*").hasRole("USER")
        .anyExchange().authenticated());

    return http.build();
  }
}
```

ServerHttpSecurity should look familiar (see the other recipes in this chapter) and is used to add security rules and do further configuration (such as adding/ removing headers and configuring the login method). With authorizeExchange, it is possible to write rules; here we secure URLs. The / is permitted for everyone, and the /orders URLs are available only for the role USER. For other requests, you have to at least be authenticated. Finally, you need to call build() to actually build and return the SecurityWebFilterChain.

In addition to authorizeExchange, it is possible to use the headers() configuration method to add security headers to requests, use csrf() to add CSRF protection, etc.

Log in to WebFlux Applications

You can override parts of the default configuration by explicitly configuring them, and you can override the authentication manager used and the repository used to store the security context. The authentication manager is detected automatically; you just need to register a bean of type ReactiveAuthenticationManager or UserDetailsRepository.

You can also configure the location where SecurityContext is stored by configuring the ServerSecurityContextRepositor. The default implementation used is the WebSessionServerSecurityContextRepository, which stores the context in WebSession. The other default implementation is NoOpServerSecurityContextRepository, which is used in stateless applications. See Listing 5-37.

Listing 5-37. Spring Security Configuration

```
@Bean
SecurityWebFilterChain springWebFilterChain(ServerHttpSecurity http) throws
Exception {
  return http
          .formLogin()
          .authenticationManager(new CustomReactiveAuthenticationManager())
          .securityContextRepository(new NoOpServerSecurityContextRepository())
          .build();
}
```

This will override the defaults with a CustomReactiveAuthenticationManager and the stateless NoOpServerSecurityContextRepository. However, for our application, we are going to stick with the defaults.

Authenticate Users

Authenticating users in a Spring WebFlux–based application is done
through a `ReactiveAuthenticationManager` interface. This is an interface
with a single `authenticate` method. You can either provide your own
implementation or use one of the provided implementations. The first is
`UserDetailsRepositoryReactiveAuthenticationManager`, which wraps an instance of
`ReactiveUserDetailsService`.

ⓘ   `ReactiveUserDetailsService` has only a single implementation,
`MapReactiveUserDetailsService`, which is an in-memory implementation.
You could provide your own implementation based on a reactive datastore (like
MongoDB or Couchbase).

As another implementation, `ReactiveAuthenticationManagerAdapter` is actually
a wrapper for a regular `AuthenticationManager`. It will wrap a regular instance, and
therefore, you can use the blocking implementations in a reactive way. This doesn't
make them reactive; they still block, but they are reusable this way. You can also use
JDBC, LDAP, etc., for your reactive application.

When configuring Spring Security in a Spring WebFlux application, you can either
add an instance of a `ReactiveAuthenticationManager` to your Java configuration class
or add a `ReactiveUserDetailsService`. When the latter is detected, it will automatically
be wrapped in a `UserDetailsRepositoryReactiveAuthenticationManager`. See
Listing 5-38.

Listing 5-38. Reactive In-Memory UserDetailsService

```
@Bean
public MapReactiveUserDetailsService userDetailsService() {
  var marten = User.withDefaultPasswordEncoder()
    .username("marten").password("secret").roles("USER").build();
  var admin = User.withDefaultPasswordEncoder()
    .username("admin").password("admin").roles("USER", "ADMIN").build();
  return new MapReactiveUserDetailsService(marten, admin);
}
```

When you now run the application, you are free to access the / page, but when accessing a URL starting with /orders, you will be greeted by a login form (see Figure 5-7). When entering the credentials of one of the predefined users, you should be allowed access to the requested URL.

Make Access Control Decisions

Table 5-9 shows the built-in expressions for access control decisions. See Listing 5-39.

Table 5-9. *Spring Security WebFlux Built-in Expressions*

Expression	Description
hasRole('role') or hasAuthority('authority')	Returns true if the current user has the given role
permitAll()	Always evaluates to true
denyAll()	Always evaluates to false
authenticated()	Returns true if the user is authenticated
access()	Use a function to determine if access is granted

🔥 Although the role and authority are almost the same, there is a slight, but important, difference in how they are processed. When using hasRole, the passed-in value for the role will be checked if it starts with ROLE_ (the default role prefix). If not, this will be added before checking the authority. So, hasRole('ADMIN') will actually check if the current user has the authority ROLE_ADMIN. When using hasAuthority, it will check the value as is.

Listing 5-39. Spring Security Custom Security Rules

```
@Bean
public SecurityWebFilterChain springWebFilterChain(ServerHttp
Security http) {
  http
    .authorizeExchange((auth) -> auth
```

```
        .pathMatchers("/").permitAll()
        .pathMatchers("/orders*").access(this::ordersAllowed)
        .anyExchange().authenticated());
    return http.build();
}

private Mono<AuthorizationDecision> ordersAllowed(
  Mono<Authentication> authentication, AuthorizationContext context) {
    return authentication
      .map(a -> a.getAuthorities().contains(new SimpleGrantedAuthority(
      "ROLE_ADMIN")))
      .map(AuthorizationDecision::new);
}
```

The access() expression can be used to write very powerful expressions. The previous snippet allows access if the current user has the ROLE_ADMIN authority. The Authentication contains the collection of GrantedAuthorities, which you can check for the ROLE_ADMIN. Of course, you can write as many complex expressions as you like; you could check for the IP address, request headers, etc.

Summary

In this chapter, you learned how to secure Spring Boot applications with Spring Security. It can be used to secure any Java application, but it's mostly used for web-based applications. The concepts of authentication, authorization, and access control are essential in the security area, so you should have a clear understanding of them.

You often have to secure critical URLs by preventing unauthorized access to them. Spring Security can help you to achieve this in a declarative way. It handles security by applying servlet filters, which can be configured with a simple Java-based configuration. Spring Security will automatically configure the basic security services for you and tries to be as secure as possible by default.

Spring Security supports multiple ways for users to log into a web application, such as form-based login and HTTP Basic authentication. It also provides an anonymous login service that allows you to handle an anonymous user just like a normal user. Remember-me support allows an application to remember a user's identity across multiple browser sessions.

Spring Security supports multiple ways of authenticating users and has built-in provider implementations for them. For example, it supports authenticating users against in-memory definitions, a relational database, and an LDAP repository. You should always store encrypted passwords in your user repository, because clear-text passwords are vulnerable to hacker attacks. Spring Security also supports caching user details locally to save you the overhead of performing remote queries.

Decisions about whether a user is allowed to access a given resource are made by access decision managers. Spring Security comes with three access decision managers that are based on the voting approach. All of them require a group of voters to be configured for voting on access control decisions.

Spring Security enables you to secure method invocations in a declarative way, either by embedding a security interceptor in a bean definition or by matching multiple methods with AspectJ pointcut expressions or annotations. Spring Security also allows you to display a user's authentication information in JSP views and to render view contents conditionally according to a user's authorities.

Spring Security provides an ACL module that allows each domain object to have an ACL for controlling access. You can read and maintain an ACL for each domain object with Spring Security's high-performance APIs, which are implemented with JDBC. Spring Security also provides facilities such as access decision voters and JSP tags for you to use ACLs consistently with other security facilities.

Spring Security also has support for securing Spring WebFlux–based applications, and you explored how you can add security to such an application.

CHAPTER 6

Data Access

Most applications use a relational database such as Oracle, MySQL, or PostgreSQL; however, there is more to data storage than just SQL databases. There are also these types:

- Document stores (MongoDB, Couchbase)

- Key-value stores (Redis, Voldemort)

- Column stores (Cassandra)

- Graph stores (Neo4j, Apache Giraph)

Each of these technologies (even different implementations of them) has its own purpose. They can also be hard to use or configure, but Spring Boot makes it easier to configure and use them. Spring Boot uses auto-configuration, which will detect which data store is in use (it detects the drivers) and will apply the configuration for it. To make it easier to work with these technologies, Spring Boot utilizes the Spring Data project.

Although each section uses a different persistence store, the `bin` directory contains scripts that set up Docker containers for each persistence store.

The Spring Data project can help make life easier; it can help configure the different technologies with the plumbing code. Each of the integration modules will have support for exception translation to Spring's consistent `DataAccessException` hierarchy and will be able to use Spring's templating approach. Spring Data also provides a cross-storage solution for some technologies, which means part of your model can be stored in a relational database with JPA, and the other part can be stored in a graph or document store.

© Marten Deinum 2024
M. Deinum, *Spring Boot 3 Recipes*, https://doi.org/10.1007/979-8-8688-0113-6_6

6-1. Configure a Data Source

When working with a relational database, the first thing you need is a connection to the database. A connection in Java is obtained through `javax.sql.DataSource`. Spring provides several out-of-the-box implementations of `DataSource` like `DriverManagerDataSource` and `SimpleDriverDataSource`. However, these implementations are not connection pools and should be considered mainly for testing use, not production use. For a live system, you want to use a proper connection pool such as HikariCP.

Problem

You need access to a database from your application.

Solution

Use the `spring.datasource.url`, `spring.datasource.username`, and `spring.datasource.password` properties to let Spring Boot configure a `DataSource` instance.

How It Works

To configure a `DataSource` instance, Spring Boot requires the presence of a connection pool such as HikariCP, a JDBC driver, or an embedded database such as H2, HSQLDB, or Derby. Spring Boot automatically detects HikariCP, Tomcat JDBC, and Commons DBCP2-based connection pools. To use the connection pool, configure the `spring.datasource.url`, `spring.datasource.username`, and `spring.datasource.password` properties (the minimum properties you need to set). Enable the JDBC support by adding the `spring-boot-starter-jdbc` dependency (see Listing 6-1). This will pull in all the required dependencies to work with JDBC.

Listing 6-1. Spring Boot JDBC Starter Dependency

```
<dependency>
    <groupId>org.springframework.boot</groupId>
    <artifactId>spring-boot-starter-jdbc</artifactId>
</dependency>
```

The dependencies included are spring-jdbc, spring-tx, and HikariCP as the default connection pool.

Use an Embedded Data Source

When Spring Boot detects the presence of H2, HSQLDB, or Derby, it will by default start an embedded database using the detected embedded implementation. This is very useful when writing a test or preparing a demonstration. Getting Spring Boot to create this is a simple matter of including the desired dependency (see Listing 6-2).

Listing 6-2. Apache Derby Dependencies for an Embedded Server

```
<dependency>
    <groupId>org.apache.derby</groupId>
    <artifactId>derby</artifactId>
    <scope>runtime</scope>
</dependency>
<dependency>
    <groupId>org.apache.derby</groupId>
    <artifactId>derbytools</artifactId>
    <scope>runtime</scope>
</dependency>
```

Spring Boot will now detect Derby and bootstrap an embedded DataSource instance. Let's write an application that lists the tables in the database (see Listing 6-3).

Listing 6-3. Spring Boot Application with TableLister

```
package com.apress.springboot3recipes.jdbc;

import javax.sql.DataSource;

import org.slf4j.Logger;
import org.slf4j.LoggerFactory;
import org.springframework.boot.ApplicationArguments;
import org.springframework.boot.ApplicationRunner;
import org.springframework.boot.SpringApplication;
import org.springframework.boot.autoconfigure.SpringBootApplication;
import org.springframework.stereotype.Component;
```

```java
@SpringBootApplication
public class JdbcApplication {

  public static void main(String[] args) {
    SpringApplication.run(JdbcApplication.class, args);
  }
}

@Component
class TableLister implements ApplicationRunner {

  private final Logger logger = LoggerFactory.getLogger(getClass());
  private final DataSource dataSource;

  TableLister(DataSource dataSource) {
    this.dataSource = dataSource;
  }

  @Override
  public void run(ApplicationArguments args) throws Exception {
    try (var con = dataSource.getConnection();
         var rs = con.getMetaData().getTables(null, null, "%", null)) {
      while (rs.next()) {
        logger.info("{}", rs.getString(3));
      }
    }
  }
}
```

When the application runs, it will create an instance of the TableLister, and the instance will receive the configured DataSource instance. Spring Boot will then detect the fact it is an ApplicationRunner and will call the run method. The run method obtains a Connection from the DataSource and uses the DatabaseMetaData (from JDBC) to obtain the tables in the database. Now when running the application, it should display output similar to that in Figure 6-1.

```
.   ____          _            __ _ _
/\\ / ___'_ __ _ _(_)_ __  __ _ \ \ \ \
( ( )\___ | '_ | '_| | '_ \/ _` | \ \ \ \
\\/  ___)| |_)| | | | | || (_| |  ) ) ) )
  '  |____| .__|_| |_|_| |_\__, | / / / /
 =========|_|==============|___/=/_/_/_/
 :: Spring Boot ::          (v3.2.1)

2023-12-30T10:51:11.401+01:00  INFO 40514 --- [        main] c.a.s.jdbc.JdbcApplication           : Starting JdbcApplication using Java 21.0.1 with |
2023-12-30T10:51:11.404+01:00  INFO 40514 --- [        main] c.a.s.jdbc.JdbcApplication           : No active profile set, falling back to 1 default
2023-12-30T10:51:12.328+01:00  INFO 40514 --- [        main] c.a.s.jdbc.JdbcApplication           : Started JdbcApplication in 1.313 seconds (proces:
2023-12-30T10:51:12.332+01:00  INFO 40514 --- [        main] com.zaxxer.hikari.HikariDataSource   : HikariPool-1 - Starting...
2023-12-30T10:51:12.337+01:00  WARN 40514 --- [        main] c.zaxxer.hikari.util.DriverDataSource : Registered driver with driverClassName=org.apach
2023-12-30T10:51:12.639+01:00  INFO 40514 --- [        main] com.zaxxer.hikari.pool.PoolBase      : HikariPool-1 - Driver does not support get/set n
2023-12-30T10:51:12.639+01:00  INFO 40514 --- [        main] com.zaxxer.hikari.pool.HikariPool    : HikariPool-1 - Added connection org.apache.derby
2023-12-30T10:51:12.644+01:00  INFO 40514 --- [        main] com.zaxxer.hikari.HikariDataSource   : HikariPool-1 - Start completed.
2023-12-30T10:51:12.917+01:00  INFO 40514 --- [        main] c.a.springboot3recipes.jdbc.TableLister : SYSALIASES
2023-12-30T10:51:12.917+01:00  INFO 40514 --- [        main] c.a.springboot3recipes.jdbc.TableLister : SYSCHECKS
2023-12-30T10:51:12.917+01:00  INFO 40514 --- [        main] c.a.springboot3recipes.jdbc.TableLister : SYSCOLPERMS
2023-12-30T10:51:12.917+01:00  INFO 40514 --- [        main] c.a.springboot3recipes.jdbc.TableLister : SYSCOLUMNS
2023-12-30T10:51:12.917+01:00  INFO 40514 --- [        main] c.a.springboot3recipes.jdbc.TableLister : SYSCONGLOMERATES
2023-12-30T10:51:12.917+01:00  INFO 40514 --- [        main] c.a.springboot3recipes.jdbc.TableLister : SYSCONSTRAINTS
2023-12-30T10:51:12.918+01:00  INFO 40514 --- [        main] c.a.springboot3recipes.jdbc.TableLister : SYSDEPENDS
2023-12-30T10:51:12.918+01:00  INFO 40514 --- [        main] c.a.springboot3recipes.jdbc.TableLister : SYSFILES
```

Figure 6-1. *TableLister output for Derby*

Use an External Database

To connect to a database, you need a JDBC driver. This recipes use PostgreSQL, so you need to include the driver for this database (Listing 6-4).

Listing 6-4. PostgreSQL Dependency

```xml
<dependency>
  <groupId>org.postgresql</groupId>
  <artifactId>postgresql</artifactId>
</dependency>
```

Configuring a single data source is a matter of including the properties in the application.properties file (Listing 6-5).

Listing 6-5. Data Source Properties to Connect to the PostgreSQL Database

```
spring.datasource.url=jdbc:postgresql://localhost:5432/customers
spring.datasource.username=customers
spring.datasource.password=customers
```

The spring.datasource.url instance tells the connection pool where to connect to, and spring.datasource.username and spring.datasource.password configure the username and password to use when connecting. You could also use

283

`spring.datasource.driver-class-name` to specify the JDBC driver class to use. Generally, Spring Boot will detect the driver to use from the passed-in URL. If you want to use a nondefault driver (for performance or logging), you could specify this as well.

When running the `JdbcApplication`, the output should be like that of Figure 6-2; there are now a bunch of different tables (compared to Derby).

```
2018-09-10 19:30:15.711  INFO 97421 --- [    main] com.zaxxer.hikari.HikariDataSource       : HikariPool-1 - Starting...
2018-09-10 19:30:15.996  INFO 97421 --- [    main] com.zaxxer.hikari.HikariDataSource       : HikariPool-1 - Start completed.
2018-09-10 19:30:16.012  INFO 97421 --- [    main] c.a.springboot2recipes.jdbc.TableLister  : pg_aggregate_fnoid_index
2018-09-10 19:30:16.012  INFO 97421 --- [    main] c.a.springboot2recipes.jdbc.TableLister  : pg_am_name_index
2018-09-10 19:30:16.012  INFO 97421 --- [    main] c.a.springboot2recipes.jdbc.TableLister  : pg_am_oid_index
2018-09-10 19:30:16.012  INFO 97421 --- [    main] c.a.springboot2recipes.jdbc.TableLister  : pg_amop_fam_strat_index
2018-09-10 19:30:16.012  INFO 97421 --- [    main] c.a.springboot2recipes.jdbc.TableLister  : pg_amop_oid_index
2018-09-10 19:30:16.012  INFO 97421 --- [    main] c.a.springboot2recipes.jdbc.TableLister  : pg_amop_opr_fam_index
2018-09-10 19:30:16.013  INFO 97421 --- [    main] c.a.springboot2recipes.jdbc.TableLister  : pg_amproc_fam_proc_index
2018-09-10 19:30:16.013  INFO 97421 --- [    main] c.a.springboot2recipes.jdbc.TableLister  : pg_amproc_oid_index
2018-09-10 19:30:16.013  INFO 97421 --- [    main] c.a.springboot2recipes.jdbc.TableLister  : pg_attrdef_adrelid_adnum_index
2018-09-10 19:30:16.013  INFO 97421 --- [    main] c.a.springboot2recipes.jdbc.TableLister  : pg_attrdef_oid_index
2018-09-10 19:30:16.013  INFO 97421 --- [    main] c.a.springboot2recipes.jdbc.TableLister  : pg_attribute_relid_attnam_index
2018-09-10 19:30:16.013  INFO 97421 --- [    main] c.a.springboot2recipes.jdbc.TableLister  : pg_attribute_relid_attnum_index
2018-09-10 19:30:16.013  INFO 97421 --- [    main] c.a.springboot2recipes.jdbc.TableLister  : pg_auth_members_member_role_index
2018-09-10 19:30:16.013  INFO 97421 --- [    main] c.a.springboot2recipes.jdbc.TableLister  : pg_auth_members_role_member_index
2018-09-10 19:30:16.013  INFO 97421 --- [    main] c.a.springboot2recipes.jdbc.TableLister  : pg_authid_oid_index
2018-09-10 19:30:16.013  INFO 97421 --- [    main] c.a.springboot2recipes.jdbc.TableLister  : pg_authid_rolname_index
2018-09-10 19:30:16.013  INFO 97421 --- [    main] c.a.springboot2recipes.jdbc.TableLister  : pg_cast_oid_index
2018-09-10 19:30:16.013  INFO 97421 --- [    main] c.a.springboot2recipes.jdbc.TableLister  : pg_cast_source_target_index
2018-09-10 19:30:16.013  INFO 97421 --- [    main] c.a.springboot2recipes.jdbc.TableLister  : pg_class_oid_index
2018-09-10 19:30:16.014  INFO 97421 --- [    main] c.a.springboot2recipes.jdbc.TableLister  : pg_class_relname_nsp_index
2018-09-10 19:30:16.014  INFO 97421 --- [    main] c.a.springboot2recipes.jdbc.TableLister  : pg_class_tblspc_relfilenode_index
2018-09-10 19:30:16.014  INFO 97421 --- [    main] c.a.springboot2recipes.jdbc.TableLister  : pg_collation_name_enc_nsp_index
2018-09-10 19:30:16.014  INFO 97421 --- [    main] c.a.springboot2recipes.jdbc.TableLister  : pg_collation_oid_index
```

Figure 6-2. *TableLister output for PostgreSQL*

Obtain a Data Source from JNDI

If you are deploying your Spring Boot application to an application server (or if you have a remote JNDI server) and want to use a preconfigured `DataSource` instance, you can use the `spring.datasource.jndi-name` property to let Spring Boot know you want to obtain a `DataSource` from JNDI (see Listing 6-6).

Listing 6-6. DataSource JNDI Lookup Property

```
spring.datasource.jndi-name=java:jdbc/customers
```

Configure the Connection Pool

The default connection pool used by Spring Boot is HikariCP. This comes automacallly when including the `spring-boot-starter-jdbc` dependency (or one of the other database-related dependencies). Spring Boot will configure the connection pool with some default settings; however, you might want to override this (increase the max connections or reduce it, set the timeouts, etc.). The configuration options for HikariCP are in the `spring.datasource.hikari` namespace (see Table 6-1).

Table 6-1. *HikariCP Common Connection Pool Settings*

Property	Description
spring.datasource. hikari.connection- timeout	Sets the maximum number of milliseconds that a client will wait for a connection from the pool. The default is 30 seconds.
spring.datasource. hikari.leak- detection-threshold	Sets the number of milliseconds that a connection can be out of the pool before a message is logged indicating a possible connection leak. The default is disabled.
spring.datasource. hikari.idle-timeout	Sets the maximum number of milliseconds that a connection is allowed to sit idle in the pool. The default is 10 seconds.
spring.datasource. hikari.validation- timeout	Sets the maximum number of milliseconds that the pool will wait for a connection to be validated as alive. The default is 5 seconds.
spring.datasource. hikari.connection- test-query	Sets the SQL query to be executed to test the validity of connections. Generally, this is not needed with JDBC 4.0 (or higher) drivers!
spring.datasource. hikari.maximum- pool-size	Sets the maximum number of connections that will be kept in the pool. The default is 10 connections.
spring.datasource. hikari.minimum-idle	Sets the minimum number of idle connections that are maintained in the pool. The default is 10 connections.
spring.datasource. hikari.data-source- properties	Sets the driver-specific properties.

There are more properties you can use (see Listing 6-7), but the list is quite long, and the properties mentioned in Table 6-1 are the most commonly used ones.

ℹ️   The properties for Tomcat JDBC are in the `spring.datasource.tomcat` namespace and for Commons DBCP2 in the `spring.datasource.dbcp2` namespace.

Listing 6-7. Additional Hikari Properties

```
spring.datasource.hikari.maximum-pool-size=5
spring.datasource.hikari.minimum-idle=2
spring.datasource.hikari.leak-detection-threshold=20s
```

This configuration will set the maximum number of connections to 5 and the minimum to 2. It will also enable leak detection with a threshold of 20 seconds.

6-2. Manage the Database Schema with Spring Boot

Problem

You need to initialize or extend the objects in the schema of the database you are using, and you want them to be triggered/managed by your Spring Boot application.

ⓘ   There is a `postgres.sh` script in the `bin` directory that will start a PostgreSQL server for use with this recipe.

Solution

Spring Boot has out-of-the-box support for simple database management as well as for Flyway and Liquibase. Include the (if needed) dependencies, and Spring Boot will automatically use the database management of your choice and provide sensible defaults as well as the ability to apply some configuration properties.

How It Works

When working with an existing database, you probably already have existing tables, views, and procedures. However, when you create a new database, it is empty, and you will need to create the tables yourself. Using Spring Boot, this is supported out of the box. You can add a `schema.sql` file to initialize the schema (tables, views, etc.) and a `data.sql` file to insert data into the tables. Spring Boot will also allow you to provide a `schema-<platform>.sql` and `data-<platform>.sql` to do database-specific initialization. When using Derby, you could add a `schema-derby.sql` file, etc. The name of the schema and data files can be changed through the `spring.sql.init.schema-locations` and `spring.sql.init.data-locations` properties. See Table 6-2 for a description of the available properties.

Table 6-2. *DataSource Initialize Properties*

Property	Description
`spring.sql.init.continue-on-error`	Sets whether to stop if an error occurs while initializing the database; the default is `false`.
`spring.sql.init.data-locations`	Sets the data (DML) script resource references; the default is `classpath:data.sql`.
`spring.sql.init.password`	Sets the password of the database to execute DML scripts; it defaults to the normal password.
`spring.sql.init.username`	Sets the username of the database to execute DML scripts; this defaults to the normal username.
`spring.sql.init.mode`	Initializes the data source with the available DDL and DML scripts. The default is `EMBEDDED` and can be changed to `NEVER` or `ALWAYS`.
`spring.sql.init.platform`	Sets the platform to use in the DDL or DML scripts (such as `schema-${platform}.sql` or `data-${platform}.sql`). The default is `all`.
`spring.sql.init.schema-locations`	Sets the data (DDL) script resource references; the default is `classpath:schema.sql`.
`spring.sql.init.separator`	Sets the statement separator in SQL initialization scripts. The default is `;`.
`spring.sql.init.encoding`	Sets the SQL script's encoding. This defaults to platform encoding.

Let's create a table called `customer` and insert some data into it. To create the table, add the `schema.sql` file to the `src/main/resources` directory (Listing 6-8).

Listing 6-8. Customer DDL

```sql
DROP TABLE IF EXISTS customer;

CREATE TABLE customer (
  id SERIAL PRIMARY KEY,
  name VARCHAR(100) NOT NULL,
  email VARCHAR(255) NOT NULL,
  UNIQUE(name)
);
```

To insert the data, add the `data.sql` file to the `src/main/resources` directory (Listing 6-9).

Listing 6-9. Customer Data Initialization SQL

```sql
INSERT INTO customer (name, email)
VALUES ('Marten Deinum', 'marten@deinum.biz'),
       ('Josh Long', 'jlong@pivotal.com'),
       ('John Doe', 'john.doe@island.io'),
       ('Jane Doe', 'jane.doe@island.io');
```

To see if this is working, let's add another `ApplicationRunner` instance that prints the content of the `customer` table using the `DataSource` instance (Listing 6-10).

Listing 6-10. CustomerLister

```java
@Component
class CustomerLister implements ApplicationRunner {

  private final Logger logger = LoggerFactory.getLogger(getClass());
  private final DataSource dataSource;

  CustomerLister(DataSource dataSource) {
    this.dataSource = dataSource;
  }

  @Override
  public void run(ApplicationArguments args) throws Exception {
    var sql = "SELECT id, name, email FROM customer";
    try (var con = dataSource.getConnection();
```

```
      var stmt = con.createStatement();
      var rs = stmt.executeQuery(sql)) {
   while (rs.next()) {
     logger.info("Customer [id={}, name={}, email={}]", rs.getLong(1),
       rs.getString(2), rs.getString(3));
   }
  }
 }
}
```

Database initialization is always enabled for embedded databases, so when using Derby, H2, or HSQLDB, this is by default enabled. When using an external database, the initialization doesn't happen by default. To change this, you can toggle the `spring.sql. init.mode` property to `always` so that it will always run (Listing 6-11).

Listing 6-11. Enable Database Initialization for Non-embedded Data Sources

```
spring.sql.init.mode=always
```

When the application starts, you will now see the list of customers from the database being printed in the logs (right before or after the tables are being logged, as shown in Figure 6-3).

```
 .   ____          _            __ _ _
/\\ / ___'_ __ _ _(_)_ __  __ _ \ \ \ \
( ( )\___ | '_ | '_| | '_ \/ _` | \ \ \ \
 \\/  ___)| |_)| | | | | || (_| |  ) ) ) )
  '  |____| .__|_| |_|_| |_\__, | / / / /
 =========|_|==============|___/=/_/_/_/
 :: Spring Boot ::                (v3.2.1)

2023-12-30T11:06:16.008+01:00  INFO 40913 --- [     main] c.a.s.jdbc.JdbcApplication               : Starting JdbcApplication using Java 21.0.1 with
2023-12-30T11:06:16.011+01:00  INFO 40913 --- [     main] c.a.s.jdbc.JdbcApplication               : No active profile set, falling back to 1 default
2023-12-30T11:06:16.602+01:00  INFO 40913 --- [     main] com.zaxxer.hikari.HikariDataSource       : HikariPool-1 - Starting...
2023-12-30T11:06:16.830+01:00  INFO 40913 --- [     main] com.zaxxer.hikari.pool.HikariPool        : HikariPool-1 - Added connection org.postgresql.
2023-12-30T11:06:16.831+01:00  INFO 40913 --- [     main] com.zaxxer.hikari.HikariDataSource       : HikariPool-1 - Start completed.
2023-12-30T11:06:16.959+01:00  INFO 40913 --- [     main] c.a.s.jdbc.JdbcApplication               : Started JdbcApplication in 1.3 seconds (process
2023-12-30T11:06:16.966+01:00  INFO 40913 --- [     main] c.a.s.jdbc.CustomerLister                : Customer [id=1, name=Marten Deinum, email=marten
2023-12-30T11:06:16.967+01:00  INFO 40913 --- [     main] c.a.s.jdbc.CustomerLister                : Customer [id=2, name=Josh Long, email=jlong@piv
2023-12-30T11:06:16.967+01:00  INFO 40913 --- [     main] c.a.s.jdbc.CustomerLister                : Customer [id=3, name=John Doe, email=john.doe@i
2023-12-30T11:06:16.967+01:00  INFO 40913 --- [     main] c.a.s.jdbc.CustomerLister                : Customer [id=4, name=Jane Doe, email=jane.doe@i
2023-12-30T11:06:16.985+01:00  INFO 40913 --- [     main] c.a.springboot3recipes.jdbc.TableLister  : customer_name_key
2023-12-30T11:06:16.985+01:00  INFO 40913 --- [     main] c.a.springboot3recipes.jdbc.TableLister  : customer_pkey
2023-12-30T11:06:16.985+01:00  INFO 40913 --- [     main] c.a.springboot3recipes.jdbc.TableLister  : customer_id_seq
```

Figure 6-3. *CustomerLister output*

Initialize the Database with Flyway

When developing an application, you want more control of the database migration. While using schema.sql and data.sql files is very quick and easy, it eventually will get cumbersome to maintain. Spring Boot also supports Flyway, which is, simply said, a version control for your database schema. It allows you to incrementally change/update your database schema. To use Flyway, the first thing to do is to add the dependency on Flyway itself (Listing 6-12).

Listing 6-12. Flyway Dependency

```xml
<dependency>
  <groupId>org.flywaydb</groupId>
  <artifactId>flyway-core</artifactId>
</dependency>
```

Spring Boot will detect the presence of Flyway, and it will assume you want to use it to do database migrations. The migration scripts should be in the db/migration folder in src/main/resources. This is the default location that can be changed by specifying spring.flyway.locations in your application.properties file. See Listing 6-13 for a migration script to use instead of schema.sql and data.sql.

Listing 6-13. Flyway Migration Script

```sql
CREATE TABLE customer (
  id SERIAL PRIMARY KEY,
  name VARCHAR(100) NOT NULL,
  email VARCHAR(255) NOT NULL,
  UNIQUE(name)
);

INSERT INTO customer (name, email) VALUES
    ('Marten Deinum', 'marten@deinum.biz'),
    ('Josh Long', 'jlong@pivotal.com'),
    ('John Doe', 'john.doe@island.io'),
    ('Jane Doe', 'jane.doe@island.io');
```

This SQL when put in a V1__first.sql file in the db/migration folder will be executed on startup (assuming an empty database). The naming convention by default is V<sequence>__<name>.sql and is used to determine what to execute. Once a script has been executed, you cannot (and shouldn't) modify the script as that will lead to Flyway preventing your application from starting. It detects changes in scripts already executed.

When running the application, the customers should still be listed, and you will notice an additional table in the table listing: flyway_schema_history. This table contains the metadata used by Flyway to detect (and guard) database changes.

```
2018-09-10 19:57:22.714  INFO 98933 --- [         main] c.a.springboot2recipes.jdbc.TableLister  : pg_user
2018-09-10 19:57:22.714  INFO 98933 --- [         main] c.a.springboot2recipes.jdbc.TableLister  : pg_user_mappings
2018-09-10 19:57:22.714  INFO 98933 --- [         main] c.a.springboot2recipes.jdbc.TableLister  : pg_views
2018-09-10 19:57:22.714  INFO 98933 --- [         main] c.a.springboot2recipes.jdbc.TableLister  : customer
2018-09-10 19:57:22.714  INFO 98933 --- [         main] c.a.springboot2recipes.jdbc.TableLister  : flyway_schema_history
2018-09-10 19:57:22.714  INFO 98933 --- [         main] c.a.springboot2recipes.jdbc.TableLister  : pg_toast_12242
2018-09-10 19:57:22.714  INFO 98933 --- [         main] c.a.springboot2recipes.jdbc.TableLister  : pg_toast_12247
2018-09-10 19:57:22.715  INFO 98933 --- [         main] c.a.springboot2recipes.jdbc.TableLister  : pg_toast_12252
```

Figure 6-4. *CustomerLister output: Flyway*

There are also several properties you can use to configure Flyway with Spring Boot; see Table 6-3 for the most commonly used properties.

Table 6-3. *Commonly Used Flyway Properties*

Property	Description
spring.flyway.enabled	Sets whether Flyway should be enabled; the default is true.
spring.flyway.encoding	Sets the encoding of the SQL migration files; this defaults to UTF-8.
spring.flyway.fail-on-missing-locations	Sets whether Flyway should fail/abort if the location is missing; the default is false.
spring.flyway.locations	Sets the locations of the migration scripts; the default is classpath:db/migration.
spring.flyway.url	Sets the JDBC URL of the database to migrate; when not set, it uses the default configured DataSource.
spring.flyway.user	Sets the username to use for the database if Flyway uses its own DataSource.

(*continued*)

Table 6-3. (*continued*)

Property	Description
`spring.flyway.password`	Sets the password to use for the database if Flyway uses its own `DataSource`.
`spring.flyway.sql-migration-prefix`	Sets the prefix to detect the SQL migration files; the default is V.
`spring.flyway.sql-migration-suffixes`	Sets the suffixes used to detect the SQL migration files; the default is `.sql`.
`spring.flyway.license-key`	Sets the license key for Flyway Teams (the paid version of Flyway).

6-3. Use JdbcTemplate or JdbcClient
Problem

You want to use `JdbcTemplate`, `NamedParameterJdbcTemplate`, or `JdbcClient` to have a better JDBC experience.

Solution

Use the automatically configured `JdbcTemplate`, `NamedParameterJdbcTemplate`, or `JdbcClient` to execute the queries and handle the results.

How It Works

Spring Boot will configure a `JdbcTemplate`, `NamedParameterJdbcTemplate`, and `JdbcClient` by default and does so when it can detect a single candidate `DataSouce`. A single candidate `DataSource` means there is either only a single `DataSource` or there is one marked as a primary resource using `@Primary`. As the `JdbcTemplate` is already available, you can use that to write your JDBC code. Rewriting the `CustomerLister` to use the `JdbcTemplate` instead of a plain `DataSource` will make the code a little easier to read and thus easier to handle (see Listing 6-14).

Listing 6-14. CustomerLister Using JdbcTemplate

```
class CustomerLister implements ApplicationRunner {

  private final Logger logger = LoggerFactory.getLogger(getClass());
  private final JdbcTemplate jdbc;

  CustomerLister(JdbcTemplate jdbc) {
    this.jdbc = jdbc;
  }

  @Override
  public void run(ApplicationArguments args) {

    jdbc.query("SELECT id, name, email FROM customer", rs -> {
      logger.info("Customer [id={}, name={}, email={}]",
        rs.getLong(1), rs.getString(2), rs.getString(3));
    });
  }
}
```

The JdbcTemplate is used to execute the query through the query method; this method takes a String and a RowCallbackHandler. The JdbcTemplate will execute the query and for each row call the RowCallbackHandler, which does the logging of the row. When running the application, the output is still the same, but the code becomes easier.

The JdbcTemplate also has the probably more familiar RowMapper interface, which can be used to map a row from the ResultSet to a Java object. Let's create a Customer class and use a RowMapper to create Customer instances from the database (Listing 6-15).

Listing 6-15. Customer Record

```
package com.apress.springboot3recipes.jdbc;

public record Customer(Long id, String name, String email) {

  public Customer(String name, String email) {
    this(null, name, email);
  }
}
```

Next we create a repository interface to define the contract and create a JDBC-based implementation (Listing 6-16).

Listing 6-16. CustomerRepository Interface

```
package com.apress.springboot3recipes.jdbc;

import java.util.List;
import java.util.Optional;

public interface CustomerRepository {

  List<Customer> findAll();
  Optional<Customer> findById(long id);
  Customer save(Customer customer);
}
```

Next the implementation uses JdbcTemplate and a RowMapper instance to map the results to Customer objects (Listing 6-17).

Listing 6-17. CustomerRepository Implementation Using JdbcTemplate

```
package com.apress.springboot3recipes.jdbc;

import org.springframework.dao.EmptyResultDataAccessException;
import org.springframework.jdbc.core.JdbcTemplate;
import org.springframework.jdbc.support.GeneratedKeyHolder;
import org.springframework.stereotype.Repository;

import java.sql.ResultSet;
import java.sql.SQLException;
import java.util.List;
import java.util.Optional;

@Repository
class JdbcCustomerRepository implements CustomerRepository {

  private static final String ALL_QUERY = "SELECT id, name, email FROM
  customer";
  private static final String BY_ID_QUERY =
    "SELECT id, name, email FROM customer WHERE id=?";
```

```java
private static final String INSERT_QUERY =
  "INSERT INTO customer (name, email) VALUES (?,?) RETURNING id";

private final JdbcTemplate jdbc;

JdbcCustomerRepository(JdbcTemplate jdbc) {
  this.jdbc = jdbc;
}

@Override
public List<Customer> findAll() {
  return jdbc.query(ALL_QUERY, (rs, rowNum) -> toCustomer(rs));
}

@Override
public Optional<Customer> findById(long id) {
  try {
    var customer = jdbc
      .queryForObject(BY_ID_QUERY, (rs, rowNum) -> toCustomer(rs), id);
    return Optional.of(customer);
  } catch (EmptyResultDataAccessException ex) {
    return Optional.empty();
  }
}

@Override
public Customer save(Customer customer) {
  var keyHolder = new GeneratedKeyHolder();
  jdbc.update( (con) -> {
    var ps = con.prepareStatement(INSERT_QUERY);
    ps.setString(1, customer.name());
    ps.setString(2, customer.email());
    return ps;
  }, keyHolder);
  var id = keyHolder.getKey().longValue();
  return new Customer(id, customer.name(), customer.email());
}
```

```
private Customer toCustomer(ResultSet rs) throws SQLException {
  var id = rs.getLong(1);
  var name = rs.getString(2);
  var email = rs.getString(3);
  return new Customer(id, name, email);
  }
}
```

JdbcCustomerRepository uses JdbcTemplate and RowMapper (through a lambda expression) to convert each row of the ResultSet object into a Customer object. CustomerLister can now use CustomerRepository to get all the Customer records from the database and print them to the console (Listing 6-18).

Listing 6-18. CustomerLister Using CustomerRepository

```
@Component
class CustomerLister implements ApplicationRunner {

  private final Logger logger = LoggerFactory.getLogger(getClass());
  private final CustomerRepository customers;

  CustomerLister(CustomerRepository customers) {
    this.customers = customers;
  }

  @Override
  public void run(ApplicationArguments args) {
    customers.findAll()
      .forEach( (customer) -> logger.info("{}", customer));
  }
}
```

As all JDBC code has been moved to JdbcCustomerRepository, the class becomes very simple. It gets a CustomerRepository instance injected, and using the findAll method, it obtains the content of the database and for each customer prints a line.

Access JDBC Through JdbcClient

A new addition to Spring JDBC is `JdbcClient`, which still uses `JdbcTemplate` or `NamedParameterJdbcTemplate` internally but offers a more fluent approach to execute SQL and map the response.

`CustomerLister` is based on `JdbcClient` and could look like Listing 6-19.

Listing 6-19. CustomerLister Using JdbcClient

```
@Component
class CustomerLister implements ApplicationRunner {

  private final Logger logger = LoggerFactory.getLogger(getClass());
  private final JdbcClient jdbc;

  CustomerLister(JdbcClient jdbc) {
    this.jdbc = jdbc;
  }

  @Override
  public void run(ApplicationArguments args) {
    jdbc.sql("SELECT id, name, email FROM customer")
        .query((rs) -> {
      logger.info("Customer [id={}, name={}, email={}]",
        rs.getLong(1), rs.getString(2), rs.getString(3));
    });
  }
}
```

The `sql` method is used to set the SQL statement to execute. Using the `param` methods, we could set positional or named parameters in the statement. The `query` method is used to execute the query and map it to a result. Here we use the `query` method that takes a `RowCallbackHandler`, much like we did with `JdbcTemplate`.

6-4. Use Spring Data JDBC

Problem

You want to map some results to objects without writing too much of the integration code. Spring Data JDBC provides an abstraction for JDBC, based on the familiar `JdbcTemplate`, and will automatically provide the mapping.

Solution

Add Spring Data JDBC as a dependency to your project, and use the base classes to create the repository.

How It Works

To use Spring Data JDBC, first you need to add the dependency to this project. Spring Boot provides the `spring-boot-starter-data-jdbc` dependency for this, which will pull in all the needed dependencies (see Listing 6-20).

Listing 6-20. Spring Data JDBC Dependency

```
<dependency>
   <groupId>org.springframework.boot</groupId>
   <artifactId>spring-boot-starter-data-jdbc</artifactId>
</dependency>
```

As we are going to store and retrieve `Customer` objects, we need a `Customer` class as well. We can reuse the one from Recipe 6-14; Listing 6-21 shows it again for completeness.

Listing 6-21. Customer Record

```
package com.apress.springboot3recipes.jdbc;

import org.springframework.data.annotation.Id;

public record Customer(@Id long id, String name, String email) { }
```

There is a small difference in this customer compared to the one in Recipe 6-15. The difference is the @Id annotation on the id property. We need to tell Spring Data which fields to use as the primary key. This is needed so things like findById will work; otherwise, Spring Data will not know which fields make up the identifier and cannot generate the query. For this we need to mark the fields with @Id. When there is only one field making up the primary key for this object and it is also named id, you could omit the @Id annotation. However, being explicit about it is never wrong and aids the expressiveness of the code.

Finally, we need a repository. In earlier recipes we defined an interface (Recipe 6-15) and provided the implementation we wanted (Recipe 6-16). With Spring Data JDBC we only need to specify an interface (Listing 6-22), which has to extend one of the Spring Data interfaces. Now Spring Data will dynamically create the appropriate repository at runtime.

Listing 6-22. CustomerRepository for Spring Data JDBC

```
package com.apress.springboot3recipes.jdbc;

import org.springframework.data.repository.CrudRepository;

public interface CustomerRepository extends CrudRepository<Customer,
Long> { }
```

CustomerRespository extends CrudRepository and contains no methods. All the methods needed are provided out of the box by Spring Data. Finally, we need to create something that uses the repository. Let's write a CustomerLister that retrieves all the Customer instances from the database and prints the output (Listing 6-23).

Listing 6-23. CustomerLister Using CustomerRepository

```
@Component
class CustomerLister implements ApplicationRunner {

  private final Logger logger = LoggerFactory.getLogger(getClass());
  private final CustomerRepository customers;

  CustomerLister(CustomerRepository customers) {
    this.customers = customers;
  }
```

```
@Override
public void run(ApplicationArguments args) {
  customers.findAll()
           .forEach( (customer) -> logger.info("{}", customer));
  }
}
```

6-5. Test JDBC Code

When writing JDBC code, eventually you want to test if your code behaves as you think it does. For this the Spring Test module can help you out. It allows for easy test setup, and Spring Boot extends it even further to make testing data-access code even easier. This recipe explores what is needed to write a test for JDBC code.

Problem

You want to test your JDBC layer against an actual database.

Solution

Use the Spring Test Context framework and the Spring Boot testing support to write a unit test using an embedded container like Apache Derby or use Testcontainers to write a dedicated integration test.

How It Works

When testing JDBC code, one requires a database, and often an embedded database like H2, Apache Derby, or HSQLDB is used for testing. Spring Boot makes it easy to write tests for JDBC code. JDBC-based tests can be annotated with @JdbcTest, and Spring Boot will create a minimal application with only the JDBC-related beans, like a DataSource and transaction manager.

Test JDBC Code with an Embedded Database

Let's write a test for JdbcCustomerRepository, and let's use H2 as the embedded database. First add H2 as a test dependency (Listing 6-24).

Listing 6-24. H2 Database as a Test Dependency

```
<dependency>
  <groupId>com.h2database</groupId>
  <artifactId>h2</artifactId>
  <scope>test</scope>
</dependency>
```

Next create JdbcCustomerRepositoryTest (Listing 6-25).

Listing 6-25. JdbcCustomerRepositoryTest Test Setup

```
@JdbcTest
@TestPropertySource(properties = "spring.flyway.enabled=false")
@Import(JdbcCustomerRepository.class)
class JdbcCustomerRepositoryTest {

  @Autowired
  private JdbcCustomerRepository repository;
}
```

The @JdbcTest annotation executes the test by a special JUnit extension (the SpringExtension) to bootstrap the Spring Test Context framework. The @JdbcTest annotation will replace the preconfigured DataSource with an embedded one (H2 in this case). As we want to test our repository, the @Import(JdbcCustomerRepository.class) annotation is added.

Finally, there is the @TestPropertySource(properties = "spring.flyway.enabled=false"), which indicates that we want to disable Flyway. The application uses Flyway to manage the schema; however, those scripts are written for PostgreSQL and not H2. For testing we want to disable Flyway and provide an H2-based schema.sql to create the schema.

> ℹ This is one of the drawbacks of using a different database for testing (H2) than actually in the live system (PostgreSQL). You either need to maintain two sets of scripts for the schema or use the same database for testing as in the live system.

Create a `schema.sql` file in `src/test/resources` and add the DDL statement in Listing 6-26.

Listing 6-26. Customer DDL for H2

```sql
CREATE TABLE customer (
  id BIGINT AUTO_INCREMENT PRIMARY KEY,
  name VARCHAR(100) NOT NULL,
  email VARCHAR(255) NOT NULL,
  UNIQUE(name)
);
```

Now write a test that tests if records get inserted correctly (Listing 6-27).

Listing 6-27. Insert Customer Test

```java
@Test
void insertNewCustomer() {
  assertThat(repository.findAll()).isEmpty();
  var newCustomer = new Customer("T. Testing", "t.testing@test123.tst");
  var customer = repository.save(newCustomer);

  assertThat(customer.id()).isNotNull();
  assertThat(customer.name()).isEqualTo("T. Testing");
  assertThat(customer.email()).isEqualTo("t.testing@test123.tst");

  assertThat(repository.findById(customer.id())).hasValue(customer);
}
```

This test first asserts that the database is empty. This is not really required but can be useful to detect if other tests pollute the database. Next a `Customer` is added to the database by calling the `save` method on the `JdbcCustomerRepository`. The resulting `Customer` is validated to have an ID and `name` and `email` attributes. Finally, the `Customer` is retrieved again and compared to be the same.

Another test you could add is the findAll method. When inserting two records, calling findAll should result in two records being retrieved (Listing 6-28).

Listing 6-28. Find All Customer Test

```
@Test
void findAllCustomers() {
  assertThat(repository.findAll()).isEmpty();

  repository.save(new Customer("T. Testing1", "t.testing@test123.tst"));
  repository.save(new Customer("T. Testing2", "t.testing@test123.tst"));

  assertThat(repository.findAll()).hasSize(2);
}
```

There could be more assertions, but saving the data is already verified in the other test method.

Test JDBC Code with Testcontainers

A better option nowadays is to use Testcontainers. Testcontainers uses Docker to bootstrap a Docker container for your given technology. In this case, we could use a PostgreSQL Docker image to boot a real database and use that in our tests. With this you are now using your actual database for testing and don't need to do with an in-memory version, meaning you can execute all the queries you want and test them. It gives you also the opportunity to test your database migration scripts (when in use).

To use Testcontainers, in this case for PostgreSQL, we need to add the appropriate dependencies (see Listing 6-29).

Listing 6-29. Testcontainers Dependency for PostgreSQL and JUnit Jupiter

```
<dependency>
  <groupId>org.springframework.boot</groupId>
  <artifactId>spring-boot-testcontainers</artifactId>
</dependency>
<dependency>
  <groupId>org.testcontainers</groupId>
  <artifactId>postgresql</artifactId>
  <scope>test</scope>
```

```
</dependency>
<dependency>
  <groupId>org.testcontainers</groupId>
  <artifactId>junit-jupiter</artifactId>
  <scope>test</scope>
</dependency>
```

Now write a test that tests if records get inserted correctly into our actual PostgreSQL database (see Listing 6-30).

Listing 6-30. JdbcCustomerRepositoryTest Test Setup for Testcontainers

```
@JdbcTest
@AutoConfigureTestDatabase(replace = AutoConfigureTestDatabase.Replace.NONE)
@Import(JdbcCustomerRepository.class)
@Testcontainers
class JdbcCustomerRepositoryTest {

  @Container
  @ServiceConnection
  static PostgreSQLContainer<?> postgres =
    new PostgreSQLContainer<>("postgres:15-alpine");
}
```

The `@JdbcTest` executes the test by a special JUnit extension (the `SpringExtension`) to bootstrap the Spring Test Context framework. The `@JdbcTest` annotation will replace the preconfigured `DataSource` with an embedded one by default. The `@AutoConfigur eTestDatabase(replace = AutoConfigureTestDatabase.Replace.NONE)` annotation prevents this replacing as we want to provide an actual `DataSource`. As we want to create an instance of our repository, the `@Import(JdbcCustomerRepository.class)` annotation is added.

Now to register the special JUnit extension for Testcontainers, the `@Testcontainers` annotation has been added. This extension finds fields annotated with `@Container` and will bootstrap the given container. For this test, that is a `PostgreSQLContainer`, which we instruct to use a PostgreSQL 15 Docker container. Testcontainers will take care of the download of this container and start an instance and then stop it after the test.

When the test runs, the provided Flyway script will automatically execute and create the schema and populate it with some data (as that was in our Flyway script; see Listing 6-8 in the previous recipe).

As the container for each test will start with a different URL, we need to tell this to our Spring Boot application. The created URL is automatically registered with the application through the use of the @ServiceConnection annotation. See also Recipe 2-3 for more information about this.

With this we can now write some tests to validate our behavior (Listing 6-31).

Listing 6-31. JdbcCustomerRepositoryTest Tests with Testcontainers

```
@Test
void insertNewCustomer() {
  var newCustomer = new Customer("T. Testing", "t.testing@test123.tst");
  var customer = repository.save(newCustomer);

  assertThat(customer.id()).isGreaterThan(0);
  assertThat(customer.name()).isEqualTo("T. Testing");
  assertThat(customer.email()).isEqualTo("t.testing@test123.tst");

  assertThat(repository.findById(customer.id())).hasValue(customer);
}

@Test
void findAllCustomers() {

  int count = repository.findAll().size();

  repository.save(new Customer("T. Testing1", "t.testing@test123.tst"));
  repository.save(new Customer("T. Testing2", "t.testing@test123.tst"));

  assertThat(repository.findAll()).hasSize(count + 2);
}
```

The tests are more or less similar to the ones used from the embedded database; however, here we have some additional data already in our database, and we have to account for that in our tests. This depends on what your database migration script looks like. If it generates an empty schema, you don't need to change the tests.

Test Spring Data JDBC Repositories

When using Spring Data JDBC, the test setup is slightly different. Instead of the @JdbcTest annotation, there is now the @DataJdbcTest annotation, which indicates the use of Spring Data JDBC and its test setup. Next, to do the setup for the needed JDBC Components (like the DataSource), it also enabled scanning for Spring Data JDBC-based repositories.

As with the @JdbcTest, this setup will also automatically try to replace the existing DataSource with an embedded one. As we use Testcontainers to bootstrap our database, we need to disable this by adding @AutoConfigureTestDatabase(replace = AutoConfigureTestDatabase.Replace.NONE).

The test class still looks a lot like the regular JDBC-based test, but the difference is the annotation (Listing 6-32).

Listing 6-32. CustomerRepositoryTest for Spring Data JDBC

```
@DataJdbcTest
@AutoConfigureTestDatabase(replace = AutoConfigureTestDatabase.
Replace.NONE)
@Testcontainers
class JdbcCustomerRepositoryTest {

  @Container
  @ServiceConnection
  static PostgreSQLContainer<?> postgres =
    new PostgreSQLContainer<>("postgres:15-alpine");

  @Autowired
  private CustomerRepository repository;
}
```

It is largely the same as the initial @JdbcTest with Testcontainers, with the differences that we now use the @DataJdbcTest annotation, indicating we want to use Spring Data JDBC, and that we autowire CustomerRepository instead of the previous JdbcCustomerRepository. We now only need the interface for testing.

6-6. Access Data with JPA

Problem

You want to use JPA in your Spring Boot application.

Solution

Spring Boot automatically detects the presence of Hibernate, and the needed JPA classes will use that information to configure the `EntityManagerFactory` instance.

How It Works

Spring Boot has out-of-the-box support for JPA through Hibernate. When Hibernate is detected, an `EntityManagerFactory` instance will be automatically configured using the earlier configured `DataSource`.

You need to add `hibernate-core` and `spring-orm` as dependencies to your project. However, it is easier to add the `spring-boot-starter-data-jpa` dependency to your project (Listing 6-33), although this will also pull in `spring-data-jpa` as a dependency.

Listing 6-33. JPA Dependencies for Spring Boot

```
<dependency>
  <groupId>org.springframework.boot</groupId>
  <artifactId>spring-boot-starter-data-jpa</artifactId>
</dependency>
```

This will add all the necessary dependencies to the classpath.

Use Plain JPA Repositories

For JPA to work, you have to annotate the classes representing entities in your system. In your system, we are going to store and retrieve `Customer` from the database. We need to mark this as an entity using the `@Entity` annotation. In addition, we need to identify the ID (primary key) of the entity (here we use `@Id` on the `id` field). A JPA entity class is required to have a default no-args constructor (although it can be `package private`).

```java
package com.apress.springboot3recipes.jpa;

import java.util.Objects;

import jakarta.persistence.Column;
import jakarta.persistence.Entity;
import jakarta.persistence.GeneratedValue;
import jakarta.persistence.GenerationType;
import jakarta.persistence.Id;

@Entity
public class Customer {

  @Id
  @GeneratedValue(strategy = GenerationType.IDENTITY)
  private Long id;

  @Column(nullable = false)
  private final String name;

  @Column(nullable = false)
  private final String email;

  public Customer() {
    this(null,null);
  }

  public Customer(String name, String email) {
    this.name = name;
    this.email = email;
  }

  public Long getId() {
    return id;
  }

  public String getName() {
    return name;
  }
```

```java
public String getEmail() {
  return email;
}

@Override
public boolean equals(Object o) {
  if (this == o) return true;
  if (o instanceof Customer other) {
    return Objects.equals(this.id, other.id);
  }
  return false;
}

@Override
public int hashCode() {
  return getClass().hashCode();
}

@Override
public String toString() {
  return String.format("Customer[id=%d, name=%s, email='%s']",
        this.id, this.name, this.email);
}
}
```

Next, create a JPA implementation of CustomerRepository (see Recipe 6-2). To use JPA you have to get EntityManager. This is done by declaring a field and annotating it with @PersistenceContext (see Listing 6-34).

Listing 6-34. Plain JPA-Based CustomerRepository Implementation

```java
package com.apress.springboot3recipes.jpa;

import org.springframework.stereotype.Repository;

import java.util.List;
import java.util.Optional;

import jakarta.persistence.EntityManager;
import jakarta.persistence.PersistenceContext;
```

```java
@Repository
class JpaCustomerRepository implements CustomerRepository {

  @PersistenceContext
  private EntityManager em;

  @Override
  public List<Customer> findAll() {
    return em.createQuery("SELECT c FROM Customer c", Customer.class).
    getResultList();
  }

  @Override
  public Optional<Customer> findById(long id) {
    var customer = em.find(Customer.class, id);
    return Optional.ofNullable(customer);
  }

  @Override
  public Customer save(Customer customer) {
    em.persist(customer);
    return customer;
  }
}
```

The following CustomerLister class (similar to the one of Recipe 6-2) will read all Customer records from the database and print them to the log (Listing 6-35).

Listing 6-35. JPA-Based CustomerLister

```java
@Component
class CustomerLister implements ApplicationRunner {

  private final Logger logger = LoggerFactory.getLogger(getClass());
  private final CustomerRepository customers;

  CustomerLister(CustomerRepository customers) {
    this.customers = customers;
  }
```

```
@Override
public void run(ApplicationArguments args) {
  customers.findAll()
        .forEach( (customer) -> logger.info("{}", customer));
  }
}
```

There are some configuration options you can use to configure
EntityManagerFactory in your application. Those properties can be found in the
spring.jpa namespace (Table 6-4).

Table 6-4. *JPA Properties*

Property	Description
spring.jpa.database	Sets the target database to operate on; this is auto-detected by default.
spring.jpa.database-platform	Sets the name of the target database to operate on; this is auto-detected by default. This can be used to specify a specific Hibernate Dialect to use.
spring.jpa.generate-ddl	Initializes the schema on startup; the default is false.
spring.jpa.show-sql	Enables logging of SQL statements; the default is false.
spring.jpa.open-in-view	Registers the OpenEntityManagerInViewInterceptor. Binds the EntityManager to the request processing thread. The default is true. This will result in a warning in the log if not explicitly enabled or disabled.
spring.jpa.hibernate.ddl-auto	Shorthand for the hibernate.hbm2ddl.auto property. The default is none and create-drop for embedded databases.
spring.jpa.hibernate.use-new-id-generator-mappings	Shorthand for the hibernate.id.new_generator_mappings property. When not explicitly set, this defaults to true.

(*continued*)

Table 6-4. (*continued*)

Property	Description
`spring.jpa.hibernate.naming.` `implicit-strategy`	Sets the FQN of the implicit naming strategy; the default is `org.springframework.boot.orm.jpa.` `hibernate.SpringPhysicalNamingStrategy`.
`spring.jpa.hibernate.naming.` `physical-strategy`	Sets the FQN of the physical naming strategy; the default is `org.springframework.boot.orm.jpa.` `hibernate.SpringImplicitNamingStrategy`.
`spring.jpa.mapping-resources`	Specifies additional XML files containing entity mappings in XML instead of Java.
`spring.jpa.properties.*`	Specifies additional properties to set on the JPA provider.

The `spring.jpa.properties` file is useful if you want to configure advanced features of Hibernate such as the fetch size (`hibernate.jdbc.fetch_size`) or batch size (`hibernate.jdbc.batch_size`) when doing batch processing (Listing 6-36).

Listing 6-36. Sample JPA Properties for Hibernate

```
spring.jpa.properties.hibernate.jdbc.fetch_size=250
spring.jpa.properties.hibernate.jdbc.batch_size=50
```

This will set the properties on the JPA provider.

Use Spring Data JPA Repositories

Instead of writing your own repositories, which can be a tedious and repetitive task, you can also let Spring Data JPA do the heavy lifting for you. Instead of writing your own implementation, you can extend the `CrudRepository` interface from Spring Data and have a repository available at runtime. This saves you from writing the data access code. Spring Boot will also autoconfigure Spring Data JPA when it detects it on the classpath (Listing 6-37).

Listing 6-37. Spring Data JPA-Based CustomerRepository

```
package com.apress.springboot3recipes.jpa;

import org.springframework.data.repository.CrudRepository;

public interface CustomerRepository extends CrudRepository<Customer,
Long> { }
```

That is all you need. The findAll, findById, and save methods, among others, are provided out of the box by Spring Data JPA. You can remove the JpaCustomerRepository implementation. Because of the CrudRepository<Customer, Long>, Spring Data knows that it can query for Customer instances and that it has a Long as an ID field.

Include Entities from Different Packages

By default Spring Boot will detect components, repositories, and entities starting from the package the @SpringBootApplication annotated class is in. But what if you have entities in a different package that still need to be included? For this you can use the @EntityScan annotation; it works like @ComponentScan but is for @Entity annotated beans.

First let's add an entity in a different package, like an Order entity (Listing 6-38).

Listing 6-38. Order Entity

```
package com.apress.springboot3recipes.order;

import jakarta.persistence.Entity;
import jakarta.persistence.Id;

import java.util.Objects;

@Entity
public class Order {

  @Id
  private Long id;

  private String number;

  public Long getId() {
    return id;
  }
```

```java
  public String getNumber() {
    return number;
  }

  public void setNumber(String number) {
    this.number = number;
  }

  @Override
  public boolean equals(Object o) {
    if (o instanceof Order other) {
      return Objects.equals(this.id, other.id);
    }
    return false;
  }

  @Override
  public int hashCode() {
    return getClass().hashCode();
  }

  @Override
  public String toString() {
    return String.format("Order[id=%d, number='%s']",
            this.id, this.number);
  }

}
```

This Order class is in the com.apress.springboot3recipes.order package, which isn't covered by the @SpringBootApplication annotated class as that is in the com.apress.springboot3.recipes.jpa package. To have this entity detected, you can add the @EntityScan annotation with the additional packages to scan to your @SpringBootApplication annotated class (or a regular @Configuration class) (Listing 6-39).

Listing 6-39. Application Class Header with @EntityScan

```
@SpringBootApplication
@EntityScan({ "com.apress.springboot3recipes.order",
              "com.apress.springboot3recipes.jpa"})
```

With this addition, the Order entity will now be detected and accessible by JPA.

6-7. Test with JPA
Problem

You want to test your JPA-based repositories using a unit or small integration test.

Solution

Use the Spring Test Context framework and the Spring Boot testing support to write a unit test using an embedded container like Apache Derby or use Testcontainers to write a dedicated integration test.

How It Works

When testing JPA code, a database is required, and often an embedded database like H2, Derby, or HSQLDB is used for testing. Spring Boot makes it easy to write tests for JPA. JPA-based tests can be annotated with @DataJpaTest, and Spring Boot will create a minimal application with only the JPA-related beans. Related beans like a DataSource, a transaction manager, and if needed Spring Data JPA repositories.

Test JPA Code with an Embedded Database

Let's write a test for CustomerRepository and use H2 as the embedded database. First add H2 as a test dependency (Listing 6-40).

Listing 6-40. H2 Dependency for Testing

```
<dependency>
  <groupId>com.h2database</groupId>
  <artifactId>h2</artifactId>
  <scope>test</scope>
</dependency>
```

Next create the `CustomerRepositoryTest` class (Listing 6-41).

Listing 6-41. CustomerRepositoryTest Class

```
@DataJpaTest
@TestPropertySource(properties = "spring.flyway.enabled=false")
class CustomerRepositoryTest {

  @Autowired
  private CustomerRepository repository;

  @Autowired
  private TestEntityManager testEntityManager;
}
```

The `@DataJpaTest` annotation executes the test with a special JUnit extension (the `SpringExtension`) to bootstrap the Spring Test Context framework. Finally, there is `@TestPropertySource(properties = "spring.flyway.enabled=false")`, which indicates that we want to disable Flyway. The application uses Flyway to manage the schema; however, those scripts are written for PostgreSQL and not H2. For testing we want to disable Flyway and provide an H2-based `schema.sql` to create the schema.

ℹ️   This is one of the drawbacks of using a different database for testing (H2) than actually in the live system (PostgreSQL). You either need to maintain two sets of scripts for the schema or use the same database for testing as in the live system.

Spring Boot offers a `TestEntityManager`, which has some convenience methods to easily store and find data for testing. Now write a test that tests if records get inserted correctly (Listing 6-42).

Listing 6-42. CustomerRepository Insert New Customer Test

```
@Test
void insertNewCustomer() {
  Assertions.assertThat(repository.findAll()).isEmpty();

  var newCustomer = new Customer("T. Testing", "t.testing@test123.tst");
  var customer = repository.save(newCustomer);

  assertThat(customer.getId()).isGreaterThan(-1L);
  assertThat(customer.getName()).isEqualTo("T. Testing");
  assertThat(customer.getEmail()).isEqualTo("t.testing@test123.tst");

  Assertions.assertThat(repository.findById(customer.getId())).
  hasValue(customer);
}
```

This test first asserts that the database is empty. This is not really required but can be useful to detect if other tests pollute the database. Next a `Customer` instance is added to the database by calling the `save` method on `CustomerRepository`. The resulting `Customer` instance is validated to make sure it has an ID and the `name` and `email` attributes. Finally, the `Customer` is retrieved again and compared to be the same.

Another test you could add is the `findAll` method. When inserting two records, calling `findAll` should result in two records being retrieved (Listing 6-43).

Listing 6-43. CustomerRepository Find All Test

```
@Test
void findAllCustomers() {
  Assertions.assertThat(repository.findAll()).isEmpty();

  testEntityManager.persist(new Customer("T. Testing1",
  "t.testing@test123.tst"));
  testEntityManager.persist(new Customer("T. Testing2",
  "t.testing@test123.tst"));
  testEntityManager.flush();
  Assertions.assertThat(repository.findAll()).hasSize(2);
}
```

There could be more assertions, but saving the data is already verified in the other test method.

Test JPA Code with Testcontainers

A better option nowadays is to use Testcontainers. Testcontainers uses Docker to bootstrap a Docker container for your given technology. In this case, we could use a PostgreSQL Docker image to boot a real database and use that in our tests. With this you are now using your actual database for testing and don't need to do with an in-memory version, meaning you can execute all the queries you want and test them. It also gives you the opportunity to test your database migration scripts (when in use).

To use Testcontainers, in this case for PostgreSQL, we need to add the appropriate dependencies (see Listing 6-44).

Listing 6-44. Testcontainers Dependency for PostgreSQL and JUnit Jupiter

```
<dependency>
  <groupId>org.springframework.boot</groupId>
  <artifactId>spring-boot-testcontainers</artifactId>
</dependency>
<dependency>
  <groupId>org.testcontainers</groupId>
  <artifactId>postgresql</artifactId>
  <scope>test</scope>
</dependency>
<dependency>
  <groupId>org.testcontainers</groupId>
  <artifactId>junit-jupiter</artifactId>
  <scope>test</scope>
</dependency>
```

Now write a test that tests if records get inserted correctly into our actual PostgreSQL database (see Listing 6-45).

Listing 6-45. CustomerRepositoryTest Test Setup for Testcontainers

```
@DataJpaTest
@AutoConfigureTestDatabase(replace = AutoConfigureTestDatabase.
Replace.NONE)
@Testcontainers
class CustomerRepositoryTest {

  @Container
  @ServiceConnection
  static PostgreSQLContainer<?> postgres =
    new PostgreSQLContainer<>("postgres:15-alpine");

  @Autowired
  private CustomerRepository repository;

  @Autowired
  private TestEntityManager testEntityManager;
```

The @DataJpaTest annotation executes the test with a special JUnit extension (the SpringExtension) to bootstrap the Spring Test Context framework. @DataJpaTest will replace the preconfigured DataSource with an embedded one by default. @AutoConfigure TestDatabase(replace = AutoConfigureTestDatabase.Replace.NONE) prevents this replacing as we want to provide an actual DataSource.

Now to register the special JUnit extension for Testcontainers, the @Testcontainers annotation has been added. This extension finds fields annotated with @Container and will bootstrap the given container. For this test, that is a PostgreSQLContainer, which we instruct to use a PostgreSQL 15 Docker container. Testcontainers will take care of the download of this container and then start an instance and stop it after the test.

When the test runs, the provided Flyway script will automatically execute and create the schema and populate it with some data (as that was in our Flyway script; see Listing 6-8).

As the container for each test will start with a different URL, we need to tell this to our Spring Boot application. For this we can use the @ServiceConnection annotation. This will pass the required and needed properties to the container automatically. See also Recipe 2-3 for more information on this.

With this we can now write some tests to validate our behavior (Listing 6-46).

Listing 6-46. CustomerRepositoryTest tests with Testcontainers

```
@Test
void insertNewCustomer() {
  var newCustomer = new Customer("T. Testing", "t.testing@test123.tst");
  var customer = repository.save(newCustomer);

  assertThat(customer.getId()).isGreaterThan(-1L);
  assertThat(customer.getName()).isEqualTo("T. Testing");
  assertThat(customer.getEmail()).isEqualTo("t.testing@test123.tst");

  testEntityManager.flush();
  testEntityManager.clear();

  Assertions.assertThat(repository.findById(customer.getId())).
    hasValue(customer);
}

@Test
void findAllCustomers() {
  var count = repository.count();
  testEntityManager.persist(new Customer("T. Testing1",
    "t.testing@test123.tst"));
  testEntityManager.persist(new Customer("T. Testing2",
    "t.testing@test123.tst"));
  testEntityManager.flush();
  Assertions.assertThat(repository.findAll()).hasSize( (int) count + 2);
}
```

The tests are more or less similar to the ones used from the embedded database; however, here we have some additional data already in our database, and we have to account for that in our tests. This depends on what your database migration script looks like. If it generates an empty schema, you don't need to change the tests.

6-8. Access Spring Data with MongoDB

Problem

You want to use MongoDB in your Spring Boot application.

Solution

Add the Mongo Driver as a dependency and use the `spring.data.mongodb` properties to let Spring Boot set up a `MongoTemplate` to the correct MongoDB.

How It Works

Spring Boot automatically detects the presence of the MongoDB driver combined with the Spring Data MongoDB classes. If those are found, MongoDB as well as the `MongoTemplate` (among others) will be automatically set up for you.

To use MongoDB with Spring Boot, first we need the proper dependencies. Using `spring-boot-starter-data-mongodb` will pull in all the needed dependencies. It will pull in `spring-data-mongodb` as well as the `mongodb-driver-sync` dependency, which is all you need to connect to MongoDB (Listing 6-47).

Listing 6-47. MongoDB Dependencies

```
<dependency>
  <groupId>org.springframework.boot</groupId>
  <artifactId>spring-boot-starter-data-mongodb</artifactId>
</dependency>
```

Next we need to specify the configuration for MongoDB. Where it is and which username/password to use are the minimum properties we need (see Listing 6-48).

Listing 6-48. MongoDB Properties

```
spring.data.mongodb.host=localhost
spring.data.mongodb.port=27017
spring.data.mongodb.database=customer
```

The application.properties file in Listing 6-45 specifies the host, username/password, and name of the database to use. This is done by setting the respective properties in the spring.data.mongodb namespace. With the dependencies in place and the properties set, upon startup Spring Boot will detect both and configure MongoDB for the application. It will create the connections to MongoDB and configure a MongoTemplate to use in your application and when detected will also detect Spring Data–based Mongo repositories.

Use the MongoTemplate

Now that the connection is set up, you can use it, ideally through MongoTemplate to make it easier to store and retrieve documents. First you need a document you want to store. Let's create a Customer that we want to persist (Listing 6-49).

Listing 6-49. Customer Record

```
package com.apress.springboot3recipes.mongo;

public record Customer(String id, String name, String email) {

  public Customer(String name, String email) {
    this(null, name, email);
  }

}
```

The id field will automatically be mapped to the _id document identifier of MongoDB. If you would like to use another field, you could use the @Id annotation from Spring Data to specify which field should be used.

Let's create a CustomerRepository instance so that instances can be saved and retrieved (Listing 6-50).

Listing 6-50. CustomerRepository Interface

```
package com.apress.springboot3recipes.mongo;

import java.util.List;
import java.util.Optional;

public interface CustomerRepository {
```

```
  List<Customer> findAll();
  Optional<Customer> findById(long id);
  Customer save(Customer customer);
}
```

The MongoDB implementation uses a `MongoTemplate`-based implementation (Listing 6-51).

Listing 6-51. CustomerRepository MongoTemplate-Based Implementation

```
package com.apress.springboot3recipes.mongo;

import org.springframework.data.mongodb.core.MongoTemplate;
import org.springframework.stereotype.Repository;

import java.util.List;
import java.util.Optional;

@Repository
class MongoCustomerRepository implements CustomerRepository {

  private final MongoTemplate mongoTemplate;

  MongoCustomerRepository(MongoTemplate mongoTemplate) {
    this.mongoTemplate = mongoTemplate;
  }

  @Override
  public List<Customer> findAll() {
    return mongoTemplate.findAll(Customer.class);
  }

  @Override
  public Optional<Customer> findById(long id) {
    return Optional.ofNullable(mongoTemplate.findById(id, Customer.class));
  }
```

```
  @Override
  public Customer save(Customer customer) {
    mongoTemplate.save(customer);
    return customer;
  }
}
```

MongoCustomerRepository uses the preconfigured MongoTemplate to store and retrieve customers in MongoDB.

To use all the parts, first there needs to be some data in MongoDB. An ApplicationRunner can be used to insert some data (Listing 6-52).

Listing 6-52. DataInitializer for MongoDB

```
@Component
@Order(1)
class DataInitializer implements ApplicationRunner {

  private final CustomerRepository customers;

  DataInitializer(CustomerRepository customers) {
    this.customers = customers;
  }

  @Override
  public void run(ApplicationArguments args) throws Exception {
    List.of(
            new Customer("Marten Deinum", "marten@deinum.biz"),
            new Customer("Josh Long", "jlong@pivotal.io"),
            new Customer("John Doe", "john.doe@island.io"),
            new Customer("Jane Doe", "jane.doe@island.io"))
            .forEach(customers::save);
  }
}
```

DataInitializer will use the CustomerRepository instance to save some Customer instances into MongoDB. Notice the @Order. We want this to execute first, which can be enforced by explicitly ordering the bean.

Next create an ApplicationRunner instance to retrieve all the customers from MongoDB (Listing 6-53).

Listing 6-53. CustomerLister Using CustomerRepository

```
@Component
class CustomerLister implements ApplicationRunner {

  private final Logger logger = LoggerFactory.getLogger(getClass());
  private final CustomerRepository customers;

  CustomerLister(CustomerRepository customers) {
    this.customers = customers;
  }

  @Override
  public void run(ApplicationArguments args) {
    customers.findAll()
            .forEach( (customer) -> logger.info("{}", customer));
  }
}
```

This CustomerLister instance will use CustomerRepository to load all customers from the database and print a line in the logs.

The application class to bootstrap all this (including the two aforementioned ApplicationRunner classes) is shown in Listing 6-54.

Listing 6-54. Full Application Class

```
package com.apress.springboot3recipes.mongo;

import org.slf4j.Logger;
import org.slf4j.LoggerFactory;
import org.springframework.boot.ApplicationArguments;
```

```java
import org.springframework.boot.ApplicationRunner;
import org.springframework.boot.SpringApplication;
import org.springframework.boot.autoconfigure.SpringBootApplication;
import org.springframework.core.annotation.Order;
import org.springframework.stereotype.Component;

import java.util.List;

@SpringBootApplication
public class MongoApplication {

  public static void main(String[] args) {
    SpringApplication.run(MongoApplication.class, args);
  }
}

@Component
@Order(1)
class DataInitializer implements ApplicationRunner {

  private final CustomerRepository customers;

  DataInitializer(CustomerRepository customers) {
    this.customers = customers;
  }

  @Override
  public void run(ApplicationArguments args) throws Exception {
    List.of(
            new Customer("Marten Deinum", "marten@deinum.biz"),
            new Customer("Josh Long", "jlong@pivotal.io"),
            new Customer("John Doe", "john.doe@island.io"),
            new Customer("Jane Doe", "jane.doe@island.io"))
            .forEach(customers::save);
  }
}
```

```
@Component
class CustomerLister implements ApplicationRunner {

  private final Logger logger = LoggerFactory.getLogger(getClass());
  private final CustomerRepository customers;

  CustomerLister(CustomerRepository customers) {
    this.customers = customers;
  }

  @Override
  public void run(ApplicationArguments args) {
    customers.findAll()
            .forEach( (customer) -> logger.info("{}", customer));
  }
}
```

When you run the application, it will automatically connect to the MongoDB instance, insert data into it, and finally retrieve it and print it to the logs.

You will need a MongoDB instance to store and retrieve documents.

Connect to an External MongoDB

ⓘ   The bin directory contains a mongo.sh script that will start a MongoDB instance using Docker.

When starting MongoApplication, it will by default try to connect to a MongoDB server on the localhost via port 27017. If that is not where you want to connect, use the spring.data.mongodb properties (see Table 6-5) to configure the correct location.

Table 6-5. *MongoDB Properties*

Property	Description
spring.data.mongodb.uri	Sets the Mongo database URI, including credentials, settings, etc. The default is mongodb://localhost/test.
spring.data.mongodb.username	Sets the login user of the Mongo server. The default is none.
spring.data.mongodb.password	Sets the login password of the mongo server. The default is none.
spring.data.mongodb.host	Sets the hostname (or IP address) of the MongoDB server. The default is to fall back to localhost.
spring.data.mongodb.port	Sets the port of the MongoDB server. The default is to fall back to 27017.
spring.data.mongodb.database	Sets the name of the MongoDB database/collection to use.
spring.data.mongodb.field-naming-strategy	Sets the FQN of the FieldNamingStrategy instance used to map object fields to document fields. This defaults to PropertyNameFieldNamingStrategy.
spring.data.mongodb.authentication-database	Sets the name of MongoDB to use for authentication. This defaults to the spring.data.mongodb.database value.
spring.data.mongodb.gridfs-database	Sets the name of MongoDB to connect to. This defaults to a spring.data.mongodb.database value.
spring.data.mongodb.replica-set-name	Sets the replica set name for the cluster; required when using a clustered MongoDB.

Although you can use Spring Boot to configure the MongoClient, if you need more control, you can always specify MongoDbFactory or MongoClient yourself as a bean, and Spring Boot will not auto-configure the MongoClient. It will still detect Spring Data MongoDB classes and will enable repository support.

Use Spring Data MongoDB Repositories

Instead of writing your own implementation of the repository, you can also use Spring Data MongoDB to create them for you (just like as with Spring Data JPA). For this you need to extend one of the Repository interfaces from Spring Data. The easiest is to extend CrudRepository or MongoRepository (Listing 6-55).

Listing 6-55. Spring Data MongoDB-Based CustomerRepository

```
package com.apress.springboot3recipes.mongo;

import org.springframework.data.mongodb.repository.MongoRepository;

public interface CustomerRepository extends MongoRepository<Customer,
String> { }
```

This is all we need to get a fully functional repository; you can remove the MongoCustomerRepository implementation. This will give you save, findAll, findById, and many more methods.

The application will still run, insert some customers, and list them in the logs (see Figure 6-4).

Use Reactive MongoDB Repositories

Instead of using regular blocking operations, MongoDB can also be used in a reactive fashion. For this, use spring-boot-starter-data-mongodb-reactive instead of spring-boot-starter-data-mongodb. This dependency will include the needed reactive libraries and reactive driver for MongoDB (Listing 6-56).

Listing 6-56. Spring Data MongoDB Dependencies for Reactive Use

```
<dependency>
  <groupId>org.springframework.boot</groupId>
  <artifactId>spring-boot-starter-data-mongodb-reactive</artifactId>
</dependency>
```

With the dependencies in order, you can make CustomerRepository reactive. This is done by simply extending ReactiveCrudRepository, ReactiveSortingRepository, or ReactiveMongoRepository depending on your needs (Listing 6-57).

Listing 6-57. Reactive CustomerRepository

```
package com.apress.springboot3recipes.mongo;

import org.springframework.data.mongodb.repository.ReactiveMongoRepository;

public interface CustomerRepository
        extends ReactiveMongoRepository<Customer, String> { }
```

Now that `CustomerRepository` extends `ReactiveMongoRepository`, all the methods return either `Flux` (zero or more elements) or `Mono` (zero or one element).

ℹ️   The default implementations use Project Reactor as the reactive framework; however, you can also use RxJava. Then, instead of `Flux` and `Mono`, you will use an `Observable` or `Single` instead. For this you need to extend `RxJava3CrudRepository` or `RxJava3SortingRepository`.

`DataInitializer` needs to be made reactive as well (Listing 6-58).

Listing 6-58. Reactive DataInitializer

```
@Component
@Order(1)
class DataInitializer implements ApplicationRunner {

  private final CustomerRepository customers;

  DataInitializer(CustomerRepository customers) {
    this.customers = customers;
  }

  @Override
  public void run(ApplicationArguments args) {
    var newCustomers = Flux.just(
            new Customer("Marten Deinum", "marten.deinum@conspect.nl"),
            new Customer("Josh Long", "jlong@pivotal.io"),
            new Customer("John Doe", "john.doe@island.io"),
            new Customer("Jane Doe", "jane.doe@island.io"));
```

```
  customers.deleteAll()
          .thenMany(customers.saveAll(newCustomers))
          .blockLast();
  }
}
```

First it deletes everything; then we create new `Customer` instances and add them to the repository. As we want to make sure everything is stored before we move on, we use `blockLast`, which will wait until the last element is written before the process continues.

Finally, `CustomerLister` needs to be made reactive (Listing 6-59).

Listing 6-59. Reactive CustomerLister

```
@Component
class CustomerLister implements ApplicationRunner {

  private final Logger logger = LoggerFactory.getLogger(getClass());
  private final CustomerRepository customers;

  CustomerLister(CustomerRepository customers) {
    this.customers = customers;
  }

  @Override
  public void run(ApplicationArguments args) {
    customers.findAll()
            .subscribe( (customer) -> logger.info("{}", customer));
  }
}
```

It will find all the customers from the repository and for each will print a line in the log file.

When starting the application, you will probably see nothing in the log files. Because of the reactive nature of the application, it finishes quickly, and `CustomerLister` doesn't have time to register itself and start listening. To prevent the shutdown of the application, add an `System.in.read()` method. This will keep the application running until you press Enter (Listing 6-60). Generally when running an application, this isn't needed because the application is exposed as a service/web application that keeps running automatically.

Listing 6-60. Keeping the Application Alive with System.in.read

```
public static void main(String[] args) throws IOException {
  SpringApplication.run(ReactiveMongoApplication.class, args);
  System.in.read();
}
```

Test Mongo Repositories

When testing MongoDB code, a running Mongo instance is needed. For testing an embedded MongoDB is often used. Spring Boot makes it easy to write tests for MongoDB, using @DataMongoTest. Spring Boot will create a minimal application with only the MongoDB-related beans and start an embedded MongoDB (if detected).

Let's write a test for CustomerRepository and use an embedded MongoDB. First add the embedded MongoDB as a test dependency (Listing 6-61).

Listing 6-61. Flapdoodle Embedded Mongo Spring Boot Starter Dependency

```
<dependency>
  <groupId>de.flapdoodle.embed</groupId>
  <artifactId>de.flapdoodle.embed.mongo.spring3x</artifactId>
  <version>4.12.0</version>
  <scope>test</scope>
</dependency>
```

To use it, we also need to specify de.flapdoodle.mongodb.embedded.version, which contains the version of MongoDB we are using (Listing 6-62). In our case, this is the 6.0.5 version (the same as the Docker container version). This together with the starter (Listing 6-61) will automatically download an embedded MongoDB version and start it, ready to use for testing.

Listing 6-62. Flapdoodle application.properties

```
de.flapdoodle.mongodb.embedded.version=6.0.5
```

Next create CustomerRepositoryTest (Listing 6-63).

Listing 6-63. MongoDB-Based Test for the CustomerRepository

```
@DataMongoTest
class CustomerRepositoryTest {

  @Autowired
  private CustomerRepository repository;

  @BeforeEach
  public void cleanUp() {
    repository.deleteAll();
  }
}
```

The @DataMongoTest annotation executes the test with a special JUnit Extension (SpringExtention) to bootstrap the Spring Test Context framework. The @DataMongoTest annotation will replace the preconfigured MongoDB with an embedded one (if on the classpath). It will also bootstrap the MongoDB components and when detected Spring Data Mongo repositories.

After each test, we want to make sure that the embedded MongoDB doesn't contain any data. This can be achieved by adding an @BeforeEach annotated method and calling deleteAll on the repository. This method will be called before each executed test method.

Now write a test that tests if records get inserted correctly (Listing 6-64).

Listing 6-64. Insert New Customer Test: MongoDB

```
@Test
void insertNewCustomer() {
  assertThat(repository.findAll()).isEmpty();

  var newCustomer = new Customer("T. Testing", "t.testing@test123.tst");
  var customer = repository.save(newCustomer);

  assertThat(customer.id()).isNotNull();
  assertThat(customer.name()).isEqualTo("T. Testing");
  assertThat(customer.email()).isEqualTo("t.testing@test123.tst");

  assertThat(repository.findById(customer.id()))
          .contains( customer);
}
```

CHAPTER 6   DATA ACCESS

This test first asserts that the database is empty, which is not really required but can be useful to detect if other tests pollute the database. Next a `Customer` is added to the database by calling the `save` method on the `CustomerRepository`. The resulting `Customer` instance is validated to have an ID and the `name` and `email` attributes. Finally, the `Customer` instance is retrieved again and compared to be the same.

Another test you could add is the `findAll` method. When inserting two records, calling `findAll` should result in two records being retrieved (Listing 6-65).

Listing 6-65. Find All Customers Test: MongoDB

```
@Test
void findAllCustomers() {
  assertThat(repository.findAll()).isEmpty();

  repository.save(new Customer("T. Testing1", "t.testing@test123.tst"));
  repository.save(new Customer("T. Testing2", "t.testing@test123.tst"));

  assertThat(repository.findAll()).hasSize(2);
}
```

Of course, there could be more assertions, but saving the data is already verified in the other test method.

When running the test, they should all succeed (Figure 6-5), and the output should show the download and start of the embedded MongoDB.

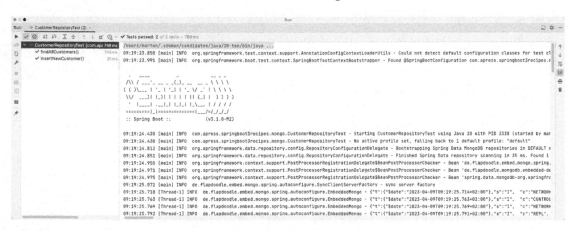

Figure 6-5. *Test output with Flapdoodle*

Test MongoDB Code with Testcontainers

Another option is to use Testcontainers. Testcontainers uses Docker to bootstrap a Docker container for your given technology. In this case, we could use a MongoDB Docker image to boot a real MongoDB instance and use that in our tests. This also you the opportunity to test your database migration scripts (when in use). This is also useful when you are combining different technologies such as SQL and MongoDB because you can use Testcontainers to bootstrap both.

To use Testcontainers, in this case for MongoDB, we need to add the appropriate dependencies (see Listing 6-66)

Listing 6-66. Testcontainers MongoDB Dependencies

```
<dependency>
  <groupId>org.springframework.boot</groupId>
  <artifactId>spring-boot-testcontainers</artifactId>
</dependency>
<dependency>
  <groupId>org.testcontainers</groupId>
  <artifactId>mongodb</artifactId>
  <scope>test</scope>
</dependency>
<dependency>
  <groupId>org.testcontainers</groupId>
  <artifactId>junit-jupiter</artifactId>
  <scope>test</scope>
</dependency>
```

Next create `CustomerRepositoryTest` (Listing 6-67).

Listing 6-67. MongoDB-Based Test Using Testcontainers for the CustomerRepository

```
@Testcontainers
class CustomerRepositoryTest {

  @Container
  @ServiceConnection
  static MongoDBContainer mongodb = new MongoDBContainer("mongo:6.0");
```

335

```
@Autowired
private CustomerRepository repository;

@BeforeEach
public void cleanUp() {
  repository.deleteAll();
}
}
```

@DataMongoTest executes the test by a special JUnit extension (SpringExtension) to bootstrap the Spring Test Context framework. Now to register the special JUnit extension for Testcontainers, the @Testcontainers annotation has been added. This extension finds fields annotated with @Container and will bootstrap the given container. For this test, that is a MongoDBContainer, which we instruct to use a MongoDB 6.0 container. Testcontainers will take care of the download of this container and start an instance and will stop it after the test.

As the container for each test will start with a different URL, we need to tell this to our Spring Boot application. For this we can use the @ServiceConnection annotation. This will pass the required and needed properties to the container automatically. See also Recipe 2-3 for more information on this.

6-9. Access Data with R2DBC

Most Java developers will know, or at least have heard of, the JDBC API (see the beginning of this chapter). JDBC, however, is blocking by nature and will not do well in an environment with reactive programming. For reactive programming and SQL databases, there is R2DBC. This is a low-level reactive API (or rather SPI) developed by the community. Several database already have a driver implementation based on this SPI, such as (but not limited to) PostgreSQL, Oracle, MySQL, and H2.

Problem

You have a reactive application but are still using a relational database. Using JDBC isn't an option as that is blocking in nature. Use R2DBC to have a reactive way to access your database.

Solution

Spring Boot will (as with JDBC) detect the presence of R2DBC and/or Spring Data R2DBC, and the properties in the `spring.r2dbc` namespace will connect to the database.

How It Works

To work with R2DBC, the first thing you need to do is to add the required dependencies: `r2dbc`, `spring-r2dbc`, and `spring-data-r2dbc`. However, to make it easier, Spring Boot provides `spring-boot-starter-r2dbc` to pull in all those dependencies at once (Listing 6-68).

Listing 6-68. Spring Data R2DBC Starter Dependency

```
<dependency>
    <groupId>org.postgresql</groupId>
    <artifactId>r2dbc-postgresql</artifactId>
</dependency>
```

It will use the properties in the `spring.r2dbc` namespace to configure the connections to the database (see Table 6-6 and Table 6-7). Just like for JDBC, the `spring.datasource` namespace is used.

Table 6-6. *R2DBC Connection Properties*

Property	Description
`spring.r2dbc.url`	Sets the R2DBC URL of the databse.
`spring.r2dbc.username`	Sets the username to use to connect to the database.
`spring.r2dbc.password`	Sets the password to use to connect to the database.
`spring.r2dbc.name`	Sets the name of the database to use if not set in the URL; the default is `testdb`.
`spring.r2dbc.generate-unique-name`	Sets whether to generate a random database name. Ignores any configured name when enabled; the default is `false`. This is useful when writing tests with an in-memory database.
`spring.r2dbc.properties`	Sets additional R2DBC driver properties.

Table 6-7. *R2DBC Connection Pool Properties*

Property	Description
spring.r2dbc.pool.enabled	Sets whether the R2DBC connection pooling is enabled; the default is true.
spring.r2dbc.pool.initial-size	Sets the initial number of connections to create; the default is 10.
spring.r2dbc.pool.max-acquire-time	Sets the maximum time to wait to obtain a connection from the pool; the default is indefinite.
spring.r2dbc.pool.max-create-connection-time	Sets the maximum time to wait to create a new connection; the default is indefinite.
spring.r2dbc.pool.max-idle-time	Sets the maximum time for a connection to sit idle in the pool; the default is 30 minutes.
spring.r2dbc.pool.max-life-time	Sets the maximum time for a connection to live; the default is indefinite.
spring.r2dbc.pool.max-size	Sets the maximum number of connections to allow to be created; the default is 10.
spring.r2dbc.pool.validation-depth	Sets the depth of the validation, LOCAL or REMOTE; the default is LOCAL.
spring.r2dbc.pool.validation-query	Sets the query to use to validate the health of the connection; the default is null.

To connect to the database, we need at least spring.r2dbc.url to be set; this can include all the information needed such as the database name, username, and password. But often spring.r2dbc.username and spring.r2dbc.password are passed separately. To connect to the database created earlier (see Recipe 6-2), we need the properties shown in Listing 6-69.

Listing 6-69. R2DBC Application Properties

```
spring.r2dbc.url=r2dbc:postgresql://localhost:5432/customers
spring.r2dbc.username=customers
spring.r2dbc.password=customers

spring.sql.init.mode=always
```

Here you see the `spring.r2dbc` properties to connect to the database as well as a `spring.sql.init.mode` property with a value of ALWAYS. This is to initialize the database and insert some data (see Recipe 6-2 for more on database initialization).

To work with the database, let's use a repository and create a different implementation for this. Listing 6-70 shows the `CustomerRepository` interface.

Listing 6-70. Reactive CustomerRepository Interface

```
package com.apress.springboot3recipes.r2dbc;

import reactor.core.publisher.Flux;
import reactor.core.publisher.Mono;

public interface CustomerRepository {

  Flux<Customer> findAll();
  Mono<Customer> findById(long id);
  Mono<Customer> save(Customer customer);
}
```

The methods return either a `Flux` or `Mono`, respectively zero or more or zero or one, which are the reactive types from Project Reactor. Project Reactor is the reactive implementation used internally with Spring, but it is also possible to work with RxJava or SmallRye Mutiny.

Next we need a class that uses this interface to retrieve the customers and prints out the results (Listing 6-71).

Listing 6-71. Reactive Customer Lister

```
@Component
class CustomerLister implements ApplicationRunner {

  private final Logger logger = LoggerFactory.getLogger(getClass());
  private final CustomerRepository customers;

  CustomerLister(CustomerRepository customers) {
    this.customers = customers;
  }
```

```
@Override
public void run(ApplicationArguments args) {
  customers.findAll()
          .subscribe( (customer) -> logger.info("{}", customer));
  }
}
```

This `CustomerLister` instance will use the `CustomerRepository` interface to call the `findAll` method and print out the given results to the console (see Figure 6-4).

Finally, we need a bootstrap class to run the code (Listing 6-72).

Listing 6-72. Spring Boot Application

```
package com.apress.springboot3recipes.r2dbc;

import org.slf4j.Logger;
import org.slf4j.LoggerFactory;
import org.springframework.boot.ApplicationArguments;
import org.springframework.boot.ApplicationRunner;
import org.springframework.boot.SpringApplication;
import org.springframework.boot.autoconfigure.SpringBootApplication;
import org.springframework.core.annotation.Order;
import org.springframework.r2dbc.core.DatabaseClient;
import org.springframework.stereotype.Component;

@SpringBootApplication
public class R2dbcApplication {

  public static void main(String[] args) throws Exception {
    SpringApplication.run(R2dbcApplication.class, args);
    System.in.read();
  }
}
```

This Spring Boot application will detect the implementation of `CustomerRepository` (see the next sections), inject it into `CustomerLister`, and execute it as an `ApplicationRunner` instance. As we have a reactive application and nothing to keep it running, we need something to prevent the shutdown. For this we can use a `System.in.read()` method. This will pause the shutdown until you press Enter.

Use DatabaseClient

When Spring Boot detects the presence of spring-r2dbc, it will automatically add DatabaseClient as a bean to the application. The most basic way to access the database is to use this preconfigured DatabaseClient, which comes from spring-r2dbc, which is part of the Spring Framework. With this DatabaseClient, you can create an implementation of CustomerRepository (Listing 6-73).

Listing 6-73. Reactive CustomerRepository Implementation with DatabaseClient

```java
package com.apress.springboot3recipes.r2dbc;

import io.r2dbc.spi.Readable;
import org.springframework.r2dbc.core.DatabaseClient;
import org.springframework.stereotype.Repository;
import reactor.core.publisher.Flux;
import reactor.core.publisher.Mono;

@Repository
class R2dbcCustomerRepository implements CustomerRepository {

  private static final String ALL_QUERY = "SELECT id, name, email FROM
  customer";
  private static final String BY_ID_QUERY =
    "SELECT id, name, email FROM customer WHERE id=:id";
  private static final String INSERT_QUERY =
    "INSERT INTO customer (name, email) VALUES (:name, :email)";

  private final DatabaseClient client;

  R2dbcCustomerRepository(DatabaseClient client) {
    this.client = client;
  }

  @Override
  public Flux<Customer> findAll() {
    return client.sql(ALL_QUERY)
```

```
          .map(this::toCustomer)
          .all();
}

@Override
public Mono<Customer> findById(long id) {
  return client.sql(BY_ID_QUERY)
          .bind("id", id)
          .map(this::toCustomer)
          .one();
}

@Override
public Mono<Customer> save(Customer customer) {
  var result = client.sql(INSERT_QUERY)
          .filter( (s) -> s.returnGeneratedValues("id"))
          .bind("name", customer.name())
          .bind("email", customer.email())
          .map( (row) -> row.get("id", Long.class))
          .first();
  return result
          .map((id) -> new Customer(id, customer.name(), customer.
          email())));
}

private Customer toCustomer(Readable row) {
  var id = row.get(0, Long.class);
  var name = row.get(1, String.class);
  var email = row.get(2, String.class);
  return new Customer(id, name, email);
}
}
```

R2dbcCustomerRepository uses DatabaseClient to execute queries, map the result, and return it. With the sql method, we can specify which SQL query we want to execute. Using map, we can transform the result into something we can use, like a Customer. In the findAll method, we execute the query to retrieve everything from the database and map the result to a Customer. The map method used here takes a Function, which maps io.r2dbc.spi.Readable (a Row is just that) to another element. The all() method instructs the DatabaseClient that we can have 0 or more results to return, and thus it will create a Flux. The findById executes a query but first uses bind to fill in the :id attribute in the query; then we map the result. The one() method instructs DatabaseClient to return a 0 or 1 result; if we get multiple results, an error will be issued.

The save method is a bit more complicated as we need to get the id; we can use the filter method to modify io.r2dbc.spi.Statement and instruct it to return the generated keys. Next we need to bind the :name and :email attributes. Using first() we get the first result returned. We could also have used one() in this case. As we get a Mono<Long>, which contains the generated ID of the Customer, we can use the map method to instruct it to create a Customer with that ID and the given Customer to save.

Use R2dbcEntityTemplate

When Spring Data R2DBC is detected on the classpath, Spring Boot will, in addition to DatabaseClient, also automatically prepare an R2dbcEntityTemplate instance. R2dbcEntityTemplate is a wrapper around DatabaseClient to make it easier to work with database entities (Listing 6-74).

Listing 6-74. Reactive CustomerRepository Implementation with DatabaseClient

```
package com.apress.springboot3recipes.r2dbc;

import static org.springframework.data.relational.core.query.Crite
ria.where;

import org.springframework.data.r2dbc.core.R2dbcEntityTemplate;
import org.springframework.data.relational.core.query.Query;
import org.springframework.stereotype.Repository;

import reactor.core.publisher.Flux;
import reactor.core.publisher.Mono;

@Repository
class R2dbcCustomerRepository implements CustomerRepository {

  private final R2dbcEntityTemplate template;
```

```
R2dbcCustomerRepository(R2dbcEntityTemplate template) {
  this.template = template;
}

@Override
public Flux<Customer> findAll() {
  return template.select(Customer.class).all();
}

@Override
public Mono<Customer> findById(long id) {
  return template
          .selectOne(Query.query(where("id").is(id)), Customer.class);
}

@Override
public Mono<Customer> save(Customer customer) {
  return template.insert(customer);
}
}
```

R2dbcCustomerRepository using the R2dbcEntityTemplate is a bit simpler than the one using a DatabaseClient instance. The mapping from the database to Customer is done automatically, as well as the binding for the insert. The findById method has some complexity still as we need to specify the where clause for the query. To make it easier to write queries, Spring Data R2DBC contains a query builder. Here we specify a limitation on the id column.

Mapping from/to database columns is done based on metadata on the Customer class. This is optional. The default is that it will use the name of the class Customer, with a lowercase first letter as the name of the table customer. If a different table is to be used, this can be supplied through the @Table annotation. For column names to field names, something similar happens: it will use the names of the field as is for the column; if something else is needed, this can be specified through an @Column annotation. A database record also needs a primary key (in general). If the class has a field named id, this will be automatically used as the primary key. If another field is to be used or if you want to make it explicit, you can annotate that field (or fields) with @Id (see Listing 6-75).

Listing 6-75. Customer Class for Use with R2DBC

```
package com.apress.springboot3recipes.r2dbc;

import org.springframework.data.annotation.Id;
import org.springframework.data.relational.core.mapping.Column;
import org.springframework.data.relational.core.mapping.Table;

@Table("customer")
public record Customer(@Column("id") @Id Long id,
                       @Column("name") String name,
                       @Column("email") String email) {
}
```

Use the R2dbcRepository

Instead of writing an implementation with Spring Data R2DBC, you can also have a dynamic implementation (just as with Spring Data JPA). For the R2DBC case, you simply extend ReactiveCrudRepository, ReactiveSortingRepository, or R2dbcRepository depending on your needs (Listing 6-76).

Listing 6-76. Reactive CustomerRepository with Spring Data Repositories

```
package com.apress.springboot3recipes.r2dbc;

import org.springframework.data.r2dbc.repository.R2dbcRepository;

import reactor.core.publisher.Flux;
import reactor.core.publisher.Mono;

public interface CustomerRepository
        extends R2dbcRepository<Customer, Long> {
}
```

As Spring Boot automatically detects the presence of Spring Data R2DBC, it will automatically pick up this interface and create a dynamic bean for it to use in our application. The output will be similar to that of Figure 6-4.

6-10. Test with Spring Data R2DBC

Problem

You want to test your R2DBC-based repositories using a unit or small integration test.

Solution

Use the Spring Test Context framework and the Spring Boot testing support to write a unit test using an embedded container such as Apache Derby, or use Testcontainers to write a dedicated integration test.

How It Works

When testing R2DBC code, a database is required. Often an embedded database such as H2, Derby, or HSQLDB is used for testing. Spring Boot makes it easy to write tests for R2DBC. R2DBC-based tests can be annotated with `@DataR2JpaTest`, and Spring Boot will create a minimal application with only the R2DBC-related beans. R2DBC related beans like a `ConnectionFactory`, a transaction manager and if needed Spring Data R2DBC repositories.

Test R2DBC Code with an Embedded Database

Let's write a test for `CustomerRepository` and use H2 as the embedded database. First add H2 as a test dependency (Listing 6-77).

Listing 6-77. Reactive H2 Dependency for Testing

```
<dependency>
    <groupId>io.r2dbc</groupId>
    <artifactId>r2dbc-h2</artifactId>
    <scope>test</scope>
</dependency>
```

As you can see, this isn't just the H2 dependency but rather the `r2dbc-h2` dependency (which pulls in the H2 database). This dependency is the reactive counterpart of the regular JDBC driver for H2.

Next create `CustomerRepositoryTest` (Listing 6-78).

Listing 6-78. CustomerRepositoryTest Class

```
@DataR2dbcTest
@TestPropertySource(properties =
        { "spring.r2dbc.url=r2dbc:h2:mem://testdb",
          "spring.r2dbc.generate-unique-name=true" })
@Import(R2dbcCustomerRepository.class)
class CustomerRepositoryTest {

  @Autowired
  private CustomerRepository repository;

  @Autowired
  private DatabaseClient db;

  @BeforeEach
  public void setup() {
    db.sql("DELETE FROM customer").fetch().first().subscribe();
  }
}
```

The @DataR2dbcTest annotation executes the test by a special JUnit extension
(SpringExtension) to bootstrap the Spring Test Context framework. The @DataR2dbcTest
annotation sets up Spring Data R2DBC (if needed) and enables all other R2DBC features.
Using @TestPropertySource, we provide spring.r2dbc.url with an H2 in-memory
database, and we set spring.r2dbc.generate-unique-name to true. As we want to test
our repository, we add @Import(R2dbcCustomerRepository.class). In @BeforeEach we
clean up the database as to not have one test interfere with another test.

Tip   When using the Spring Data R2DBC-based repository, you don't need
@Import as the repository will be automatically detected.

Now write a test that tests if records get inserted correctly (Listing 6-79).

Listing 6-79. CustomerRepository Inserting New Customer Test

```
@Test
void insertNewCustomer() {
  var newCustomer = new Customer("T. Testing", "t.testing@test123.tst");
  repository.save(newCustomer)
            .as(StepVerifier::create)
              .assertNext( (c) -> assertThat(c.id()).isNotNull())
              .verifyComplete();
}
```

A Customer instance is added to the database by calling the save method on CustomerRepository. The resulting Customer instance is validated to have an ID and verify if the reactive pipeline has finished.

Another test you could add is the findAll method. When inserting two records, calling findAll should result in two records being retrieved (Listing 6-80).

Listing 6-80. CustomerRepository Find All Tests

```
@Test
void findAllCustomers() {

  var customers = Flux.just(
          new Customer("T. Testing1", "t.testing@test123.tst"),
          new Customer("T. Testing2", "t.testing@test123.tst"));

  customers.doOnNext(repository::save)
          .as(StepVerifier::create)
          .expectNextCount(2)
          .verifyComplete();
}
```

Of course, there could be more assertions, but saving the data is already verified in the other test method.

Test Spring Data R2DBC Code with Testcontainers

A better option nowadays is to use Testcontainers. Testcontainers uses Docker to bootstrap a Docker container for your given technology. In this case, we could use a PostgreSQL Docker image to boot a real database and use that in our tests. With this you are now using your actual database for testing and don't need to have an in-memory version, meaning you can execute all the queries you want and test them. It also gives you the opportunity to test your database migration scripts (when in use).

To use Testcontainers, in this case for PostgreSQL, we need to add the appropriate dependencies (see Listing 6-81). We need the PostgreSQL dependency from Testcontainers as well as the JUnit Jupiter one and a special one for R2DBC.

Listing 6-81. Testcontainers Dependency for PostgreSQL and JUnit Jupiter

```
<dependency>
  <groupId>org.springframework.boot</groupId>
  <artifactId>spring-boot-testcontainers</artifactId>
  <scope>test</scope>
</dependency>
<dependency>
  <groupId>org.testcontainers</groupId>
  <artifactId>postgresql</artifactId>
  <scope>test</scope>
</dependency>
<dependency>
  <groupId>org.testcontainers</groupId>
  <artifactId>r2dbc</artifactId>
  <scope>test</scope>
</dependency>
```

Now write a test that tests if records get inserted correctly into our actual PostgreSQL database (see Listing 6-82).

Listing 6-82. CustomerRepositoryTest Test Setup for Testcontainers

```
@Import(R2dbcCustomerRepository.class)
@Testcontainers
class CustomerRepositoryTest {

  @Container
  @ServiceConnection
  static PostgreSQLContainer<?> postgres = new PostgreSQLContainer<>
  ("postgres:15-alpine");

  @Autowired
  private CustomerRepository repository;
```

The `@DataR2dbcTest` annotation executes the test by a special JUnit extension (the `SpringExtension`) to bootstrap the Spring Test Context framework. Now to register the special JUnit extension for Testcontainers, the `@Testcontainers` annotation has been added. This extension finds fields annotated with `@Container` and will bootstrap the given container. For this test, that is a `PostgreSQLContainer`, which we instruct to use a PostgreSQL 15 Docker container. Testcontainers will take care of the download of this container and start an instance and stop it after the test.

As the container for each test will start with a different URL, we need to tell this to our Spring Boot application. For this we can the `@RServiceConnection` annotation. This is a Spring Boot Test support annotation that registers the needed properties based on this container instance in the application. Properties such as `spring.r2dbc.url`, etc., are thus added automatically for the tests. This can also be done manually using the `@DynamicPropertySource` annotation on a static method (see also Recipe 2-3).

With this we can now write some tests to validate our behavior (Listing 6-83).

Listing 6-83. CustomerRepositoryTest Tests with Testcontainers

```
@Test
void insertNewCustomer() {
  var newCustomer = new Customer("T. Testing", "t.testing@test123.tst");
  repository.save(newCustomer)
            .as(StepVerifier::create)
```

```
        .assertNext( (c) -> assertThat(c.id()).isNotNull())
        .verifyComplete();
}

@Test
void findAllCustomers() {
  var customers = Flux.just(
        new Customer("T. Testing1", "t.testing@test123.tst")
        ,new Customer("T. Testing2", "t.testing@test123.tst"));

  customers.flatMap(repository::save)
        .as(StepVerifier::create)
        .expectNextCount(2)
        .verifyComplete();

  repository.findAll()
        .count()
        .as(StepVerifier::create)
        .expectNext(6L)
        .verifyComplete();
}
```

The tests are more or less similar to the ones used from the embedded database; however, here we have some additional data already in our database, and we have to account for that in our tests. This depends on what your database migration script looks like. If it generates an empty schema, you don't need to change the tests.

CHAPTER 7

Java Enterprise Services

In this chapter, you will learn about Spring Boot's support for the most common Java enterprise services: using Java Management Extensions (JMX), sending email with Jakarta Mail, and scheduling tasks.

JMX is part of Java SE and is a technology for managing and monitoring system resources such as devices, applications, objects, and service-driven networks. These resources are represented as managed beans (MBeans). Spring supports JMX by exporting any bean as a model MBean without programming against the JMX API.

Jakarta Mail is the standard API and implementation for sending email in Java. Spring further provides an abstract layer to send email in an implementation-independent fashion, and Spring Boot adds automatic configuration when detected.

There are two main options for scheduling tasks on the Java platform: JDK Timer and Quartz Scheduler. JDK Timer offers simple task scheduling features that are bundled with the JDK. Compared with JDK Timer, Quartz offers more powerful job scheduling features. For both options, Spring supplies utility classes to configure scheduling tasks in a bean configuration file, without using either API directly.

We will also cover how you can use the Java Flight Recorder as well as the Micrometer API to get insights into your application's behavior and usage.

7-1. Configure Spring Asynchronous Processing
Problem

You want to asynchronously invoke a method with a long-running method.

© Marten Deinum 2024
M. Deinum, *Spring Boot 3 Recipes*, https://doi.org/10.1007/979-8-8688-0113-6_7

Solution

Spring has support to configure a `TaskExecutor` and the ability to asynchronously execute methods annotated with `@Async`. This can be done in a transparent way without the normal setup for doing asynchronous execution. Spring Boot, however, will not automatically detect the need for asynchronous method execution. This support has to be enabled with the `@EnableAsync` configuration annotation.

How It Works

Let's write a component that prints something in an asynchronous way to the console. See Listing 7-1.

Listing 7-1. Simple HelloWorldService

```java
package com.apress.springboot3recipes.scheduling;

import org.slf4j.Logger;
import org.slf4j.LoggerFactory;
import org.springframework.scheduling.annotation.Async;
import org.springframework.stereotype.Component;

@Component
public class HelloWorldService {

    private final Logger logger = LoggerFactory.getLogger(getClass());

    @Async
    public void printMessage() {
      try {
        Thread.sleep(500);
      } catch (InterruptedException ex) {
        Thread.currentThread().interrupt();
      }
      logger.info("Hello World, from Spring Boot 3!");
    }
}
```

The class will wait for 500 milliseconds before printing something to the logger. The @Async annotation on the method indicates that the method will be executed in an asynchronous manner. However, this support has to be explicitly enabled for a Spring Boot application.

To enable asynchronous processing, the @EnableAsync configuration annotation is needed. The easiest solution is to add this annotation to your application class. See Listing 7-2.

Listing 7-2. Spring Boot Application to Enable Async Processing

```
package com.apress.springboot3recipes.scheduling;

import org.springframework.boot.ApplicationRunner;
import org.springframework.boot.SpringApplication;
import org.springframework.boot.autoconfigure.SpringBootApplication;
import org.springframework.context.annotation.Bean;
import org.springframework.scheduling.annotation.EnableAsync;

import java.io.IOException;

@SpringBootApplication
@EnableAsync
public class ThreadingApplication {

    public static void main(String[] args) throws IOException {
        SpringApplication.run(ThreadingApplication.class, args);

        System.out.println("Press [ENTER] to quit:");
        System.in.read();
    }

    @Bean
    public ApplicationRunner startupRunner(HelloWorldService hello) {
        return (args) -> hello.printMessage();
    }
}
```

The @EnableAsync annotation registers the needed components for the async execution of methods as well as the detection of @Async annotated methods. Spring Boot will, if not explicitly configured, add a TaskExecutor.

ℹ️   `System.in.read` is in there to prevent the application from shutting down so that the background tasks can finish processing. When you press the Enter key, the program will quit. Generally when developing a web application, you don't need things like this.

When running the application, the output will be similar to Figure 7-1.

```
.   ____          _            __ _ _
/\\ / ___'_ __ _ _(_)_ __  __ _ \ \ \ \
( ( )\___ | '_ | '_| | '_ \/ _` | \ \ \ \
 \\/  ___)| |_)| | | | | || (_| |  ) ) ) )
  '  |____| .__|_| |_|_| |_\__, | / / / /
 =========|_|==============|___/=/_/_/_/
 :: Spring Boot ::                (v3.2.1)

2023-12-29T15:27:27.285+01:00  INFO 35566 --- [           main] c.a.s.scheduling.ThreadingApplication    : Starting ThreadingApplication using Java 21.0.
2023-12-29T15:27:27.288+01:00  INFO 35566 --- [           main] c.a.s.scheduling.ThreadingApplication    : No active profile set, falling back to 1 defau
2023-12-29T15:27:27.958+01:00  INFO 35566 --- [           main] c.a.s.scheduling.ThreadingApplication    : Started ThreadingApplication in 1.102 seconds
Press [ENTER] to quit:
2023-12-29T15:27:28.468+01:00  INFO 35566 --- [         task-1] c.a.s.scheduling.HelloWorldService       : Hello World, from Spring Boot 3!
```

Figure 7-1. *Async execution output*

Configure the TaskExecutor

By default Spring Boot will use a `ThreadPoolTaskExecutor` to run the async tasks. This can be configured through properties in the `spring.task.execution` namespace (see Table 7-1) unless `spring.threads.virtual.enabled` is set to `true`, in which case it will use a `SimpleAsyncTaskExecutor` configured to create virtual threads (available in Java 21).

Table 7-1. *Task Properties*

Property	Description
spring.task.execution. thread-name-prefix	Sets the prefix for the threads; the default is task-.
spring.task.execution. pool.core-size	Sets the default number of threads to create; the default is 8.
spring.task.execution. pool.max-size	Sets the maximum number of threads to create; the default is Integer.MAX_VALUE.
spring.task.execution.pool. allow-core-thread-timeout	Allows core threads to time out; enables the growing and shrinking of the pool. The default is true.
spring.task.execution. pool.keep-alive	Sets the idle limit for threads, before being terminated. The default is 60 seconds.
spring.task.execution. pool.queue-capacity	Sets the task queue capacity. The default is Integer.MAX_VALUE. New threads will be created only if the queue reaches its capacity. Using an unbounded queue will effectively ignore the max-size property.
spring.task.execution. shutdown.await-termination	Sets whether the task executor should wait for tasks to complete on shutdown; the default is false.
spring.task.execution. shutdown.await-termination- period	Sets the time to wait for tasks to complete.
spring.threads.virtual. enabled	Sets whether we use virtual or platform threads. The default is false.

These properties can be used to configure the Spring Boot–managed `TaskExecutor`. As shown in Figure 7-1, the default thread name is prefixed with `task-`, as that is the default. Let's add the `spring.task.execution.thread-name-prefix` property to the `application.properties` file with a value of `sb3r-exec-`. When also configuring `spring.task.execution.shutdown.await-termination`, we could remove `System.in.read()` as now Spring Boot will wait for the task to complete. See Listing 7-3.

Listing 7-3. Spring Task Application Properties

```
spring.task.execution.thread-name-prefix=sb3r-exec-
spring.task.execution.shutdown.await-termination=true
spring.task.execution.shutdown.await-termination-period=45S
```

With the property in place, you can see that the name of the thread has changed to `sb3r-exec-1`, as shown in Figure 7-2.

```
  .   ____          _            __ _ _
 /\\ / ___'_ __ _ _(_)_ __  __ _ \ \ \ \
( ( )\___ | '_ | '_| | '_ \/ _` | \ \ \ \
 \\/  ___)| |_)| | | | | || (_| |  ) ) ) )
  '  |____| .__|_| |_|_| |_\__, | / / / /
 =========|_|==============|___/=/_/_/_/
 :: Spring Boot ::                (v3.2.1)

2023-12-29T15:29:51.375+01:00  INFO 35636 --- [        main] c.a.s.scheduling.ThreadingApplication   : Starting ThreadingApplication using Ja
2023-12-29T15:29:51.379+01:00  INFO 35636 --- [        main] c.a.s.scheduling.ThreadingApplication   : No active profile set, falling back to
2023-12-29T15:29:52.135+01:00  INFO 35636 --- [        main] c.a.s.scheduling.ThreadingApplication   : Started ThreadingApplication in 1.257
2023-12-29T15:29:52.647+01:00  INFO 35636 --- [ sb3r-exec-1] c.a.s.scheduling.HelloWorldService      : Hello World, from Spring Boot 3!
```

Figure 7-2. *Async execution output*

If there are, for some reason, multiple `TaskExecutor` instances in your application, you would need to either mark one of them as `@Primary` to be used as the default `TaskExecutor` or use the `AsyncConfigurer` interface and implement the `taskExecutor` method to return the `TaskExecutor` to use. See Listing 7-4.

Listing 7-4. Explicitly Configured Executor with AsyncConfigurer

```
package com.apress.springboot3recipes.scheduling;

import org.springframework.boot.ApplicationRunner;
import org.springframework.boot.SpringApplication;
import org.springframework.boot.autoconfigure.SpringBootApplication;
import org.springframework.context.annotation.Bean;
import org.springframework.core.task.VirtualThreadTaskExecutor;
```

```
import org.springframework.scheduling.annotation.AsyncConfigurer;
import org.springframework.scheduling.annotation.EnableAsync;

import java.io.IOException;
import java.util.concurrent.Executor;

@SpringBootApplication
@EnableAsync
public class ThreadingApplication implements AsyncConfigurer {

    public static void main(String[] args) throws IOException {
        SpringApplication.run(ThreadingApplication.class, args);

        System.out.println("Press [ENTER] to quit:");
        System.in.read();
    }

    @Bean
    public VirtualThreadTaskExecutor taskExecutor() {
        return new VirtualThreadTaskExecutor();
    }

    @Override
    public Executor getAsyncExecutor() {
        return taskExecutor();
    }

    @Bean
    public ApplicationRunner startupRunner(HelloWorld hello) {
        return (args) -> hello.printMessage();
    }
}
```

7-2. Configure Spring Task Scheduling
Problem

You want to schedule a method invocation in a consistent manner, using either a cron expression, an interval, or a rate.

Solution

Spring has support to configure TaskExecutors and TaskSchedulers. This capability, coupled with the ability to schedule method execution using the @Scheduled annotation, makes Spring scheduling support work with a minimum of fuss: all you need are a method and an annotation, and you need to switch on the scanner for annotations. Spring Boot will not automatically detect the need for scheduling, so you will have to enable it yourself using the @EnableScheduling annotation.

How It Works

Let's write a component that prints a message to the log every four seconds. Create a Java class and use the @Scheduled annotation on a method to indicate that this needs to be invoked. When using fixedRate=4000 as an argument, it will run every four seconds. If you want to use a cron expression, you can set the cron attribute on the @Scheduled annotation instead.

```
package com.apress.springboot3recipes.scheduling;

import org.slf4j.Logger;
import org.slf4j.LoggerFactory;
import org.springframework.boot.SpringBootVersion;
import org.springframework.scheduling.annotation.Scheduled;
import org.springframework.stereotype.Component;

@Component
public class HelloWorld {

  private static final Logger logger = LoggerFactory.getLogger
  (HelloWorld.class);

  @Scheduled(fixedRate = 4000L)
  public void printMessage() {
    logger.info("Hello World, from Spring Boot {}", SpringBootVersion.
    getVersion());
  }
}
```

The @Component annotation will make sure that it will be detected by Spring Boot.

The next thing to do is enable scheduling for your application. The easiest solution is to annotate the application class with @EnableScheduling. Of course, you can also place it on other @Configuration annotated classes.

```
package com.apress.springboot3recipes.scheduling;

import org.springframework.boot.SpringApplication;
import org.springframework.boot.autoconfigure.SpringBootApplication;
import org.springframework.scheduling.annotation.EnableScheduling;

@SpringBootApplication
@EnableScheduling
public class SchedulingApplication {

    public static void main(String[] args) {
        SpringApplication.run(SchedulingApplication.class, args);
    }
}
```

The @EnableScheduling annotation will enable the detection of @Scheduled annotated methods and will register a TaskScheduler to use for scheduling tasks. When a single TaskScheduler is detected in the application context, it will use that one rather than creating a new one.

Running SchedulingApplication will give you an output in the logs about every four seconds (Figure 7-3).

```
  .   ____          _            __ _ _
 /\\ / ___'_ __ _ _(_)_ __  __ _ \ \ \ \
( ( )\___ | '_ | '_| | '_ \/ _` | \ \ \ \
 \\/  ___)| |_)| | | | | || (_| |  ) ) ) )
  '  |____| .__|_| |_|_| |_\__, | / / / /
 =========|_|==============|___/=/_/_/_/
 :: Spring Boot ::                (v3.2.1)

2023-12-29T15:35:10.437+01:00  INFO 35831 --- [           main] c.a.s.scheduling.SchedulingApplication   : Starting SchedulingApplication using Ja
2023-12-29T15:35:10.440+01:00  INFO 35831 --- [           main] c.a.s.scheduling.SchedulingApplication   : No active profile set, falling back to
2023-12-29T15:35:11.000+01:00  INFO 35831 --- [           main] c.a.s.scheduling.SchedulingApplication   : Started SchedulingApplication in 0.91 s
2023-12-29T15:35:11.004+01:00  INFO 35831 --- [  scheduling-1] c.a.s.scheduling.HelloWorld              : Hello World, from Spring Boot 3.2.1
2023-12-29T15:35:15.001+01:00  INFO 35831 --- [  scheduling-1] c.a.s.scheduling.HelloWorld              : Hello World, from Spring Boot 3.2.1
2023-12-29T15:35:19.000+01:00  INFO 35831 --- [  scheduling-1] c.a.s.scheduling.HelloWorld              : Hello World, from Spring Boot 3.2.1
```

Figure 7-3. *Scheduled execution output*

Instead of using the @Scheduled annotation, you could schedule a method using Java. You might want to do this if you cannot place an @Scheduled annotation on the method you want to execute periodically or you just want to limit the amount of annotations. For this you can use the `SchedulingConfigurer`, which has a single callback method to configure additional tasks.

```
package com.apress.springboot3recipes.scheduling;

import org.springframework.beans.factory.annotation.Autowired;
import org.springframework.boot.SpringApplication;
import org.springframework.boot.autoconfigure.SpringBootApplication;
import org.springframework.scheduling.annotation.EnableScheduling;
import org.springframework.scheduling.annotation.SchedulingConfigurer;
import org.springframework.scheduling.config.ScheduledTaskRegistrar;

import java.time.Duration;

@SpringBootApplication
@EnableScheduling
public class SchedulingApplication implements SchedulingConfigurer {

  @Autowired
  private HelloWorld helloWorld;

  public static void main(String[] args) {
    SpringApplication.run(SchedulingApplication.class, args);
  }

  @Override
  public void configureTasks(ScheduledTaskRegistrar taskRegistrar) {
    taskRegistrar.addFixedRateTask(
        () -> helloWorld.printMessage(), Duration.ofSeconds(4));
  }
}
```

The output from this application is still the same as that shown in Figure 7-3.

7-3. Send Email

Spring Boot will automatically configure the ability to send mail when mail properties and the Java mail library is detected on the classpath. In this recipe, we will take a look at how to set the properties and how to send an email using Spring Boot.

Problem

You want to send email from a Spring Boot application using the standard Jakarta Mail API.

Solution

Spring's email support makes it easier to send email by providing an abstract and implementation-independent API for sending email. The core interface of Spring's email support is `MailSender`. The `JavaMailSender` interface is a subinterface of `MailSender` that includes specialized JavaMail features such as Multipurpose Internet Mail Extensions (MIME) support. To send an email message with HTML content, inline images, or attachments, you have to send it as a MIME message. Spring Boot will automatically configure the `JavaMailSender` when the `jakarta.mail` classes are found on the classpath and when the appropriate `spring.mail` properties have been set.

How It Works

The first thing to do is add the `spring-boot-starter-mail` dependency to your list of dependencies. This will add the necessary `jakarta.mail` as well as the `spring-context` dependencies on the classpath.

```
<dependency>
    <groupId>org.springframework.boot</groupId>
    <artifactId>spring-boot-starter-mail</artifactId>
</dependency>
```

Configure the JavaMailSender

To be able to send mail, you need to configure the appropriate `spring.mail` properties; see Table 7-2. The `spring.mail.host` property is required; the other properties are optional.

Table 7-2. *Mail Properties*

Property	Description
spring.mail.host	The SMTP server host
spring.mail.port	The SMTP server port (default 25)
spring.mail.username	The username to use for connecting to the SMTP server
spring.mail.password	The password to use for connecting to the SMTP server
spring.mail.protocol	The protocol used by the SMTP server (default smtp)
spring.mail.test-connection	Tests if the SMTP server is available at startup (default false)
spring.mail.default-encoding	Encoding used for MIME messages (default UTF-8)
spring.mail.properties	Additional properties to be set on the JavaMail Session
spring.mail.jndi-name	JNDI name of the JavaMail Session; can be used when deploying to an JEE server with preconfigured JavaMail sessions in JNDI

Next you need to define at least the `spring.mail.host` property to be able to send mail.

```
spring.mail.host=localhost
spring.mail.port=3025
```

ⓘ   The code for this recipe uses GreenMail as an SMTP server. A configured instance can be run using the `smtp.sh` script from the `bin` directory. It will, by default, expose an SMTP server on port 3025.

Send a Plain-Text Email

With the added dependencies and `spring.mail` properties, Spring Boot will add a preconfigured `JavaMailSenderImpl` as a bean to the `ApplicationContext`. This bean can be autowired into components by using an `@Autowired` field, by using constructors, or, as shown here, by using dependencies in the `@Bean` annotated methods. See Listing 7-5.

Listing 7-5. SpringBootApplication Sending Email

```java
package com.apress.springboot3recipes.mailsender;

import org.springframework.boot.ApplicationRunner;
import org.springframework.boot.SpringApplication;
import org.springframework.boot.autoconfigure.SpringBootApplication;
import org.springframework.context.annotation.Bean;
import org.springframework.mail.javamail.JavaMailSender;
import org.springframework.mail.javamail.MimeMessageHelper;

@SpringBootApplication
public class MailSenderApplication {

  public static void main(String[] args) {
    SpringApplication.run(MailSenderApplication.class, args);
  }

  @Bean
  public ApplicationRunner startupMailSender(JavaMailSender mailSender) {
    return (args) -> mailSender.send((msg) -> {
      var helper = new MimeMessageHelper(msg);
      helper.setTo("recipient@some.where");
      helper.setFrom("spring-boot-3-recipes@apress.com");
      helper.setSubject("Status message");
      helper.setText("All is well.");
    });
  }
}
```

The `MailSenderApplication` will send an email when the application has finished starting. The `startupMailSender` is an `ApplicationRunner` (see Chapter 2), which takes the preconfigured `JavaMailSender` to send a mail message.

Test the Sending of Email

To test this, we can use the GreenMail JUnit5 support to bootstrap an SMTP server. For this you will need to add the `greenmail-junit5` dependency to the list of dependencies. See Listing 7-6.

Listing 7-6. GreenMail JUnit5 Dependency

```
<dependency>
  <groupId>com.icegreen</groupId>
  <artifactId>greenmail-junit5</artifactId>
  <version>2.0.1</version>
  <scope>test</scope>
</dependency>
```

Next we can use the @SpringBootTest annotation to boot our application. The application that was written sends a message after startup, so in our test we can verify that this has happened. See Listing 7-7.

Listing 7-7. Test for Mail Sending Application

```
package com.apress.springboot3recipes.mailsender;

import com.icegreen.greenmail.junit5.GreenMailExtension;
import com.icegreen.greenmail.util.ServerSetupTest;
import jakarta.mail.Message;
import jakarta.mail.internet.InternetAddress;
import jakarta.mail.internet.MimeMessage;
import org.junit.jupiter.api.Test;
import org.junit.jupiter.api.extension.RegisterExtension;
import org.springframework.boot.test.context.SpringBootTest;

import static org.assertj.core.api.Assertions.assertThat;

@SpringBootTest
class MailSenderApplicationTest {

  @RegisterExtension
  static GreenMailExtension greenMail = new GreenMailExtension(
  ServerSetupTest.ALL)
      .withPerMethodLifecycle(false);

  @Test
  void shouldHaveSendMail() throws Exception {
    MimeMessage[] receivedMessages = greenMail.getReceivedMessages();
    assertThat(receivedMessages).hasSize(1);
```

```
    assertThat(receivedMessages[0].getSubject())
        .isEqualTo("Status message");
    assertThat(receivedMessages[0]
        .getRecipients(Message.RecipientType.TO))
        .contains(new InternetAddress("recipient@some.where"));
  }
}
```

The test first starts the GreenMail test mail server; this is done as a Junit5 extension using the @RegisterExtension annotation. The ServerSetupTest.ALL starts all available mail protocols such as IMAP, POP3, SMTP, etc., and will expose the ports.

ℹ   The withPerMethodLifecycle(false) is needed here because we are sending mail at startup. If we didn't specify this, the mail server would start and stop per the test method, which means the application would fail to start as there isn't a mail server.

In the test method, we can verify if we received the message, and using AssertJ we can verify if it was the message that we expected to receive. Of course, this applies to other or larger use cases as well.

Use Thymeleaf for Email Templates

Spring Boot has some nice support for using Thymeleaf as a templating solution; however, the default setup is mainly for using Thymeleaf for web pages. It is, however, possible to use Thymeleaf for other templating solutions as well, like here for email.

First add spring-boot-starter-thymeleaf as a dependency. This will pull in all the needed Thymeleaf dependencies and will automatically configure the Thymeleaf TemplateEngine, which we need to generate the HTML content. See Listing 7-8.

Listing 7-8. Spring Boot Thymeleaf Dependency

```
<dependency>
  <groupId>org.springframework.boot</groupId>
  <artifactId>spring-boot-starter-thymeleaf</artifactId>
</dependency>
```

By default the Spring-configured Thymeleaf `TemplateEngine` will resolve the HTML templates from the `templates` directory under `src/main/resources`. Add a file named `email.html` to this directory and make a nice-looking email message from it. See Listing 7-9.

Listing 7-9. Email HTML Template

```html
<!DOCTYPE html>
<html xmlns:th="http://www.thymeleaf.org">
<head>
    <meta http-equiv="Content-Type" content="text/html; charset=UTF-8" />
</head>
<body>
<p><strong th:text="${msg}">Some email content will be here.</strong></p>

<p>
Kind Regards,
    Your Application
</p>
</body>
</html>
```

The `th:text` is a Thymeleaf tag and will replace the content with the value of that attribute. Of course we would need to pass in a value for that attribute from our mail-sending/generating code. See Listing 7-10.

Listing 7-10. MailSender with Templating

```java
package com.apress.springboot3recipes.mailsender;

import org.springframework.boot.ApplicationRunner;
import org.springframework.boot.SpringApplication;
import org.springframework.boot.autoconfigure.SpringBootApplication;
import org.springframework.context.annotation.Bean;
import org.springframework.context.i18n.LocaleContextHolder;
import org.springframework.mail.javamail.JavaMailSender;
import org.springframework.mail.javamail.MimeMessageHelper;
import org.thymeleaf.context.Context;
import org.thymeleaf.spring6.ISpringTemplateEngine;
```

```java
import java.util.Collections;

@SpringBootApplication
public class MailSenderApplication {

  public static void main(String[] args) {
    SpringApplication.run(MailSenderApplication.class, args);
  }

  @Bean
  public ApplicationRunner startupMailSender(
      JavaMailSender mailSender, ISpringTemplateEngine templateEngine) {
    return (args) -> mailSender.send((msg) -> {
      var helper = new MimeMessageHelper(msg);
      helper.setTo("recipient@some.where");
      helper.setFrom("spring-boot-3-recipes@apress.com");
      helper.setSubject("Status message");

      var context =  new Context(
          LocaleContextHolder.getLocale(),
          Collections.singletonMap("msg", "All is well!"));
      var body = templateEngine.process("email.html", context);
      helper.setText(body, true);
    });
  }
}
```

The code is similar to the previous code, with the difference that we also now have an ISpringTemplateEnginge at our disposable to generate the HTML content for our email. We use the process method to select the template we want to render, email.html, and pass in a Context object. The Context object is used by Thymeleaf to resolve the attributes, in our case the msg one.

7-4. Register a JMX MBean

Problem

You want to register an object in your Spring Boot application as a JMX MBean, to have the ability to look at services that are running and manipulate their state at runtime. This will allow you to run tasks such as rerunning batch jobs, invoking methods, and changing configuration metadata.

Solution

Spring Boot has support for registering beans through the Spring JMX support; it will detect the @ManagedResource annotated beans and register them with the JMX server. However, by default JMX is disabled and must be enabled by adding `spring.jmx.enabled=true` to `application.properties`.

How It Works

First let's inspect the JMX support offered by Spring Boot. Let's create a simple Spring Boot application that will keep running and use JConsole to inspect the running application. See Listing 7-11.

Listing 7-11. Basic Spring Boot Starting Application

```
package com.apress.springboot3recipes.jmx;

import org.springframework.boot.SpringApplication;
import org.springframework.boot.autoconfigure.SpringBootApplication;

import java.io.IOException;

@SpringBootApplication
public class JmxApplication {

  public static void main(String[] args) throws IOException {
    SpringApplication.run(JmxApplication.class, args);
```

```
    System.out.println("Press [ENTER] to quit:");
    System.in.read();
  }
}
```

ℹ️   Don't forget `spring.jmx.enabled=true` in `application.properties`; otherwise, it won't register.

When the application is running, you can start `jconsole`, and you will be prompted with a screen in which you can select the local process to connect to. Select the one that is running the `JmxApplication` (Figure 7-4).

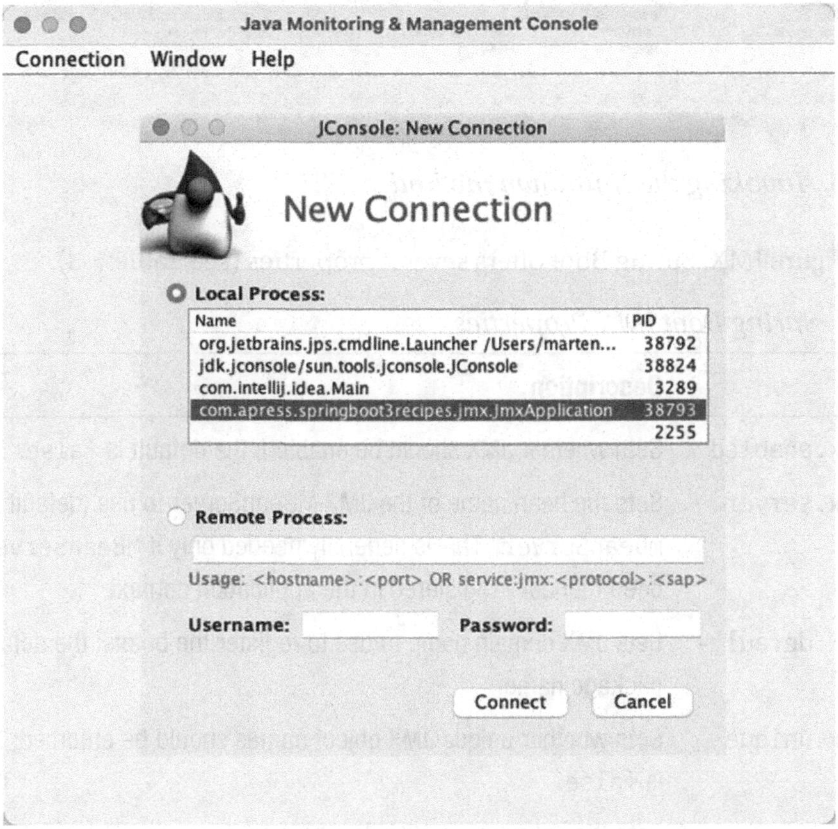

Figure 7-4. JConsole process selection

After selecting the process, go to the MBeans tab and open the `org.springframework.boot` menu and everything under it on the left side of the screen. There is a `shutdown` operation on the `SpringApplication` that you can invoke. When invoked, it will shut down the application. See Figure 7-5.

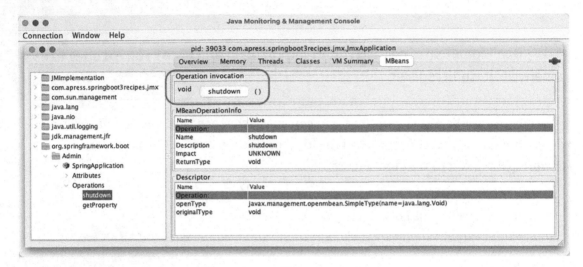

Figure 7-5. *Invoking the shutdown method*

To configure JMX, Spring Boot offers several properties (see Table 7-3).

Table 7-3. *Spring Boot JMX Properties*

Property	Description
`spring.jmx.enabled`	Sets whether JMX should be enabled; the default is `false`.
`spring.jmx.server`	Sets the bean name of the JMX MBeanServer to use (default `mbeanServer`). This is generally needed only if `MBeanServer` has been manually registered in the application context.
`spring.jmx.default-domain`	Sets JMX domain name to use to register the beans; the default is the package name.
`spring.jmx.unique-names`	Sets whether unique JMX object names should be enforced; the default is `false`.
`spring.jmx.registration-policy`	Sets the policy on what to do when duplicate beans are detected. The allowed options are `FAIL_ON_EXISTING`, `IGNORE_EXISTING`, and `REPLACE_EXISTING`. The default is `FAIL_ON_EXISTING`.

Spring Boot by default (see Table 7-3) has JMX disabled. This first needs to be enabled by setting `spring.jmx.enabled` to `true`. After that, exposing a bean is pretty straightforward. For a bean to be exposed, it needs to have an `@ManagedResource` annotation and the operations to expose the `@ManagedOperation` annotation. See Listing 7-12.

Listing 7-12. HelloWorld with JMX Metadata

```
package com.apress.springboot3recipes.jmx;

import org.slf4j.Logger;
import org.slf4j.LoggerFactory;
import org.springframework.jmx.export.annotation.ManagedOperation;
import org.springframework.jmx.export.annotation.ManagedResource;
import org.springframework.stereotype.Component;

@Component
@ManagedResource
public class HelloWorld {

  private static final Logger logger = LoggerFactory.
  getLogger(HelloWorld.class);

  @ManagedOperation
  public void printMessage() {
    logger.info("Hello World, from Spring Boot 3.2!");
  }
}
```

When the application has been restarted and JConsole has reconnected to the process running the `JmxApplication`, you will notice a `com.apress.springboot3recipes.jmx` leaf in the menu on the left side. Open all the nodes, and in the operations leaf you will find the `printMessage` operation (Figure 7-6).

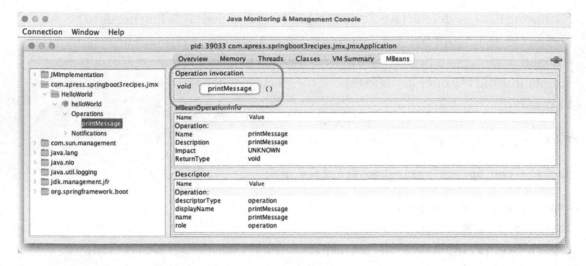

Figure 7-6. *Invoking the printMessage method*

When invoking the `printMessage` method, the console will print the message (Figure 7-7).

```
  /\\ / ___'_ __ _ _(_)_ __  __ _ \ \ \ \
 ( ( )\___ | '_ | '_| | '_ \/ _` | \ \ \ \
  \\/  ___)| |_)| | | | | || (_| |  ) ) ) )
   '  |____| .__|_| |_|_| |_\__, | / / / /
 =========|_|==============|___/=/_/_/_/
 :: Spring Boot ::                (v3.2.1)

2023-12-30T09:26:14.124+01:00  INFO 39033 --- [           main] c.a.s.jmx.JmxApplication                 : Starting JmxApplication using Java :
2023-12-30T09:26:14.128+01:00  INFO 39033 --- [           main] c.a.s.jmx.JmxApplication                 : No active profile set, falling back
2023-12-30T09:26:14.860+01:00  INFO 39033 --- [           main] c.a.s.jmx.JmxApplication                 : Started JmxApplication in 1.182 sec
Press [ENTER] to quit:
2023-12-30T09:33:45.815+01:00  INFO 39033 --- [(2)-192.168.2.6] c.a.springboot3recipes.jmx.HelloWorld    : Hello World, from Spring Boot 3!
2023-12-30T09:33:51.550+01:00  INFO 39033 --- [(2)-192.168.2.6] c.a.springboot3recipes.jmx.HelloWorld    : Hello World, from Spring Boot 3!
```

Figure 7-7. *Console output*

7-5. Use Java Flight Recorder to Investigate Application Startup

Problem

You want to investigate the startup of your Spring Boot application and determine what can be improved using the Java Flight Recorder (JFR). The JFR is a tool for recording diagnostic and profiling information about a running application on a JVM. It does this with almost no performance overhead, which makes it useful in almost every environment. The JFR will collect data about the JVM it runs on as well as the application it runs.

Solution

The core Spring container provides an API to monitor the setup and start of the application context. This API, the `ApplicationStartup` interface, has one implementation, `FlightRecorderApplicationStartup`, which can be used to publish JFR events. However, by default the `ApplicationStartup` is no-op and doesn't do anything, so you will need to activate it.

After enabling the `FlightRecorderApplicationStartup`, you also need to instruct the JDK to record the JFR events. Finally, to investigate the events, you need a tool such as Java Mission Control.

How It Works

First we need to set the proper `ApplicationStartup` implementation we want to use. Next we start with the proper command-line properties, and finally we can inspect the events.

Enable JFR Event Processing

To enable JFR event publishing, we need to configure Spring Boot with the `FlightRecorderApplicationStartup` class, instead of the default no-op one. You can do this by calling the `setApplicationStartup` method, which is defined in a base class used by most, so not all, application context implementations. After the registration, you call `refresh` to start loading the application context. See Listing 7-13.

Listing 7-13. Main Class with ApplicationStartup Configuration

```
package com.apress.springboot3recipes.order;

import org.springframework.boot.ApplicationRunner;
import org.springframework.boot.SpringApplication;
import org.springframework.boot.autoconfigure.SpringBootApplication;
import org.springframework.context.annotation.Bean;
```

```
import org.springframework.core.metrics.jfr.
FlightRecorderApplicationStartup;

@SpringBootApplication
public class OrderApplication {

  public static void main(String[] args) {
    var app = new SpringApplication(OrderApplication.class);
    app.setApplicationStartup(new FlightRecorderApplicationStartup());
    app.run(args);
  }

  @Bean
  ApplicationRunner orderInitializer(OrderService orders) {
    return args -> {
      OrderGenerator.generate(5)
          .subscribe(orders::save);
    };
  }
}
```

Instead of the convenient SpringApplication.run, we now construct an instance of SpringApplication, which allows to do some more configuration before the actual start of the application. Here we set the applicationStartup property to the mentioned FlightRecorderApplicationStartup.

However, with only this in place, the events won't be recorded. For that you would need to add the StartFlightRecording attribute to the JVM. Adding an attribute for the JVM is done by passing it with -XX to the java command. See Listing 7-14.

Listing 7-14. Java Launch Command

```
java -XX:StartFlightRecording:filename=recording.jfr,duration=30s -jar
target/recipe_7_5_i-3.0.0.jar
```

This will start the application with the JFR enabled. It will write the events in a file named recording.jfr and will record 30 seconds of data.

Another option is to enable the JFR in-flight, meaning in a running application. You can use the jcmd command for that. Using the Process Explorer (Windows) of the ps command on Unix-based systems, you need to determine the process ID of the Java process you want to enable the JFR. Let's say the process ID is 4321; then Listing 7-15 would enable the JFR.

Listing 7-15. JCMD Launch Command

```
jcmd 4321 JFR.start duration=30s filename=recording.jfr
```

When enabling the JFR, you will see some output on the console indicating this, as shown in Listing 7-16.

Listing 7-16. Recording Enabled Output

```
[0,524s][info][jfr,startup] Started recording 1. The result will be
written to:
[0,524s][info][jfr,startup]
[0,524s][info][jfr,startup] /Users/marten/Repositories/apress/spring-
boot-3-recipes/code/ch07/recipe_7_5_i/recording.jfr
```

After stopping the application, you can open the recording.jfr file in Java Mission Control to observe the events. See Figure 7-8.

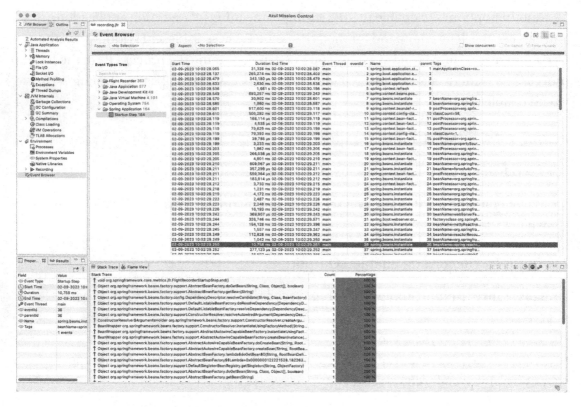

Figure 7-8. *Java Mission Control*

As you can see, there are several `spring.*` events all corresponding to part of the life cycle of the application context or the beans in it. This makes the JFR a powerful tool to help identifying which parts of the application startup are slowing things down.

7-6. Observe Your Application with Micrometer

In Recipe 7-5 you looked at the Java Flight Recorder. While that is a powerful tool, for Spring Boot applications it's mainly useful for monitoring the startup of an application. It is no replacement for a Java profiler or metrics library like Micrometer. When the need arises, Spring and Spring Boot integrate with Micrometer out of the box, as do many of the Spring portfolio projects such as Spring Security, Spring Data, etc.

In recent years, the Micrometer API has become the de facto standard for recording metrics and applying tracing to your applications. Micrometer can integrate with many different monitoring systems, such as Prometheus, Influx, and New Relic. More and more monitoring systems are being added, and if it isn't supported out of the box, it is fairly easy to integrate it with Micrometer yourself.

To provide better integration, Spring and Spring Boot have embedded support for the Micrometer API in its internals, by default using a no-op registry, but it can be configured to send data to one of the supported monitoring systems. Spring Boot will automatically configure the metrics as well as expose them to the monitoring systems of choice. Including `spring-boot-starter-actuator` adds the support to expose the metrics. As we are using a web application for this example, the metrics are automatically exposed as a Spring Boot Actuator endpoint.

Problem

You want to gather metrics for your applications, and you want your Spring-based application to publish these metrics over JMX.

Solution

Micrometer defines a concept of an `Observation`, which allows for both metrics as well as tracing to be supported in your application. Metrics are timers, gauges, and counters and provide a way to collect statistics on the runtime behavior of your application such as the number of HTTP requests that are being handled and the respective outcome. Metrics help in analyzing performance, application usage patterns, and error rates. Tracing allows a more holistic view of your application landscape and enables you to track requests (HTTP, messages, etc.) through your entire system.

Micrometer Concepts

Here is a quick overview of the concepts of Micrometer `Observation`:

- `Observation` is the actual recording of something happening in your application. The `Observation` instance is handled by an `ObservationHandler` to provide metrics and/or traces.

- Every observation has an `ObservationContext` implementation, which holds all relevant metadata for the `Observation`. For example, in the case of an HTTP request, it will hold the HTTP method, response status, etc.

- Each `Observation` consists of one or more `KeyValues`. In the case of an HTTP request, this will be the HTTP method, response status, processing time, etc. The `KeyValues` are provided to an `ObservationConvention` implementation (for which there are many), which is tied to specific `ObservationContext` implementations.

- `KeyValues` are called *low-cardinality* when there are a low and bound number of possible values for the `KeyValue` (for instance, an HTTP method for which there are just a few). Low-cardinality values are contributed to metrics only.

- `KeyValues` are called *high-cardinality* when there are an unbounded number of possibilities (like the URL). High-cardinality values are contributed to traces only.

- Finally, there is an `ObservationDocumentation` that documents all possible observations in a domain, describing the expected key names and their meaning.

To record metrics, Micrometer needs a `MeterRegistry` so the `Observation` instance can use it to create the counters, timers, etc. Different technologies have different `MeterRegistry` implementations (this is the integration part to the specific monitoring tool in use). Here we are going to use the default Spring Boot Actuator endpoint to show the metrics.

How It Works

To publish metrics, we need to add a dependency to the Spring Boot Actuator starter. This will add the automatic configuration for the Micrometer metrics as well as expose them as an endpoint. If you included one of the supported Micrometer integrations like Prometheus, it would be configured automatically as well. See Listing 7-17.

Listing 7-17. Maven Dependency

```
<dependency>
  <groupId>org.springframework.boot</groupId>
  <artifactId>spring-boot-starter-actuator</artifactId>
</dependency>
```

With this dependency, the metrics collection will be automatically configured. To expose them over the Actuator endpoint, we need to add the `metrics` endpoint to it. By default, only the `health` endpoint is being exposed over HTTP. To do so, we can configure `management.endpoints.web.exposure.include`. See Listing 7-18.

Listing 7-18. Application Property to Enable Exposing Metrics

```
management.endpoints.web.exposure.include=health,metrics
```

This property can take a list of what to expose (depending on the used dependencies and technologies, this list can grow); here we expose the `health` and `metrics`. It is also possible to use *, which will expose all the available endpoints (such as `info`, `shutdown` if enabled, `threaddump`, etc.).

⚠️   Exposing all the endpoints can be a security risk as this can either leak information as it exposes the beans and configuration and, when configured incorrectly, can allow external parties to shut down your application.

Now when accessing the `metrics` endpoint through `http://localhost:8080/actuator/metrics`, it will show you a list of all the available metrics (Figure 7-9).

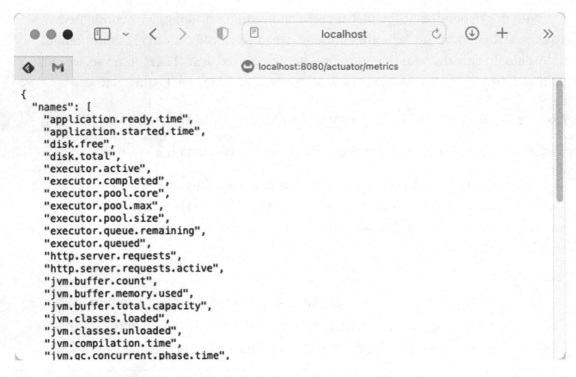

Figure 7-9. *Available metrics*

Spring Boot will detect the metrics to expose based on the technologies in use. When Kafka is detected, it will add metrics for that, Hibernate, etc.

When looking at a specific metric (`name-of-metrics`), it will show you what is available. When looking at `http.server.requests` (Figure 7-10), it will show you how many there have been, what the max execution time it was, and the total time. It will also show the available tags; those tags are also propagated to monitoring tools such as Prometheus and can be used to group metrics.

```
{
  "name": "http.server.requests",
  "baseUnit": "seconds",
  "measurements": [
    {
      "statistic": "COUNT",
      "value": 2
    },
    {
      "statistic": "TOTAL_TIME",
      "value": 0.12344502600000001
    },
    {
      "statistic": "MAX",
      "value": 0
    }
  ],
```

Figure 7-10. *Specific metric*

In reality you will be using a monitoring tool to monitor your application, as you probably have multiple instances. But the Actuator endpoint can be a nice helper while developing or to look at a single instance in a live environment.

Summary

In this chapter, we looked at how we can use some enterprise technologies from within Spring Boot such as executing asynchronous tasks, sending email, integrating with JMX, and exposing metrics. We took a brief look at Spring Boot Actuator and the support JFR events. The JFR events can be a great help in identifying problems during application startup.

The next chapter will explore various messaging solutions that are supported out of the box by Spring Boot and how to apply the configurations.

CHAPTER 8

Spring Messaging

The Spring Portfolio provides extensive support for integrating with various messaging systems. From a fairly simple JMS API to RabbitMQ and Kafka. Spring Boot provides auto-configuration when these frameworks and technologies are detected.

8-1. Configure JMS
Problem

You want to use JMS in a Spring Boot application and need to connect to the JMS broker.

Solution

Spring Boot supports auto-configuration for ActiveMQ and Artemis. By adding one of those libraries and setting some properties, the `spring.activemq` or `spring.artemis` namespace will be all you need.

How It Works

By declaring a dependency on the JMS provider of your choice, Spring Boot will automatically configure `ConnectionFactory` and enable a strategy to look up destinations, `DestinationResolver`, for your environment. This can also be done by using JNDI. Another solution is to do all the configuration yourself; this might be necessary if you need more control over the `ConnectionFactory` instance or want to use a non-auto-configured JMS provider.

Adding dependencies for the supported JMS providers is pretty easy as Spring Boot provides starter projects for them. For JNDI, you need to include the JMS dependencies yourself.

© Marten Deinum 2024
M. Deinum, *Spring Boot 3 Recipes*, https://doi.org/10.1007/979-8-8688-0113-6_8

Use ActiveMQ

When using ActiveMQ, the first thing to do is to include `spring-boot-starter-activemq`. This will pull in all the needed JMS and ActiveMQ dependencies to get started. It will include the `spring-jms` dependency and the client libraries for ActiveMQ. See Listing 8-1.

Listing 8-1. Spring Boot ActiveMQ Starter Dependency

```
<dependency>
  <groupId>org.springframework.boot</groupId>
  <artifactId>spring-boot-starter-activemq</artifactId>
</dependency>
```

By default Spring Boot will start an embedded broker if no explicit broker configuration is given. The configuration can be changed by using properties from the `spring.activemq` namespace (see Table 8-1).

Table 8-1. *ActiveMQ Configuration Properties*

Property	Description
`spring.activemq.broker-url`	Sets the URL of the broker to connect to. The default is `vm://localhost?broker.persistent=false` for an in-memory broker; otherwise, it's `tcp://localhost:61616`.
`spring.activemq.user`	Sets the username to use to connect to the broker; the default is empty.
`spring.activemq.password`	Sets the password to use to connect to the broker; the default is empty.
`spring.activemq.in-memory`	Sets whether an embedded broker should be used; the default is `true`. This is ignored when `spring.activemq.broker-url` has been explicitly set.
`spring.activemq.non-blocking-redelivery`	Sets the stop message delivery before re-delivering rolled-back messages. When it's enabled, the message order will not be preserved; the default is `false`.

(continued)

Table 8-1. (*continued*)

Property	Description
spring.activemq.close-timeout	Sets the time to wait to consider a close to be effective; the default is 15 seconds.
spring.activemq.send-timeout	Sets the time to wait for a response from the broker; the default is 0 (unlimited).
Spring.activemq.packages.trust-all	When using Java serialization to send JMS messages, this sets whether classes from all packages should be trusted; the default is none (which requires explicitly setting the packages).
spring.activemq.packages.trusted	Is a comma-separated list of specific packages to trust.

The following is a simple application to list all the beans with jms in their name. This should include a bean named jmsConnectionFactory.

```
package com.apress.springboot3recipes.jms;

import org.springframework.boot.SpringApplication;
import org.springframework.boot.autoconfigure.SpringBootApplication;

import java.util.Comparator;
import java.util.stream.Stream;

@SpringBootApplication
public class JmsApplication {

  private static final String MSG = "\tName: %100s, Type: %s\n";

  public static void main(String[] args) {
    var ctx = SpringApplication.run(JmsApplication.class, args);

    System.out.println("# Beans: " + ctx.getBeanDefinitionCount());

    var names = ctx.getBeanDefinitionNames();
    Stream.of(names)
```

```
    .filter(name -> name.toLowerCase().contains("jms") || ctx.
getType(name).getName().contains("jms"))
        .sorted(Comparator.naturalOrder())
        .forEach(name -> {
    var bean = ctx.getBean(name);
    System.out.printf(MSG, name, bean.getClass().getSimpleName());
    });
  }
}
```

When running this, the program will print all the names and types of the beans containing jms in their name to the console. The output should look like Figure 8-1.

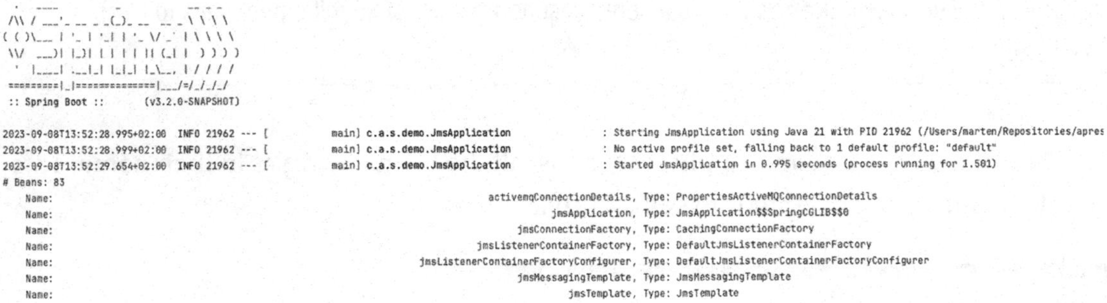

Figure 8-1. ActiveMQ beans output

When using ActiveMQ, it is also possible to use a pool of JMS connections (much like a JDBC-based connection pool). By default this is disabled. To enable and configure it, you can use the properties in the spring.activemq.pool namespace (see Table 8-2).

Table 8-2. *ActiveMQ Pooling Configuration Properties*

Property	Description
`spring.activemq.pool.enabled`	Sets whether a connection pool should be used; the default is `false`.
`spring.activemq.pool.max-connections`	Sets the maximum number of connections; the default is 1.
`spring.activemq.pool.maximum-active-session-per-connection`	Sets the maximum number of active JMS sessions that are allowed per connection; the default is 500.
`spring.activemq.pool.idle-timeout`	Sets how long a connection can be idle; the default is 30 seconds.
`spring.activemq.pool.expiry-timeout`	Sets how long before a connection is expired; the default is 0 (never).
`spring.activemq.pool.reconnect-on-exception`	Resets the connection when a `JMSException` occurs; the default is `true`.
`spring.activemq.pool.block-if-full`	Blocks when a connection is requested or throws a `JMSException` instead; the default is `true`.
`spring.activemq.pool.block-if-full-timeout`	Sets how long to block before throwing a `JMSException`; the default is -1 (block until a connection is available).
`spring.activemq.pool.create-connection-on-startup`	Sets whether a connection should be eagerly created on startup of the application; the default is `true`.

Using the pooling facility requires the `pooled-jms` dependency to be added to your build file. See Listing 8-2.

Listing 8-2. JMS ConnectionPool Dependency

```
<dependency>
  <groupId>org.messaginghub</groupId>
  <artifactId>pooled-jms</artifactId>
</dependency>
```

When running the application again, you will notice that the type of ConnectionFactory has changed to PooledConnectionFactory.

Use Artemis

When using Artemis, the first thing to do is to include spring-boot-starter-artemis. This will pull in all the needed JMS and Artemis dependencies to get started. It will include the spring-jms dependency and the libraries for Artemis (see Table 8-3). See Listing 8-3.

Listing 8-3. Spring Boot Artemis Starter Dependency

```
<dependency>
    <groupId>org.springframework.boot</groupId>
    <artifactId>spring-boot-starter-artemis</artifactId>
</dependency>
```

Table 8-3. *Artemis Configuration Properties*

Property	Description
spring.artemis.broker-url	Sets the Artemis broker URL.
spring.artemis.user	Sets the username for connecting to the Artemis broker; the default is empty.
spring.artemis.password	Sets the password for connecting to the Artemis broker; the default is empty.
spring.artemis.mode	Sets the mode of operation, either native or embedded; the default is none, leading to auto-detection of the mode. When the embedded classes are found, it will run in embedded mode.

The following is a simple application to list all the beans with jms in their name. This should include a bean named jmsConnectionFactory.

```
package com.apress.springboot3recipes.jms;

import org.springframework.boot.SpringApplication;
```

```java
import org.springframework.boot.autoconfigure.SpringBootApplication;

import java.util.Comparator;
import java.util.stream.Stream;

@SpringBootApplication
public class JmsApplication {

  private static final String MSG = "\tName: %100s, Type: %s\n";

  public static void main(String[] args) {
    var ctx = SpringApplication.run(JmsApplication.class, args);

    System.out.println("# Beans: " + ctx.getBeanDefinitionCount());

    var names = ctx.getBeanDefinitionNames();
    Stream.of(names)
      .filter(name -> name.toLowerCase().contains("jms") || ctx.
    getType(name).getName().contains("jms"))
          .sorted(Comparator.naturalOrder())
          .forEach(name -> {
      var bean = ctx.getBean(name);
      System.out.printf(MSG, name, bean.getClass().getSimpleName());
    });
  }
}
```

When run, the output will look like Figure 8-2.

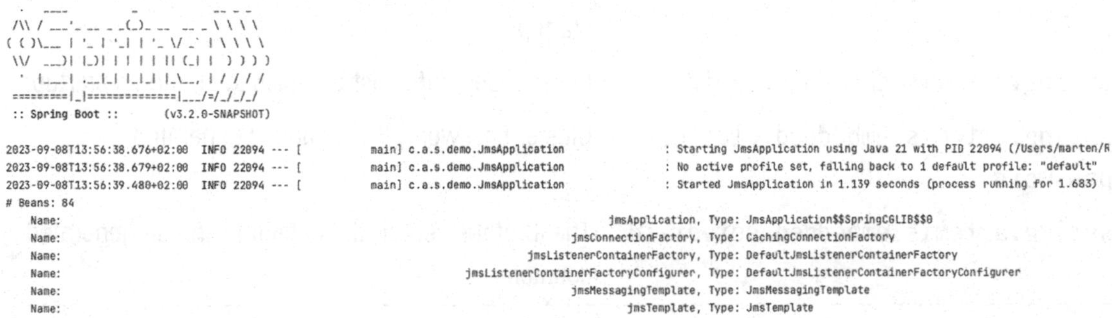

Figure 8-2. *Artemis beans output*

ℹ️   You might wonder when using Artemis if there is still an
`ActiveMQConnectionFactory` in your configuration. Artemis is based on
ActiveMQ and as such shares classes with it.

Artemis can be used in embedded mode (just like ActiveMQ); it will then start an
embedded broker. To configure it, there are several properties exposed in the `spring.`
`artemis.embedded` namespace. The embedded mode requires `artemis-jakarta-server`
as an additional dependency (see Table 8-4).

```
<dependency>
  <groupId>org.apache.activemq</groupId>
  <artifactId>artemis-jakarta-server</artifactId>
</dependency>
```

Table 8-4. *Artemis Embedded Configuration Properties*

Property	Description
`spring.artemis.embedded.enabled`	Sets whether embedded mode should be enabled; the default is `true`.
`spring.artemis.embedded.persistent`	Sets whether messages are persisted; the default is `false`.
`spring.artemis.embedded.data-directory`	Sets the directory used to store the journal; this is useful only when `persistent` is true.
`spring.artemis.embedded.queues`	Comma-separated list of queues to create on startup.
`spring.artemis.embedded.topics`	Comma-separated list of topics to create on startup.
`spring.artemis.embedded.cluster-password`	Cluster password; the default is generated.
`spring.artemis.embedded.server-id`	The ID of the server; the default is an autogenerated counter.

Use Artemis with a Connection Pool

When using Artemis, it is also possible to use a pool of JMS connections (much like a JDBC-based connection pool). By default this is disabled. To enable and configure it, you can use the properties in the `spring.artemis.pool` namespace (see Table 8-5).

Table 8-5. *ActiveMQ Pooling Configuration Properties*

Property	Description
`spring.artemis.pool.enabled`	Sets whether a connection pool should be used; the default is `false`.
`spring.artemis.pool.max-connections`	Sets the maximum number of connections; the default is 1.
`spring.artemis.pool.maximum-active-session-per-connection`	Sets the maximum number of active JMS sessions allowed per connection; the default is 500.
`spring.artemis.pool.idle-timeout`	Sets how long a connection can be idle; the default is 30 seconds.
`spring.artemis.pool.expiry-timeout`	Sets how long before a connection is expired; the default is 0 (never).
`spring.artemis.pool.reconnect-on-exception`	Rests the connection when a `JMSException` occurs; the default is `true`.
`spring.artemis.pool.block-if-full`	Blocks when a connection is requested or throws a `JMSException` instead; the default is `true`.
`spring.artemis.pool.block-if-full-timeout`	Sets how long to block before throwing a `JMSException`; the default is -1 (which blocks until a connection is available).
`spring.artemis.pool.create-connection-on-startup`	Sets whether a connection should be eagerly created on startup of the application; the default is `true`.

Using the pooling facility requires the `pooled-jms` dependency to be added to your build file. See Listing 8-4.

Listing 8-4. JMS ConnectionPool Dependency

```
<dependency>
  <groupId>org.messaginghub</groupId>
  <artifactId>pooled-jms</artifactId>
</dependency>
```

When running the application again, you will notice that the type of the
ConnectionFactory has changed to PooledConnectionFactory.

Use JNDI

When deploying a Spring Boot application to a JEE container, there is a big change that
you want to use a preregistered ConnectionFactory from that container as well. To
enable this, you would need a dependency on the spring-jms library and the jakarta.
jms-api (the latter can then probably be marked provided that it will be supplied by your
JEE container). You could use one of the starters and exclude the explicit ActiveMQ or
Artemis dependencies; however, declaring only the needed dependencies is easier and
clearer. See Listing 8-5.

Listing 8-5. Bare JMS Dependencies

```
<dependency>
  <groupId>org.springframework</groupId>
  <artifactId>spring-jms</artifactId>
</dependency>
<dependency>
  <groupId>jakarta.jms</groupId>
  <artifactId>jakarta.jms-api</artifactId>
</dependency>
```

When JNDI is available, Spring Boot will first try to detect ConnectionFactory in
the JNDI register under one of the well-known names such as java:/JmsXA and java:/
XAConnectionFactory or by the name specified in the spring.jms.jndi-name property.
Furthermore, it will also automatically create a JndiDestinationResolver so that the
queues and topics will also be detected in JNDI; by default a fallback to dynamic creation
of destinations is allowed.

```
spring.jms.jndi-name=java:/jms/connectionFactory
```

With that in place and having built your artifact, you can now deploy your application to the JEE container and reuse the existing `ConnectionFactory`.

Configure Manually

The final way to configure JMS is to do it manually. For this you will need at least the `spring-jms` and `jakarta.jms-api` dependencies and probably some client libraries for the JMS broker you are using. Manual configuration can be needed when:

- Spring Boot cannot auto-configure your `ConnectionFactory`
- Extensive setup of the `ConnectionFactory` instance is needed
- Multiple `ConnectionFactory` instances are needed

To configure a `ConnectionFactory` instance, you add an `@Bean` annotated method that constructs a `ConnectionFactory` instance. See Listing 8-6.

Listing 8-6. ConnectionFactory Bean Configuration

```
@Bean
public ConnectionFactory connectionFactory() {
  var connectionFactory =
    new ActiveMQConnectionFactory("vm://localhost?broker.
    persistent=false");
  connectionFactory.setClientID("someId");
  return connectionFactory;
}
```

This will create a `ConnectionFactory` instance for Artemis; it will use an embedded nonpersistent broker and set the `clientId` instance. When Spring Boot detects a preconfigured `ConnectionFactory`, it doesn't attempt to create one itself. When running it, the output should look like Figure 8-3.

```
/\\ /___'_ _ _ _()_ __ _ _\ \ \ \
( ( )\___ | '_ | '_| | '_ \/ _` | \ \ \ \
 \\/  ___)| |_)| | | | | || (_| |  ) ) ) )
  '  |____| .__|_| |_|_| |_\__, | / / / /
 =========|_|==============|___/=/_/_/_/
 :: Spring Boot ::                (v3.2.1)

2023-12-29T10:39:29.855+01:00  INFO 31249 --- [        main] c.a.s.jms.JmsActiveMQApplication      : Starting JmsActiveMQApplication using Java 21.0.1 with PID 31249 (/Users/mar
2023-12-29T10:39:29.861+01:00  INFO 31249 --- [        main] c.a.s.jms.JmsActiveMQApplication      : No active profile set, falling back to 1 default profile "default"
2023-12-29T10:39:30.622+01:00  INFO 31249 --- [        main] c.a.s.jms.JmsActiveMQApplication      : Started JmsActiveMQApplication in 1.102 seconds (process running for 1.762)
# Beans: 82
   Name:                                                        jmsActiveMQApplication, Type: JmsActiveMQApplication$$SpringCGLIB$$0
   Name:                                                        connectionFactory, Type: ActiveMQConnectionFactory
   Name:         org.springframework.boot.autoconfigure.jms.JmsAutoConfiguration$JmsTemplateConfiguration, Type: JmsTemplateConfiguration
   Name:                                                        jmsTemplate, Type: JmsTemplate
```

Figure 8-3. *Artemis beans output*

8-2. Send Messages Using JMS

Problem

You want to send messages to other systems over JMS.

Solution

Use the Spring Boot–provided JmsTemplate to send and (optionally) convert messages.

How It Works

When using Spring Boot, if it detects JMS and a single ConnectionFactory, it will also automatically configure a JmsTemplate, which can be used to send and convert messages. Spring Boot exposes properties in the spring.jms.template namespace, which can be used to configure the JmsTemplate instance.

Send a Message with JmsTemplate

To send a message through JMS, you can use the send or sendAndConvert method on JmsTemplate. Let's write a component that every second places a message with the current date and time on a queue. See Listing 8-7.

Listing 8-7. JMS Message Sender Component

```
@Component
class MessageSender {

  private final JmsTemplate jms;
```

```
MessageSender(JmsTemplate jms) {
  this.jms = jms;
}

@Scheduled(fixedRate = 1000)
public void sendTime() {
  var msg = "Current Date & Time is: " + LocalDateTime.now();
  jms.convertAndSend("time-queue", msg);
}
}
```

The `JmsTemplate` instance is automatically injected through the constructor, and because of scheduling, we will get a message containing the current date and time on a queue called `time-queue`. To run this code, you will need an `@SpringBootApplication` class with the `@EnableScheduling` annotation so that `@Scheduled` will be processed. See Listing 8-8.

Listing 8-8. Spring Boot Application for the JMS Sender

```
@SpringBootApplication
@EnableScheduling
public class JmsSenderApplication {

    public static void main(String[] args) {
      SpringApplication.run(JmsSenderApplication.class, args);
    }
}
```

Now when running this class, it appears as if nothing much is happening, but the messages are filling up the queue. We can write an integration test to check if this code is working. See Listing 8-9.

Listing 8-9. Spring Boot JMS Integration Test

```
package com.apress.springboot3recipes.jms;

import jakarta.jms.JMSException;
import jakarta.jms.TextMessage;
import org.junit.jupiter.api.Test;
```

```
import org.springframework.beans.factory.annotation.Autowired;
import org.springframework.boot.test.context.SpringBootTest;
import org.springframework.jms.core.JmsTemplate;

import static org.assertj.core.api.Assertions.assertThat;

@SpringBootTest
class JmsSenderApplicationTest {

  @Autowired
  private JmsTemplate jms;

  @Test
  void shouldSendMessage() throws JMSException {

    var message = jms.receive("time-queue");

    assertThat(message)
      .isInstanceOf(TextMessage.class);
    assertThat(((TextMessage) message).getText())
      .startsWith("Current Date & Time is: ");
  }
}
```

This JUnit test will bootstrap the application and start sending messages. In the test, we use a `JmsTemplate` instance to `receive` a message, and we do some assertions on it to see if messages are really sent and contain what we expected them to contain. The test will use the embedded JMS broker as we haven't configured anything. When running the test, it should be green as a message will be sent and received. To see if it fails, you can remove the @Scheduled annotation from `MessageSender`. The test will then fail indicating a message wasn't received.

💡   When writing tests for messaging, you might want to set the `receive-timeout` property of `JmsTemplate` because the default is to indefinitely wait for a message to come. However, after 500 ms, you might want to fail your test.

Configure JmsTemplate

Spring Boot provides properties in the `spring.jms.template` namespace to configure JmsTemplate (see Table 8-6).

Table 8-6. *JmsTemplate Properties*

Property	Description
spring.jms.template.default-destination	Sets the default destination to use for send and receive operations when a specific destination isn't specified.
spring.jms.template.delivery-delay	Sets the delivery delay for sending a message.
spring.jms.template.delivery-mode	Sets the delivery mode, persistent or non-persistent. When explicitly set, it sets qos-enabled to true.
spring.jms.template.priority	Sets the priority of the message when sending. The default is none; when explicitly set, it sets qos-enabled to true.
spring.jms.template.qos-enabled	Sets whether quality of service (QOS) should be enabled. When enabled, the priority, delivery-mode, and time-to-live of a message will be set. The default is false.
spring.jms.template.receive-timeout	Sets the timeout to use for receive calls. The default is indefinite.
spring.jms.template.time-to-live	Sets the time-to-live of a JMS message; when set, it sets qos-enabled to true.
spring.jms.pub-sub-domain	Sets the default destination to a topic or queue. The default is false, meaning queue.

In addition to these properties, JmsTemplate will also be auto-configured with a DestinationResolver and MessageConverter if a unique instance of the beans can be found. If no unique instance can be found, the defaults will be used, DynamicDestinationResolver and SimpleMessageConverter (see Table 8-7).

Table 8-7. *SimpleMessageConverter Class to JMS Message Converter*

Type	JMS Message Type
java.lang.String	javax.jms.TextMessage
java.util.Map	javax.jms.MapMessage
java.io.Serializable	javax.jms.ObjectMessage
byte[]	javax.jms.BytesMessage

Let's send an Order to the orders queue, and let's use Jackson to send JSON instead of using the Java Serialization mechanism. See Listing 8-10.

Listing 8-10. Order Class

```
package com.apress.springboot3recipes.order;

import java.math.BigDecimal;

public record Order (String id, BigDecimal amount) { }
```

That is the Order class we are going to send. To be able to generate an order, let's create an OrderGenerator class that will create an order with an ID and a random amount. See Listing 8-11.

Listing 8-11. OrderGenerator Class

```
package com.apress.springboot3recipes.order;

import java.math.BigDecimal;
import java.math.RoundingMode;
import java.util.UUID;
import java.util.concurrent.ThreadLocalRandom;

public class OrderGenerator {
  public static Order generate() {
    var rnd = ThreadLocalRandom.current().nextDouble(1000.00);
    var amount = BigDecimal.valueOf(rnd).setScale(2, RoundingMode.
    HALF_EVEN);
```

```
    var id = UUID.randomUUID().toString();
    return new Order(id, amount);
  }
}
```

Now we need a sender that generates an `Order` and places it on the queue using `JmsTemplate`. See Listing 8-12.

Listing 8-12. JMS-Based OrderSender

```
@Component
class OrderSender {

  private final JmsTemplate jms;

  OrderSender(JmsTemplate jms) {
    this.jms = jms;
  }

  @Scheduled(fixedRate = 500)
  public void sendOrder() {
    var order = OrderGenerator.generate();
    jms.convertAndSend("orders", order);
  }
}
```

It isn't that different from `MessageSender` written earlier, but now it generates an `Order` with some random generated data (see the `OrderGenerator`) and sends it on the `orders` queue. When running this, it would actually fail. Because `Order` doesn't implement `Serializable`, it won't be converted into an `ObjectMessage`. However, we wanted to use JSON. To make this happen, a different `MessageConverter` is needed: the `MappingJackson2MessageConverter` to be exact. This uses Jackson to marshal and unmarshal objects to JSON. It should be added as a bean to the configuration.

First you will need to add the dependency to add Jackson (or, rather, JSON support) to your application. Add `spring-boot-starter-json` to get the needed dependencies. See Listing 8-13.

Listing 8-13. Spring Boot JSON Starter Dependency

```xml
<dependency>
  <groupId>org.springframework.boot</groupId>
  <artifactId>spring-boot-starter-json</artifactId>
</dependency>
```

> ℹ️   When you already have `spring-boot-starter-web` or `spring-boot-starter-webflux` in your list of dependencies, `spring-boot-starter-json` is already included.

Next you can configure `MappingJackson2MessageConverter`. See Listing 8-14.

Listing 8-14. MessageConverter Configuration

```java
@Bean
public MappingJackson2MessageConverter messageConverter() {
  var converter = new MappingJackson2MessageConverter();
  converter.setTypeIdPropertyName("content_type"); ①
  converter.setTypeIdMappings(Map.of("order", Order.class)); ②
  return converter;
}
```

① The `typeIdPropertyName` is a required property and indicates the name of the property in which the actual type of the message is stored. Without any further configuration, the FQN of the class will be used.

② This is the mapping for which type identifier (`typeId`) to use for a given class. Instead of sending the FQN of a class, it will use the type in the mapping to identify the type. When sending an `Order`, the `content-type` header will contain the value order.

💡 It generally is a good idea to explicitly define type mappings. This way you don't explicitly bind two or more applications together on the Java level. They can use their own mapping for order to their own Order class.

With all this in place, we can write a test to see if orders are actually being sent.

```java
package com.apress.springboot3recipes.jms;

import com.apress.springboot3recipes.order.Order;
import com.fasterxml.jackson.databind.ObjectMapper;
import jakarta.jms.BytesMessage;
import org.junit.jupiter.api.Test;
import org.springframework.beans.factory.annotation.Autowired;
import org.springframework.boot.test.context.SpringBootTest;
import org.springframework.jms.core.JmsTemplate;

import static org.assertj.core.api.Assertions.assertThat;

@SpringBootTest
class JmsSenderApplicationTest {

  @Autowired
  private JmsTemplate jms;

  @Test
  void shouldReceiveOrderPlain() throws Exception {

    var message = jms.receive("orders");

    assertThat(message)
            .isInstanceOf(BytesMessage.class);

    var msg = (BytesMessage) message;

    var mapper = new ObjectMapper();
    var content = new byte[(int) msg.getBodyLength()];
    msg.readBytes(content);
    var order = mapper.readValue( content, Order.class);
```

```
    assertThat(order).hasNoNullFieldsOrProperties();
  }

  @Test
  void shouldReceiveOrderWithConversion() throws Exception {

    var order = (Order) jms.receiveAndConvert("orders");
    assertThat(order).hasNoNullFieldsOrProperties();
  }
}
```

There are two test methods here. The plain one does manual conversion of the message to an `Order`, whereas the second uses the `receiveAndConvert` method to have the conversion done for you. This to show what the `MessageConverter` is doing and that it makes your code more readable. As you can see, `MappingJackson2MessageConverter` converts the `Order` into a `BytesMessages`. If you want to use `TextMessage` instead, you can set the `targetType` property to `TEXT`; you will then recieve a `TextMessage` with a JSON as a `String` as the payload.

8-3. Receive Messages Using JMS

Problem

You want to read messages from a JMS destination so that you can handle them in your application.

Solution

Create a class and annotate methods with `@JmsListener` to bind it to a destination and handle incoming messages.

How It Works

You can create a POJO and annotate its methods with `@JmsListener`. Spring will detect this and create a JMS listener for it. Spring Boot exposes properties to configure the listeners under the `spring.jms.listener` namespace.

Receive mMessages

Let's create a service that listens to the message sent by the sender from Recipe 8-2. See Listing 8-15.

Listing 8-15. JMS-Based Spring JMS Listener

```
@Component
class CurrentDateTimeService {

  @JmsListener(destination = "time-queue")
  public void handle(TextMessage msg) throws JMSException {
    System.out.println("[RECEIVED] - " + msg.getText());
  }
}
```

It is a regular class and has a method annotated with @JmsListener, which requires at least a destination so that it knows where to retrieve messages from. It accepts a jakarta.jms.TextMessage and prints the content to the console. The method signature of a @JmsListener annotated method is somewhat flexible as it allows for several arguments either annotated or from a specific type (see Table 8-8).

Table 8-8. *Allowed Method Parameter Types*

Type	Description
java.lang.String	Gets message payload as String only for TextMessage
java.util.Map	Gets message payload as Map only for MapMessage
byte[]	Gets message payload as byte[] only for BytesMessage
Serializable object	Deserializes Object from ObjectMessage
jakarta.jms.Message	Gets the actual JMS message
jakarta.jms.Session	Accesses the Session for access, sending a custom reply, for instance
@Header annotated element	Extracts a header from the JMS message
@Headers annotated element	Only usable on a java.util.Map to get all the JMS message headers
org.springframework.messaging.Message	Representation of the incoming JMS message

The listener could be simplified by using a `String` as a method argument instead of handling the `jakarta.jms.Message` configuration ourselves. See Listing 8-16.

Listing 8-16. String-Based Spring JMS Listener

```
@Component
class CurrentDateTimeService {

    @JmsListener(destination = "time-queue")
    public void handle(String msg) {
            System.out.println("[RECEIVED] - " + msg);
    }
}
```

The output of both application should look like Figure 8-4.

```
  .   ____          _            __ _ _
 /\\ / ___'_ __ _ _(_)_ __  __ _ \ \ \ \
( ( )\___ | '_ | '_| | '_ \/ _` | \ \ \ \
 \\/  ___)| |_)| | | | | || (_| |  ) ) ) )
  '  |____| .__|_| |_|_| |_\__, | / / / /
 =========|_|==============|___/=/_/_/_/
 :: Spring Boot ::               (v3.2.1)

2023-12-29T11:09:17.465+01:00  INFO 31864 --- [         main] c.a.s.jms.JmsReceiveApplication       : Starting JmsReceiveApplication using
2023-12-29T11:09:17.469+01:00  INFO 31864 --- [         main] c.a.s.jms.JmsReceiveApplication       : No active profile set, falling back t
2023-12-29T11:09:18.893+01:00  INFO 31864 --- [         main] c.a.s.jms.JmsReceiveApplication       : Started JmsReceiveApplication in 1.9
[RECEIVED] - Current Date & Time is: 2023-12-29T11:09:18.982079
[RECEIVED] - Current Date & Time is: 2023-12-29T11:09:19.891393
[RECEIVED] - Current Date & Time is: 2023-12-29T11:09:20.891206
[RECEIVED] - Current Date & Time is: 2023-12-29T11:09:21.892838
```

Figure 8-4. *JMS receive output*

Configure the Listener Container

Spring uses a `JmsListenerContainerFactory` to create the infrastructure needed to support the `@JmsListener` annotation. Spring Boot configures a default one, which can be configured using properties from the `spring.jms.listener` namespace. If that isn't sufficient, you can always configure your own instance and do all the configuration options manually. Spring Boot will refrain from creating `JmsListenerContainerFactory` when it already detects one in the context (see Table 8-9).

Table 8-9. *JMS Listener Properties*

Property	Description
`spring.jms.listener.acknowledge-mode`	Acknowledges the mode of the container; the default is automatic.
`spring.jms.listener.auto-startup`	Starts the container automatically on startup. The default is true.
`spring.jms.listener.concurrency`	Sets the minimum number of concurrent consumers. The default is none, leading to one concurrent consumer (the Spring default).
`spring.jms.listener.max-concurrency`	Sets the maximum number of concurrent consumers. The default is none, leading to one concurrent consumer (the Spring default).
`spring.jms.receive-timeout`	Sets the timeout to use for receiving messaged; the default is one second.
`spring.jms.pub-sub-domain`	Sets whether the default destination is a topic or queue. The default is `false`, meaning queue.

The default configured `JmsListenerContainerFactory` will also detect a single, unique `DestinationResolver` and `MessageConverter` and when found will use that; otherwise, it will use the Spring defaults `DynamicDestinationResolver` and `SimpleMessageConverter` (see Recipe 8-2 for more information).

Use a Custom MessageConverter

What if you want to send objects as JSON to the next system over JMS? You could rely on Java Serialization, but that generally is frowned upon as that is a tightly coupled system. Using JSON or XML to transfer objects/messages is a better way to do it. With Spring JMS, it is a matter of configuring a different `MessageConverter` (see also Recipe 8-2 for the sending part). See Listing 8-17.

Listing 8-17. MessageConverter Configuration

```
@Bean
public MappingJackson2MessageConverter messageConverter() {
  var messageConverter = new MappingJackson2MessageConverter();
  messageConverter.setTypeIdPropertyName("content_type");
  messageConverter.setTypeIdMappings(singletonMap("order", Order.class));
  return messageConverter;
}
```

MappingJackson2MessageConverter by default requires a property name to put the identifier for the content type in. This will be read from a header in the JMS message (here we set it to content_type). Next we can, optionally, define a mapping between a type and the class. As we want to be able to map objects to the Order class, we specify that as the mapping for the content-type order. See Listing 8-18.

Listing 8-18. JMS MessageListener Receiving an Order

```
@Component
class OrderService {

  @JmsListener(destination = "orders")
  public void handle(Order order) {
    System.out.println("[RECEIVED] - " + order);
  }
}
```

The listener receives the Order object as Spring JMS will take care of receiving and converting the messages. If you combine this listener with the order sender from Recipe 8-2, you will see a steady stream of orders coming in (Figure 8-5).

```
/\\ / ___'_ __ _ _(_)_ __  __ _ \ \ \ \
( ( )\___ | '_ | '_| | '_ \/ _` | \ \ \ \
 \\/  ___)| |_)| | | | | || (_| |  ) ) ) )
  '  |____| .__|_| |_|_| |_\__, | / / / /
 =========|_|==============|___/=/_/_/_/
 :: Spring Boot ::                (v3.2.1)

2023-12-29T11:14:37.056+01:00  INFO 32045 --- [      main] c.a.s.jms.JmsSenderApplication    : Starting JmsSenderApplication using Java 21.0.
2023-12-29T11:14:37.061+01:00  INFO 32045 --- [      main] c.a.s.jms.JmsSenderApplication    : No active profile set, falling back to 1 defau
2023-12-29T11:14:38.870+01:00  INFO 32045 --- [      main] c.a.s.jms.JmsSenderApplication    : Started JmsSenderApplication in 2.376 seconds
[RECEIVED] - Order[id=a0f4be43-c088-4a6e-89a3-d97a4b770be4, amount=251.53]
[RECEIVED] - Order[id=a3346779-d41a-43a4-96ce-7542e951d7e4, amount=336.38]
[RECEIVED] - Order[id=e8a36f36-d312-4626-9fd4-398a6f1cb0fd, amount=994.58]
```

Figure 8-5. *JMS receive output, orders*

Send a Reply

Sometimes when receiving a message you want to return an answer or trigger another part of the process. With Spring messaging, this is pretty easy; you can simply return what you want to send from your handler method. To determine where to send the response, you can add an additional @SendTo annotation to specify the destination. Let's modify the sample to send an OrderConfirmation to the order-confirmation queue. See Listing 8-19.

Listing 8-19. OrderService Sending OrderConfirmation

```
@Component
class OrderService {

  @JmsListener(destination = "orders")
  @SendTo("order-confirmations")
  public OrderConfirmation handle(Order order) {
    System.out.println("[RECEIVED] - " + order);
    return new OrderConfirmation(order.id());
  }
}
```

The OrderService configuration changed slightly; it now returns an OrderConfirmation after processing the order. With the @SendTo annotation, we specify which destination to put the result on.

Let's create another listener for the OrderConfirmation objects so that we can see them coming in. See Listing 8-20.

Listing 8-20. JMS OrderConfirmationService

```
@Component
class OrderConfirmationService {

  @JmsListener(destination = "order-confirmations")
  public void handle(OrderConfirmation confirmation) {
    System.out.println("[RECEIVED] - " + confirmation);
  }
}
```

The OrderConfirmation class so that we know what to marshal into. See Listing 8-21.

Listing 8-21. Simple OrderConfirmation

```
package com.apress.springboot3recipes.order;

public record OrderConfirmation(String orderId) { }
```

When running the application, you will see that first the order is received and next that the OrderConfirmation is being received (Figure 8-6).

```
  .   ____          _            __ _ _
 /\\ / ___'_ __ _ _(_)_ __  __ _ \ \ \ \
( ( )\___ | '_ | '_| | '_ \/ _` | \ \ \ \
 \\/  ___)| |_)| | | | | || (_| |  ) ) ) )
  '  |____| .__|_| |_|_| |_\__, | / / / /
 =========|_|==============|___/=/_/_/_/
 :: Spring Boot ::                (v3.2.1)

2023-12-29T11:17:34.295+01:00  INFO 32132 --- [          main] c.a.s.jms.JmsSenderApplication      : Starting JmsSenderApplication using Java 21.0
2023-12-29T11:17:34.299+01:00  INFO 32132 --- [          main] c.a.s.jms.JmsSenderApplication      : No active profile set, falling back to 1 defa
2023-12-29T11:17:35.806+01:00  INFO 32132 --- [          main] c.a.s.jms.JmsSenderApplication      : Started JmsSenderApplication in 1.99 seconds
[RECEIVED] - Order[id=5266d351-4f74-4eeb-8210-a7c7caf6a2fa, amount=227.05]
[RECEIVED] - OrderConfirmation[orderId=5266d351-4f74-4eeb-8210-a7c7caf6a2fa]
[RECEIVED] - Order[id=3c03a78e-98b6-4b92-8330-1fa043405b47, amount=834.82]
[RECEIVED] - OrderConfirmation[orderId=3c03a78e-98b6-4b92-8330-1fa043405b47]
[RECEIVED] - Order[id=0c7369f5-6bf4-420c-b1aa-e98c928a64ca, amount=71.79]
[RECEIVED] - OrderConfirmation[orderId=0c7369f5-6bf4-420c-b1aa-e98c928a64ca]
```

Figure 8-6. *JMS receive output, orders and confirmations*

8-4. Configure RabbitMQ

Problem

You want to use AMQP messaging in a Spring Boot application and need to connect to the RabbitMQ broker.

Solution

Configure the appropriate `spring.amqp` properties (minimal `spring.amqp.host`) to connect to the exchange and be able to send and receive messages.

How It Works

Spring Boot will automatically create a `ConnectionFactory` instance when it detects the RabbitMQ library on the classpath. To get started, you need to add the `spring-boot-starter-amqp` dependencies. This will pull in all the required dependencies. See Listing 8-22.

Listing 8-22. Spring Boot Starter AMQP Dependency

```
<dependency>
  <groupId>org.springframework.boot</groupId>
  <artifactId>spring-boot-starter-amqp</artifactId>
</dependency>
```

Now you can use the `spring.amqp` properties to connect to the broker. See Listing 8-23.

Listing 8-23. Spring AMQP Basic Configuration

```
spring.amqp.host=localhost
spring.amqp.port=5672
spring.amqp.username=guest
spring.amqp.password=guest
```

This configuration is all that is needed to connect to a default instance of RabbitMQ using the Spring Boot defaults (see Table 8-10).

Table 8-10. RabbitMQ Properties

Property	Description
`spring.amqp.addresses`	A comma-separated list of addresses to which the client should connect.
`spring.amqp.connection-timeout`	Sets a connection timeout. The default is none; 0 means never timeout.
`spring.amqp.host`	Sets the RabbitMQ host.
`spring.amqp.port`	Sets the RabbitMQ port.
`spring.amqp.username`	Sets the username to use for connecting; the default is `guest`.
`spring.amqp.password`	Sets the password to use for connecting; the default is `guest`.
`spring.amqp.publisher-confirms`	Sets whether to enable publisher confirms. The default is `false`.
`spring.amqp.publisher-returns`	Sets whether to enable publisher returns. The default is `false`.
`spring.amqp.requested-heartbeat`	Sets the requested heartbeat timeout. The default is none; 0 means no heartbeat.
`spring.amqp.virtual-host`	Sets the virtual host to use when connecting to the broker.

8-5. Send Messages Using RabbitMQ

Problem

You want to send a message to a RabbitMQ broker so that the message can be delivered to the receiver.

Solution

Using `RabbitTemplate`, you can send messages to an exchange and provide a routing key.

How It Works

Spring Boot automatically configures a RabbitTemplate when it finds a unique ConnectionFactory; this template can be used to send a message to a queue.

Configure the RabbitTemplate

Spring Boot will automatically configure a RabbitTemplate if it can find a unique ConnectionFactory and if no RabbitTemplate exists in the configuration. Spring Boot allows you to modify the configured RabbitTemplate through properties in the spring.rabbitmq.template namespace (see Table 8-11).

Table 8-11. RabbitTemplate Configuration Properties

Property	Description
spring.rabbitmq.template.exchange	Sets the name of the default exchange to use for send operations; the default is none.
spring.rabbitmq.template.routing-key	Sets the value of a default routing key to use for send operations; the default is none.
spring.rabbitmq.template.receive-timeout	Sets the timeout for send and receive operations.
spring.rabbitmq.template.reply-timeout	Sets the timeout for receive operations.

Spring Boot also makes it easy to configure retry logic with RabbitTemplate, but by default it is disabled. Putting spring.rabbitmq.template.retry.enabled=true in application.properties will enable it. Now when sending fails, it will try an additional two times to send the message. To change the number of retries or the interval, you can use properties from the spring.rabbitmq.template.retry namespace (see Table 8-12).

Table 8-12. *RabbitTemplate Retry Configuration*

Property	Description
`spring.rabbitmq.template.retry.enabled`	Enables publishing retries; the default is false.
`spring.rabbitmq.template.retry.max-attempts`	Sets the number of attempts to deliver a message; the default is 3.
`spring.rabbitmq.template.retry.initial-interval`	Sets the duration between the first and second publishing attempts; the default is 1 second.
`spring.rabbitmq.template.retry.max-interval`	Sets the number of attempts to deliver a message; the default is 10 seconds.
`spring.rabbitmq.template.retry.multiplier`	Sets the multiplier to apply to the previous interval; the default is 1.0.

Send a Simple Message

Sending a message with RabbitTemplate can be done by the convertAndSend method. It takes, at least, the routing key and the object to send in the message.

```
@Component
class HelloWorldSender {

  private final RabbitTemplate rabbit;

  HelloWorldSender(RabbitTemplate rabbit) {
    this.rabbit = rabbit;
  }

  @Scheduled(fixedRate = 500)
  public void sayHello() {
```

```
    var msg =  "Hello World, from Spring Boot 3, over RabbitMQ!";
    rabbit.convertAndSend("hello", msg);
  }
}
```

HelloWorldSender will be injected with RabbitTemplate through the constructor. Each 500 ms, a message will be sent on the default exchange with the hello routing key. As it is sent to the default exchange, a queue with the name hello will be automatically created. You can check the number of messages on the queue in the RabbitMQ management console.

Write a test to verify the correct behavior of the application. As there isn't an embedded broker for RabbitMQ, you need to mock the RabbitTemplate with @MockBean. In the @Test method, validate the method call with the proper arguments. See Listing 8-24.

Listing 8-24. Spring Boot Test for RabbitMQ with Mocks

```
package com.apress.springboot3recipes.rabbit;

import org.junit.jupiter.api.Test;
import org.mockito.Mockito;
import org.springframework.amqp.rabbit.core.RabbitTemplate;
import org.springframework.boot.test.context.SpringBootTest;
import org.springframework.boot.test.mock.mockito.MockBean;

import static org.mockito.Mockito.verify;

@SpringBootTest
class RabbitSenderApplicationTest {

  @MockBean
  private RabbitTemplate rabbitTemplate;

  @Test
  void shouldSendAtLeastASingleMessage() {

    verify(rabbitTemplate, Mockito.atLeastOnce())
      .convertAndSend("hello", "Hello World, from Spring Boot 3, over
      RabbitMQ!");
  }
}
```

Another option is to use the Spring Boot Testcontainer support to start a RabbitMQ broker in Docker and use that to communicate. See Listing 8-25.

Listing 8-25. Spring Boot Test for RabbitMQ with Testcontainers

```
package com.apress.springboot3recipes.rabbit;

import org.junit.jupiter.api.Test;
import org.springframework.amqp.core.Binding;
import org.springframework.amqp.core.BindingBuilder;
import org.springframework.amqp.core.DirectExchange;
import org.springframework.amqp.core.Queue;
import org.springframework.amqp.core.QueueBuilder;
import org.springframework.amqp.rabbit.core.RabbitTemplate;
import org.springframework.beans.factory.annotation.Autowired;
import org.springframework.boot.test.context.SpringBootTest;
import org.springframework.boot.test.context.TestConfiguration;
import org.springframework.boot.testcontainers.service.connection.ServiceC
onnection;
import org.springframework.context.annotation.Bean;
import org.testcontainers.containers.RabbitMQContainer;
import org.testcontainers.junit.jupiter.Container;
import org.testcontainers.junit.jupiter.Testcontainers;

import static org.assertj.core.api.Assertions.assertThat;

@SpringBootTest
@Testcontainers
class RabbitSenderApplicationIntegrationTest {

  @ServiceConnection
  @Container
  static RabbitMQContainer rabbitmq =
    new RabbitMQContainer("rabbitmq:3.12.11-management-alpine");

  @Autowired
  private RabbitTemplate rabbitTemplate;

  @Test
```

```
void shouldSendAtLeastASingleMessage() {

  String msg = (String) rabbitTemplate.receiveAndConvert("hello", 1500);
  assertThat(msg).isEqualTo("Hello World, from Spring Boot 3, over
  RabbitMQ!");
}

@TestConfiguration
static class RabbitMqQueueConfiguration {

  @Bean
  public Queue helloQueue() {
    return QueueBuilder.nonDurable("hello").build();
  }

  @Bean
  public Binding helloQueueBinding(Queue queue) {
    return BindingBuilder
      .bind(queue)
      .to(DirectExchange.DEFAULT)
      .withQueueName();
  }
  }
 }
}
```

Send an Object

To send a message to RabbitMQ, the message payload has to be converted into a byte[].
For a String, that is pretty easy by calling String.getBytes. However, when sending
an object, this becomes more cumbersome. The default implementation will check if
the object is Serializable and, if so, will use Java serialization to convert the object to
a byte[]. Using Java serialization isn't the best solution, especially if you need to send
messages to non-Java clients.

RabbitTemplate uses a MessageConverter to delegate the message creation
to. By default it uses the SimpleMessageConverter, which implements the strategy
outlined earlier. There are, however, various implementations that use XML
(MarshallingMessageConverter) or JSON (Jackson2JsonMessageConverter) for the
actual payload (instead of Java serialization).

Spring Boot will automatically detect the configured `MessageConverter` and use it for both `RabbitTemplate` as well as the listeners (see Recipe 8-6). See Listing 8-26.

Listing 8-26. MessageConverter Configuration

```
@Bean
public Jackson2JsonMessageConverter jsonMessageConverter() {
  return new Jackson2JsonMessageConverter();
}
```

This is enough to change `SimpleMessageConverter` into a `Jackson2JsonMessageConverter`. Next create an `Order` and let's use the `RabbitTemplate` to send it to the `orders` exchange using a `new-order` routing key. See Listing 8-27.

Listing 8-27. Order Class

```
package com.apress.springboot3recipes.order;

import java.math.BigDecimal;

public record Order (String id, BigDecimal amount) { }
```

Now that we have an order, let's create a scheduled method that periodically sends a message with a random order. See Listing 8-28.

Listing 8-28. OrderSender for RabbitMQ

```
package com.apress.springboot3recipes.rabbit;

import com.apress.springboot3recipes.order.OrderGenerator;
import org.springframework.amqp.rabbit.core.RabbitTemplate;
import org.springframework.scheduling.annotation.Scheduled;
import org.springframework.stereotype.Component;

@Component
class OrderSender {

  private final RabbitTemplate rabbit;

  OrderSender(RabbitTemplate rabbit) {
    this.rabbit = rabbit;
  }
```

```
@Scheduled(fixedRate = 250)
public void sendTime() {
  var order = OrderGenerator.generate();
  rabbit.convertAndSend("orders", "new-order", order);
}
}
```

It will create an Order with a random amount of max 1000.00. It will then send it, using the convertAndSend method to the orders exchange, with the new-order routing key.

The test will create a mock of RabbitTemplate using @MockBean again and will test the method invocation. See Listing 8-29.

Listing 8-29. OrderSender Test with Mocks

```
package com.apress.springboot3recipes.rabbit;

import com.apress.springboot3recipes.order.Order;
import org.junit.jupiter.api.Test;
import org.springframework.amqp.rabbit.core.RabbitTemplate;
import org.springframework.boot.test.context.SpringBootTest;
import org.springframework.boot.test.mock.mockito.MockBean;

import static org.mockito.ArgumentMatchers.any;
import static org.mockito.ArgumentMatchers.eq;
import static org.mockito.Mockito.atLeastOnce;
import static org.mockito.Mockito.verify;

@SpringBootTest
class RabbitSenderApplicationTest {

  @MockBean
  private RabbitTemplate rabbitTemplate;

  @Test
  void shouldSendAtLeastASingleMessage() {

    verify(rabbitTemplate, atLeastOnce())
            .convertAndSend(
                    eq("orders"),
```

```
                    eq("new-order"),
                    any(Order.class));
    }
}
```

To write an integration test, we can leverage the Testcontainers support to do so much as in the previous sample, but we need some additional configuration for the queue and exchange. See Listing 8-30.

Listing 8-30. OrderSender Test with Testcontainers

```
package com.apress.springboot3recipes.rabbit;

import org.junit.jupiter.api.Test;
import org.springframework.amqp.core.Binding;
import org.springframework.amqp.core.BindingBuilder;
import org.springframework.amqp.core.Exchange;
import org.springframework.amqp.core.ExchangeBuilder;
import org.springframework.amqp.core.Queue;
import org.springframework.amqp.core.QueueBuilder;
import org.springframework.amqp.rabbit.core.RabbitTemplate;
import org.springframework.beans.factory.annotation.Autowired;
import org.springframework.boot.test.context.SpringBootTest;
import org.springframework.boot.test.context.TestConfiguration;
import org.springframework.boot.testcontainers.service.connection.ServiceC
onnection;
import org.springframework.context.annotation.Bean;
import org.testcontainers.containers.RabbitMQContainer;
import org.testcontainers.junit.jupiter.Container;
import org.testcontainers.junit.jupiter.Testcontainers;

import static org.assertj.core.api.Assertions.assertThat;

@SpringBootTest
@Testcontainers
class RabbitSenderApplicationIntegrationTest {

  @ServiceConnection
  @Container
```

```java
  static RabbitMQContainer rabbitmq =
    new RabbitMQContainer("rabbitmq:3.12.4-management-alpine");

  @Autowired
  private RabbitTemplate rabbitTemplate;

  @Test
  void shouldSendAtLeastASingleMessage() {

    var msg = rabbitTemplate.receive("new-order", 1500);

    assertThat(msg).isNotNull();
    assertThat(msg.getBody()).isNotEmpty();
    assertThat(msg.getMessageProperties().getReceivedExchange())
            .isEqualTo("orders");
    assertThat(msg.getMessageProperties().getReceivedRoutingKey())
            .isEqualTo("new-order");
    assertThat(msg.getMessageProperties().getContentType())
            .isEqualTo("application/json");
  }

  @TestConfiguration
  static class RabbitMqQueueConfiguration {

    @Bean
    public Queue newOrderQueue() {
      return QueueBuilder.durable("new-order").build();
    }

    @Bean
    public Exchange ordersExchange() {
      return ExchangeBuilder.topicExchange("orders").durable(true).build();
    }

    @Bean
    public Binding newOrderQueueBinding(Queue queue, Exchange exchange) {
      return BindingBuilder.bind(queue).to(exchange).with("new-order").noargs();
    }
  }
}
```

The included @TestConfiguration adds the queue, exchange, and needed bindings. The queue and bindings are needed to be able to receive the messages; otherwise, they would reside only on the exchange (or depending on the configuration be discarded).

The integration test will load the application and the additional configuration. It will use RabbitTemplate to receive the message.

8-6. Receive Messages Using RabbitMQ

Problem

You want to receive messages from RabbitMQ.

Solution

Annotating a method with @RabbitListener will bind it to a queue and will let it receive messages.

How It Works

A bean that has @RabbitListener and/or @RabbitHandler annotated methods will be used as message listeners from incoming messages. A message listener container is constructed, and the annotated method will receive the incoming message. The message listener container can be configured through properties in the spring.rabbitmq. listener namespace (see Table 8-13).

Table 8-13. *Rabbit Listener Properties*

Property	Description
spring.rabbitmq.listener.type	Sets the listener container type direct or simple; the default is simple.
spring.rabbitmq.listener.simple.acknowledge-mode	Sets the container acknowledge mode; the default is none.
spring.rabbitmq.listener.simple.prefetch	Sets the number of messages to be handled in a single request; the default is none.
spring.rabbitmq.listener.simple.default-requeue-rejected	Sets whether rejected deliveries should be re-queued.
spring.rabbitmq.listener.simple.concurrency	Sets the minimum number of listener invoker threads.
spring.rabbitmq.listener.simple.max-concurrency	Sets the maximum number of listener invoker threads.
spring.rabbitmq.listener.simple.transaction-size	Sets the number of messages processed in a single transaction. For best results, this should be smaller or equal to the prefetch size.
spring.rabbitmq.listener.direct.acknowledge-mode	Sets the container acknowledge mode; the default is none.
spring.rabbitmq.listener.direct.prefetch	Sets the number of messages to be handled in a single request; the default is none.
spring.rabbitmq.listener.direct.default-requeue-rejected	Sets whether rejected deliveries should be re-queued.
spring.rabbitmq.listener.direct.consumers-per-queue	Sets whether rejected deliveries should be re-queued.

Receive a Simple Message

A component with an @RabbitListener annotation is all that is needed to start receiving messages from RabbitMQ. See Listing 8-31.

Listing 8-31. RabbitMQ Listener for String Messages

```
@Component
class HelloWorldReceiver {

  @RabbitListener( queues = "hello")
  public void receive(String msg) {
    System.out.println("Received: " + msg);
  }
}
```

This component will receive all the messages from the hello queue and print them to the console (Figure 8-7). This works fine for simple payloads or if the receiving object can be deserialized from the payload of the message. However, when sending objects or complex messages, you might prefer to use JSON or XML.

```
/\\ / ___'_ __ _ _(_)_ __  __ _ \ \ \ \
( ( )\___ | '_ | '_| | '_ \/ _` | \ \ \ \
 \\/  ___)| |_)| | | | | || (_| |  ) ) ) )
  '  |____| .__|_| |_|_| |_\__, | / / / /
 =========|_|==============|___/=/_/_/_/
 :: Spring Boot ::              (v3.2.1)

2023-12-29T11:45:35.213+01:00  INFO 33009 --- [           main] c.a.s.rabbit.RabbitSenderApplication     : Starting RabbitSenderApplication using Java 21.0.1 with PID 33009 (/Users/mar
2023-12-29T11:45:35.220+01:00  INFO 33009 --- [           main] c.a.s.rabbit.RabbitSenderApplication     : No active profile set, falling back to 1 default profile: "default"
2023-12-29T11:45:36.458+01:00  INFO 33009 --- [           main] o.s.a.r.c.CachingConnectionFactory       : Attempting to connect to: [localhost:5672]
2023-12-29T11:45:36.506+01:00  INFO 33009 --- [           main] o.s.a.r.c.CachingConnectionFactory       : Created new connection: rabbitConnectionFactory#a7ad6e5:0/SimpleConnection@aS
2023-12-29T11:45:36.513+01:00  INFO 33009 --- [           main] o.s.amqp.rabbit.core.RabbitAdmin         : Auto-declaring a non-durable, auto-delete, or exclusive Queue (hello) durable
2023-12-29T11:45:36.579+01:00  INFO 33009 --- [           main] c.a.s.rabbit.RabbitSenderApplication     : Started RabbitSenderApplication in 1.803 seconds (process running for 2.559)
Received: Hello World, from Spring Boot 3, over RabbitMQ!
Received: Hello World, from Spring Boot 3, over RabbitMQ!
Received: Hello World, from Spring Boot 3, over RabbitMQ!
Received: Hello World, from Spring Boot 3, over RabbitMQ!
```

Figure 8-7. RabbitMQ listener output

Receive an Object

To receive a more complex object without relying on Java serialization, you need to configure a MessageConverter (see also Recipe 8-4). The configured MessageConverter will be used by the message listener container to convert incoming payloads into an object required by the @RabbitListener annotated method. See Listing 8-32.

Listing 8-32. JSON MessageConverter Configuration

```
@Bean
public Jackson2JsonMessageConverter jsonMessageConverter() {
  return new Jackson2JsonMessageConverter();
}
```

To configure the MessageConverter, create an @Bean annotated method and construct the converter you want to use; here the converter is a Jackson 2–based one, but there is also one for unmarshaling XML: MarshallingMessageConverter. See Listing 8-33.

Listing 8-33. Rabbit Listener for Orders

```
@Component
class OrderService {

  @RabbitListener(bindings =
    @QueueBinding(
          exchange =@Exchange(name="orders", type = ExchangeTypes.TOPIC),
          value = @Queue(name = "incoming-orders"),
          key = "new-order"
  ))
  public void handle(Order order) {
    System.out.println("[RECEIVED] - " + order);
  }
}
```

The previous listener will user the orders exchange (which is a fanout exchange) and create a binding for the incoming-orders using the new-order routing key. When started, the exchange and queue will automatically be created if they don't already exist. The incoming message is converted into an Order using Jackson2JsonMessageConverter. The output should be similar to Figure 8-8.

```
  .   ____
 /\\ / ___'_ __ _ _(_)_ __  __ _ \ \ \ \
( ( )\___ | '_ | '_| | '_ \/ _` | \ \ \ \
 \\/  ___)| |_)| | | | | || (_| |  ) ) ) )
  '  |____| .__|_| |_|_| |_\__, | / / / /
 =========|_|==============|___/=/_/_/_/
 :: Spring Boot ::              (v3.2.1)

2023-12-29T11:48:29.207+01:00  INFO 33121 --- [          main] c.a.s.rabbit.RabbitReceiverApplication   : Starting RabbitReceiverApplication using Java 2
2023-12-29T11:48:29.217+01:00  INFO 33121 --- [          main] c.a.s.rabbit.RabbitReceiverApplication   : No active profile set, falling back to 1 defaul
2023-12-29T11:48:30.615+01:00  INFO 33121 --- [          main] o.s.a.r.c.CachingConnectionFactory       : Attempting to connect to: [localhost:5672]
2023-12-29T11:48:30.672+01:00  INFO 33121 --- [          main] o.s.a.r.c.CachingConnectionFactory       : Created new connection: rabbitConnectionFactory
2023-12-29T11:48:30.732+01:00  INFO 33121 --- [          main] c.a.s.rabbit.RabbitReceiverApplication   : Started RabbitReceiverApplication in 2.063 seco
[RECEIVED] - Order[id=62fcc442-ae6e-4276-9c6d-1a2b347b7072, amount=745.95]
[RECEIVED] - Order[id=2f3bde5b-cd00-44ed-8bbc-09f8dd77f961, amount=255.26]
[RECEIVED] - Order[id=9ce9313c-a5d3-4f61-97f5-6beea15e1f3b, amount=452.12]
```

Figure 8-8. *RabbitMQ listener output: orders*

Receive a Message and Send a Reply

When receiving a message, it might be necessary to send a response to the client or communicate with a different message; using an @RabbitListener on a nonvoid method is possible. It will create a result message and place it on an exchange with a routing key; this needs to be specified in the @SendTo annotation. See Listing 8-34.

Listing 8-34. Rabbit Listener for Orders with Reply

```
@Component
class OrderService {

  @RabbitListener(bindings = @QueueBinding(
          exchange = @Exchange(name="orders", type = ExchangeTypes.TOPIC),
          value = @Queue(name = "incoming-orders"),
          key = "new-order"

  ))
  @SendTo("orders/order-confirmation")
  public OrderConfirmation handle(Order order) {
    System.out.println("[RECEIVED] - " + order);
    return new OrderConfirmation(order.id());
  }
}
```

When receiving an Order and processing it, an OrderConfirmation will be sent; the @SendTo annotation (from the general Spring Messaging component) contains the exchange and routing key. The part before the / is the exchange, and the part afterward is the routing key; thus, `<exchange>/<routing-key>` is the pattern used. An empty exchange or routing key value is possible (or both); in that case, the default configured exchange and routing key will be used. Here it will use the `orders` exchange and use `order-confirmation` as the routing key.

Another listener could be used to process the `OrderConfirmation` messages. See Listing 8-35.

Listing 8-35. OrderConfirmationService for RabbitMQ

```
@Component
class OrderConfirmationService {

  @RabbitListener(bindings = @QueueBinding(
          exchange = @Exchange(name="orders", type = ExchangeTypes.TOPIC),
          value = @Queue(name = "order-confirmations"),
          key = "order-confirmation"
  ))
  public void handle(OrderConfirmation confirmation) {
    System.out.println("[RECEIVED] - " + confirmation);
  }
}
```

It will create a queue `order-confirmations` using the `order-confirmation` routing-key and bind that on the `orders` exchange (just as the `OrderService` created earlier). When running the code, together with the sender from Recipe 8-4, you should receive `Order` instances and see that they will be confirmed as well (Figure 8-9).

```
 .   ____          _            __ _ _
/\\ / ___'_ __ _ _(_)_ __  __ _ \ \ \ \
( ( )\___ | '_ | '_| | '_ \/ _` | \ \ \ \
 \\/  ___)| |_)| | | | | || (_| |  ) ) ) )
  '  |____| .__|_| |_|_| |_\__, | / / / /
 =========|_|==============|___/=/_/_/_/
 :: Spring Boot ::                (v3.2.1)

2023-12-29T11:51:10.175+01:00  INFO 33246 --- [    main] c.a.s.rabbit.RabbitReceiverApplication   : Starting RabbitReceiverApplication using Java 21
2023-12-29T11:51:10.179+01:00  INFO 33246 --- [    main] c.a.s.rabbit.RabbitReceiverApplication   : No active profile set, falling back to 1 default
2023-12-29T11:51:11.517+01:00  INFO 33246 --- [    main] o.s.a.r.c.CachingConnectionFactory       : Attempting to connect to: [localhost:5672]
2023-12-29T11:51:11.573+01:00  INFO 33246 --- [    main] o.s.a.r.c.CachingConnectionFactory       : Created new connection: rabbitConnectionFactory#
2023-12-29T11:51:11.674+01:00  INFO 33246 --- [    main] c.a.s.rabbit.RabbitReceiverApplication   : Started RabbitReceiverApplication in 1.941 secon
[RECEIVED] - Order[id=e840c0f5-d917-4c2e-9809-4fa1c2c33061, amount=83.27]
[RECEIVED] - OrderConfirmation[orderId=e840c0f5-d917-4c2e-9809-4fa1c2c33061]
[RECEIVED] - Order[id=8e07cffd-cd47-457f-9f16-45157f19c66c, amount=985.97]
[RECEIVED] - OrderConfirmation[orderId=8e07cffd-cd47-457f-9f16-45157f19c66c]
```

Figure 8-9. *RabbitMQ listener output for orders and confirmations*

8-7. Configure Spring for Apache Kafka

Problem

You want to use Spring for Apache Kafka in a Spring Boot application and need to connect to the Kafka cluster.

Solution

Configure the appropriate `spring.kafka` properties (minimally `spring.kafka.bootstrap-servers`) to connect to the cluster and be able to send (or receive) messages.

How It Works

Spring Boot will automatically create a `ConnectionFactory` instance when it detects the Spring Kafka and Kafka libraries on the classpath. To get started, you need to add the `spring-kafka` dependency. This will pull in all the required dependencies. See Listing 8-36.

Listing 8-36. Spring Kafka Dependency

```
<dependency>
  <groupId>org.springframework.kafka</groupId>
  <artifactId>spring-kafka</artifactId>
</dependency>
```

ⓘ   This recipe uses the Spring Boot Docker Compose support to bootstrap Kafka, so a dependency on `spring-boot-docker-compose` is needed as well.

Now you can use the `spring.kafka` properties to connect to the broker. See Listing 8-37.

Listing 8-37. Minimal Spring Kafka Properties to Connect and Receive Messages

```
spring.kafka.bootstrap-servers=localhost:9092
```

This configuration is all that is needed to connect to the Kafka container and send and receive messages through Kafka. Table 8-14 describes the global Kafka properties that can be set. In the `spring.kafka.consumer` and `spring.kafka.producer` namespaces, you can set the respective properties for Kafka Consumer (Table 8-15) or Producer (Table 8-16).

Table 8-14. *Common Kafka Properties*

Property	Description
`spring.kafka.bootstrap-servers`	Comma-separated list of addresses to which the client should connect
`spring.kafka.client-id`	ID to pass to the server when making requests, mainly used for server-side logging
`spring.kafka.properties`	Additional properties, common for the producer and consumer, used to configure the client

To configure the receiving side of the Kafka support, you can add the `spring.kafka.consumer` properties to your configuration (Table 8-15).

Table 8-15. *Kafka Consumer Properties*

Property	Description
`spring.kafka.consumer.auto-commit-interval`	Sets the frequency in which the consumer offsets are committed to Kafka, if `enable-auto-commit` is true.
`spring.kafka.consumer.auto-offset-reset`	Sets what to do when there is no initial offset in Kafka or if the current offset is no longer available.
`spring.kafka.consumer.bootstrap-servers`	Is a comma-separated list of addresses to which the client should connect. This overrides the global setting.
`spring.kafka.consumer.client-id`	Sets the ID to pass to the server when making requests; used in server logging.
`spring.kafka.consumer.enable-auto-commit`	Sets whether the offset should be automatically committed.

(continued)

Table 8-15. (*continued*)

Property	Description
`spring.kafka.consumer.fetch-max-wait`	Sets the amount of time to block before answering the fetch request.
`spring.kafka.consumer.fetch-min-size`	Sets the minimal amount of data the server should return for a fetch request.
`spring.kafka.consumer.group-id`	Sets the unique string to identify the consumer group; this is required!
`spring.kafka.consumer.heartbeat-interval`	Sets the heartbeat time between signals to the consumer coordinator.
`spring.kafka.consumer.isolation-level`	Sets the isolation level for reading messages that have been written transactionally. The default is READ_UNCOMMITTED.
`spring.kafka.consumer.key-deserializer`	Sets the deserializer for the keys; the default is `StringDeserializer`.
`spring.kafka.consumer.value-deserializer`	Sets the deserializer for the values; the default is `StringDeserializer`.
`spring.kafka.consumer.max-poll-records`	Sets the maximum number of records to return in a single call to `poll()`.
`spring.kafka.consumer.properties`	Sets the additional consumer-specific properties used to configure the client.
`spring.kafka.consumer.security.protocol`	Sets the security protocol to use when communicating with the Kafka broker.
`Spring.kafka.consumer.ssl.*`	Sets the SSL configuration used for connecting to the Kafka broker, used to set keystore, trust store, etc.

To configure the producing side of the Kafka support, you can add the `spring.kafka.producer` properties to your configuration (Table 8-16).

Table 8-16. *Kafka Producer Properties*

Property	Description
`spring.kafka.producer.acks`	Sets the number of acks needed by the producer from the broker to consider a request complete.
`spring.kafka.producer.batch-size`	Sets the default batch size.
`spring.kafka.producer.bootstrap-servers`	Sets the comma-separated list of addresses to which the client should connect. This overrides the global setting.
`spring.kafka.producer.buffer-memory`	Sets the total memory size the producer is allowed to use for buffering records waiting to be sent to the server.
`spring.kafka.producer.client-id`	Sets the ID to pass to the server when making requests; used in server logging.
`spring.kafka.producer.compression-type`	Sets the compression type for all data generated by the producer.
`spring.kafka.producer.key-deserializer`	Sets the deserializer for the keys; the default is `StringDeserializer`.
`spring.kafka.producer.value-deserializer`	Sets the deserializer for the values; the default is `StringDeserializer`.
`spring.kafka.producer.retries`	Sets the number of allowed retries; the default is 0.
`spring.kafka.producer.transaction-id-prefix`	When nonempty, this enables transaction support for the producer.
`spring.kafka.producer.properties`	Sets the additional producer-specific properties used to configure the client.
`spring.kafka.producer.security.protocol`	Sets the security protocol to use when communicating with the Kafka broker.
`Spring.kafka.producer.ssl.*`	Sets the SSL configuration used for connecting to the Kafka broker; used to set keystore, trust store, etc.

When adding the minimal configuration (Listing 8-35) and the needed dependencies, Kafka auto-configuration will kick in. It will automatically connect to the Kafka server and configure `KafkaTemplate` and the needed beans to enable `@KafkaListener`. The default (and most basic configuration) is to allow for sending and receiving `String`-based messages.

8-8. Send Messages Using Spring Kafka

Problem

You want to send a message to a Kafka server so that the messages can be delivered to the receiver.

Solution

Using `KafkaTemplate`, you can send messages to a topic and provide a key.

How It Works

Spring Boot automatically configures a `KafkaTemplate` instance when Kafka is available and configured.

Configure the KafkaTemplate

Spring Boot will automatically configure a `KafkaTemplate` instance if no `KafkaTemplate` exists in the configuration. Spring Boot allows you to modify the configured `KafkaTemplate` instance through properties in the `spring.kafka.template` namespace (see Table 8-17).

Table 8-17. *KafkaTemplate Configuration Properties*

Property	Description
`spring.kafka.template.default-topic`	Sets the name of the default topic to use for send operations; the default is none.
`spring.kafka.template.transaction-id-prefix`	Sets the transaction ID prefix; overrides the transaction ID specified in the producer configuration.

Send a Simple Message

Sending a message with the KafkaTemplate can be done with the send method. It takes, at least, the topic (if no default is configured) and the object to send in the message.

```java
@Component
class HelloWorldSender {

  private final KafkaTemplate<String, String> kafka;

  HelloWorldSender(KafkaTemplate<String, String> kafka) {
    this.kafka = kafka;
  }

  @Scheduled(fixedRate = 50)
  public void sayHello() {
    String msg = "Hello World, from Spring Boot 3, over Apache Kafka!";
    kafka.send("hello", msg);
  }
}
```

HelloWorldSender will be injected with KafkaTemplate through the constructor. Each 50 ms, a message will be sent on the hello topic.

Write a test to verify the correct behavior of the application. We can create a mock for the KafkaTemplate and verify if it calls the correct methods. See Listing 8-38.

Listing 8-38. Spring Boot Test for Kafka with Mock

```java
package com.apress.springboot3recipes.kafka;

import org.junit.jupiter.api.Test;
import org.mockito.Mockito;
import org.springframework.boot.test.context.SpringBootTest;
import org.springframework.boot.test.mock.mockito.MockBean;
import org.springframework.kafka.core.KafkaTemplate;

import static org.mockito.Mockito.verify;
```

```
@SpringBootTest
class KafkaSenderApplicationTest {

  @MockBean
  private KafkaTemplate<String, String> kafka;

  @Test
  void shouldSendAtLeastASingleMessage() {

    var msg = "Hello World, from Spring Boot 3, over Apache Kafka!";
    verify(kafka, Mockito.atLeastOnce()).send("hello", msg);
  }
}
```

Another option is to use the Spring Boot Testcontainer support to start a broker in Docker and use that to communicate with. See Listing 8-39.

Listing 8-39. Spring Boot Test for Kafka with Testcontainers

```
package com.apress.springboot3recipes.kafka;

import org.junit.jupiter.api.Test;
import org.springframework.beans.factory.annotation.Autowired;
import org.springframework.boot.test.context.SpringBootTest;
import org.springframework.boot.testcontainers.service.connection.ServiceC
onnection;
import org.springframework.kafka.core.ConsumerFactory;
import org.testcontainers.containers.KafkaContainer;
import org.testcontainers.junit.jupiter.Container;
import org.testcontainers.junit.jupiter.Testcontainers;
import org.testcontainers.utility.DockerImageName;

import java.time.Duration;
import java.util.List;

import static org.assertj.core.api.Assertions.assertThat;

@SpringBootTest(properties = "spring.kafka.consumer.group-id=test-group")
@Testcontainers
class KafkaSenderApplicationIntegrationTest {
```

```
@ServiceConnection
@Container
static KafkaContainer kafkaContainer =
  new KafkaContainer(DockerImageName.parse("confluentinc/cp-
  kafka:latest"));

@Autowired
private ConsumerFactory<String, String> consumerFactory;

@Test
void shouldSendAtLeastASingleMessage() {
  try (var consumer = consumerFactory.createConsumer()) {
    consumer.subscribe(List.of("hello"));
    var records = consumer.poll(Duration.ofSeconds(2));
    assertThat(records).isNotNull();
    assertThat(records).isNotEmpty();

  }
 }
}
```

To determine whether the message has been sent, we need a Kafka Consumer. For this we can use the ConsumerFactory from Spring Kafka to easily create one. We subscribe to the topic and check if we get any messages.

💡   The default KafkaTemplate doesn't come preconfigured with ConsumerFactory. If this is being set (or you are using a custom configured KafkaTemplate), that could be used as well.

Send an Object

To send a message to Kafka, the message payload has to be converted into a byte[]. For a String, that is pretty easy by calling String.getBytes. However, when sending an object, this becomes more cumbersome. The default Spring Kafka auto-configuration will set up the sending of String-based messages.

To be able to send a different type of value, you need to configure a `Serializer` for the producer. This can be done through the `spring.kafka.producer.value-serializer` property. Additional configuration can be passed through the `spring.kafka.producer.` `properties` namespace. Here we will set up the `JsonSerializer`, which will create JSON from our passed-in `Order` object. See Listing 8-40.

Listing 8-40. Serializer Configuration

```
spring.kafka.bootstrap-servers=localhost:9092 spring.kafka.producer.value-
serializer=org.springframework.kafka.support.serializer.JsonSerializer
spring.kafka.properties.spring.json.trusted.packages=com.apress.
springboot3recipes.order
```

`spring.kafka.producer.value-serializer` is set to `JsonSerializer`; by default only a few types are allowed to be sent. Hence, setting `spring.json.trusted.packages` will allow classes from that package to be sent.

Let's create an `Order` and use the `KafkaTemplate` to send it to the `orders` topic. See Listing 8-41.

Listing 8-41. Order Class

```
package com.apress.springboot3recipes.order;

import java.math.BigDecimal;

public record Order (String id, BigDecimal amount) { }
```

Now that we have an order, let's create a scheduled method that periodically sends a message with a random order. See Listing 8-42.

Listing 8-42. OrderSender for Kafka

```
@Component
class OrderSender {

  private final KafkaTemplate<String, Order> kafka;

  OrderSender(KafkaTemplate<String, Order> kafka) {
    this.kafka = kafka;
  }
```

```
@Scheduled(fixedRate = 50)
public void sendOrder() {
  var order = OrderGenerator.generate();
  kafka.send("orders", order);
  }
}
```

It will create an Order with a random amount and a max of 1000.00. It will then send it using the send method to the orders topic. Using JsonDeserializer, it will create JSON from the object and eventually convert that into a byte[] that is being sent out to Kafka.

8-9. Receive Messages Using Kafka

Problem

You want to receive messages from a Kafka topic.

Solution

Annotating a method with @KafkaListener will bind it to a topic and will let it receive messages.

How It Works

A bean that has the @KafkaListener and/or @KafkaHandler annotated methods will be used as message listeners from incoming messages. A message listener container is constructed, and the annotated method will receive the incoming message. The message listener container can be configured through properties in the spring.rabbitmq. listener namespace (see Table 8-18).

Table 8-18. *Kafka Listener Properties*

Property	Description
spring.kafka. listener.type	Sets the listener container type SINGLE or BATCH; the default is SINGLE.
spring.kafka. listener.ack-mode	Sets the container acknowledge mode; the default is none.
spring.kafka. listener.async-acks	Sets whether we acknowledge async; the default is none. This is useful only with ack-mode set to MANUAL or MANUAL-IMMEDIATE.
spring.kafka. listener.client-id	Sets the prefix for the client-id property.
spring.kafka. listener.concurrency	Sets the minimum number of listener invoker threads.
spring.kafka. listener.poll-timeout	Sets the timeout to use when polling the consumer.
spring.kafka. listener.no-poll- threshold	Sets the multiplier to apply to the poll-timeout to determine whether a consumer is nonresponsive.
spring.kafka. listener.ack-count	Sets the number of records between offset commits for ack-mode COUNT or COUNT_TIME.
spring.kafka. listener.ack-time	Sets the time between offset commits for ack-mode TIME or COUNT_TIME.
spring.kafka. listener.idle- between-polls	Sets the interval between consumer polls.
spring.kafka. listener.idle-event- interval	Sets the time between publishing idle consumer events.
spring.kafka. listener.idle- partition-event- interval	Sets the time between publishing idle partition consumer events.

(continued)

Table 8-18. (*continued*)

Property	Description

`spring.kafka.`
`listener.monitor-`
`interval`
	Sets the time between checks for nonresponsive consumers.

`spring.kafka.`
`listener.log-`
`container-config`
	Sets whether the container configuration should be logged during startup; the default is none.

`spring.kafka.`
`listener.missing-`
`topics-fatal`
	Sets whether the container will fail if topics are missing; the default is `false`.

`spring.kafka.`
`listener.immediate-`
`stop`
	Sets whether the container stops after the current record is processed or after all the records from previous polls have been processed. The default is `false`.

`spring.kafka.` `listener.auto-startup`	Sets whether to automatically start the container. The default is `true`.

`spring.kafka.`
`listener.change-`
`consumer-thread-name`
	Sets whether the consumer thread should be changed during startup. The default is none.

Receive a Simple Message

A component with an `@KafkaListener` annotation is all that is needed to start receiving messages from Kafka. See Listing 8-43.

Listing 8-43. Kafka Listener for String Messages

```
@Component
class HelloWorldReceiver {

  @KafkaListener(
    topics = "hello",
    groupId = "recipe_8_9_i" )
```

```
public void handle(String msg) {
  System.out.println("[RECEIVED] - " + msg);
  }
}
```

This component will receive all the messages from the hello topic and print it to the console. This works fine for String-based payloads. However, when sending objects or complex messages, one might prefer to use JSON, XML, or maybe even AVRO.

Receive an Object

To receive a more complex object without relying on Java serialization, you need to configure a Serializer (see also Recipe 8-8). The configured Serializer will be used by the message listener container to convert incoming payloads into an object required by the @KafkaListener annotated method. See Listing 8-44.

Listing 8-44. JSON Serializer Configuration

```
spring.kafka.bootstrap-servers=localhost:9092
spring.kafka.consumer.value-deserializer=\
org.springframework.kafka.support.serializer.JsonDeserializer
spring.kafka.properties.spring.json.trusted.packages=\
  com.apress.springboot3recipes.order
```

To configure the Serializer used by the Kafka client, we can add some configuration properties to application.properties. In this case, we can add the spring.kafka.consumer.value-deserializer property. This will register the serializer to convert the actual value being sent from a Java object to JSON. We also need to specify spring.json.trusted.packages as we need to allow it to serialize our classes. This can be done by specifying it using spring.kafka.properties, which can be used to set additional properties. See Listing 8-45.

Listing 8-45. Kafka Listener for Orders

```
@Component
class OrderService {

  @KafkaListener(topics = "orders")
  public void handle(Order order) {
```

```
System.out.println("[RECEIVED] - " + order);
  }
}
```

This listener will user the `orders` topic to receive messages. When started, the topic will automatically be created if they don't already exist. The incoming message is converted into an `Order` using the configured `JsonDeserializer`. The output should be similar to that of Figure 8-10.

```
  /\\ / ___'_ __ _ _(_)_ __  __ _ \ \ \ \
 ( ( )\___ | '_ | '_| | '_ \/ _` | \ \ \ \
  \\/  ___)| |_)| | | | | || (_| |  ) ) ) )
   '  |____| .__|_| |_|_| |_\__, | / / / /
  =========|_|==============|___/=/_/_/_/
  :: Spring Boot ::                (v3.2.1)

2023-12-29T12:03:04.752+01:00  INFO 33697 --- [         main] c.a.s.kafka.KafkaReceiverApplication       : Starting KafkaReceiverApplication using Java 21.
2023-12-29T12:03:04.757+01:00  INFO 33697 --- [         main] c.a.s.kafka.KafkaReceiverApplication       : No active profile set, falling back to 1 default
2023-12-29T12:03:04.856+01:00  INFO 33697 --- [         main] .s.b.d.c.l.DockerComposeLifecycleManager   : Using Docker Compose file '/Users/marten/Reposit
2023-12-29T12:03:06.340+01:00  INFO 33697 --- [utReader-stderr] o.s.boot.docker.compose.core.DockerCli    : Container zookeeper  Created
2023-12-29T12:03:06.341+01:00  INFO 33697 --- [utReader-stderr] o.s.boot.docker.compose.core.DockerCli    : Container broker  Created
2023-12-29T12:03:06.347+01:00  INFO 33697 --- [utReader-stderr] o.s.boot.docker.compose.core.DockerCli    : Container zookeeper  Starting
2023-12-29T12:03:06.564+01:00  INFO 33697 --- [utReader-stderr] o.s.boot.docker.compose.core.DockerCli    : Container zookeeper  Started
2023-12-29T12:03:06.564+01:00  INFO 33697 --- [utReader-stderr] o.s.boot.docker.compose.core.DockerCli    : Container broker  Starting
2023-12-29T12:03:06.910+01:00  INFO 33697 --- [utReader-stderr] o.s.boot.docker.compose.core.DockerCli    : Container broker  Started
2023-12-29T12:03:06.910+01:00  INFO 33697 --- [utReader-stderr] o.s.boot.docker.compose.core.DockerCli    : Container zookeeper  Waiting
2023-12-29T12:03:06.910+01:00  INFO 33697 --- [utReader-stderr] o.s.boot.docker.compose.core.DockerCli    : Container broker  Waiting
2023-12-29T12:03:07.417+01:00  INFO 33697 --- [utReader-stderr] o.s.boot.docker.compose.core.DockerCli    : Container zookeeper  Healthy
2023-12-29T12:03:07.417+01:00  INFO 33697 --- [utReader-stderr] o.s.boot.docker.compose.core.DockerCli    : Container broker  Healthy
2023-12-29T12:03:20.415+01:00  INFO 33697 --- [         main] fkaConsumerFactory$ExtendedKafkaConsumer   : [Consumer clientId=consumer-recipe_8_9_ii-1, gro
2023-12-29T12:03:20.430+01:00  INFO 33697 --- [         main] c.a.s.kafka.KafkaReceiverApplication       : Started KafkaReceiverApplication in 16.175 secor
2023-12-29T12:03:23.568+01:00  INFO 33697 --- [ntainer#0-0-C-1] o.s.k.l.KafkaMessageListenerContainer     : recipe_8_9_ii: partitions assigned: [orders-0]
[RECEIVED] - Order[id=87457896-419f-466a-b080-7375c0859d0b, amount=542.91]
[RECEIVED] - Order[id=fc224b34-8283-4f6e-8d3f-5e7149bb99d9, amount=494.46]
[RECEIVED] - Order[id=e3365502-1b20-4a59-99bd-c124c28ff235, amount=605.52]
[RECEIVED] - Order[id=708f644b-7128-4886-b276-ec114b4dee50, amount=777.36]
```

Figure 8-10. *Kafka listener output for orders*

ℹ   The sample recipe uses the Spring Boot Docker support to launch a Kafka container to send and receive messages.

Receive a Message and Send a Reply

When receiving a message, it might be necessary to send a response to the client or communicate with a different message. Using an `@KafkaListener` on a nonvoid method is possible. This will create a result message and place it on the topic, which needs to be specified in the `@SendTo` annotation. See Listing 8-46.

Listing 8-46. Kafka Listener for Orders with Reply

```
@Component
class OrderService {

  @KafkaListener(topics = "orders")
  @SendTo("order-confirmations")
  public OrderConfirmation handle(Order order) {
    System.out.println("[RECEIVED] - " + order);
    return new OrderConfirmation(order.id());
  }
}
```

When receiving an Order after processing it, an OrderConfirmation will be sent. The @SendTo annotation (from the general Spring Messaging component) contains the topic name. Another listener could be used to process the OrderConfirmation messages. See Listing 8-47.

Listing 8-47. OrderConfirmationService for Kafka

```
@Component
class OrderConfirmationService {

  @KafkaListener(topics = "order-confirmations")
  public void handle(OrderConfirmation confirmation) {
    System.out.println("[RECEIVED] - " + confirmation);
  }
}
```

When running the code, together with the sender from Recipe 8-8, you should receive Order instances and see that they will be confirmed as well.

Summary

In this chapter, we looked at the messaging support from Spring and how to use it with Spring Boot. We covered JMS, RabbitMQ, and Kafka. However, support for messaging doesn't end there. There is also support for Apache Pulsar and more; they all follow the same pattern for receiving and sending messages.

CHAPTER 9

Spring Boot Actuator

When developing an application, you want to be able to monitor the behavior of the application once it's launched. Spring Boot makes it easy to enable this by introducing Spring Boot Actuator. Spring Boot Actuator exposes the health status and metrics from the application to interested parties. This can be over JMX or HTTP, or data can be exported to an external system.

The health endpoints tell something about the health of your application and/or the system it is running on. They will detect if the database is up, report the disk space available, etc. The metrics endpoints expose usage and performance statistics such as the number of requests, the longest request, the fastest request, the utilization of your connection pool, etc.

All these metrics can be viewed through either JMX or HTTP when enabled and can also be automatically exported to an external system such as Graphite, InfluxDB, and many others.

9-1. Enable and Configure Spring Boot Actuator

Problem

You want to enable health and metrics in your application so that you can monitor the status of the application.

Solution

Add a dependency for `spring-boot-starter-actuator` to your project to enable and expose the health status and metrics for your application. Additional configuration can be done through properties in the `management` namespace.

© Marten Deinum 2024
M. Deinum, *Spring Boot 3 Recipes*, https://doi.org/10.1007/979-8-8688-0113-6_9

How It Works

When adding `spring-boot-starter-actuator`, Spring Boot will automatically set up the health checks and metrics based on the beans in the application context. Which health checks and metrics are exposed depends on the beans and features that are enabled. When a data source is detected, metrics for that data source will be collected and exposed, and Spring Boot will monitor the health of the data source. Spring Boot does this for many components such as Hibernate, RabbitMQ, Kafka, caches, etc.

To enable Spring Boot Actuator, add the dependency to your application (here we assume Recipe 3-3 sources), as shown in Listing 9-1.

Listing 9-1. Spring Boot Starter Actuator Dependency

```xml
<dependency>
  <groupId>org.springframework.boot</groupId>
  <artifactId>spring-boot-starter-actuator</artifactId>
</dependency>
```

Now when starting the application, Spring Boot will have the Spring Boot Actuator configured. It is accessible through the Web (by default under the `/actuator` path), as shown in Figure 9-1. It is also possible to expose Spring Boot Actuator over JMX (Figure 9-2); this needs to be explicitly enabled by setting the `spring.jmx.enabled` property to `true`.

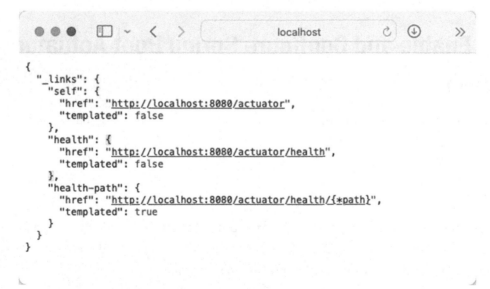

Figure 9-1. *Access Spring Boot Actuator through the Web*

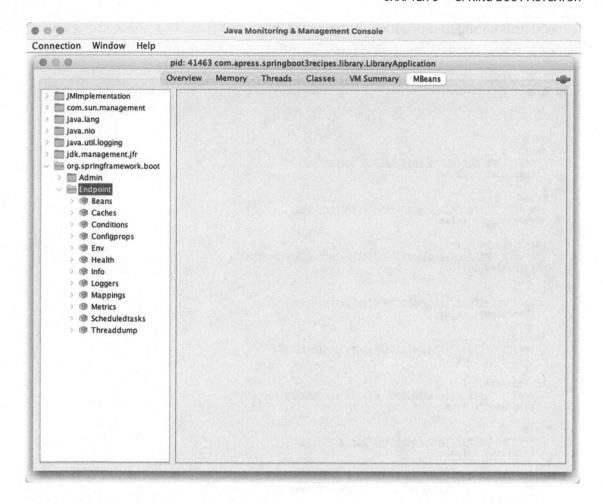

Figure 9-2. *HTTP exposed metrics*

You will notice that JMX exposes more endpoints than HTTP does. HTTP, by default, exposes only /actuator/health and /actuator/info. This is done with security in mind. The /actuator is exposed publicly, and as such you don't want everyone to see this information. You can configure what to expose through the `management.endpoints.web.exposure.include` and `management.endpoints.web.exposure.exclude` properties. Using a * for the include will expose all endpoints to the Web. See Listing 9-2.

Listing 9-2. Expose Properties Through the Web

```
management.endpoints.web.exposure.include=*
```

With this configuration added to `application.properties`, the same features will be exposed to the Web as through JMX (see Figure 9-3).

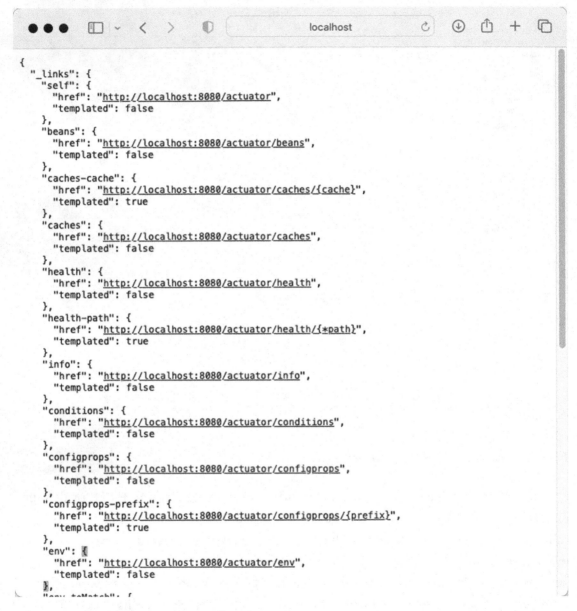

Figure 9-3. *HTTP exposing all metrics*

Configure the Management Server

By default Spring Boot Actuator is available on the same port and address (`http://localhost:8080`) as the regular application. It is, however, common to run the management endpoints on a different port. You can configure this through properties in the `management.server` namespace. Most of the properties mimic the ones in the regular `server` namespace (see Table 9-1).

Table 9-1. *Management Server Properties*

Property	Description
`management.server.add-application-context-header`	Adds an X-Application-Context header to the response, containing the application context name
`management.server.port`	Sets the port to run the management server on; the default is the same as `server.port`
`management.server.address`	Sets the network address to bind to; the default is the same as `server.address` (which is 0.0.0.0 or all addresses)
`management.server.base-path`	Sets the management endpoint base path; the default is /, which requires a port to be set
`management.server.ssl.*`	Sets the SSL properties to configure SSL for the management server

Add Listing 9-3 to the `application.properties` file, which will run the management endpoints on a separate port and add the X-Application-Context header.

Listing 9-3. Management Server Properties

```
management.server.add-application-context-header=true
management.server.port=8090
```

When restarting the application, the management endpoints are now available on `http://localhost:8090/actuator`. Running Spring Boot Actuator on a different port has the benefit of hiding it from the public Internet by blocking the port on the firewall and allowing only local access.

447

ⓘ The management.server properties are effective only when using an embedded server. When deploying to an external server, these properties don't apply anymore!

Configure Individual Management Endpoints

Individual endpoints can be configured through properties in the management. endpoint.<endpoint-name> namespace. Most of them have at least an enabled property and a cache.time-to-live property. The first will enable or disable the endpoint. The other one specifies how long to cache the result of the endpoint (see Table 9-2).

Table 9-2. *Endpoint Configuration Properties*

Property	Description
management.endpoint.<endpoint-name>. enabled	Sets whether the specific endpoint is enabled; generally defaults to true and sometimes depends on availability of a feature. For example, if Flyway isn't present, then enabling the flyway endpoint wouldn't have any effect.
management.endpoint.<endpoint-name>. cache.time-to-live	Sets the time to cache a response; the default is is 0ms, meaning no caching.
management.endpoint.health.show-details	Sets whether to show details for the health endpoint; the default is never and can be changed to always or when_authorized.
management.endpoint.configprops.show-values management.endpoint.env.show-values management.endpoint.quartz.show-values	Sets when to show unsanitized values for the endpoint; the default is never. This can be changed to always or when_authorized.
management.endpoint.configprops.roles management.endpoint.env.roles management.endpoint.health.roles management.endpoint.quartz.roles	Sets the roles that are allowed to see the details (use with when_authorized for show-details/show-values).

Adding `management.endpoint.health.show-details=always` to `application.properties` will show more information about the health of the application, as shown in Figure 9-4.

```
{
  "status": "UP",
  "components": {
    "diskSpace": {
      "status": "UP",
      "details": {
        "total": 499963170816,
        "free": 128622997504,
        "threshold": 10485760,
        "path": "/Users/marten/Repositories/apress/spring-boot-3-recipes/code/ch09/recipe_9_1/.",
        "exists": true
      }
    },
    "ping": {
      "status": "UP"
    }
  }
}
```

Figure 9-4. *Extended health endpoint output*

Secure Management Endpoints

When Spring Boot detects both Spring Boot Actuator and Spring Security, it will enable secure access to management endpoints automatically. When accessing the endpoint, a basic login prompt will be shown and will ask for a username and password. Spring Boot will generate a default user named `user` with a generated password (see Recipe 5-1) for logging in.

Adding `spring-boot-starter-security` in addition to `spring-boot-starter-actuator` is enough to secure your management endpoints. See Listing 9-4.

Listing 9-4. Spring Boot Security Starter Dependency

```
<dependency>
  <groupId>org.springframework.boot</groupId>
  <artifactId>spring-boot-starter-security</artifactId>
</dependency>
```

This will enable security in your application and for the management endpoints. Now when accessing the endpoint `http://localhost:8090/actuator`, a basic login prompt will be shown. After entering the correct credentials, you should still be able to see the results.

449

Configure Health Checks

One of the features of Spring Boot Actuator is to do health checks. They are exposed under `http://localhost:8090/actuator/health`. This produces a result if the application is UP or DOWN. The health endpoint calls all the available `HealthIndicators` in the system and reports them in the endpoint. You can control which `HealthIndicators` are present by setting the `management.health.<health-indicator>.enabled` property. Setting a property to `true` for a not available feature (such as trying to get information on `DataSource` while one isn't available) won't work. See Listing 9-5.

Listing 9-5. Disabling a Health Indicator

```
management.health.diskspace.enabled=false
```

This will disable the health check for the disk space, and it won't be part of the health checks anymore.

Configure Metrics

One of the features of Spring Boot Actuator is to expose metrics. They are exposed under `http://localhost:8090/actuator/metrics`. This will produce a list of available metrics for your application (see Figure 9-5).

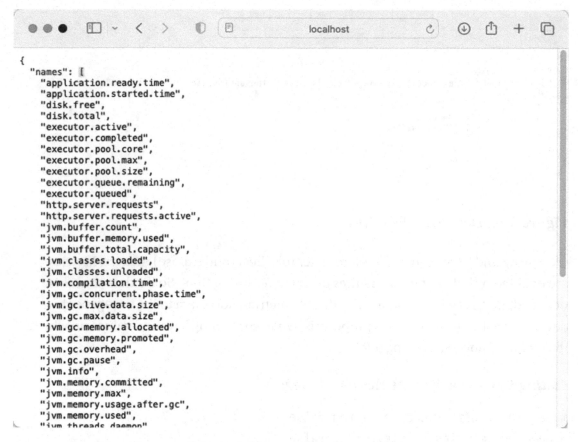

Figure 9-5. *List of currently available metrics*

You can contain more information about a metric by accessing http://
localhost:8090/actuator/metrics/{name-of-metric}. For example, http://
localhost:8090/actuator/metrics/system.cpu.usage will show the current CPU
usage (Figure 9-6).

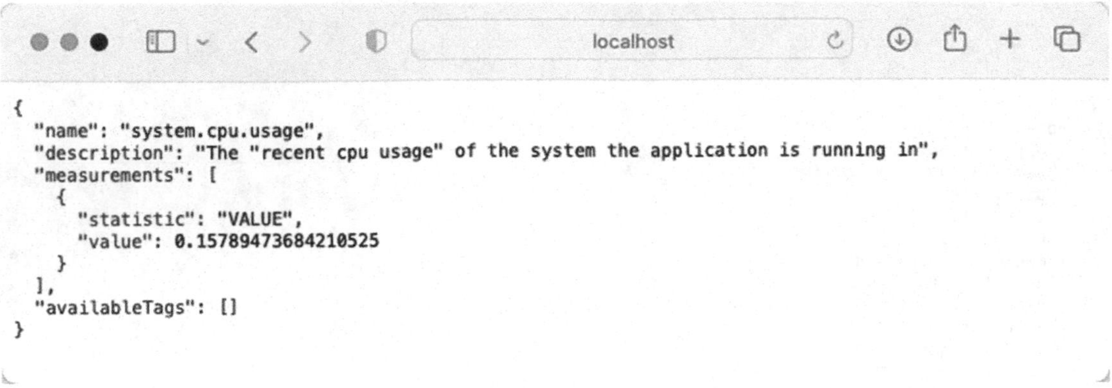

```
{
  "name": "system.cpu.usage",
  "description": "The "recent cpu usage" of the system the application is running in",
  "measurements": [
    {
      "statistic": "VALUE",
      "value": 0.15789473684210525
    }
  ],
  "availableTags": []
}
```

Figure 9-6. *Detailed CPU metrics*

Spring and Spring Boot use Micrometer to collect (and expose) metrics. Metrics are enabled by default for the features detected by Spring Boot. So if a data source is detected, metrics will be enabled. To disable metrics, add them to the `management.metrics.enable` property. This property is a map containing keys and values on which metrics to enable. See Listing 9-6.

Listing 9-6. Disabling Metrics for a Category

```
management.metrics.enable.system=false
management.metrics.enable.tomcat=false
```

This configuration will disable `system` and `tomcat` metrics. When viewing the metrics at `http://localhost:8090/actuator/metrics`, you can see they aren't part of the list anymore.

9-2. Create Custom Health Checks and Metrics Problem

Your application needs to expose certain metrics and have health checks that aren't available by default.

Solution

Health checks and metrics are pluggable, and beans of type `HealthIndicator` and `MetricBinder` are automatically registered to provide additional health checks and metrics. You just need to create a class implementing the desired interface and register an instance of that class as a bean in the context to have it contribute to the health and metrics.

How It Works

Assuming that a dependency on Spring Boot Actuator is already present, you can start writing an implementation right away. Assume you have an application using a `TaskScheduler` and you want to have some metrics and health checks on it. (Adding @ `EnableScheduling` is enough to have Spring Boot create a default `TaskScheduler`.)

First let's write the `HealthIndicator` interface. You can either directly implement the `HealthIndicator` interface (and implement the `health()` method) or use the convenience `AbstractHealthIndicator` method as a base class (which adds some logic and exception handling out of the box). We can use Recipe 3-3 as the starting point for this recipe. See Listing 9-7.

Listing 9-7. HealthIndicator Implementation

```
package com.apress.springboot3recipes.library;

import org.springframework.boot.actuate.health.AbstractHealthIndicator;
import org.springframework.boot.actuate.health.Health;
import org.springframework.scheduling.concurrent.ThreadPoolTaskScheduler;
import org.springframework.stereotype.Component;

@Component
class TaskSchedulerHealthIndicator extends AbstractHealthIndicator {

  private final ThreadPoolTaskScheduler taskScheduler;

  TaskSchedulerHealthIndicator(ThreadPoolTaskScheduler taskScheduler) {
    this.taskScheduler = taskScheduler;
  }
```

```java
@Override
protected void doHealthCheck(Health.Builder builder) throws Exception {

    int poolSize = taskScheduler.getPoolSize();
    int active = taskScheduler.getActiveCount();
    int free = poolSize - active;

    builder
            .withDetail("active", active)
            .withDetail("poolsize", poolSize);

    if (poolSize > 0 && free <= 1) {
      builder.down();
    } else {
      builder.up();
    }
  }
}
```

The TaskSchedulerHealthIndicator interface operates on the given ThreadPoolTaskExecutor. It reports the status as down if there are 1 or fewer threads available to schedule tasks. The condition on poolSize > 0 is there because the creation of the underlying Executor is delayed until needed; until then, the poolSize will report 0. The returned value includes the poolsize and active thread count.

The TaskSchedulerMetrics implementation extends the MeterBinder interface from Micrometer.io. It exposes the active and pool-size values to the metrics registry. See Listing 9-8.

Listing 9-8. MeterBinder Implementation to Expose Metrics

```java
package com.apress.springboot3recipes.library;

import io.micrometer.core.instrument.FunctionCounter;
import io.micrometer.core.instrument.MeterRegistry;
import io.micrometer.core.instrument.binder.MeterBinder;
import org.springframework.scheduling.concurrent.ThreadPoolTaskScheduler;
import org.springframework.stereotype.Component;
```

```
@Component
class TaskSchedulerMetrics implements MeterBinder {

  private final ThreadPoolTaskScheduler taskScheduler;

  public TaskSchedulerMetrics(ThreadPoolTaskScheduler taskScheduler) {
    this.taskScheduler = taskScheduler;
  }

  @Override
  public void bindTo(MeterRegistry registry) {
    FunctionCounter
            .builder("task.scheduler.active", taskScheduler,
                    ThreadPoolTaskScheduler::getActiveCount)
            .register(registry);

    FunctionCounter
            .builder("task.scheduler.pool-size", taskScheduler,
                    ThreadPoolTaskScheduler::getPoolSize)
            .register(registry);

  }
}
```

Now when placing an @EnableScheduling annotation on LibraryApplication and restarting the application, metrics and health will be reported for TaskScheduler (see Figure 9-7).

```
{
  "status": "UP",
  "components": {
    "diskSpace": {
      "status": "UP",
      "details": {
        "total": 499963170816,
        "free": 126091550720,
        "threshold": 10485760,
        "path": "/Users/marten/Repositories/apress/spring-boot-3-recipes/code/ch09/recipe_9_2/.",
        "exists": true
      }
    },
    "ping": {
      "status": "UP"
    },
    "taskScheduler": {
      "status": "UP",
      "details": {
        "active": 0,
        "poolsize": 0
      }
    }
  }
}
```

Figure 9-7. *TaskScheduler health check*

9-3. Export Metrics

Problem

You want to export the metrics to an external system to create a dashboard to monitor the application.

Solution

Use one of the supported systems such as Graphite and periodically push the metrics to that system. Include a Micrometer.io registry dependency in your application (in addition to the `spring-boot-starter-actuator` dependency), and metrics will automatically be exported. By default, every minute the data will be pushed to the server.

How It Works

The ability to export metrics is part of the Micrometer.io library, and it supports a wide variety of services such as Graphite, DataDog, Prometheus, or regular StatsD. This recipe uses Graphite, so a dependency to `micrometer-registry-graphite` needs to be added. See Listing 9-9.

Listing 9-9. Micrometer Graphite Registry Dependency

```
<dependency>
  <groupId>io.micrometer</groupId>
  <artifactId>micrometer-registry-graphite</artifactId>
</dependency>
```

In theory, this could be enough to have metrics published to Graphite if Graphite is running on `localhost` and with the default ports. However, Spring Boot makes it easy to configure this by exposing some properties. Generally, this is in the `management.metrics.export.<registry-name>` namespace (see Table 9-3).

Table 9-3. *Common Metrics Export Properties*

Property	Description
management.`<registry-name>`.metrics.export.enabled	Sets whether to enable metrics exporting. The default is true when the library is detected on the classpath.
management.`<registry-name>`.metrics.export.host	Sets the host to send metrics to, mostly `localhost` or a well-known URL of the service (like SignalFX, DataDog, etc.).
management.`<registry-name>`.metrics.export.port	Sets the port to send metrics to; this defaults to the well-known port of the desired service.
management.`<registry-name>`.metrics.export.step	Sets how often to send metrics; the default is 1 minute.
management.`<registry-name>`.metrics.export.rate-units	Sets the base time unit used to report rates; the default is seconds.
management.`<registry-name>`.metrics.export.duration-units	Sets the base time unit used to report durations; the default is `milliseconds`.

To report the metrics every 10 seconds instead of each minute, add Listing 9-10 to the `application.properties` file.

Listing 9-10. Graphite Configuration

```
management.graphite.metrics.export.step=10s
```

> ℹ️   The bin directory contains a graphite.sh file that uses Docker to start a Graphite instance.

Now the metrics will be published to Graphite every 10 seconds. If you start the application and open Graphite on http://localhost/ (assuming you are running the aforementioned Docker container), you could, for example, create a graph of the CPU usage and load (see Figure 9-8).

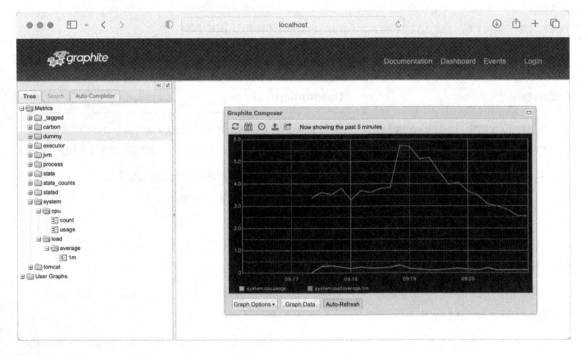

Figure 9-8. *Graphite CPU graph*

9-4. Tracing with Zipkin

Problem

You want to correlate log lines in your logfiles to incoming requests, messages, and call flows as well as record traces to a tracing solution like Zipkin.

Solution

When using Spring Boot, it comes with out-of-the-box and embedded support for the Micrometer Metrics and Tracing API, and it can auto-configure the tracer for OpenTelemetry or OpenZipkin Brave. For auto-configuration, `spring-boot-starter-actuator` is needed, as is the respective tracer bridge for Micrometer (either `io.micrometer:micrometer-tracing-bridge-otel` or `io.micrometer:micrometer-tracing-bridge-brave`). The final component is the exporter for either Brave or OpenTelemetry. In Listing 9-11, we are going to use OpenZipkin Brave (the other integrations have very similar setup options).

Listing 9-11. Tracing Dependencies for Brave with Zipkin

```
<dependency>
  <groupId>org.springframework.boot</groupId>
  <artifactId>spring-boot-starter-actuator</artifactId>
</dependency>
<dependency>
  <groupId>io.micrometer</groupId>
  <artifactId>micrometer-tracing-bridge-brave</artifactId>
</dependency>
<dependency>
  <groupId>io.zipkin.reporter2</groupId>
  <artifactId>zipkin-reporter-brave</artifactId>
</dependency>
```

These dependencies are enough to trigger the auto-configuration and to set up the tracing, logging, and exporting. When enabling debug logging, you can now see the trace and span ID in the logging.

Console   Actuator

```
2023-11-10T16:16:04.401+01:00 DEBUG 3958 --- [Library] [mcat-handler-10] [654e49343a04a502f26acb06fa4a875f-f26acb06fa4a875f] o.s.web.servlet.DispatcherServlet    : GET "/books", parameters={}
2023-11-10T16:16:04.403+01:00 DEBUG 3958 --- [Library] [mcat-handler-10] [654e49343a04a502f26acb06fa4a875f-f26acb06fa4a875f] o.s.web.servlet.DispatcherServlet    : Completed 200 OK
```

Figure 9-9. *Logging output with trace and span IDs*

This information is also sent to Zipkin and can be viewed.

> ℹ️ The sources for this recipe include a Docker compose file, which will automatically start Zipkin at the start of the application (if not yet started). This Zipkin instance can be viewed by accessing `http://localhost:9411/zipkin` (see Figure 9-10).

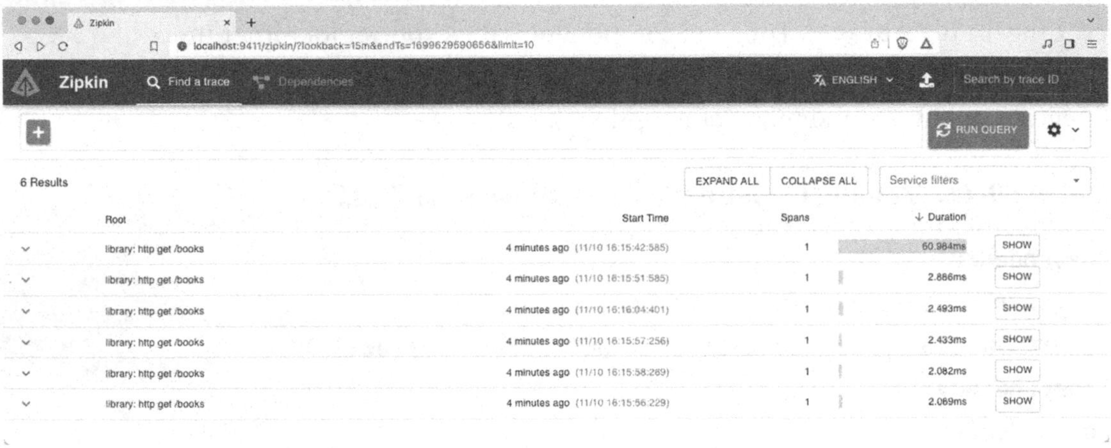

Figure 9-10. *Zipkin UI*

However, this is just a trace with a single component. When there are more components, they would also appear, as shown in Figure 9-11.

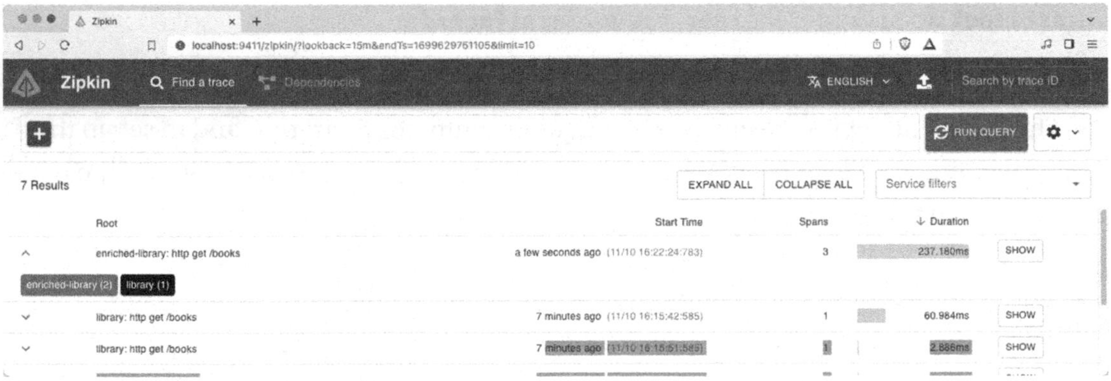

Figure 9-11. *Zipkin UI, multiple spans*

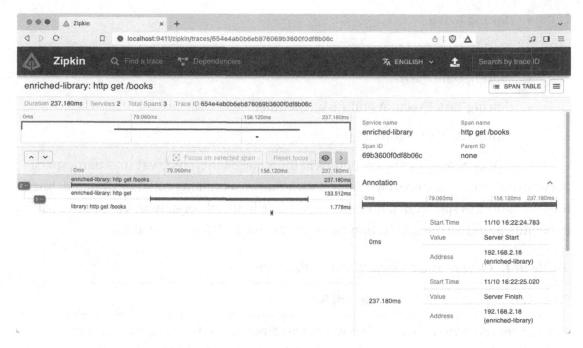

Figure 9-12. *Zipkin UI, multiple span details*

In Figure 9-12, you can see the details of each call and that they belong to a single trace.

How It Works

Spring Boot uses the Micrometer observation to observe calls to pass through your applications. When `spring-boot-starter-actuator` is included as a dependency, Spring Boot will automatically pull in the Micrometer observation.

With this, Spring Boot will automatically set up an `ObservationHandler` for use in your application. This `ObservationHandler` will be injected in an `ObservationRegistry`. The `ObservationRegistry` is the component that is injected into various places of the framework and libraries. At the moment of writing, the `ObservationRegistry` will automatically be applied to components from the following:

- Spring JMS

- Spring Web and Spring WebFlux

- Spring Security

461

- Spring Kafka

- Spring Data for MongoDB

- Spring Data R2DBC

- Spring Task Executor and Task Scheduler

- Spring AMQP (RabbitMQ)

Spring Boot exposes some properties in the `management.observations` namespace to configure certain features (see Table 9-4). Some observations could be disabled, but it is also possible to specify default values to include in the observations. This can be useful to include parts like the application name or version as default key/values.

Table 9-4. *Observation Configuration Properties*

Property	Description
`management.observations.` `enable.<key>`	Sets whether the given observation of `<key>` should be enabled; the default is `true`. The `all` is a special keyword to enable or disable all observations.
`management.observations.` `http.client.requests.name`	Sets the name of the observation for the client requests; the default is `http.client.requests`.
`management.observations.` `http.server.requests.name`	Sets the name of the observation for the client requests; the default is `http.server.requests`.
`management.observations.` `key-values.<key>`	Sets the common key/values that are applied to all observations. The default is empty.
`management.observations.` `r2dbc.include-parameter-` `values`	Sets whether to include the query parameters for the R2DBC observations; the default is `false`.

⚠️ When Spring Boot detects a preconfigured `ObservationHandler`, it will not configure one for you, and the properties from Table 9-4 won't be applied as it is expected that you do the full configuration!

Next you need to include a tracing bridge (needed to connect Micrometer with the tracing solution of choice). This will pull in the necessary Micrometer tracing dependencies (see Listing 9-12 for a sample Brave with Zipkin implementation).

Listing 9-12. Tracing Dependencies for Brave with Zipkin

```
<dependency>
  <groupId>org.springframework.boot</groupId>
  <artifactId>spring-boot-starter-actuator</artifactId>
</dependency>
<dependency>
  <groupId>io.micrometer</groupId>
  <artifactId>micrometer-tracing-bridge-brave</artifactId>
</dependency>
<dependency>
  <groupId>io.zipkin.reporter2</groupId>
  <artifactId>zipkin-reporter-brave</artifactId>
</dependency>
```

With all these dependencies in place, the auto-configuration of Spring Boot will configure an `ObservationHandler`. By default it will set up an `io.micrometer.tracing.handler.DefaultTracingObservationHandler`. When a preconfigured `ObservationHandler` is detected, Spring Boot will not create the default one but will reuse the preconfigured one.

In addition to configuring an `ObservationHandler`, Spring Boot will also slightly modify the logging pattern that is being used to automatically include the `span-id` and `trace-id` that have been detected or generated. This way, logs will also contain the necessary information, which can be useful while troubleshooting a certain call. It is also possible to manually configure the log pattern by specifying the `logging.pattern.correlation` property in your application properties. The `span-id` and `trace-id` are available in the Mapped Diagnostic Context (MDC) under the names `traceId` and `spanId`. Listing 9-13 shows the default pattern that Spring Boot will apply for log correlation. This can of course be modified if you need.

Listing 9-13. Correlation Logging Properties

```
logging.pattern.correlation=[${spring.application.name:},
%X{traceId:-},%X{spanId:-}]
```

Configure Tracing

Spring Boot exposes some properties to make it easier to configure tracing. You can configure the propagation type it should and how many of the calls should be sampled (the default is 10%). By default it will be enabled if detected, but you can also disable it.

Table 9-5. *Tracing Configuration Properties*

Property	Description
management. tracing.enabled	Sets whether the auto-configuration of tracing should be enabled; the default is true.
management. tracing.sampling. probability	Sets the probability of the sample range, from 0 to 1.0; the default is 0.1.
management. tracing. propagation.type	Lists supported tracing context propagations (can contain W3C, B3, or B3_ MULTI); the default is null. When set, it takes precedence over the more fine-grained consumes and produces properties.
management. tracing. propagation. consume	Lists supported tracing context propagations for receiving (can contain W3C, B3, or B3_MULTI); the default is all values.
management. tracing. propagation. produce	Lists supported tracing context propagations for sending (can contain W3C, B3, or B3_MULTI); the default is W3C.
management. tracing.sampling. probability	Probability in the range from 0.0 to 1.0 that a trace will be sampled.

Next, it is possible to configure Zipkin. Mainly the URL to the endpoint and some connection timeouts can be set (see Table 9-6). This applies to other solutions such as Wavefront, Open Telemetry, and Prometheus.

Table 9-6. *Zipking Configuration Properties*

`management.zipkin.tracing.endpoint`	Sets the URL to the Zipkin API; the default is `http://localhost:9411/api/v2/spans`.
`management.zipkin.tracing.connect-timeout`	Sets the connection timeout for requests to Zipkin; the default is 1 second.
`management.zipkin.tracing.read-timeout`	Sets a read timeout for requests to Zipkin; the default is 10 seconds.

Set Up Tracing with an ObservationRegistry

Spring Boot will automatically construct an `ObservationRegistry`. This `ObservationRegistry` can also be injected into regular beans for manual use (if needed). See Listing 9-14.

Listing 9-14. Using an ObservationRegistry

```
package com.apress.springboot3recipes.library;

import io.micrometer.observation.Observation;
import io.micrometer.observation.ObservationRegistry;
import io.micrometer.observation.annotation.Observed;
import org.springframework.stereotype.Service;

import java.util.Map;
import java.util.Optional;
import java.util.concurrent.ConcurrentHashMap;

@Service
class InMemoryBookService implements BookService {

  private final Map<String, Book> books = new ConcurrentHashMap<>();

  private final ObservationRegistry observations;

  InMemoryBookService(ObservationRegistry observations) {
    this.observations = observations;
  }
```

```
public Optional<Book> find(String isbn) {
  var observation = Observation
    .createNotStarted("BookService.find", this.observations);
  observation.lowCardinalityKeyValue("isbn", isbn);
  return observation.observe(() -> Optional.ofNullable(books.get(isbn)));
  }
}
```

Here an observation is added to the find method. To do this, an Observation is created with a name and the injected ObservationRegistry. Next we invoke the actual code we want to have observed by using the observe() method. The Observation. observe() method takes either a Runnable or a Supplier depending on whether you need to return a result. With this small adaptation, we will now be able to see how long it takes to look up a book, and it will display as an additional part of the trace in Zipkin.

Set Up Tracing with AspectJ

When AspectJ is detected, it will also register an io.micrometer.observation. aop.ObservedAspect. The ObservedAspect will detect methods with an @Observed annotation and create a new observation for it. See Listing 9-15.

Listing 9-15. Using the @Observed Annotation

```
package com.apress.springboot3recipes.library;

import io.micrometer.observation.Observation;
import io.micrometer.observation.ObservationRegistry;
import io.micrometer.observation.annotation.Observed;
import org.springframework.stereotype.Service;

import java.util.Map;
import java.util.Optional;
import java.util.concurrent.ConcurrentHashMap;

@Service
class InMemoryBookService implements BookService {

  private final Map<String, Book> books = new ConcurrentHashMap<>();

  private final ObservationRegistry observations;
```

```
InMemoryBookService(ObservationRegistry observations) {
  this.observations = observations;
}
@Override
@Observed(name = "BookService.create")
public Book create(Book book) {
  books.put(book.isbn(), book);
  return book;
}
}
```

The @Observed annotation will trigger the creation of a new Observation with the
given name. If name is omitted, it will use method.observed as the default. Additionally,
the class name and method name are added as low-cardinality keys to the observation.
It is also possible to supply static values as low-cardinality keys in the @Observed
annotation; it isn't possible (at the time of writing) to specify an expression to retrieve,
for instance, the isbn value from the Book parameter.

CHAPTER 10

Packaging

In this chapter, you will learn about different solutions for packaging a Spring Boot application, from creating an executable JAR to using GraalVM to create a native image from the code.

10-1. Create an Executable Archive

By default Spring Boot creates a JAR or WAR that can be run with `java -jar your-application.jar`. However, you might want to run the application as part of the startup of your server (currently tested and supported for Debian- and Ubuntu-based systems). For this you can use the Maven or Gradle plugins to create an executable JAR.

Problem

You want an executable file so that it can be installed as a service in your environment.

Solution

The Spring Boot Maven and Gradle plugins both have the option to make the created artifact executable.[1] When doing so, the archive also becomes/behaves like a Unix shell script to start/stop a service.

How It Works

To make an artifact executable, you need to configure the Maven or Gradle plugin as such.

---

[1] https://docs.spring.io/spring-boot/docs/current/reference/html/deployment-install.html

© Marten Deinum 2024
M. Deinum, *Spring Boot 3 Recipes*, https://doi.org/10.1007/979-8-8688-0113-6_10

Make the Archive Executable

In the Maven plugin, you can set the executable property to true, and the archive will be executable. See Listing 10-1.

Listing 10-1. Spring Boot Maven Plugin to Create Executable

```
<plugin>
    <groupId>org.springframework.boot</groupId>
    <artifactId>spring-boot-maven-plugin</artifactId>
    <configuration>
        <executable>true</executable>
    </configuration>
</plugin>
```

For Gradle you need to specify launchScript() to achieve this. See Listing 10-2.

Listing 10-2. Spring Boot Gradle Plugin to Create Executable

```
tasks.named('bootJar') {
    launchScript()
}
```

Now after building your artifact, the artifact itself is executable and can be used to launch the application. Instead of java -jar your-application.jar, you can now simply type ./your-application.jar and it will start.

ⓘ   It might be necessary to make the archive executable; you can use chmod +x your-application.jar for that.

When making the archive executable, what happens is the archive will be prefixed with a bash script. You might think that doing so will break the Java archive. However, because of the way Java reads archives (bottom to top) and the way the shell reads the archives (top to bottom), this actually does work.

ⓘ   You can see the bash script using head -n 309 your-application.jar.

Specify the Configuration

Normally when you launch a Spring Boot–based application, there are several options for providing additional configuration (see Chapter 2).[2] However, when using the archive as a script (or as a service), some of them don't apply anymore. What you can do instead is make use of a `.conf` file next to your executable archive (it must be named `your-application.conf`) to contain additional configuration options for your application. See Table 10-1.

Table 10-1. *Available Properties*

Property	Description
MODE	Sets the "mode" of operation. The default is `auto`, which will detect the mode. When launched from a symlink, it will behave like `service`. Change to `run` if you want to run the process in the foreground.
RUN_AS_USER	Sets the user that is used to run the application; the default is the owner of the JAR file.
USE_START_STOP_DAEMON	Sets whether to use the `start-stop-daemon` command. By default this will detect if the command is available.
PID_FOLDER	Sets the name of the folder to write the PID to; the default is `/var/run`.
LOG_FOLDER	Sets the name of the folder to write the logging to; the default is `/var/log`.
CONF_FOLDER	Sets the name of the folder to read `.conf` from; the default is the same directory as the JAR file.
LOG_FILENAME	Sets the name of the logfile to write to; the default is `<appname>.log`.
APP_NAME	Sets the name of the application. If the JAR file is run from a symlink, the script guesses the app name.
RUN_ARGS	Sets the arguments to pass to the Spring Boot application.
JAVA_HOME	By default, this will be discovered from the $PATH but can be explicitly defined if needed.

(*continued*)

---

[2]https://docs.spring.io/spring-boot/docs/current/reference/html/boot-features-external-config.html

Table 10-1. (*continued*)

Property	Description
JAVA_OPTS	Sets the options to pass to the JVM (like memory settings, GC settings, etc.).
JARFILE	Sets the explicit location of the JAR file, in case the script is being used to launch a JAR that is not actually embedded.
DEBUG	If not empty, sets the -x flag on the shell process, making it easy to see the logic in the script.
STOP_WAIT_TIME	Sets the time to wait before forcing a shutdown (the default is 60 seconds).

When using an embedded script (the default), the JARFILE and APP_NAME properties aren't configurable using a .conf file. See Listing 10-3.

Listing 10-3. Properties for Executable

```
JAVA_OPTS=-Xmx1024m
DEBUG=true
```

With this, you will assign a max of 1 GB of memory to your application, and it will do some additional logging for the shell script. It is of course possible to add any of the properties from Table 10-1 to this file.

10-2. Create a WAR File for Deployment

Problem

Instead of creating a JAR file, you want a WAR file to deploy to a servlet container or Jakarta EE container. This so-called traditional deployment can be necessary if you are in an organization that still uses servers such as Oracle WebLogic, IBM WebSphere, or Tomcat.

Solution

Change the packaging of the application from JAR to WAR and let your Spring Boot application extend `SpringBootServletInitializer` so that it can bootstrap itself as a regular application. Lastly, make sure the server you use for development is included as a provided dependency so that it can be filtered while generating the deployable artifact.

How It Works

To make Recipe 3-1 into a deployable WAR, three things need to be done.

1. Change the packaging from JAR to WAR.

2. Extend `SpringBootServletInitializer` to bootstrap the application on deployment.

3. Change the scope of the embedded server to `provided`.

In the `pom.xml` file, change the packaging from JAR to WAR. See Listing 10-4.

Listing 10-4. Create a WAR File with Maven

```
<packaging>war</packaging>
```

To prevent the embedded container from adding its classes to the web application, the scope of the embedded container needs to be changed to `provided` instead of the default `compile`.

When using an embedded Tomcat (the default), add Listing 10-5 to `pom.xml`.

Listing 10-5. Scoped Dependency

```
<dependency>
    <groupId>org.springframework.boot</groupId>
    <artifactId>spring-boot-starter-tomcat</artifactId>
    <scope>provided</scope>
</dependency>
```

When using a different embedded container, see Recipe 3-7; then change the scope of that container to `provided` by including `<scope>provided</scope>`. When doing so, the Spring Boot plugin will not add the libraries to the default `WEB-INF/lib`. However, they will still be part of the created WAR file, but in the special `WEB-INF/lib-provided`

473

directory. Spring Boot knows this location, and as such you can also use the WAR to start the embedded container. Starting an embedded container is very nice for development; however, as it is a WAR file, it is also deployable to a container like Tomcat of WebSphere.

To make sure that the application will start, you need your application to extend `SpringBootServletInitializer`. This is a special class needed to bootstrap Spring Boot in a servlet or JEE container. See Listing 10-6.

Listing 10-6. SpringBootApplication with SpringBootServletInitializer

```
package com.apress.springboot3recipes.helloworld;

import org.springframework.boot.SpringApplication;
import org.springframework.boot.autoconfigure.SpringBootApplication;
import org.springframework.boot.builder.SpringApplicationBuilder;
import
org.springframework.boot.web.servlet.support.SpringBootServletInitializer;

@SpringBootApplication
public class HelloWorldApplication extends SpringBootServletInitializer {

  public static void main(String[] args) {
    SpringApplication.run(HelloWorldApplication.class, args);
  }

  @Override
  protected SpringApplicationBuilder configure(SpringApplicationBuilder
  builder) {
    return builder.sources(HelloWorldApplication.class);
  }
}
```

When extending the `SpringBootServletInitializer`, you need to override the `configure` method. The `configure` method gets a `SpringApplicationBuilder`, which you can use to configure the application. One of the things to add is the main configuration class, just as with `SpringApplication.run`. That is what the line `builder.sources(HelloWorldApplication.class)` does. This will be used to bootstrap the application.

For completeness, Listing 10-7 shows the controller.

Listing 10-7. HelloWorldController

```
package com.apress.springboot3recipes.helloworld;

import org.springframework.web.bind.annotation.GetMapping;
import org.springframework.web.bind.annotation.RestController;

@RestController
public class HelloWorldController {

  @GetMapping
  public String hello() {
    return "Hello World, from Spring Boot 3!";
  }
}
```

> ⚠️ When deploying something to a servlet or JakartaEE container, Spring Boot is no longer in control of the server. Therefore, configuration options from the `server` and `management.servlet` namespaces don't apply anymore. So when `server.port` has been defined, it will be ignored when deploying to an external server.

When the application has been deployed, it is no longer available at the root URL `/` as it would be when using the embedded server. It will be available at the `<name-of-war>` URL instead. Generally, it is something like `http://<name-of-server>:8080/<name-of-war>` to access the application.

When deployed to a standard Tomcat installation and looking at the Management GUI, you will see a screen like that in Figure 10-1.

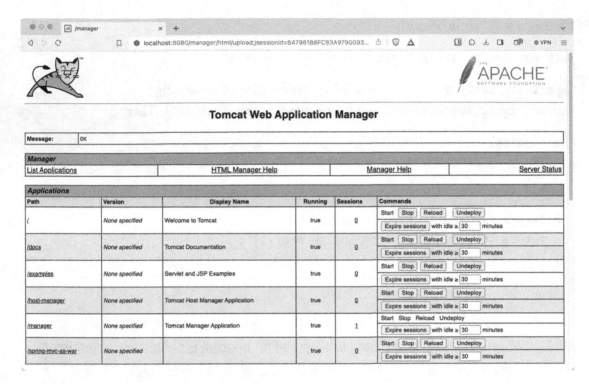

Figure 10-1. *Tomcat Management GUI*

Click the /spring-mvc-as-war link to open the application (see Figure 10-2).

Hello World, from Spring Boot 3!

Figure 10-2. *Result of deployed application*

10-3. Reduce the Archive Size Through the Thin Launcher

Problem

Spring Boot by default generates a *fat JAR*, which is a JAR file with all the dependencies inside it. This has some obvious benefits as the JAR file is fully self-contained. However, the JAR size can grow considerably, and when using multiple applications, you might want to reuse already downloaded dependencies to reduce the overall footprint.

Solution

When packaging the application, you can specify a custom layout to use. This behavior can be changed by using a custom layout. One such custom layout is the Thin Launcher. This launcher will result in the dependencies to be downloaded before starting the application, instead of the dependencies packaged inside the application.

How It Works

When using the Spring Boot plugin as is, all the needed libraries are included in the archive in the BOOT-INF/lib folder. However, one might want to reduce the size of the JAR and enable reuse of dependencies to create an even smaller overall footprint. For example, the archive generated with Recipe 10-1 is around 7.1 MB. Most of this comes from included dependencies.

It is possible to add a custom layout and launcher to the Spring Boot plugin. A layout defines where the sources are loaded from, and the launcher uses this information to load those dependencies. The Thin Launcher will download the artifacts from Maven Central and place them in a shared repository. So when multiple applications share the dependencies, they are downloaded only once.

To use the Thin Launcher, add a dependency to the Spring Boot plugin. See Listing 10-8.

Listing 10-8. Thin Layout Configuration

```
<plugin>
    <groupId>org.springframework.boot</groupId>
    <artifactId>spring-boot-maven-plugin</artifactId>
    <dependencies>
        <dependency>
            <groupId>org.springframework.boot.experimental</groupId>
            <artifactId>spring-boot-thin-layout</artifactId>
            <version>1.0.31.RELEASE</version>
        </dependency>
    </dependencies>
</plugin>
```

This is enough to create a considerably smaller archive (there is no BOOT-INF/lib directory inside the archive anymore). When running mvn verify, the resulting JAR is around 12 KB. The drawback is, however, that it needs to download the dependencies when the application is started, so starting the application might take longer depending on the number of dependencies.

What happens is that a class named ThinJarWrapper has been added, and that will be the entrypoint of your application. Now your application contains a pom.xml and/or META-INF/thin.properties file to determine the dependencies. The thinJarWrapper will locate another JAR file (the "launcher"). The wrapper downloads the launcher (if it needs to) or else uses the cached version in your local Maven repository.

The launcher then takes over and reads pom.xml (if present) and META-INF/thin. properties, downloading the dependencies (and all transitives) as necessary. It will now create a custom class loader with all the downloaded dependencies on the classpath. Then it runs the application's own main method with that class loader.

ℹ   When downloading the dependencies from Maven, it will respect the settings made in the Maven settings.xml file as it uses regular Maven tooling. When using a mirror, like Nexus, for Maven repositories, include thin.repo in the META-INF/ thin.properties file to point to that mirror. Otherwise, downloading the launcher will fail.

10-4. Containerize a Spring Boot Application

Using Docker to build and ship containers is a common practice nowadays. When using Spring Boot, it is quite easy to wrap that into a Docker container.

Problem

You want to run your Spring Boot–based application inside a Docker container.

Solution

Create a `Dockerfile` and use one of the Docker plugins available to Maven to build the Docker container.

ℹ️   In this recipe we choose to use `docker-maven-plugin` from Fabric8, but there are others that work equally well.

How It Works

First you will need a `Dockerfile` containing the information needed to build the container. When the container has been built, you can launch it using the `docker run` command.

Update a Build Script to Produce a Docker Container

To create a Docker container, first create a `Dockerfile`. The `Dockerfile` is the file containing the information on how to build the container. Place this file in the root of the project. See Listing 10-9.

Listing 10-9. Dockerfile

```
FROM eclipse-temurin:21-jre-alpine
ARG JAR_FILE
COPY ${JAR_FILE} app.jar
ENTRYPOINT ["java","-Djava.security.egd=file:/dev/./urandom","-jar",
"/app.jar"]
```

With this `Dockerfile` we use the Eclipse Temurin–provided container to build our own. We are going to add our application to it using the `ADD` command, and finally we need to tell the container what to start during startup. For this you can use the `ENTRYPOINT` command.

🔥   Using publicly available containers as a starting point might seem like a good idea, but you have to be aware of the possible security implications this can have. As you don't control that specific container, you cannot guarantee what is built into (or not into) the container. For real-life situations, you might want to build your own base containers.

The `ARG` in the `JAR_FILE` argument is telling the build that there is a variable `JAR_FILE` available that can be used in the build script. We will provide the value of that variable through the plugin configuration.

The `ENTRYPOINT` simply specifies that it will run `java -jar /app.jar`; you could also combine this with Recipe 14-1 and install an executable JAR as a script, making the entrypoint a little smaller.

Now that there is a `Dockerfile`, you need to add `docker-maven-plugin` to your build section of the `pom.xml` file. See Listing 10-10.

Listing 10-10. Docker Maven Plugin

```
<plugin>
  <groupId>io.fabric8</groupId>
  <artifactId>docker-maven-plugin</artifactId>
  <version>0.43.4</version>
  <configuration>
    <buildArgs>
      <JAR_FILE>target/${project.build.finalName}.jar</JAR_FILE>
    </buildArgs>
  </configuration>
</plugin>
```

The `buildArgs` elements are for passing arguments to the `docker build` command so that they can be made available when processing the `Dockerfile`. As we have specified a `JAR_FILE`, we also declare that in the configuration and point it to the location of the generated artifact.

Build and Start the Container

Now that everything is in place, you can use `mvn package docker:build` to generate a Docker container.

To launch the container, you can run it with something like Listing 10-11.

Listing 10-11. Docker Command

```
docker run -d springboot3recipes/recipe_10_4_i:latest
```

This will start a container in the background, and it will start to print messages to the console. To see the logs, do `docker logs <name-of-container> --follow`, and you will see a message printed every two seconds (see Figure 10-3).

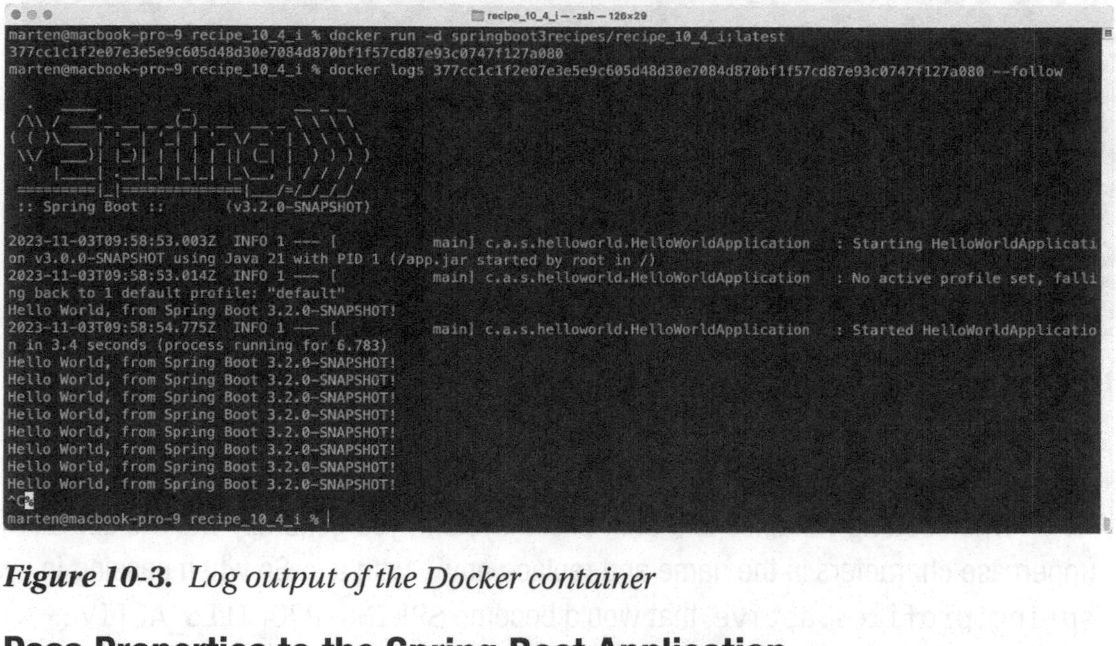

Figure 10-3. *Log output of the Docker container*

Pass Properties to the Spring Boot Application

When running a Spring Boot application in a Docker container, you probably want to be able to change properties based on the environment the application gets deployed on. You can use Spring profiles for this (see also Chapter 2), but you still need to provide a

variable specifying which profile to use. Normally you would start the application like
`java -jar your-applicarion.jar --spring.profiles.active=profile1,profile2`;
however, as you have a Docker container, that isn't possible.

Luckily, with Docker you can use the `-e` switch to pass in environment variables, and
Spring Boot also takes into consideration the variables in the local environment.[3]

For the simple application we have here, we can pass the `audience` property (by
default it will say `World` and the message becomes `Hello World, from Spring Boot
3!`). Let's change it to `Docker`. To do this, you need to add `-e AUDIENCE='Docker'` to the
run command. See Listing 10-12.

Listing 10-12. Docker Command

```
docker run -d -e AUDIENCE='Docker' springboot3recipes/recipe_10_4_i:latest
```

When looking at the logging of the newly started container, the message has changed
to `Hello Docker, from Spring Boot 3!` (see Figure 10-4).

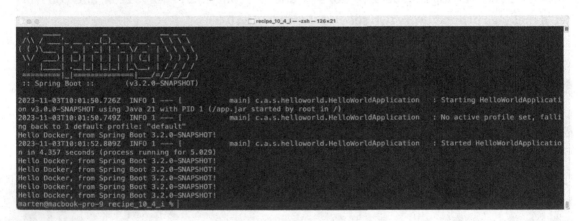

Figure 10-4. *Log output of the Docker container*

> 🛈 When setting variables to a Unix-based system, you generally want to use all
> uppercase characters in the name and replace any `.` with a `_`. So when passing in
> `spring.profiles.active`, that would become `SPRING_PROFILES_ACTIVE`.

---

[3] https://docs.spring.io/spring-boot/docs/current/reference/html/boot-features-
external-config.html

Build a Better Docker Container

While the simple Dockerfile we have will work, it is far from efficient from a Docker standpoint. It would be better to include some additional layers that could be reused. When building a Spring Boot runnable JAR, it will include some layers already in the structure of the JAR and placement of files. We can utilize this to create a more efficient container.

Spring Boot has support for extracting the layers; we can do this by starting the application with some parameters. Using `java -Djarmode=layertools -jar app.jar extract`, it will extract the content of the application in separate directories, which can then be used to create additional layers in the container.

With this it is possible to create a multistage Dockerfile, which first extracts the needed information and finally builds the container image we need. This could allow for reusable layers in our container. Reusable layers will reduce build time and the total size used for the images. See Listing 10-13.

Listing 10-13. Multistage Dockerfile with Layers

```
FROM eclipse-temurin:21-jre-alpine as builder
WORKDIR application
ARG JAR_FILE
COPY ${JAR_FILE} app.jar
RUN java -Djarmode=layertools -jar app.jar extract

FROM eclipse-temurin:21-jre-alpine
WORKDIR application
COPY --from=builder application/dependencies/ ./
COPY --from=builder application/spring-boot-loader/ ./
COPY --from=builder application/snapshot-dependencies/ ./
COPY --from=builder application/application/ ./

ENTRYPOINT ["java", "org.springframework.boot.loader.launch.JarLauncher"]
```

The first part (or stage) of this Docker file copies our JAR file and extracts the different layers. The next part (or stage) copies the different layers to the resulting image. When layers haven't changed, they wouldn't need re-creating and will be thus reused. This is generally the case when modifying application code but not upgrading dependencies.

The container can be built in the same way as before through running `mvn package docker:build`.

Use Buildpacks to Build a Container

Although you can use a Dockerfile to build a container, there are other options. One of those is to use cloud-native buildpacks. Cloud-native buildpacks are part of cloud platforms like Heroku and Cloud Foundry, which allow pushed JAR files to run on the cloud. You can, however, also use these buildpacks to generate a Docker-compatible container.

The Spring Boot plugins for Maven and Gradle both have support for this. Invoking mvn `spring-boot:build-image` is enough to create the container image. When executing, it will first download a container to run the build and a container to use to create the final image. This will take some time; however, this is a one-time (until there is a new version of the container) download. Subsequent builds will run much faster. See Listing 10-14.

Listing 10-14. Build Output with Buildpacks

```
mvn spring-boot:build-image

[INFO] --- spring-boot:3.2.0-SNAPSHOT:build-image (default-cli)
        @ recipe_10_4_iii ---
[INFO] Building image 'docker.io/library/recipe_10_4_iii:3.0.0-SNAPSHOT'
[INFO]
[INFO]  > Pulling builder image 'docker.io/paketobuildpacks/builder-jammy-
        base:latest' 100%
[INFO]  > Pulled builder image 'paketobuildpacks/builder-jammy-base@sha256:
        ca071f8c4a22d61e6a381422570f3885e070bca988caccff4ae3a099253116ef'
[INFO]  > Pulling run image 'docker.io/paketobuildpacks/run-jammy-
        base:latest' 100%
[INFO]  > Pulled run image 'paketobuildpacks/run-jammy-base@sha256:722
        5e689826c84a7e04e65178324ba5ead17205f558bbf55ca1def685b515362'
[INFO]  > Executing lifecycle version v0.17.2
[INFO]  > Using build cache volume 'pack-cache-7433cad4bf70.build'
...
[INFO]     [creator]      ===> EXPORTING
[INFO]     [creator]      Warning: no analyzed metadata found at path
                          '/layers/analyzed.toml'
```

```
[INFO]     [creator]     Timer: Exporter started at 2023-10-25T14:18:30Z
[INFO]     [creator]     Reusing layer 'paketo-buildpacks/ca-
                         certificates:helper'
[INFO]     [creator]     Reusing layer 'paketo-buildpacks/bellsoft-
                         liberica:helper'
[INFO]     [creator]     Reusing layer 'paketo-buildpacks/bellsoft-
                         liberica:java-security-properties'
[INFO]     [creator]     Reusing layer 'paketo-buildpacks/bellsoft-
                         liberica:jre'
[INFO]     [creator]     Reusing layer 'paketo-buildpacks/executable-
                         jar:classpath'
[INFO]     [creator]     Reusing layer 'paketo-buildpacks/spring-
                         boot:helper'
[INFO]     [creator]     Reusing layer 'paketo-buildpacks/spring-
                         boot:spring-cloud-bindings'
[INFO]     [creator]     Reusing layer 'paketo-buildpacks/spring-boot:web-
                         application-type'
[INFO]     [creator]     Reusing layer 'buildpacksio/lifecycle:launch.sbom'
[INFO]     [creator]     Reusing 5/5 app layer(s)
[INFO]     [creator]     Reusing layer 'buildpacksio/lifecycle:launcher'
[INFO]     [creator]     Reusing layer 'buildpacksio/lifecycle:config'
[INFO]     [creator]     Reusing layer 'buildpacksio/
                         lifecycle:process-types'
[INFO]     [creator]     Adding label 'io.buildpacks.lifecycle.metadata'
[INFO]     [creator]     Adding label 'io.buildpacks.build.metadata'
[INFO]     [creator]     Adding label 'io.buildpacks.project.metadata'
[INFO]     [creator]     Adding label 'org.opencontainers.image.title'
[INFO]     [creator]     Adding label 'org.opencontainers.image.version'
[INFO]     [creator]     Adding label 'org.springframework.boot.version'
[INFO]     [creator]     Setting default process type 'web'
[INFO]     [creator]     Timer: Saving docker.io/library/
                         recipe_10_4_iii:3.0.0-SNAPSHOT... started at
                         2023-10-25T14:18:30Z
[INFO]     [creator]     *** Images (973964c80779):
```

```
[INFO]     [creator]               docker.io/library/recipe_10_4_
                                   iii:3.0.0-SNAPSHOT
[INFO]     [creator]     Timer: Saving docker.io/library/recipe_10_4_
                                   iii:3.0.0-SNAPSHOT... ran for 3.201896923s and
                                   ended at 2023-10-25T14:18:33Z
[INFO]     [creator]     Timer: Exporter ran for 3.320421063s and ended at
                                   2023-10-25T14:18:33Z
[INFO]     [creator]     Timer: Cache started at 2023-10-25T14:18:33Z
[INFO]     [creator]     Reusing cache layer 'paketo-buildpacks/syft:syft'
[INFO]     [creator]     Reusing cache layer 'buildpacksio/
                                   lifecycle:cache.sbom'
[INFO]     [creator]     Timer: Cache ran for 247.300377ms and ended at
                                   2023-10-25T14:18:34Z
[INFO]
[INFO] Successfully built image 'docker.io/library/recipe_10_4_iii:3.0.0'
```

Now after the build we can use docker run recipe_10_4_iii:3.0.0 to run our container and see the hello world message again every two seconds.

10-5. Use Spring Boot GraalVM Native Images

GraalVM native images are single-image executables that can be run without Java and other dependencies. They are generated by compiling the Java application ahead of time instead of just in time with the JVM. These native images will most likely have a smaller size, have a smaller memory footprint, and are quicker to start. The native image is a platform-specific executable; there is no need to include a JVM on those environments.

Native images are very suitable to run in containerized environments, especially when using functions as a service, like AWS Lambda.

There are some drawbacks, however, when using native images.

- The classpath is fixed and needs to be fully defined at build time.

- The beans defined in the application cannot be changed at runtime.

- @Profile support isn't available in native images; the profile to run with needs to be supplied at build time.

- @Conditional beans, which rely on the Environment, are available only at build time.

- Bean definitions that are defined as Lambda expressions or method references cannot be used.

All of the restrictions come from the fact that GraalVM operates in a closed world, which means that all classes and bytecode that are needed at runtime need to be there at build time. Using Spring ahead-of-time (AOT) processing, we can help GraalVM get a full and clear view on which classes and bytecode are needed. Spring itself already does a great job of providing as much information as it can, but we can also help the AOT processing a little by providing additional metadata and information.

Problem

You want to create a native executable for your Spring Boot application.

Solution

Spring Boot can leverage the GraalVM plugins for both Maven and Gradle to create a native image. For Maven there is a special profile that adds additional configuration to generate the proper image. Running mvn -Pnative native:compile will run the regular compilation, the AOT processing, and finally the GraalVM compiler.

Build a Native Image Using Native Build Tools

To build the image on your local machine using the Maven (or Gradle) plugins, you will need to install GraalVM and include the plugin in your build. See Listing 10-15.

Listing 10-15. Maven GraalVM Plugin

```
<plugin>
  <groupId>org.graalvm.buildtools</groupId>
  <artifactId>native-maven-plugin</artifactId>
</plugin>
```

With this in place, you can run `mvn -Pnative native:compile`, and the application will be built, started, and analyzed, and eventually it will result in an executable for the platform you are compiling on. It will take a while even for this small Hello World application for the binary to be created.

> ℹ️ At the moment of writing, it isn't possible to do cross compilation, so it isn't possible to create a Windows executable on macOS; you would need to use a build container that would contain Windows and GraalVM.

The resulting binary can be found in the `target` directory and is named `recipe_10_5_i` (the name of the artifact). Starting it will show the same output as the Java way of running it. With one difference, it will start blazingly fast.

Some of the trade-offs are longer compilation for faster startup times and lower memory footprint.

Build a Native Image Using Buildpacks

Another way of building a native image is to use a buildpack (see also Recipe 10-4). When using a buildpack, you wouldn't need to have a GraalVM installed on your local system as it would be downloaded as part of the image. You would need the GraalVM Maven plugin in your build. See Listing 10-16.

Listing 10-16. Maven GraalVM Plugin

```
<plugin>
  <groupId>org.graalvm.buildtools</groupId>
  <artifactId>native-maven-plugin</artifactId>
</plugin>
```

To use a buildpack, running the regular build with the desired Maven profile is enough. `mvn -Pnative spring-boot:build-image` is all that is needed. After the process has finished, you have a container image with a native executable, which you can run using Docker, K8S, or another container technology.

How It Works

When building, a GraalVM native image is created based on the code that is currently available in the JVM. Based on that, the GraalVM will compile a native executable. GraalVM assumes that all the code that is needed to run the application is present in the JVM at the moment the application is being inspected. If the code isn't there, it will not be part of the resulting native executable. The process to compile the bytecode in native code is called *ahead-of-time (AOT) compilation*, instead of what the JVM does with just-in-time compilation (JIT).

Spring has support for contributing information ahead of time to GraalVM, and Spring Boot leverages that support in the Spring Boot plugins. When running `mvn -Pnative native:compile`, you will see a line in the output that reads something like `[INFO] --- spring-boot:3.2.1:process-aot (process-aot) @ recipe_10_5_i ---`. See Figure 10-5.

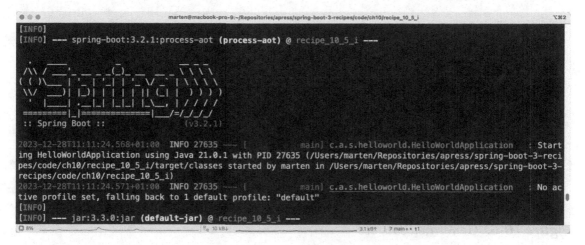

Figure 10-5. *Maven plugin output*

While executing `process-aot`, Spring Boot will do a couple of things.

- Generate source code for bean definitions

- Generate a file containing GraalVM hints

- Generate bytecode for proxy classes

All of these steps are needed for GraalVM to do a proper static analysis of the code needed to run the application.

Generate Source Code for Bean Definitions

As we cannot have dynamic code in a GraalVM native image, we need to have a static configuration. Normally an @Configuration class is parsed while starting the application, and based on the @Bean annotated methods, Spring will create special BeanDefinition source files. The actual @Bean methods are being invoked with reflection, something we cannot do in a native image.

Now when creating a native image instead of parsing the @Configuration classes at runtime and parsing the beans, it generates the bean definitions during the AOT processing. It will actually generate a source file for the @Configuration class. These classes can be found in the target/spring-aot/main/sources directory. See Figure 10-6.

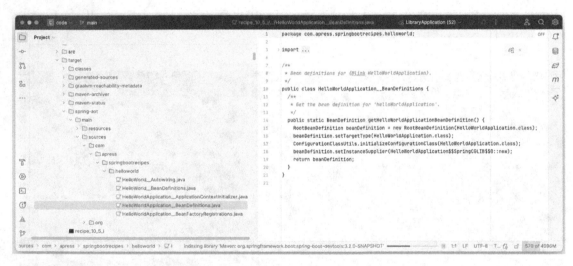

Figure 10-6. *Generated sources*

As you can see, there is also an org directory, as it will generate sources for all @Configuration classes it generates. This also works for the Spring Boot auto-configuration classes and other @Configuration classes that are loaded.

Generate GraalVM Hints

In addition to generating sources, Spring AOT will also generate a hints file that is used by the GraalVM. The hint file contains data, in JSON format, that describes how GraalVM should deal with situations it cannot understand directly, like in the case of reflection, multiple constructors, or dynamic class loading.

The hint file is automatically generated in the `target/spring-aot/main/resources` directory. See Figure 10-7.

Figure 10-7. *Generated hint files*

While Spring Boot will do its best to infer the hints to generate based on the code, it might be that it cannot determine what to generate, and it might need some help. Spring AOT can help here and provides the `RuntimeHintsRegistrar` interface, which allows you to register additional hints for the code in question. After defining the specific hints, you can use the `@ImportRuntimeHints` annotation to make Spring AOT aware of this class. See Listing 10-17.

Listing 10-17. Register Runtime Hints

```
package com.apress.springboot3recipes.helloworld;

import org.springframework.aot.hint.RuntimeHints;
import org.springframework.aot.hint.RuntimeHintsRegistrar;
import org.springframework.boot.SpringApplication;
import org.springframework.boot.autoconfigure.SpringBootApplication;
import org.springframework.context.annotation.ImportRuntimeHints;
import org.springframework.scheduling.annotation.EnableScheduling;

@SpringBootApplication
@EnableScheduling
@ImportRuntimeHints(HelloWorldApplication.HelloWorldRuntimeHints.class)
```

```
public class HelloWorldApplication {

  public static void main(String[] args) {
    SpringApplication.run(HelloWorldApplication.class, args);
  }

  static class HelloWorldRuntimeHints implements RuntimeHintsRegistrar {

    @Override
    public void registerHints(RuntimeHints hints, ClassLoader cl) {
      hints.resources().registerPattern("classpath:/*.properties");
    }
  }
}
```

Here we create resource hints for including all `.properties` files in the root of the classpath. This can be needed if files are dynamically loaded and Spring or GraalVM isn't able to detect this. When registering runtime hints, we can register hints for `jni`, `proxies`, `reflection`, `resources`, and/or `serialization`. All of these will contribute entries to one of the available hint files.

Generate Bytecode for Proxy Classes

Finally, Spring AOT will generate actual class files containing the bytecode for the proxies created at runtime. Proxies are dynamically created classes, and this is something that isn't possible with GraalVM; thus, they are exported at build time. The code is generated in the regular `target/classes` directory and can be noticed by the `$SpringCGLIB$$<number>` suffix. See Figure 10-8.

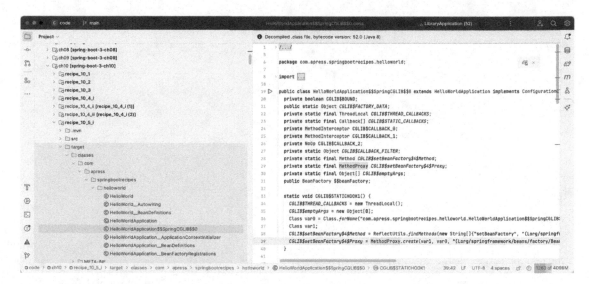

Figure 10-8. *Generated class files*

This proxy is created because of @SpringBootApplication also being an @Configuration class, which has the proxyBeanMethods attribute set to true. The classfiles will be generated for all classes that use AOP like @Transactional and security annotations, so in a regular application there might be a few classes being generated.

Index

© Marten Deinum 2024
M. Deinum, *Spring Boot 3 Recipes*, https://doi.org/10.1007/979-8-8688-0113-6

Printed in the United States
by Baker & Taylor Publisher Services